D1541586

Without Benefit of Clergy

Recent titles in
RELIGION IN AMERICA SERIES
Harry S. Stout, General Editor

Taking Heaven by Storm: Methodism and the Rise of Popular Christianity in America
John H. Wigger

Encounters with God: An Approach to the Theology of Jonathan Edwards
Michael J. McClymond

Evangelicals and Science in Historical Perspective
Edited by David N. Livingstone,
D. G. Hart, and Mark A. Noll

Methodism and the Southern Mind, 1770–1810
Cynthia Lynn Lyerly

Princeton in the Nation's Service: Religious Ideals and Educational Practice, 1868–1928
P. C. Kemeny

Church People in the Struggle: The National Council of Churches and the Black Freedom Movement, 1950–1970
James F. Findlay Jr.

Tenacious of Their Liberties: The Congregationalists in Colonial Massachusetts
James F. Cooper Jr.

In Discordance with the Scriptures: American Protestant Battles over Translating the Bible
Peter J. Thuesen

The Gospel Working Up: Progress and the Pulpit in Nineteenth-Century Virginia
Beth Barton Schweiger

Black Zion: African American Religious Encounters with Judaism
Edited by Yvonne Chireau and
Nathaniel Deutsch

God Forbid: Religion and Sex in American Public Life
Edited by Kathleen M. Sands

American Methodist Worship
Karen B. Westerfield Tucker

Transgressing the Bounds: Subversive Enterprises among the Puritan Elite in Massachusetts, 1630–1692
Louise A. Breen

The Church on the World's Turf: An Evangelical Christian Group at a Secular University
Paul A. Bramadat

The Universalist Movement in America, 1770–1880
Ann Lee Bressler

A Republic of Righteousness: The Public Christianity of the Southern New England Clergy, 1783–1833
Jonathan D. Sassi

Noah's Curse: The Biblical Justification of American Slavery
Stephen R. Haynes

A Controversial Spirit: Evangelical Awakening in the South
Philip N. Mulder

Identifying the Image of God: Radical Christians and Nonviolent Power in the Antebellum United States
Dan Buchanan

Some Wild Visions: Autobiographies by Female Itinerant Evangelists in Nineteenth-Century America
Elizabeth Elkin Grammer

Black Puritan, Black Republican: The Life and Thought of Lemuel Haynes, 1753–1833
John Saillant

Without Benefit of Clergy: Women and the Pastoral Relationship in Nineteenth-Century American Culture
Karin E. Gedge

Without Benefit of Clergy

Women and the Pastoral Relationship in Nineteenth-Century American Culture

KARIN E. GEDGE

OXFORD

UNIVERSITY PRESS

2003

OXFORD
UNIVERSITY PRESS

Oxford   New York
Auckland   Bangkok   Buenos Aires   Cape Town   Chennai
Dar es Salaam   Delhi   Hong Kong   Istanbul   Karachi   Kolkata
Kuala Lumpur   Madrid   Melbourne   Mexico City   Mumbai   Nairobi
São Paulo   Shanghai   Taipei   Tokyo   Toronto

Copyright © 2003 by Karin E. Gedge

Published by Oxford University Press, Inc.
198 Madison Avenue, New York, New York 10016

www.oup.com

Oxford is a registered trademark of Oxford University Press

Library of Congress Cataloging-in-Publication Data
Gedge, Karin E. (Karin Erdevig), 1949–
    Without benefit of clergy : women and the pastoral relationship in
nineteenth-century American culture / Karin E. Gedge.
        p. cm.—(Religion in America series)
Includes bibliographical references.
    ISBN 0-19-513020-0 (cloth)
    1. Clergy—United States—History—19th century.   2. Christian
women—Religious life—United States—19th century.   3. Clergy—United
States—Sexual behavior—History—19th century.   4. Christian
women—Pastoral counseling of—United States—19th century.   5. United
States—Church history—19th century.   I. Title.   II. Religion in America
series (Oxford University Press)
    BR525 .G43 2003
    259'.082'0973—dc21   2002011539

9 8 7 6 5 4 3 2 1

Printed in the United States of America
on acid-free paper

Acknowledgments

I incurred many debts in the course of this project, too numerous to
make clear here. A mere listing of some of the institutions and individuals who have contributed the most to this project must suffice.
First and foremost, I thank my advisors in the American Studies
program at Yale, who guided and supported me from the project's
conception as a dissertation to its accomplishment as this book. Jon
Butler offered the first and longest-lasting assistance; Harry Stout
the benefit of his seminars, discussions, and editorship of this series;
and Nancy Cott her attention to detail and her deep historical knowledge. I also benefited from discussions with John Demos, Bryan
Wolf, Lynn Wardley, and James Fisher in the earliest stages of the
project. I have presented papers based on portions of this book at
the Yale Graduate Students Seminar, the American Historical Association annual meeting, the Organization of American Historians
annual meeting, the American Society of Church History annual
meeting, the Institute for the Study of American Evangelicals Conference on Theological Education, the Young Scholars in American
Religion at Indiana University-Purdue University Indianapolis, and
the Chester County Historical Society, among others, and thank the
many listeners and commentators who offered encouragement and
substantive suggestions. A few stand out and deserve special thanks:
Nell Painter, Patricia Cline Cohen, Margaret Thompson, Richard
Wightman Fox, Glenn T. Miller, Beth Barton Schweiger, and Judy
Gunston.

The generous financial assistance I received in the form of research grants and fellowships from several institutions has ensured
completion of the project. I am most grateful to the Schlesinger Library at Radcliffe College, the Institute for the Study of American

Evangelicals at Wheaton College, the Institute for the Study of Protestantism in American Culture at Louisville Seminary, and the Pew Program in Religion and American History at Yale University. West Chester University and the Department of History provided an educational leave of absence and travel funds. Whenever I contemplated giving up, I remembered the interest and confidence in the value of this book that these scholars displayed, and I took up the laptop again. I also thank those research librarians and archivists who offered assistance, encouragement, and permission to use their collections at the American Antiquarian Society, the Schlesinger Library, Hartford Seminary, Princeton Seminary Archives, Firestone Library at Princeton University, Oberlin College Archives, the University of Rochester Rare Books Collection, Hobart and William Smith Colleges, Cornell University, the American Baptist Historical Society, Colgate-Rochester Divinity School/Bexley Hall/Crozier Theological Seminary/St. Bernard's Institute, Bentley Historical Library at the University of Michigan, George Arents Special Collections at Syracuse University, Fairfield Historical Society, New York Historical Society, New York Public Library, Notre Dame University Library, Brown University Library, Yale Divinity School Library, Yale Manuscripts and Archives, and the Yale Law Library.

Many friends in and outside the academy have offered invaluable help and support. Elizabeth Abrams, Scott Reisinger, and Robert Guffin offered timely assistance. Bridget Gillespie and Erin Holland offered eleventh-hour help. Catherine Brekus and Nancy Rosoff offered the most persistent support—to the point where I just could not impose on them any more. Catherine, through most of this project, has served as my scholarly exemplar and an endless font of knowledge and sources. Nancy, through the last few years, has served as a trusted reader and nagging conscience, both of us engaged in seemingly endless projects and burdened with overwhelming teaching and administrative loads. Pat Beairsto, Pat and Jane Conaway, John Erdevig and Ruth Shamraj, Laurel and Karl Zimmermann, and Rose Rosoff provided generous hospitality. My editor at Oxford University Press, Cynthia Read, displayed cheerful encouragement, much patience, and the ability to find thoughtful, helpful anonymous readers, for which I am very grateful. Most of all, I thank my family for their reading, forbearance, financial and moral support, and their love—my mother, Eileen Liebman; my sister, Jeanne Christiansen; my sons, Erick and Charlie Gedge; and my husband, Chuck. I am blessed.

Contents

Introduction: Dim Views of the Pastoral Relationship, 3

PART I   The Pastoral Relationship as Perception

1. The Bellwether; or, What the Traveler Saw, 11

2. Gone Astray; or, What the Public Feared, 23

3. Mending Fences; or, What the Public Saw, 49

PART II   The Pastoral Relationship in the Literary Imagination

4. Paradoxical Pastors; or, What the Novelist Imagined, 77

PART III   The Pastoral Relationship as Ideal

5. Forbidden and Forgotten Territory; or, Where the Pastor Feared to Tread, 111

PART IV   The Pastoral Relationship in Experience

6. The Unsteady Shepherd; or, What the Pastor Experienced, 141

7. Sheep without a Shepherd; or, What Women Experienced, 163

Epilogue: Separating the Ewes from the Rams; or, Seeing through a New Lens, 197

Appendix: Historiographical Essay: Counting Sheep; or, What the Historian Did, 209

Notes, 221

Selected Bibliography, 261

Index, 285

A photo gallery follows page 74

Without Benefit of Clergy

Introduction

Dim Views of the Pastoral Relationship

Nathaniel Hawthorne wrote *The Scarlet Letter* in the middle of the nineteenth century, even though he set the novel in the seventeenth century. A well-known work at the time, a "timeless classic" assigned to millions of high school students today, Hawthorne's romance plumbed the psychological depths of an adulterous relationship between a minister and his female parishioner. In the mid-1870s, Henry Ward Beecher, arguably the most famous preacher in Victorian America, earned widespread and lasting notoriety in the so-called trial of the century. Newspapers and magazines all over the nation followed more than a year of his trials, first in a church hearing and later in a civil suit for adultery. Though no jury found Beecher culpable, most historians of the event judged him guilty. In the 1970s, Ann Douglas, a noted cultural historian, examined the novels of the nineteenth century, the Beecher case, and the writings and relationships of several other well-known liberal clergymen and female writers and discovered a peculiar alliance between the two groups. Illicit sexual relations did not necessarily characterize the alliance. Worse than sex, in Douglas's view, was sentiment. The alliance resulted in the "feminization" of American culture: a mushy sentimental theology and popular literature replaced a vigorous Calvinist orthodoxy.[1]

These three prominent case studies—one "fiction," one "fact," one "history"—all took a dim view of the pastoral relationship that prompted me to look more carefully at the nineteenth century and to test the assumption that clergymen and women enjoyed a close, often dangerously intimate relationship with each other. In addition to Douglas, I found more historians who assumed that the preponderance of women in most churches signaled a special attraction between women and their pastors. I also found European travelers to America who reported a mutual admiration between clergy and women. I found dozens of additional trials of clergymen accused of sexual misconduct. I found ministers as romantic heroes and lecherous villains in a variety of literary genres throughout the period. In short, the evidence from both primary and secondary sources seemed overwhelming: Women and their ministers enjoyed a dangerously intimate pastoral relationship during the nineteenth century. However, the evidence and the interpretations begged two important, previously unanswered questions. First, *why* did this relationship fascinate and preoccupy nineteenth-century Americans? Second, did the *perception* of an alliance reflect the *experience* of ordinary ministers and laywomen? Did pastors fashion a particular ministry toward women? Did women find spiritual enlightenment and comfort in the person of their pastor?

To answer those questions, I cast my net widely over a broad range of additional sources, looking for the experiences of ordinary men and women, not just the extraordinary public persons who attracted the attention of Ann Douglas. I looked for sources in the decades roughly between 1800 and 1880. I confined my search mostly to the New England states but wandered occasionally into New York, New Jersey, Ohio, and Michigan. There I discovered the manuscripts and publications of men and women, young and old, rural and urban, who represented many Protestant denominations, some without any denominational affiliation, and a few of the Catholic faith. I discovered men and women who enjoyed scant means and little education and also those with comfortable livings and advanced learning. I discovered mostly men and women who escaped the stigma of color, but a few who did not. I have tried to be sensitive to the differing perspectives of my sources and to alert the reader whenever possible that important distinctions in social status or theological orientation sometimes affected participation in the pastoral relationship. But for the most part I have looked for the common denominators and broad cultural forces that most significantly influenced the men and women within that relationship.

When I first began organizing these sources, I tended to divide them into two categories: either "fiction" or "fact," "image" or "reality." But those simple dichotomies soon proved unworkable, and I began to see the sources falling instead into four broad classes. In the first category (part I), a variety of outsiders—travelers, pamphleteers, cartoonists, and the public at large—recorded *perceptions* of the pastoral relationship from their various perspectives. They saw what *appeared* to be true. In the second category (part II), numerous writers, mostly novelists, recorded the relationship in the *imagination*. They saw what *might* be true. In the third section (part III), a few writers, mostly pastoral theologians, prescribed an *ideal* relationship. They saw what *ought* to be true. Finally, in the fourth category (part IV), quite a few mostly ordinary pastors and women recorded the pastoral relationship of their own *experience*. They saw what *was* true for these individuals from their intimate perspectives within the relationship. (Readers who wish to review historians' perceptions of the time period in general and the pastoral relationship in particular should read the historiographical essay in the appendix.)[2]

Examining and comparing the pastoral relationship as it was perceived, imagined, idealized, and experienced revealed some enlightening and surprising answers to the question of why nineteenth-century Americans seemed so obsessed with the pastoral relationship and whether a dangerous alliance characterized that relationship in reality as well as in the popular imagination. The pastoral relationship both attracted and disturbed these Americans because it undermined their faith in an evolving and problematic gender ideology. That ideology generally posited separate spheres of activity for men and women. However, that ideology also presumed that clergy and women could transcend separate spheres to share a mission as moral guardians of the republic. Nineteenth-century Americans found deeply unsettling any evidence that pastors and female parishioners failed to fulfill that role: It boded ill for the health of families, society, and the republic.

As with most ideals, these new gender models failed to describe a social reality. Like all prescriptions, they proved difficult for most men and women to attain. Furthermore, the experienced relationship, from both pastors' and women's perspectives, fell far short of the ideal because of that same emerging gender ideology. Pastors and women failed to share a mission not because they were too close but because they were too distant—separated by the very gender ideology they were supposed to transcend. The disjuncture between the ideal and the experience of most men's and women's lives caused tension, discomfort, and even fear. For many nineteenth-century Americans, the pastoral relationship between clergymen and their female parishioners proved an unsettling reminder of the many ways that the pervasive ideology of separate spheres failed to serve as a useful guide to gender relations.

The false perception of a dangerous intimacy in the pastoral relationship obscures a much more complicated and interesting story of gender relations. First, it hides the distance and dysfunction these men and women experienced. Pastors avoided women more often than they reached out to them with a special ministry. Women suffered neglect, but they demonstrated a spiritual independence and resourcefulness to compensate for that neglect. These men and women not only struggled within the boundaries of separate spheres but also struggled against them. Both men and women tried to define themselves *within* gender boundaries by enhancing their gender identities—clergymen by valiantly trying to conform to masculine ideals of intellectual authority and competition, women by striving to conform to feminine ideals of piety, purity, and submission. Both men and women also tried to *transcend* gender boundaries in more or less successful ways—men by promulgating an ideal of spiritual equality, women by asserting it.

In 1977, the pioneer historian of women, Gerda Lerner, wrote a positive review of Ann Douglas's *Feminization of American Culture*, accepting with qualifications her portrait of the alliance between clergy and women. The title of that review, "Benefit of Clergy," suggested that women gained some advantage from the familiar relationship, even if clergy were stigmatized by their closeness to the feminine sphere. I argue that exactly the opposite notion ought to characterize our understanding of the pastoral relationship in the nineteenth century. Women were without benefit of clergy. One popular meaning of the phrase "benefit of clergy" connotes ecclesiastical sanction or "church blessing." Sexual intercourse "without benefit of clergy" implies that the couple neglected to gain recognition from the church for a marriage and that therefore their union is unlawful. As we shall see, the ubiquitous negative perceptions of the pastoral relationship raised suspicions that clergy regularly enjoyed physical access to women and illicit sexual relationships with them. They might facetiously be described as engaging in fornication "without benefit of clergy." A more precise definition of the term "benefit of clergy," however, refers to a special privilege enjoyed by the medieval clergy: They were exempt from trial or punishment except in a church court. Again, we shall see that although nineteenth-century American clergymen stood trial in civil, criminal, and ecclesiastical courts, those trials frequently ended in an equivocal verdict that spared the clergyman punishment, if not the ordeal of a trial. They might be described as enjoying the traditional rewards of their status even though they were legally "without benefit of clergy." But in the end, I hope readers will use the phrase "without benefit of clergy" to question and counter the paradigm of the feminization of religion. Numbers alone do not tell the story. The assumption that women and clergymen possessed a close bond, even an alliance, is not borne out in the testimony of dozens of participants in the pastoral relationship. Women rarely noted or expressed their appreciation for a pastor's individual spiritual attentions. If they did, it was likely that the man served primarily as a romantic lover, suitor, or husband rather than as a religious counselor. Contrary to popular opinion then and scholarly opinion now, nineteenth-century American women were "without benefit of clergy." This insight should help us better understand the tension that an ideology of separate spheres imposed on those who tried to live up to its ideals. In addition, the tension between men and women in the church helps us understand why some women chose alternatives to the institutionalized churches of the nineteenth century.[3]

Two graphic images and one textual image from the latter half of the century illuminate the new perspective I hope to bring to the study of nineteenth-century American religion and culture. The first graphic, a sentimental print that appeared in the *New York Daily Graphic* of 1875, portrays the pastoral relationship as many contemporaries and historians have mistakenly viewed it. "A Present to the Pastor" (figure 1 in the photo gallery) is set in an intimate domestic space where a cupboard of dishes serves as the background and toys and pets occupy the foreground. A large family group of women, children, and female servants clusters around—even embraces—a patient and kindly pastor in the act of receiving a gift they have jointly prepared for him. The man of the house does not participate in this sentimental ritual: He remains in another room taking pleasure in a beverage that the pastor may or may not be invited to share with him. This print clearly delineates the popular perception that pastors were men who enjoyed a peculiar intimacy with their female flock. In turn, they were welcomed into the bosom of the family, with or without the supervision of a paterfamilias.[4]

A front-page cartoon in the *Daily Graphic* of a few months before provides an alternative and perhaps more accurate portrait of the pastoral relationship than the sentimental print. The top half of "The Churches and the Women" (figure 2) shows the "Rev. Hereticus," a Protestant clergyman with a look of dismay on his face and his arms outstretched, barring the door of his church to three disappointed women. The caption has him telling the women: "We can take your money, my good woman; but the places of honor in our churches are only for men." Although the cartoon as a whole makes a pro-Catholic statement, the message that Protestant churches counted on the support of women without offering them recognition and acceptance in return reflects an attitude prevalent in many sources. The third document (figure 3), the type-script text of a lecture delivered to the theological students of Oberlin College somewhat later in the century, makes that prevailing attitude explicit. Professor James H. Fairchild characterized the "relations of the pastor to the women of his church" as a neglected, even taboo, subject. In the first draft, he described the relationship as "forbidden territory"; in a revision, he described it as "forgotten territory." These last two images of alienation, I argue, are more descriptive of the experiences of women and pastors than the widely accepted portrait of cozy intimacy.[5]

This study is not an exposé, despite a focus on the sexual relationship between clergymen and women and the sensational forms it sometimes assumed. I don't want to be accused of "tabloid history"—the deliberate exposure of feet of clay in previously well-respected historical figures. My purpose, above all, is to understand the very human circumstances and tensions that shaped gender relations in general and the pastoral relationship in particular. Men were both agents and victims; women were both agents and victims. Men, of course, wielded more power. They shared, albeit unequally, in the constraints that gender constructs imposed on both sexes. Women on the other hand were permitted—and thus wielded—much less institutional and social power. Yet within these social and ideological strictures, they, too, fashioned social and spiritual lives of surprising independence and complexity.[6]

This study reveals the ways that human beings negotiate the tensions between ideology and lived experience and the cultural consequences of that negotiation. In the early twenty-first century, Americans still are attempting to reconcile an evolving and problematic gender ideology in the midst of changing social realities. Only three decades old, our relatively new ideals of gender equality in the home and in the workplace fail to conform to our social reality and prove devilishly difficult to attain. Our inability to realize our ideals causes frustration, tension, and fear, just as it did for our nineteenth-century predecessors. Over the past few decades of change, our popular media have been preoccupied with such issues as sexual harassment in the workplace, neglected children, sexual abuse in day-care centers, rising divorce rates, abortion, teen pregnancy, welfare mothers, and violence in our schools. All of these issues in some way reveal our failures to impose and live up to the new ideal of gender equality at home and at work. Social psychologists worry about the psychological development of adolescent girls and, more recently, of adolescent boys— another clear sign that gender socialization is deeply problematic. At the turn of the twenty-first century, widespread accusations of the sexual abuse of boys by Roman Catholic priests have confused and blurred ideological boundaries that long seemed to safely separate children, adolescents, and adults or heterosexuals, homosexuals, and celibates. These obsessions, evident in high-profile trials and throughout other cultural expressions from literature to cinema, reflect and shape our fears and frustration as we negotiate between gender ideals and experienced realities. I hope this study affords some additional insight into the complexity of our own problems, as well as those of our forebears.

PART I

The Pastoral Relationship as Perception

I

The Bellwether; or, What the Traveler Saw

During the decades before the Civil War, many European travelers to the young United States felt obliged to record their observations of the novel "experiment" in democracy, to assess the viability of this new form of government, and to publish their reports for both European and American audiences. Dozens of these writers described not just politics but everything from geography to the social conditions to the "manners and morals" of the new republic. Observations of American women—their appearance, dress, education, and manners—constituted one obligatory topic. The state of religion in the absence of an established national church also demanded comment. Both topics were important measurements of the future success of the nation. If a nation that espoused equality could count on its weakest members, its women, to uphold republican ideals and if a nation that rejected state-sponsored religion could still count on its churches to maintain moral order, then there was reasonable hope for democracy's growth and maturity.

Historians frequently quote these accounts since they provide a kind of sketch in words—a picture of the young nation by outsiders who brought a fresh, apparently disinterested perspective to the subject. However, these outsiders also brought with them political orientations and preconceived notions about the efficacy of democracy. Too frequently, historians employ these quotations uncritically, as if the sketch were not designed and framed by the traveler's perspective and bias. A critical examination of the travelers' opinions about women, religion, and clergy reveal that, despite their widely differing experiences and perspectives on the American scene, they reached a curious, surprising, and disconcerting consensus that continues to influence our picture of the subject today. Travelers from both the right and the left of the political spectrum discovered a possibly fatal flaw in the new nation—the remarkable devotion of American women to their religious leaders. Oddly, this relationship failed to reassure travelers of the moral strength of America. Rather, it seriously undermined their faith in democracy or confirmed their suspicions of its inherent instability. Travelers saw flocks of sheep without responsible moral leaders, an image that reflected their concerns about democratic leadership in politics as well as religion.[1]

Travelers frequently disagreed or at least interpreted similar phenomena in distinctly different ways. Some, like the oft-quoted Frenchman Alexis de Tocqueville, generally praised the new republic. Others, like the Englishwoman Frances Trollope, found little to laud. Yet even those who supported most things American could disagree on specific topics. In his observations on American women, for instance, de Tocqueville claimed that although they were "confined within the narrow circle of domestic life, and their situation . . . in some respects one of extreme dependence," still they occupied a "loftier position" than any women he had encountered in his wide travels. In fact, he credited the prosperity and strength of the American people largely to the "superiority of their women." Frederika Bremer, a Swedish admirer of American people and ideals, agreed their women were held in high esteem for their spiritual character. Yet, she noticed, "[m]en have in general . . . more *gallantry* than actual esteem for women." Men rarely sought women's society "when they seek strengthening food for soul or thought." Women might rule at home, Bremer argued, but it was men's acknowledgment of women's weaknesses rather than their virtues that allowed them to do so. Still, she claimed American girls received the same educational opportunities as boys and found a "peculiar vocation" in the public sphere through teaching. Frances Wright, an eccentric reformer from England, muddled the portrait of American women even further when she allowed that American women had more "liberty" in public places than their European sisters but believed that young girls needed a much better education to fulfill their roles as republican mothers. In short, the travelers' accounts are externally and internally inconsistent. Many were convinced that American women were not just beautiful but also morally and educationally fit to perform important domestic duties in the new nation. Others disagreed— often, explicitly—about the strength and status of women. Clearly, they also contradicted themselves, producing confusing and ambiguous images within the same report.[2]

The differences in reports on women are not easily explained, but the differences in the reports on religion seem linked to the political or religious orientation of the author. For example, those travelers who favored a strong national church were most likely to deplore the profusion of sects, the fanaticism those groups incited, and the ignorance, immorality, materialism, or contentious spirit of their clergy. Conversely, those who favored disestablishment and the voluntary system were most impressed by the profusion of churches, the widespread piety, the climate of religious harmony, and the high quality of preaching. Frances Wright acknowledged this controversy. Some travelers observed *no* religion while others saw fanaticism, she reported. Neither was true in her view. Instead, a "perfect cordiality" among religious fraternities reigned, thanks to the religious freedom permitted by a voluntary system.[3]

Travelers created especially confusing and ambiguous images of the clergyman in the new voluntary system. In the Church of England, as in other national churches on the Continent, the church hierarchy, not the congregation, appointed a rector or vicar to serve in a given parish. Tithes, not voluntary contributions from the parish, went to the hierarchy, who, in turn, determined the salaries of the parish priests. In short, the minister was directly accountable to his church superiors, not to the members of his parish. Travelers to America, therefore, worried about the relationship between a minister and his congregation in a system where the man could be wholly independent from any ecclesiastical authority and wholly dependent on his clients or, worse, inferiors for his position and his income. At best, he was more businessman than churchman, of necessity too interested in this world and less interested in the next. At worst, he was a craven servant of the people rather than a noble servant of Christ.

Two European visitors maintained an optimistic view of the American clergy in this new situation. "The minister," Frederika Bremer argued, "is exclusively the shepherd of souls, and occupies himself with nothing excepting the care of souls, by public preaching and private admonition and sympathy." She observed that congregations were genuinely attached to men who performed their duties in a selfless manner. They were not, as other writers had complained, "fortune-hunters." In fact, the "intelligent and interesting individuals" she had met among the clergy favorably impressed her. Francis Grund, a sympathetic observer from Germany, opined that "every clergyman may be said to do business on his own account, and under his own firm." Each minister could take full credit for his successes and full blame for his deficiencies. "He always acts as principal, and is, therefore, more anxious, and will make greater efforts to obtain popularity, than one who serves for wages," Grund maintained. He saw an additional advantage—the American clergy was a bargain. Ministers were plentiful and their price cheaper than that of an established clergy.[4]

Other writers doubted the advantages of the voluntary system. English traveler Sarah Maury questioned the allegiance of men who took their careers into their own hands. Although the system "contributes greatly to the excellencies of preaching," she admitted, it was "because the ties between the pastor and his flock are remote and sordid, liable to be broken before they are well begun." The minister could easily pick up stakes and move to a better-paying congregation. "He therefore sedulously studies the one branch of his profession which is the most likely to obtain for him another ministry; of course his sermons are his capital." His attention to the mundane duties of pastoral visiting thus suffered, she implied, since those efforts were not easily transferred or recycled in the next post. Maury was unusual in perceiving American clergy as men on the make—competing in the public sphere on terms very similar to those of political and commercial competitors, ambitious for their own self-interest, and maintaining only slim attachments to the people nominally under their care. Although Maury generally applauded the experiment in democracy, she favored the social hierarchy of the Catholic church and slavery. Thus, her view of the clergy as men more interested in themselves than in those in their care reflected an unspoken suspicion that American leaders—whether political or religious—were unreliable.[5]

Englishman Henry Fearon noted the same lack of attachment between the congregation and the pastor as early as the 1810s. "The great proportion of attendants at any particular church," he perceived, "appear to select it either because they are acquainted with the preacher, or that it is frequented by fashionable company, or their great grandmother went there before the Revolution. . . ." The most important reason, however, was that "*their interest will be promoted by their so doing,*" he emphatically stated. The congregation's interest was not spiritual, but social: a self-interest. In fact, Fearon doubted that they thought very much at all about Christianity. "Whatever degree of religious intelligence exists, is confined to the clergy," he conceded, "who, perhaps, have lost no advantage by the abolition of a state religion." However, the same Henry Fearon who worried about the "deadness of feeling" in American churches also observed that "*Clerical* gentlemen have here an astonishing hold upon the minds of men: the degree of reverential awe for the sanctity of their office, and the attention paid to the *external forms* of religion, approach almost to idolatry. . . ." In short, Fearon believed that Americans attended church for much the same reasons that Maury believed young men became ministers—they were ambitious and self-interested. Yet Fearon nonetheless noted an inexplicable clerical power over a largely unthinking people. Although he used the term *men*, he probably meant it as a generic reference to all Americans, not just American males. Confused and negative assessments such as Fearon's, taken together with the more positive but still ambivalent appraisals of other European travelers, produced an altogether equivocal judgment upon the state of religion and the status of the clergy in the wake of disestablishment.[6]

How surprising to find, then, that writers who so disagreed in their views on American women and American religion could agree on the peculiar topic of the pastoral relationship specifically between clergy and women. Across the spectrum, from the radical reform-minded Harriet Martineau on one end to the conservative and sardonic Frances Trollope on the other, travelers to America perceived an unusual and unfortunate attraction between women and their pastors. Three visitors confirmed Fearon's observations about the power of the clergy but were more specific, claiming that reverence for the clergy was confined almost exclusively to the women of America. English writer Charles Dickens noted the "evangelical ladies" who, devoted to religion and horrified by "theatrical entertainments," flocked to church, chapel, and lecture room. "In the kind of provincial life which prevails in cities such as this [Boston], the Pulpit has great influence." In fact, the tedium of women's restricted sphere drove them to the most entertaining preachers. "Wherever religion is resorted to as a strong drink, and as an escape from the dull, monotonous round of home," Dickens contended, "those of its ministers who pepper the highest will be the surest to please."[7]

Francis Grund, a German nobleman generally sympathetic to voluntary churches, further complicated the view of the clergy's influence. He claimed that "parsons" had more power in the United States than in any other country. He declared that "they have the power of breaking any man they please; for they possess the most complete control over the women." Unfortunately, Grund failed to explain just exactly how this enormously coercive power was exerted on men through women. He recounted a lively dispute that followed a sermon he had heard by Dr. Channing, an abolitionist preacher in Boston. The men in the group debated the preacher's controversial antislavery stand while the women remained silent. At the end of the lively debate, one woman offered the insipid comment that Channing was "a charming preacher," and another said that she preferred reading Channing's sermons to hearing them at church. Grund might have intended to show that Channing exerted influence on men by engaging them in debate over controversial issues while his female listeners attended more to the man and his manner than to his message. Yet the generally uncritical response of the women provided little evidence of Grund's claim for the clergy's "control" over the females and even less support for his hyperbolic contention that the men thus suffered under the clergy's power, too. Nevertheless, Grund's unsubstantiated argument is important, if only because he links the pastoral relationship between clergy and women to the larger question of its effects on American society as a whole.[8]

Richard Gooch, an Englishman of the conservative Tory High-Church party, echoed some of Grund's concerns but confined the clergy's influence entirely to women. He asserted, without reservations, "It is a fact that the females of all classes of fanatics in America are under a complete state of subjection to their *spiritual* pastors, and that they alone ought to be looked upon as their hearers & supporters. . . . It is to the women all their appeals are addressed, it is upon them all the baser purposes of fanatical preachers are made to operate." Gooch based his assertion on his own observations: "I have been in many of their most crowded congregations, and amongst several thousands never saw above a hundred men present at the same time." His astonishment was not singular. "[I]n fact, the disproportion of the sexes never fails to create surprise in strangers," he assured his readers. In short, then, Dickens, Grund, and Gooch all perceived a remarkable and potentially threatening clerical influence over women. Their criticisms cannot be dismissed as cynical or misogynist rants, however, because more thoughtful, critical, and apprehensive female writers, from opposite ends of the political spectrum, seconded and elaborated on that image.[9]

Harriet Martineau occupied a political position far to the left of Dickens, Grund, or Gooch but shared their concerns about the pastoral relationship. She heartily endorsed American ideals of equality and religious freedom but consistently faulted American institutions for failing to achieve their stated goals. She chastised the clergy, for instance, on their moral bankruptcy regarding slavery and disputed the claims that clergy held a respected position in antebellum society. In part, she blamed the problem on small salaries that rendered clergy beholden to wealthy patrons in the congregation. She pitied them this "disadvantageous position," an unfortunate by-product of the very voluntary system that she herself supported. Still, she refused to excuse their vices. "The American clergy are the most backward and timid class in the society in which they live," she insisted, "self-exiled from the great moral questions of the time [primarily slavery]; the least informed with true knowledge; the least efficient in virtuous action; the least conscious of that christian and republican freedom which, as the native atmosphere of piety and holiness, it is their duty to cherish and diffuse."[10]

Martineau argued that the clergy's timidity and unworldliness commanded little respect from the men of the community. After observing a group of merchants mock the efforts of a preacher to condemn their high prices, she ascertained that the men "esteem his services highly for keeping their wives, children and domestics in strict religious order." A "liberal-minded" acquaintance of Martineau cautioned her against believing all clergymen's statements, so out of touch with reality were they. "You know," he informed her, "the clergy are looked upon by all grown men as a sort of people between men and women." The characterization of the clergy as androgynous placed them in an ambiguous sphere, somewhere between the feminine domestic sphere and the masculine public sphere. But it also clearly banished them to a social netherworld—certainly beneath consideration, almost beneath contempt—by "all grown men."[11]

Given her view of the clergy's extremely limited status and authority, Martineau might be expected to disagree with the travelers who noted an unusually strong clerical influence and power over women. She did not. Instead, the clergy's influence was merely "confined to the weak members of society: women and superstitious men." That influence might be benign, she admitted, if the character of the minister was good and his conduct strictly professional, restricted to "friendship or acquaintance." But Martineau abhorred the "ill effects of the practice of parochial visiting" on women without specifically naming the problems. She advised ministers to call only on the "poor and afflicted persons, who have little other resource of human sympathy." Finally, she contrived an invidious comparison between the custom of parochial visiting and the Catholic ritual of auricular confession, counting on the deep and continuing anti-Catholicism of a Protestant England and America to detect the inherent evil in the practice. Although she never explicitly described the "evils" she perceived, her circumspection on the subject suggests that she feared an immoral sexual attraction between clergy and women.[12]

Whether or not Martineau suspected sexual misconduct, she was most disturbed by the political consequences of the sorry relationship between clergy and women. "I cannot enlarge upon the disagreeable subject of the devotion of the ladies to the clergy," she protested. "I believe there is no liberal-minded minister who does not see, and too sensibly feel, the evil of women being driven back upon religion as a resource against vacuity; and of there being a professional class to administer it." She especially condemned as "mischief" women's efforts to raise money to help educate young ministers. Clearly, Martineau, like Dickens, blamed women's dedication to the clergy on the rigidity

of the regnant gender ideology of separate spheres. In that constrictive configuration of gender roles, women had few opportunities outside the family and
the church to develop and exercise their talents. Their restricted sphere of
activity and their consequent intellectual purposelessness afforded them little
alternative to doting on children, husband, and priest. In her account, Martineau's wider purpose was to urge Americans to live up to their stated ideals
of equality, including the radical notion of women's political equality. She condemned religion only if it proved a source of cant and superstition. If either
the clergy or women employed religion to advance moral issues such as antislavery, she approved. Thus, Martineau's critique of the pastoral relationship
springs directly from her political beliefs that women should demand entrance
into a fully democratic society and expand their sphere of moral influence
beyond the narrow confines of the family and, especially, of the pastoral relationship. In short, their attention to their pastors prevented women from seeing and resisting the gendered boundaries that circumscribed their influence
and activity on moral issues in the political sphere.[13]

Martineau's radical political beliefs inspired one further criticism of the
pastoral relationship—namely, that gender difference created an unbridgeable
gap between male pastors and their female parishioners. With more contempt
than pity, she related the story of a young clergyman who complained to her
that his "parochial visiting afflicted him much. He had been visiting and exhorting a mother who had lost her infant," she reported, "a sorrow which he
always found he could not reach." He believed such visits yielded nothing but
harm. "How should it be otherwise?" Martineau expostulated. "What should
he know of the grief of a mother for her infant?" As usual, she assigned blame
for this ineffectual relationship equally to both mother and pastor. She accused
the mother of sending for the pastor as a "kind of charmer, to charm away the
heart's pain. Such pain is not sent to be charmed away." A pastor's sympathy
might render the mother's pain more endurable, but it would neither eliminate
it nor teach the necessary moral lesson. The minister, Martineau claimed, "of
necessity" had no sympathy to offer "but only a timid pain with which to
aggravate [hers]." In other words, Martineau believed the mother called on the
pastor not as the explicator of the theological reasons and implications of her
loss but rather as on a shaman who would relieve her anguish with the aid of
magic. And the pastor, because of his inadequate training and notions of pastoral counseling, but also because of his masculine experience and orientation,
must ultimately fail to provide her any spiritual or human comfort. From Martineau's perspective, the pastoral relationship was too dependent on both sides.
She also saw that, despite the clergyman's dubious gender status somewhere
between male and female, the relationship was also dysfunctional because of
gender differences. Women could not call on men to understand and alleviate
their pain because men could never "know" the special grief of a mother. In
the end, the relationship bred only superstition, mindlessness, and timidity—
an inhospitable environment for the growth of the vigorous and courageous
democratic Christianity she hoped would eventually flourish on American
soil.[14]

Martineau never doubted that democracy was a worthy goal, but she was impatient with the social restrictions that prevented immediate implementation of democratic processes. Conservatives, on the other hand, already doubted the worthiness and ultimate success of American ideals and institutions. Yet, just like Martineau, they reserved a special condemnation for the pastoral relationship. One of the most quoted travelers of the antebellum era, Frances Trollope, repeatedly directed her piercing gaze at clergy and women. Throughout her best-selling and oft-reprinted account, her mordant wit etched an indelible portrait of a morally impaired relationship. Much of Trollope's work in general, and her criticisms of religion more specifically, focused on the crude manners, language, and education of the rustic Americans. Thus, a frontier preacher who straddles the back of a chair as his pulpit, chews tobacco and spits, and endlessly repeats the same scriptural verse in a variety of accents and tones without actually expounding on it constitutes one target of her reproach. Trollope visited churches, prayer meetings, revivals, and camp meetings, excoriating each for the superficiality, ignorance, narrow-mindedness, or enthusiastic fanaticism of the participants. Before either Grund or Martineau published (both in 1837) their negative opinions of female-dominated congregations, Trollope (in 1832) had already declared that she had "never [seen], or read, of any country where religion had so strong a hold upon the women, or a slighter hold upon the men." That dangerous imbalance she blamed on the "influence which the ministers of all the innumerable religious sects throughout America, have on the females of their respective congregations."[15]

Trollope likened the situation to "what we read of in Spain, or in other strictly Roman Catholic countries," evoking among Protestant readers the same images of superstition and idolatry that Martineau had summoned in her criticism. In a democratic society that had erased most forms of social hierarchy, Trollope claimed that only the clergy enjoyed such high status, giving them "high importance in the eyes of the ladies." She also believed that the inordinate esteem women accorded clergy was reciprocal. "[I]t is from the clergy only that the women of America receive that sort of attention which is so dearly valued by every female heart throughout the world." But where Martineau had blamed the unhealthy pastoral relationship on gender roles that circumscribed women's talents, Trollope blamed a democratic society that withheld from American women the "influential importance" granted to upper- and middle-class European women. In the absence of deference from the general population of men, American women earned respect only from the clergy and consequently gave "their hearts and souls into [the clergy's] keeping."[16]

Where Martineau had only hinted of sexual misconduct, Trollope repeatedly accused the clergy of base sexual motives. A venal clergy easily abused the inordinate confidence women placed in their pastors, Trollope complained. At a prayer meeting, she noted the "coaxing affectionate tone" preachers employed to exhort sinners, mostly young girls, to the anxious benches. The "priests," as she called them, "began whispering to the poor tremblers" and "from time to time" applied a "mystic caress." "More than once," Trollope declared, "I saw a young neck encircled by a reverend arm." In her devastating account of a camp meeting, Trollope described in detail the "[h]ysterical sobbings, convulsive groans, shrieks and screams" that emanated from the hundreds of women in attendance. The preachers moved among them, "at once exciting and soothing their agonies." "I saw the insidious lips approach the cheeks of the unhappy girls," she reported with disgust.[17]

Unlike Martineau, who cast blame for the sinister relationship on both clergy and women, Trollope placed the responsibility for these "atrocities" squarely on the shoulders of American men. They failed to value their women, forcing their wives and daughters into the arms of sympathetic ministers. How could they leave the women they love best "bound in the iron chains of a most tyrannical fanaticism?" she implored. "Do they fear these self-elected, self-ordained priests, and offer up their wives and daughter to propitiate them?" Just as Henry Fearon feared but could not explain the American clergy's indirect control over men through their control of women, so Trollope shaped a distorted rhetoric that defies logic. Why would American men fear the clergy and offer up their women as a virtual human sacrifice when, as Trollope asserted, so few men even bothered to attend church? Were men so uncomfortable with pastoral denunciations of their lives and values that they stayed away but let their wives go in their stead? That writers such as Fearon and Trollope failed to explicate their fears in the descriptions and denunciations of the pastoral relationship only underscores, rather than undermines, their surprise, confusion, dismay, anger, and fear.[18]

Trollope's prescription for curing the unhappy and unhealthy pastoral relationship was simple: She desperately wanted American men to assert their patriarchal authority and to step in and defend women from the depredations of an illegitimate clergy. She confirmed her suspicions of the physical as well as spiritual dangers inherent in the pastoral relationship with hearsay evidence she acquired from sources "on whose veracity I perfectly rely." One storyteller recounted for her the visit of an itinerant preacher who inspired "a curious mixture of spiritual awe and earthly affection" in a vulnerable young girl. The girl's father, fortunately, "remarked the sort of covert passion that gleamed through the eyes of his godly visitor" and, alerted by rumors of other young women singled out for the preacher's attentions, banished the man from his household. The clergyman quickly left town, but "no less than seven unfortunate girls produced living proofs of the wisdom of . . . [the] worthy father," Trollope reported sarcastically. For Trollope, the "worthy father" was the heroic papa, not the priest. In him she found an American man who merited praise for protecting the females of his family from a predatory preacher. Trollope certainly had personal motives for admiring men who assumed the role of paternal guardian. Her own husband was an improvident and unreliable bread-winner. Frances became an ambitious entrepreneur who undertook extraordinary risks—crossing the Atlantic and journeying to the frontier city of Cincinnati to set up a commercial bazaar—to compensate for the financial ineptitude of her husband. When that venture failed, she published her travel diaries and finally found a lucrative profession for herself as a very prolific and successful writer. No doubt a deep desire to be better cared for by her own husband inspired some of the real fear and anger in her denunciation of American men's response to the moral threat of the pastoral relationship.[19]

Trollope's *personal* fear of an absent paternal protector never surfaced in her writing. Instead, she articulated a *political* fear that the national government of the United States, the representatives of American men, failed to protect its weakest citizens from religious fanatics. Trollope deplored a family she met "where one was a Methodist, one a Presbyterian, and a third a Baptist." In another, "one was a Quaker, one a declared Atheist, and another a Universalist." In both these contemptible families, it was females who, though "moving in the best society that America affords," were "one and all of them as incapable of reasoning on things past, present, and to come, as the infants they nourish." These childlike women acted on the misbegotten national principle that "each had a right to choose a creed and mode of worship for herself." Trollope could summon no admiration for "so loose, unstable, and unscriptural a system" and ultimately blamed "short-sighted legislation" for producing such chaos. In effect, the revolutionary founding fathers had sired a democratic government and a disestablished religion whose legacy was the frightful religious enthusiasm and sectarianism of American women, the craven, predatory nature of their clergy, and the loathsome religious indifference of the nation's men. Likewise, an unholy union of women and clergy produced not just bastard children but illegitimate and fatherless religions. In Trollope's view, only the patriarchal authority and monarchical institutions (to which she returned in England) could prevent America's precipitous descent into moral disorder.[20]

Why did travel writers relentlessly target and condemn the pastoral relationship in America, and what were the consequences of the image they constructed? These writers at least dimly sensed that the pastoral relationship was a crucial predictor of the health and viability of democracy in the new nation. The portrait they collectively created did not herald democracy's success. By painting a picture of an ineffectual or exploitative religious leader and his hopelessly gullible female flock, travel writers overturned the traditional scriptural image of a shepherd and his flock. Indeed, the word *pastor* literally and figuratively evoked the shepherd. But travel writers effected a disturbing metamorphosis in this reassuring paternalistic image. Gone was the man—the shepherd—who clearly possessed an authority delegated from God and demonstrated intellectual qualities of judgment and wisdom far superior to those in his flock. In a democracy and a voluntary church system, travelers feared the shepherd's role had been usurped by a religious guide with neither legitimacy nor leadership abilities. They saw instead a bellwether—the traditional term for the male sheep (often castrated) who wore a bell and led his female counterparts in the flock. The term *bellwether* connoted an unreliable leader, usually self-appointed, and often a noisy, clamorous fellow followed blindly by a foolish flock. With only a little imagination, a nineteenth-century reader of these travel accounts might see the fatuous women of American churches as stand-ins for the voting public at large and see their boisterous, self-anointed preachers as substitutes for the popularly elected political leaders in the new republic. Although no writer used the word *bellwether*, the word was in current use during the period to describe the futility of true democracy. And writers delighted in describing and condemning the emotional and spiritual anarchy of the rural camp meeting, the perfect pastoral illustration of the potential chaos of democracy. Those who ultimately hoped for democracy's success, such as Martineau, believed the sheep would, through proper education, acquire reason and learn to follow the most rational and moral leaders among them. Trollope, on the contrary, believed the sheep were, by nature, incapable of leading themselves.[21]

Few Americans today openly question the health and longevity of American democracy, though the prominence of campaign reform on the national political scene points to some of the same fears of illegitimacy in political leaders. In the first half of the nineteenth century, however, the life span of the democratic "experiment" was still very much in doubt for both its supporters and its detractors. No wonder, then, that nineteenth-century European travel writers were so ineluctably fascinated by the pastoral relationship. This peculiar relationship between women and pastors in a voluntary church served as a synecdoche—the part that represented the whole. It seemed to indicate a possibly fatal defect in democracy itself. By generally making women, rather than men *and* women, the gullible sheep, these writers safely confined the danger to the female portion of the society. Women and clergy together became the scapegoats for democracy's potential failure. Although the reformer Martineau might have hoped for women's eventual full participation in the democratic experiment, she probably retarded women's progress toward that goal by helping to create such a negative image of the pastoral relationship between clergy and women. Similarly, Trollope's prescription that men assert their patriarchal authority in the dangerous pastoral relationship proved an effective and enduring antidote to arguments for women's rights for almost a century to come.

2

Gone Astray; or, What the Public Feared

The American clergy suffered from moral corruption, charged the acerbic Frances Trollope, and her fellow English traveler Richard Gooch emphatically agreed. Gooch supported this contention with evidence extracted from the newspapers and trial pamphlets of the early 1830s. He reported that "abandoned characters" emigrated to the United States to become popular preachers. By crossing international boundaries, English scoundrels assumed a new and respectable identity and preyed on a fresh and innocent American population. Gooch devoted one entire chapter of his travel account to the best known clerical scandal of the antebellum period, the Rev. Ephraim Avery's trial for the murder of a mill girl in Fall River, Massachusetts. European travelers such as Gooch came to the United States in the antebellum period to search for evidence of the vitality of democracy. Instead, as we have just read, many discovered in the relationship between ministers and women a disquieting symptom of political ill health.[1]

Although travelers' views of the pastoral relationship were outsiders' perceptions, so, too, were the views of most ordinary Americans. Although many men and women knew and worshiped with a regular pastor, many more had no ongoing connection with a particular clergyman. They might read of an idealized image—a constructive relationship between a minister and his female flock—in the numerous Sunday school tracts and pious memoirs. But many undoubtedly accepted the much more destructive relationship portrayed in the secular press. Nineteenth-century Americans, like their European visitors, shared a suspicion of clergy and women largely because the most powerful representations of the pastoral relationship were highly publicized sensational trials of clergymen for sexual misconduct. Americans and Europeans both saw in the pastoral relationship a disquieting image, but for Americans the threat was much more immediate. It jeopardized not just their republic but their churches and their families, too.

For centuries, anticlerical writers had employed clerical scandals in the cause of free thought. Freethinkers in the United States attacked organized religion, especially Christianity, and its clergy as "a source of danger to the American republic." W. F. Jamieson claimed that clergymen occupied a special privileged "class" that assumed too much power and influence for the good of a democratic society. In addition, the clergy's unhealthy political power was matched by a dangerous antinomianism that ignored social controls. "No man in the world has so few conditions imposed upon him at the threshold of society as the clergyman. His passport to social life is almost *carte blanche*. . . . The rules of social intercommunication between the sexes are, in his case, virtually suspended." To radical defenders of religious freedom and the separation of church and state, the clergyman posed not merely a political threat but a serious social risk because he was not bound by the same rules of decorum as ordinary men. The minister too easily transgressed the very moral codes he prescribed for everyone else. Indeed, Americans throughout much of the nineteenth century complained that clergy regularly wandered outside the social and moral enclosures constructed for a republican society. These perceptions became frighteningly real during a series of trials that profoundly distressed ordinary Americans and not merely those anticlerical philosophers who already harbored deep suspicions of unmerited ministerial influence in the new republic.[2]

The public trials of clergymen created dynamic and disturbing images of the pastoral relationship for thousands of readers by portraying ministers and women in a variety of characterizations and plots. The adversarial format of the trials shaped the plots and interpretations available to jurors and readers. The opposing sides, in court and in trial publications, created competing melodramas that forced the audience to choose between simplistic, sensational, and stereotypical renderings of very complex human relationships. In the most common scenario, the enemies of the accused clergyman depicted the minister as a monster, an unholy predator on innocent women, who masqueraded as a servant of God and invaded the domestic fold. Neither the stalwart shepherd nor the bumbling bellwether, the pastor in this scenario became a beastly and rapacious "wolf in sheep's clothing." In the opposing scenario, the minister's supporters portrayed the clergyman as a martyr, the victim of an unholy conspiracy that dragged women into the public arena in order to bring down a hapless pastor. The women hauled before the court might be cast as deliberate temptresses, traitors to the ideal of true womanhood, or conversely they might appear as confused beneficiaries of the pastor's spiritual affections, weak and vulnerable lost sheep cruelly manipulated and exploited by his ruthless male enemies. Despite their enduring power, none of these polarizing plots emerged triumphant from the press reports. Instead, Americans struggled to reconcile the contradictory scripts. Most readers chose their interpretations of these problematic relationships by focusing only on the errant individuals rather than viewing them as part of an endemic social, cultural, political, or religious pathology. They saw a particular leader of a flock who breached moral and social boundaries and led his followers astray. In the process of transgressing borders, the protagonists changed both character and shape. The minister, more than the women, metamorphosed into a frightful freak of nature, a hybrid creature that displayed confusing physical and moral characteristics. He was both wolf and sheep, at once evil and good.[3]

These simplistic and contradictory characterizations of the minister both obscured the complexity of each individual and his relationship with women and masked deeper cultural tensions. As European travelers saw it, the unhealthy alliance between clergy and women was a symptom of democracy's real or potential failure. Many nineteenth-century Americans, however, saw the threat to the nation not in political terms, but in moral ones: They worried that these public trials threatened the moral strength of the nation by undermining religion and encouraging anticlericalism, skepticism, and infidelity. Yet these clerical sexual misconduct cases inspired such horror and fascination not merely because they challenged cherished political or religious ideals but because they seriously threatened the almost universally held ideals of gender loosely articulated as "separate spheres." Like political and religious ideals, gender norms served as powerful sources of social and moral control in the young republic.

Cases of sexual misconduct in the pastoral relationship tragically exposed the differences between what *ought* to be and what *appeared* to be the proper relations between men and women. Men ought to protect women. Men ought to participate in the rough-and-tumble of the competitive public sphere, earn bread enough for themselves and their families, and return home to the harmonious domestic haven created by women. Women ought to uphold the strictest moral standards in themselves and encourage them in their husbands and children. Ministers ought to be the partners of women in protecting the moral sanctity of the home, the church, and the society at large. Yet these trials dramatically demonstrated that ideals might not represent reality and that the ideal itself might be dangerously flawed, contributing to misconduct rather than preventing it. The trust in the partnership between ministers and women was dangerously misplaced because that pastoral relationship ignored the separation of public masculine and private feminine spheres and occupied a terrifying no-man's-land where the ideological rules failed to apply.

The Rev. Ephraim Avery and three other ministers from succeeding decades garnered an unusual level of public attention because they all revealed serious violations of the borders constructed by the separate spheres ideology. In 1832, the Rev. Avery allegedly strayed from his marriage and clerical vows to prey upon a female factory worker, herself an outcast from middle-class feminine norms. In 1844, the Right Rev. Benjamin Onderdonk's inappropriate conduct betrayed his elevated position in the church and society and confounded his Episcopal peers and contemporaries. In 1857, the Rev. Isaac Kalloch overstepped his pastoral role by appearing in a compromising place with a married woman from his congregation. In 1875, the Rev. Henry Ward Beecher baffled and amused an entire nation by wandering across the indistinct boundaries between friendship, love, and pastoral responsibility. Each case eroded Americans' trust in their ideology of gender and their trust in the relationship between women and their pastors, forcing generations of Americans to acknowledge and try to shore up the fragile boundaries between men's and women's spheres. The first and most tragic of the four stories clearly illustrates the dismay, morbid interest, and distorted perceptions generated by clergymen who failed to stay within the accepted bounds of gender roles and conduct.[4]

The Reverend Ephraim K. Avery

This crime first attracted local media attention in late December 1832, when a farmer in Tiverton, Rhode Island, walked out over his frosted fields early one morning and discovered a grim sight. The crumpled and half-frozen body of Sarah Maria Cornell, a thirty-year-old unmarried mill worker from nearby Fall River, Massachusetts, hung on the stackpole the farmer used to mound and dry his hay. On first observation, the coroner and other witnesses confirmed the death a suicide and buried the body. But rumors and testimony at the inquest soon undermined this determination. Authorities subsequently exhumed, examined, and reburied the body, not once but twice, in an effort to confirm or dispel the possibility of murder. The accumulated evidence raised troubling questions. First, the knot in the cord from which Cornell was suspended could not have been tightened by the weight of her slumping body. Second, Cornell died carrying a fetus three or four months from conception. Third, the family with whom the young woman boarded claimed she was not in a suicidal frame of mind the day of her death and brought forward several significant documents from her trunk. Most incriminating was a note that read, "If I should be missing enquire of the Rev Mr Avery of Bristol he will know where I am Dec 20th S M Cornell." In addition, bruises on the corpse's abdomen suggested either sexual assault or a crude attempt at abortion. Finally, prosecutors discovered and presented several credible witnesses, including a ferryman, who testified to seeing Avery in the vicinity of Tiverton on the night of the girl's death. Both Cornell's family and her doctor told prosecutors she had named Avery as the author of her troubles. Although suicide still appeared likely to many observers, credible circumstantial evidence of foul play pointed toward the minister.

Ephraim K. Avery, an ordained preacher in the Methodist Connection, withstood a barrage of damning testimony at a preliminary hearing in his hometown of Bristol, Rhode Island, where two friendly justices again ruled the death a suicide. The public uproar that followed this decision inspired Avery to go into hiding with friends in New Hampshire. But a dogged detective, on retainer from a committee of Fall River mill owners determined to bring Avery to justice, followed his trail and served Avery with new warrants and extradition papers. The minister spent the next five months in jail, awaiting his criminal trial before the Rhode Island Supreme Court and preparing his defense with two distinguished attorneys funded by the Methodist church. The trial itself lasted nearly a month, then a record for duration in American jurisprudence. In the end, Avery was acquitted of all charges by the criminal courts as well as by his clerical brethren. A furious public, however, whipped up by the barrage of newspaper coverage, refused to allow Avery to secure a pulpit anywhere in New England. The grisly crime, the pathetic status of the victim, the minister's flight, the formation of an organized opposition, the preeminence of the attorneys enlisted on both sides, and the contrast between the official and popular verdicts all combined to guarantee this intriguing story a widespread and continuing audience.[5]

During the trial, the confident prosecutors pinned their case on the wide array of circumstantial evidence against Avery, portraying him as Cornell's wicked seducer at a camp meeting and her violent abortionist and murderer in the stackyard. However, the judge never allowed witnesses such as the doctor and Cornell's family to testify that Sarah had named Avery as the father of her child, deeming it hearsay evidence. In contrast, the judge allowed Avery's defense attorneys to introduce numerous witnesses whose secondhand evidence detailed the victim's aberrant and unhappy sexual past. The defense scenario convincingly cast Cornell as a depraved young woman so distraught by her illegitimate pregnancy that she took her own life. The Rev. Avery merely defended the purity of his church by refusing her readmission to his church or a letter of transfer to another church. Each side in the case claimed the other side represented not merely a base and loathsome individual but also a foul conspiracy. The prosecutors painted the Methodist clergy as a dangerous cabal ready to defend their minister at all costs. Similarly, Avery's defense counsel blamed the false charges against him on a conspiracy of anti-Masonic and anti-Methodist mill owners anxious to absolve themselves of their failure to protect their young female workers from contamination by abandoned women such as Cornell. The media coverage of the trial both reflected and fueled this bitter partisanship. Throughout the proceedings, spectators and reporters mobbed the courtroom. The judge enjoined reporters not to publish any accounts until the jury rendered a verdict. His gag rule held until the last few days, when New York and Boston papers competed to be first to publish the testimony. More than a dozen pamphlets followed the newspaper reports in the coming months. A few publications claimed to present the trial testimony in an impartial manner, but most argued fiercely for Avery's guilt or innocence.[6]

The print coverage was extraordinary not merely for its volume but for its variety as well. Some pamphlets reported the testimony in embarrassingly explicit detail, and others offered expurgated versions. Avery quickly denounced as a forgery one pamphlet containing his alleged confession. Poems warning young women of the depredations of false lovers appeared in newspapers and broadsides. Catherine Williams produced an early version of the true-crime novel by augmenting the trial testimony with interviews of family and friends of the protagonists that gave her readers more detailed and sympathetic character sketches of the participants than the pamphleteers had provided. In addition, engraved portraits of the protagonists (figures 4 and 5) gave viewers an opportunity to judge the main characters for themselves. Avery might appear imposing and upright to his defenders but dark and brooding to his doubters. Likewise, Cornell might appear the ingenue to her supporters but the hussy to her detractors. At least one play staged in New York made the melodramatic quality of the case explicit.[7]

Perhaps the most elaborate publication resulting from the case was a portfolio of facsimiles of the alleged correspondence between Sarah Cornell and Ephraim Avery. The lithographs were such faithful reproductions of the original documents that they duplicated the color of the stationery, inscribed the back with the address of the recipient, and contained fold lines—only the wax wafers that sealed them were missing. The publishers of the facsimile encouraged readers to compare the samples of Avery's and Cornell's handwriting to determine the authors and their motivations. Readers pondered whether Sarah's note pointing to Avery (figure 6) was written in a state of fear, hope, or revenge. The lithographers also included maps of the area so that readers of the testimony might judge the accuracy of Avery's accounts of his peregrinations on the day of the murder. The attention to authenticity and claims of it, the questions of authorship, and the corroboration of trial testimony in these documents were intended not for passive readers but rather for active consumers of evidence. All invited readers to engage in a careful analysis of the letters, to construct their own interpretations, and to reach their own verdicts in the case. The public carefully studied these documents in an attempt to resolve the apparently contradictory scripts.[8]

Although the facsimiles left the verdict up to the reader, a lithograph entitled "A Minister Extraordinary Taking Passage & Bound on a Foreign Mission to the Court of His Satanic Majesty!" made no such claims to impartiality (figure 7). A New York City entrepreneur named Robinson published the hand-colored engraving (nine and one-eighth inches by sixteen and one-eighth inches) suitable for framing, which offered viewers a dramatic interpretation of the case. In the left foreground, Cornell's body, in cloak and bonnet, hangs limply from a pole. Behind her stands a stack or rustic outbuilding that evokes the pastoral or rural setting so inconsistent with the scene of a crime. In front of the corpse, the artist has scattered some of the circumstantial evidence in the case—a pair of slippers, a white handkerchief, and an abbreviated note inscribed, "If missing, enquire of Rev . . . ," even though this evidence was actually discovered far from the scene of the crime. In the center of the print, Avery sits hunched over in a small ferryboat, his head turned awkwardly toward the viewer, staring back in an expression of surprise or fear or intimidation. In the boat, in the air, in the water, on an island in the background, and on the far right side of the print, fantastic creatures nearly surround the minister, ushering him along to a diabolical realm in marked contrast to the pastoral scene he leaves behind him.[9]

The trial testimony suggested that Avery had indeed crossed over water several times on the day before and the day after the murder, and he perhaps crossed the boundary between Massachusetts and Rhode Island, too. In this print, however, he crosses a far more treacherous and significant symbolic border, apparently a traitor to his profession and his faith. The caption played on the double meaning of the term *minister*. Instead of an ordinary minister of God, Avery is an extraordinary agent on a special but undetermined mission to God's archenemy, His Satanic Majesty. The artist emphasized Avery's crossing this charged boundary by drawing on classical themes of the underworld and Christian notions of supernatural evil. Like Avery, the devilish creatures surrounding him cross a variety of boundaries and thus defy easy categorization. For example, a bat resists classification as either a bird or a rodent: It flies but has fur; it is blind in the light but sees in the dark. Similarly, the other beasts defy boundaries by living on both land and in the air or in the water. A skeleton horse can still carry a rider and fly, no less. Even humanlike figures fly, wear horns or tails, and display both human and animal characteristics. Several administer death, pitching or leading humans off an island or boiling their remains in a grisly stew. In other words, the freaks that challenge supposedly natural categories of human and beast, regularly transgress the boundaries of land, water, and air, and toss humans from life to a horrible death are *extra*ordinary, *un*natural, even *super*natural. They are monstrous and evil. These monsters, not the pathetic lifeless creature hanging on the stackpole, are Avery's soul mates. In this context, Avery transforms himself from a humane pastor into an inhumane monster, from a minister of Christ into a supernatural consort of the Devil.[10]

No document better illustrates the source of the public's fascination with the Avery case. The minister performed an unnatural act by literally turning his back on the young woman, exactly the type of poor creature (one of his flock) he was charged with protecting and saving. His reptilian eyes stare back into the viewer's eyes, yet his character remains inscrutable. While he shares the title, clothing, and status of an emissary of God and a superior moral authority, still he appears to commune with and inhabit a supernatural nether realm of evil and death. Like a wolf in sheep's clothing, he is a ravening beast masquerading as a docile domestic animal. No more frightening apparition could adorn the walls of an antebellum home (or perhaps more appropriately a tavern) than the image of a clergyman as a debaucher of innocent womanhood and a fiendish murderer.

Other publications similarly explored the ways both protagonists in the case crossed natural boundaries to become monsters, illustrating the power of these mythical creatures to terrify and captivate audiences. In her novel, Catherine Williams imagined the distraction of the local people facing preachers in the pulpit on the Sunday after the murder. Some stayed home from church, thinking "ministers were such wicked creatures, they did not want to hear them." Others declined to condemn all ministers for the failings of one and struggled to listen with reverence to their pastor. But "their thoughts, in spite of themselves, would wander after him, who in their mind was guilty of this foul deed, and at this very time calling *sinners* to repentance." The difficulty of reconciling the minister and the murderer in the same person produced images of both a moral monster and a shameless play actor. Williams concluded a poem on the subject by declaring, "No verdict can the monster clear / Who dies a hypocrite must wake to weep." She deemed Avery not merely a mutation, something between human and beast, but a conscious pretender who only played the part of a minister to disguise the heart of a seducer and murderer.[11]

A number of broadside poems sympathetic to Cornell also exposed Avery as the beast in pastoral disguise, the dangerous deceiver. In "The Death of Sarah M. Cornell," the lyricist warned,

> Young maidens all a warning take
> From truth's herein revealed,
> You oft beneath a righteous robe
> May find a wolf concealed.

"The Factory Maid," to be sung to the tune of the national anthem, made explicit the false perception, even blindness, that Cornell took to her meeting with Avery and the terrifying double take she must have experienced just before her death.

> Her lover? Ah, no! her deceiver drew nigh,
> Her fears flew away, for the false one came smiling;
> How sightless in love is fair woman's bright eye,
> She saw not that round her a serpent was coiling. . . .
> Those hands that in her's had been tenderly laid,
> Like paws of the tiger, now fiercely did clutch her. . . .

Readers perceived Avery as both a lover and a deceiver, a snake and a wild cat, nothing less than a terrifying shape-shifter who crossed the boundaries between human and beast, good and evil, minister and devil, with impunity. In "Lines Written on the Death of Sarah M. Cornell" (figure 8), the bard lamented "when cruel men break nature's laws" and declared that readers' hearts "must bleed, when Shepherds murder lambs indeed." "Hellish lust," he intoned, had transformed Avery into a "monster dire."[12]

In the many publications suspicious of Avery, Sarah Cornell conformed to the ideal of innocent womanhood and Avery assumed the shape of the wolf in sheep's clothing. The same unsettling perceptions of shape-shifting also afflicted those observers who defended the minister. In their eyes, Cornell became the monster by forfeiting her claims to virtuous womanhood. Avery's attorney claimed that when women were "chaste and pure," they far excelled men. But "when profligate," women sank just as far below them. "[I]f you were to seek for some of the vilest monsters in wickedness and depravity," he assured the men of the jury, "you would find them in the female form." Not merely flawed, women with damaged sexual reputations were monstrous inversions of the ideal type of true womanhood, more evil than any man. The novelist Catherine Williams, at least, recognized that Avery's defense team constructed a work of creative drama far more imaginative than her own work. Their version of the crime, she claimed, was "a romance, not to be equalled by any thing we know or read of Spanish or Italian vengeance, . . . dress[ed]

. . . up in a most ingenious manner, [and] presented . . . to the Jury." In short, Sarah shifted from innocent victim to depraved harlot. Her story shifted, too, from factual reporting to fanciful romance. Both were works of dangerous artifice.[13]

Sarah Cornell and Ephraim Avery fascinated antebellum Northerners because both of them, much like the creatures in Richardson's lithograph, defied classification within the emergent ideology of gendered spheres and dramatized the disturbing consequences of failing to live within its bounds. Both Cornell and Avery crossed the prescribed boundaries of gender in significant ways. Cornell, at thirty years old, still worked as an itinerant mill worker. She had failed to secure for herself a position in the domestic sphere as wife and mother. Equally unsettling, she lost her place in the Methodist church and thus her status as a moral exemplar. At times, Cornell had earned membership in good standing but more than once had been expelled or refused admission for lying, stealing, and loose behavior. Novelist Catherine Williams recognized that Sarah's marginal status as a female factory worker contributed to her unfortunate end but wondered, "How different her fate would have been could she have been settled in life and tied to the duties of a wife and mother." She believed that Cornell would have made a "much better wife than ordinary" and that marriage would have spared her the grisly death she met as a single mill girl. Instead, Sarah was denied the chance to prove her worth as a woman. Unfettered by marriage, she stepped out of the bounds of virtuous womanhood that antebellum culture so rigidly imposed on women and too easily assumed a monstrous aspect as a result.[14]

Ephraim Avery, like many of his clerical brothers, failed to reside securely within the bounds of enterprising masculinity that the culture promoted for men. In the new division of labor, ministers shuttled between the two spheres and shared with women the responsibility for upholding moral standards. They split their time between, on the one hand, the masculine duties of theological study and controversial preaching and, on the other, the feminine duties of visiting and comforting. Too often, their ministrations appeared to be a service almost strictly to women, creating at once an "uneasy alliance" and a dangerous intimacy. Frances Trollope was perceptive when she claimed that American men considered the clergy effeminate, in some androgynous sphere all their own.

In disconcerting ways, a minister shared the monstrous, hermaphroditic shape of the "man-mid-wife," the male physician who increasingly, during the nineteenth century, crossed gender borders to intrude on the traditional female domain of childbirth and displace the female midwife. Critics of this new masculine profession charged that the man-mid-wife's unnatural familiarity with women inspired lust in both the doctor and his patient. Husbands, the critics urged, should avoid being cuckolded by refusing to employ a man-mid-wife except in extreme emergencies. The controversy over male midwifery produced an explicit visual image of a half-man, half-woman, a creature labeled "a newly discoverr'd animal," a "*Monster*" uncatalogued by eighteenth-century naturalists (figure 9). Although the dual sex of the man-mid-wife image is more explicit than any visual images of the ministers, the same confusion over sexual identity and the fear over transgressed gender boundaries haunted Americans contemplating clerical misconduct in the pastoral relationship.[15]

In sum, both accusers and defenders of the minister viewed one (or both) of the two protagonists in the Avery story as menacing tricksters, creatures who changed physical form as well as moral character. These liminal figures navigated across the imaginary boundaries of acceptable gendered behavior with destabilizing social effects, indeed, terrifyingly evil consequences. This case and others exposed not just the failings of the individual protagonists but also the fragility and permeability of separate spheres. These concerns, nonetheless, usually remained below the surface of rhetoric surrounding each case. Evidence of such cultural confusion emerges not in explicit discourse but in the ambiguity of the outcome of the trial. In Avery's case, the monster of public opinion eventually defeated the martyr of official verdicts. Public opinion rendered Avery anathema despite his acquittal in both the church and criminal courts. For decades afterward, Americans invoked Avery's name whenever a new clerical scandal or hypocrisy surfaced. The embattled Avery finally capitulated to public opposition, moved to the Western Reserve of Ohio, and ended his days quietly as a farmer. No longer trusted in relationships with women outside his own family, Avery was exiled to the traditional rural confines of his own domestic sphere, one he had worked so hard to escape as a youth.[16]

The Right Reverend Benjamin Onderdonk

The Avery case by itself would illumine important tensions in antebellum culture, but a spate of trials that appeared in the following decades explored, each in a quite different way, the threat to social stability posed by clerical wrongdoing. The most celebrated case of the 1840s, judging by the number of publications it generated, was that of the Right Reverend Benjamin Onderdonk, Episcopal bishop of the state of New York and one of the most powerful of the eighteen bishops in that hierarchical and aristocratic denomination. Onderdonk's case displayed many of the same characteristics as the Avery case, particularly in the inordinate number of highly partisan pamphlets it produced. But notable differences between the Avery and Onderdonk cases still show that a clergyman's crossing of social boundaries was profoundly disconcerting. In the Onderdonk story, all the protagonists seemed to fall neatly within their prescribed gender roles. The bishop, unlike Avery, was no upstart, uneducated preacher: He descended from an old and wealthy New York family, enjoyed the privileges of a university education, served in New York City's leading congregations, and taught at General Theological Seminary. The Episcopal church, unlike Methodism, made a stronger claim as the legitimate descendant of the established Church of England. Moreover, Onderdonk favored the high church ritual and liturgy inherited from Roman Catholicism over the emotional evangelicalism of Avery's camp meetings. Onderdonk's superior status within his church guaranteed him a secure position in the public, masculine sphere as well as high visibility for his trial in the court of his peers. Just as Onderdonk laid an unassailable claim to a confident masculinity, the women who testified against him laid an unassailable claim to true womanhood: All were pious, respected, active members of their churches, and two were clergymen's wives. Both accused and accuser apparently held firm to the tenets of separate spheres. It was not the bishop's social status that betrayed his claim to masculinity. It was, instead, his social behavior that strayed beyond the limits of the regnant gender ideology.

Years before his trial, rumors of the bishop's intemperance and indiscretion had circulated among Episcopal clergy and laity. However, the august prelate faced a presentment before his fellow bishops for nine counts of "immoralities and impurities" only after a political feud between Onderonk's high-church (or liturgical) party and the low-church (or evangelical) opposition reached a boiling point in late 1844. Four female witnesses reluctantly offered supporting testimony. Unlike the Avery case, however, none of their charges or testimony alleged any serious physical assault. Contemporaries noted that the case never would have appeared in a civil or criminal court.[17]

The lack of a clearly defined crime posed a special problem for the female witnesses because none had offered any vigorous physical resistance to the groping they alleged they had suffered. The prim young wife of an evangelical Episcopal clergyman tearfully recounted her ordeal with Onderdonk to his fellow prelates. She claimed that she and Onderdonk had shared the rear seat of a carriage on a nightlong journey through the upstate New York countryside. Onderdonk, smelling of spiritous liquors, had tried to touch her breast and thigh, despite her quiet attempts to fend him off without attracting the attention of her husband or the driver in the front seat. Finally, in desperation, she crawled into the forward seat and spent the rest of the trip on her husband's lap. On arriving at their destination, she privately reported the bishop's unwanted fondling to her young husband. The couple debated whether to confront his superior. Because the bishop was scheduled to ordain the young man that afternoon, the couple wondered whether the sacred ceremony of laying on hands would be spiritually legitimate when the bishop's hands seemed so corrupt. In the end, the prudent young couple decided that silence would best secure the husband's career in the church. Only several years later, under intense political pressure and testimony from a number of other women, did the two agree to add their story to the accusations of others. Still, their story was met with deep skepticism. Onderdonk's behavior seemed so inconsistent with his upper-class and ecclesiastical status that the young woman failed to convince her own father, himself an Episcopal priest, that the bishop had committed such an offense.[18]

During the trial, three more women braved the public light to tell their tales of Onderdonk's pathetic clutching at their naked flesh. Most of the attacks occurred in public places, even in a crowded room. Additional witnesses, too embarrassed or intimidated, failed to testify in support of a number of other vague charges. "The whole of the testimony against Bishop Onderdonk amount . . . to embracings, caressing, and paternal salutations of that kind," the *New*

York Herald reported dismissively. In the absence of strong corroborative evidence and any explicit crime, Onderdonk's peers reached a very unsatisfactory compromise decision: He kept his title, continued to collect his salary and to reside in the mansion, but surrendered all responsibilities and duties as bishop. This controversial situation continued for the remaining fifteen years of Onderdonk's life and guaranteed the church continuing embarrassment and confusion. The editorialist at the *Herald* predicted with some accuracy that "the attempt of 21 bishops to give solemnity to this ridiculous farce, will only fall on their heads, and create nothing but shouts of laughter, wherever the matter is heard of."[19]

Most reporters of the day, as well as denominational historians in the twentieth century, overlooked the Bishop's possible moral shortcomings and focused on the political battle as the source of all his problems. More than a dozen pamphlets appeared in the months after the trial, and nearly all made partisan presentations. Those attacking the bishop relied on the women's testimony of indecent assaults but also painted the bishop as subject to a host of self-indulgent aristocratic behaviors, from eating and drinking at extravagant dinner parties to officiating in elaborate vestments. He was even accused of visiting one of New York's many upscale bordellos. Onderdonk's defenders, on the other hand, emphasized that the reputedly virtuous victims had failed to publicly protest their mistreatment. The best explanation that his supporters could muster in Onderdonk's defense was that the young brides, flush with recently acquired sexual knowledge, had misinterpreted his innocent paternal embraces. Most important, Onderdonk's defenders alleged that a conspiracy of low church theological opponents had turned over every stone in hopes of finding something morally incriminating. Because the verdict votes followed strict party lines, that charge seemed credible then and ever since.

Although graphic images of the bishop are few, they offer striking contrasts between the competing interpretations of the bishop's behavior and help in explaining what the public saw, or struggled to reconcile, in this case. A professional oil portrait of Onderdonk by William Sydney Mount approximately fourteen years before the trial shows a conventional image of the clergyman markedly different from the stern, almost malevolent pose of Avery during the same time period (figures 10 and 5). Whereas Avery appeared stern, dark, and judgmental, his piercing gaze magnified by his spectacles, Onderdonk's glance falls gently on his viewer, a ring of cherubic curls encircling a face of youthful and candid piety. Little wonder that supporters found it difficult to reconcile the bishop's saintly appearance with his roguish behavior. A broadside cartoon, on the other hand, gave readers a very different way to understand Onderdonk's conduct: It cast the melodrama in blackface (figure 11). The bishop's angelic aspect in the formal portrait was transformed into a scurrilous caricature, accentuating his reduced and liminal status not only by rendering him in blackface but also by demoting him to deacon. Like the bishop described in the testimony, Deacon Doughlips clutches at his colleague's wife's bosom. Instead of the prim half-smile of the portrait, however, the deacon's enormously exaggerated lips envelop his victim's mouth. Instead of the delicate, rather feminine hand laid modestly on his own breast, the "Feelin Deacon's" huge paw plunges rudely into her bodice. As Patricia Cline Cohen has argued, Onderdonk so far transgressed the boundaries of Anglo-upper-class notions of decorum that he could be portrayed only by dramatically and drastically changing his physical shape and appearance. Only overdrawn racial stereotypes easily explained his rudeness, hypocrisy, and sensuality to "refined" nineteenth-century white Americans familiar with blackface minstrelsy and its racial caricatures. Simultaneously, the crude cartoon reinforced a white middle-class sense of cultural and moral superiority. Instead of the supernatural monster, the bishop became an inferior human.[20]

At the turn of the twenty-first century, psychologists might label the bishop's actions as the behavior of an insecure man compelled to demonstrate his masculine power over his feminine constituents (and, perhaps, his high-church authority over their evangelical menfolk). He bolstered his masculine status by exercising his male sexual privilege—his physical and psychological power over them. In the early twenty-first century, however, Americans identify this behavior as the crime of sexual harassment, a deliberate discriminatory behavior that transgresses both the recently constructed ideology of gender equality and the legislation that supports it. But nineteenth-century Americans assumed that sexual discrimination—maintaining distinctions between women and men—was proper and desirable. Even if they thought that Onderdonk's behavior was immoral, few would have deemed it part of a system of oppressing women. With no psychological theory or legal lexicon to explain Onderdonk's failings, his contemporaries considered his behavior something more than playful but much less than sinful or criminal.

Instead, Americans in the 1840s pictured Onderdonk's deviance by resorting to racial and class stereotypes that effectively erased his privileged status as a white, wealthy, and powerful male—the status that allowed him to abuse the women in the first place. They failed to recognize that his status, rather than guaranteeing his morality, protected his immorality. In the broadside, the deacon, by grabbing at a female breast, engages in an act of "dark underdonkation." In effect, Onderdonk gave his name to the conduct his contemporaries could neither define, excuse, nor condemn. The case blurs those boundaries between race and class, calling into question the physical and behavioral characteristics that separate white from black, the reputable from the disreputable, the moral from the immoral. Albeit intended as a humorous rendering, the sketch depicts a creature somewhere between a civilized gentleman and a beast, in order to illustrate Onderdonk's mutable character. The surprise and dismay on the victim's face and the satisfaction and delight at her discomfiture inscribed on all the men's faces showed a world where men were not obliged to protect women. This blackface world stood in stark contrast to the world guided by Victorian gender ideology, the one Onderdonk has so perversely violated. Indeed, in neither the white world nor the black were white men obliged, or black men permitted, to protect black women. So, at the same time as the broadside print blurred race and class boundaries, it reinforced a different, less ideal gender boundary, one in which men enjoyed a sexual privilege that women, both black and white, were bound to resist but found difficult to actually do. In short, nineteenth-century Americans more easily "saw" Onderdonk's behavior as the clownish fumblings of a vulgar social inferior rather than the oppressive depredations of a highly powerful and privileged criminal. He fell not from grace but merely from middle-class respectability.[21]

Just as in the Avery trial, the Onderdonk case reveals the cultural fear that clergymen enjoyed too much access to women. Despite his angelic, even feminine façade, Onderdonk cannot help exercising the male sexual privilege that antebellum culture implicitly endorsed. Unlike Avery, Onderdonk was portrayed less as a wolf in sheep's clothing than a clown in clerical garb. Perhaps the ludicrous quality of the behavior charged against him encouraged his supporters to disbelieve it and helped Onderdonk successfully claim the status of martyr to the high-church cause among so many of his contemporaries and later historians. The equivocal verdict reflected the ambivalence and confusion over the case. Only one aspect of the sentence was unequivocal: It removed Onderdonk from the domestic female sphere by relieving him of his pastoral duties. He could no longer indulge his immature sexual impulses with the implicit imprimatur of his church.

The Reverend Isaac Kalloch

The Avery and Onderdonk cases portrayed protagonists or behavior that challenged categorization within the ideology of gender. The Isaac Kalloch case, however, illustrates how the physical setting of the behavior shaped perceptions of the "crime," especially when it defied categorization and upset assumptions about the utility of gendered separate spheres to regulate behavior. Kalloch, a popular and charismatic Baptist preacher who attracted hundreds of worshipers and visitors to Boston's Tremont Temple in the 1850s, also gave well-attended lectures throughout the New England area. He subscribed to the temperance and abolitionist sympathies of many of his fellow reformers but was hardly their most ardent activist. Still, his trial in criminal court on charges of adultery attracted nationwide attention in 1857.[22]

Neither Kalloch's supposed paramour, her husband, nor any members of his congregation ever testified against him. In fact, they publicly defended his innocence. The public prosecutors in this criminal case instead produced a handful of hotel employees who claimed that Kalloch, in a Boston suburb to give an evening lecture, registered for a room for himself and a female companion and signed them in as man and wife. The maid and steward, attracted by the sounds of what they claimed was sexual intercourse, peeked through cracks in a door frame. Although they couldn't swear to seeing the couple in the act of fornication, they reported hearing fragments of incriminating conversation and watching the couple get up from the floor, tidy themselves, re-arrange their clothing, and replace the pillows on the bed.

The media attention was, again, prompt and overwhelming. Again, the clergyman's supporters claimed a conspiracy against him, this time by the enemies he had made as a popular supporter of reform. Again, the woman was reluctant—and indeed, refused—to testify against the minister. Again, a hung jury produced an equivocal verdict. Again, the case reveals the nineteenth-century fascination with the men and women who transgressed cultural boundaries of gender. In the illustration contained in a pamphlet on the case, Kalloch defies the stereotype of the effeminate clergyman—his broad chest, stubborn chin, and shock of virile hair proclaim his masculinity (figure 12). He appears both a worthy opponent and a plausible sexual aggressor. "The Lady in Black," his alleged correspondent, appears exotic by contemporary standards of femininity: proud, mysterious, alluring, dark-eyed, sensual, and dangerous (figure 13). Although both claimed to adhere faithfully to Victorian norms, either or both could be terrifying exceptions to the ideal of the minister and the true woman as moral guardians of the republic. Significantly, the best-selling pamphlet promised readers not only portraits of the pair but also an intimate view of the scene of the crime: the "reading room" the two shared at the Lechmere Hotel (figure 14).[23]

At first glance, the caption contradicts the print because the scene appears to be set in a domestic space—a bed is clearly visible in the background. The nineteenth-century viewer reasonably assumed, in that case, that the couple sharing this intimate space must be husband and wife. He sits in a relaxed position, preoccupied by the papers on his lap. She seems equally at ease, absorbed in her own reflection in the mirror at the dressing table. A second glance quickly challenges the assumption of a domestic scene, however. The man's hat sits close at hand, as if he only temporarily occupies this room. The most incongruous and disturbing aspect of the print is the audience that immediately transforms the private space into a public one. Under the bed and over the transom are three voyeurs whose incredulous gaze now completely overturns the assumption of a domestic space and a married couple. Like an optical illusion, the room oscillates between public and private, masculine and feminine, space.

Kalloch relied on an able defense attorney, his good friend and the famous author Richard Henry Dana, to dispel the assumptions of illicit intercourse that the witnesses testified they saw in the hotel bedroom. Dana spent much time reviewing the testimony and re-creating the scene, "showing the size of the room, the position of the furniture, and the size of the aperture over the door," to prove the impossibility of the witnesses seeing what they claimed to have seen. In addition, Dana insisted that Kalloch had requested a "private parlor"—a room without a bed—in order to rest briefly before and after his lecture. Unfortunately, asserted Dana, the Lechmere Hotel had been able to offer him only a bedroom. Dana labored to convince the jury that despite its private character, the bedroom was indeed a public space—too public to shield the crime of adultery. "No curtain drawn, no blind closed, a bright gas-light burning, with two doors, two key-holes," Dana argued, all rendered the entire space visible from the corridor or the yard. How ludicrous for a public man to display his lechery in such a public place! "Here is a man holding a high and sacred position," said Dana, "committing adultery, with everything at stake on secresy, and that door is never once locked! And if it had been locked," he conceded, "how fatal, fatal, fatal would have been that fact!" In short, Dana claimed that only a locked door, prima facie evidence of privacy, would have been "conclusive of guilt; more so than any evidence we have before us now." Without the locked door, only the cynical and suspicious eyes of the hotel employees had transformed a public space into a private space. Dana argued that the workers' experience in an inn of doubtful repute had colored their perceptions. They falsely interpreted the innocent behavior of Kalloch and his female friend as criminal behavior because of the physical environment, the *setting*. Trying desperately to support this contention with biblical references, Dana shouted, "It is the ground on which seed fell, that determined what the fruit would be." Then, mixing his scriptural metaphors, Dana reminded the jury that "the Scripture speaks of 'eyes full of adultery.' There was more adultery in the eyes that looked on, than in the hearts of those who were there," he insisted. Dana used the phrase "eyes full of adultery," perhaps from 2 Peter 2:14–15, to condemn the hotel employees for their misperception. However, listeners familiar with that particular Bible verse might have recognized Kalloch and his parishioner, rather than the hotel staff, as "cursed children" who had "gone astray."[24]

The depiction of the reading room that appeared in the pamphlet was *not* an accurate rendering of the witnesses' testimony. For example, *no* witness claimed to be under the bed during the encounter. Yet the print provides an interesting graphic representation of not only the Kalloch case but also the pastoral relationship in the antebellum period. Although the couple appear to be as intimate as man and wife, they are instead a pastor and parishioner sharing a public space under constant public scrutiny and suspicion. The public gaze, not any identifiably illicit behavior of the subjects, transforms an innocent domestic scene into a sensational and sexually charged vignette. The Kalloch case, like those of Avery and Onderdonk, called into question the capacity of an ideology of separate spheres to adequately regulate relationships between men and women in general and between pastors and female parishioners in particular. In the same way that separate spheres ideals failed to help antebellum Americans define some women as true women, some ministers as real men, and some behavior as true crimes, it also failed to help them clearly define space as either wholly private or wholly public.

The new, large, luxury hotels that opened in Boston, New York, and Philadelphia during the 1850s posed an especially vexing example of this problem. Hotels were highly public spaces constructed by men, where men socialized and engaged in commerce. They were open to women travelers and even solicited them, but only within segregated spaces. Hotels accommodated women with separate parlors and dining rooms where husbands and fathers might join their families but single men were unwelcome. The largest hotels even offered women separate entrances when they complained that they were subject to the unwelcome stares—the public gaze—of men and boys who congregated at the front entrance. Still, the elegant shops and ballrooms in the hotel provided space that was neither completely public nor private, neither masculine nor feminine. There, men and women mingled together anonymously without the supervision that had regulated their behavior in more intimate, rural communities. The Lechmere Hotel fell somewhere between the new and the old—not large enough to offer a variety of rooms for different social purposes yet not small enough to adequately superintend the activities of all its patrons. Thus the inability to adequately label the space within as purely public or private, as clearly "masculine" or "feminine," led to the equally frustrating inability to judge the propriety of the couple who occupied those liminal spaces. Kalloch and his parishioner, then, endured the intrusive gaze of a suspicious public who saw them, with or without hard evidence, as straying beyond their respective spheres and caught in compromising surroundings.[25]

The Reverend Henry Ward Beecher

In 1875, the most famous preacher in America became embroiled in the most famous sexual scandal of the century. Henry Ward Beecher "has gone as a preacher and teacher of the public too far, very much too far," pronounced an editorial in the New York *Staats Zeitung*. "But for the previous transgressions of certain necessary bounds, such a scandal would never have been possible." Beecher had become entirely "too powerful"; he had attained a "dangerous importance . . . in consequence of his unequaled influence." Henry Bowen, one of Beecher's long-time parishioners—a founding member of his church and the publisher of the journal Beecher edited—reportedly said that "Henry Ward Beecher is a wolf in the fold, and I know it; he ought never to preach another sermon nor write another word in a religious newspaper; he endangers families and disgraces religion; he should be blotted out." In short, the most celebrated trial of the century repeated the same fears of transgressing boundaries—cultural, physical, and psychological—that the earlier cases exposed. And despite the numerous trials of errant clergymen in the nineteenth century, the church hearing and the civil trial of Beecher received more public attention for a more sustained length of time than any other case.[26]

For decades before his trial, domestic and foreign travelers made his Plymouth church an essential stop on their itineraries. The Swedish traveler Frederika Bremer saw the "young preacher from the West" a few years after he arrived in Brooklyn. Bremer, like many supporters, admired Beecher for his "life and energy," his lack of contentious spirit, his extemporaneous style, his use of his own experience, and the combination of laughter and tears he evoked from his audience. Beecher's influence extended far beyond his church, however. Besides the sermons he preached to his large congregation and thousands of visitors, his teachings also circulated in lyceum lectures, newspapers, pamphlets, and books, including a novel and a biography of Christ. In those lessons, Beecher perfected a brand of evangelicalism that broke the bonds of Calvinist orthodoxy to espouse an emotional, sentimental, naturalist Christianity. Critics, however, called it a "Gospel of Gush" that substituted *feeling* good for *doing* good. One of his orthodox critics among the Congregational clergy thought

Beecher strayed too far from the intellectual and ecclesiastical discipline of his fellow clergy. He "appeared to crave the approval and applause of men of the world rather than of the fathers of the church."[27]

Beecher's unequaled prominence and the extensive publicity that attended his trial derived from his extra-orthodox theology and also from the political writing and speaking that periodically took him down the path of radical politics. Like his famous sister, Harriet Beecher Stowe (author of *Uncle Tom's Cabin*), Beecher in the 1850s actively supported abolitionism, including the arming of Kansas antislavery settlers. Like his half-sister, Isabella Beecher Hooker, a prominent suffragist, he lent his name and efforts to an Equal Rights Association dedicated to women's suffrage as well as to freedmen's rights in the 1860s. Despite these decidedly radical positions, however, Beecher tried to navigate a path of moderate reform. After the Civil War, he opposed the Radical Republicans in the impeachment of President Andrew Johnson and sided with the conservative wing of the suffrage movement. Yet in a bizarre incident in late 1869, Beecher stepped into a high-profile case that appeared once again to ally him with the social radicals. He performed a marriage ceremony between a divorced woman, Mrs. Daniel McFarland, and her lover, Albert D. Richardson, who lay dying of a gunshot wound inflicted by her ex-husband. Friend and foe alike interpreted Beecher's actions in this case as support of marriage reform or, worse, "free love." Clearly, Beecher was a fellow traveler with political and social radicals. The first printed public accusations of an extramarital affair between Beecher and one of his parishioners appeared in the newspaper of a true challenger of accepted boundaries. Victoria Woodhull—notorious spiritualist, suffragist, stockbroker, presidential candidate, and free-love advocate—hoped to expose Beecher as an adherent of the radical doctrine of free love in his private behavior, if not in his public statements. Thus, Beecher's prominent pulpit and publishing career, his unorthodox theology, and his controversial political activities all took him well outside the boundaries of most nineteenth-century clergymen's roles and beliefs and made his case more fascinating in the public eye.

When the infamous Woodhull first published her report of the scandalous story of a sexual affair between Beecher and a married woman, the writer landed in court for violating new federal obscenity charges, later known as Comstock laws. The charges lay dormant in the regular press for nearly three more years, suppressed with the help of a "mutual friend" of Beecher and the husband of the alleged adultress. Unfortunately for the protagonists, however, too many additional friends, family, and religious and political associates heard the story from participants and witnesses. As a result of the relentless rumors, Theodore Tilton, the wounded husband and editor of a respected periodical, found himself accused of libeling Beecher in private, if not in print. To defend himself, Tilton finally published his own accusations of adultery against Beecher. This action prompted a general call for a hearing before a group of Beecher's fellow Congregational ministers. Beecher opposed such a forum and, instead, appointed a committee of his own Plymouth church parishioners to investigate the libelous charges. During the summer of 1874, local and national press covered the hearing proceedings and the witnesses' statements and testimony, stimulating widespread editorial comment and public reaction. When Beecher's handpicked committee exonerated him, some of the public and press suspected a whitewash and demanded a more impartial forum. Though the beleaguered pastor enjoyed much public sympathy, Tilton's supporters gave him confidence enough to file a civil case against his former friend and pastor. He charged Beecher with "criminal conversation" with his wife, Elizabeth Tilton, and with "alienating her affections" while he was gone on frequent lecture tours. When the civil trial ended in July 1875, a hung jury had failed to resolve the yearlong, internationally publicized controversy.[28]

The Beecher-Tilton scandal, as it became known, captivated the American public of the Gilded Age because the Tilton couple and their pastor proved a most fascinating trinity and welcome distraction from the seemingly endless partisan conflict over Reconstruction. The relationships between the three epitomized the highest ideals of Victorian love in the forms of church fellowship, friendship, and marriage. Beecher, twenty years older than the Tiltons, played the roles of pastor, father, friend, and mentor. Theodore and Elizabeth had joined his church as teenagers. Beecher married them when Theodore turned twenty and Elizabeth was twenty-one. Young Theodore developed an extremely close professional, personal, and even physical relationship with Beecher in the years before the alleged affair with Elizabeth. As Beecher's protégé, Theodore led the Plymouth Church Sunday school, wrote for *The Independent*, a religious journal edited by Beecher, and later took over as editor himself. Theodore shared Beecher's radical politics and eventually went much further than Beecher in his public support of the Radical Republicans, women's rights, and free-love principles. Like his mentor, Tilton was a popular editorialist and lyceum lecturer. The two men, almost as close (or closer) than father and son, displayed their affection for each other by exchanging expensive gifts, but also by hugging, kissing, sitting on one another's laps, and walking arm in arm through the streets of Brooklyn. In letters exchanged a decade before the trial, both had confirmed their high esteem for each other. Beecher called Tilton "so near and dear to me." Likewise, Tilton considered Beecher his "minister, teacher, father, brother, friend, companion" and begged Beecher to love his children, who had been taught to "reverence you and to regard you as the man of men." When asked during the trial if the acquaintance had grown to intimacy, Beecher replied, "Yes, it was downright loving on my part." Despite such a passionate friendship, Beecher and Theodore Tilton occupied secure positions in a masculine homosocial public sphere of friendship, work, and politics—a world that valued fraternal association and tolerated a much closer physical bond between men than the homophobic American culture of the mid-twentieth century.[29]

As a pious, submissive wife and mother, Elizabeth, too, conformed to Victorian expectations for women. She bore six children, lost three as infants, and miscarried another, all the while counting on her church and her pastor to provide consolation in her grief. She supervised a busy household, entertained her husband's many political and literary acquaintances, and developed many

friendships of her own. A literate and patient woman, she critiqued her husband's writing and participated in political discussions in her parlor but did
not write or speak publicly herself. Her most public activity was teaching a
Sunday school class for poor mothers and, with Theodore, listening attentively
to the preaching of her famous pastor. The Tiltons' marriage appeared to be
the Victorian ideal: a companionate union based on mutual affection and trust.
Elizabeth's letters to Theodore consistently reiterated her marriage vows. "My
soul is satisfied, our union is perfect," she wrote in early 1867. Two years later
she vowed, "I consecrate myself to you so long as I shall live." Theodore, in
return, asked Elizabeth to "accept my undivided and ever-growing love." But
in another letter Theodore's image of Elizabeth as the ideal wife carried an
implicit threat that foreshadowed their eventual split. "If you should ever appear to me anything less than the ideal woman—the Christian saint that I
know you to be—I shall not care to live a day longer."[30]

Theodore and Elizabeth expressed their affection for each other and lived
up to the highest ideals of Victorian marriage. Likewise, Beecher and Theodore
expressed their deep affection for each other and still sat securely within contemporary expectations for masculine friendship. Theodore and Elizabeth, together, could maintain a cordial pastoral relationship with Beecher and openly
express their love for him without provoking jealousy. An 1863 letter from
Theodore Tilton addresses Beecher as "My Best of Friends." The same letter
appends a message from Elizabeth: "Tell him [Beecher] I love him dearly."
Then, extravagantly, Tilton added, "So does her husband—now, henceforth,
and forever. Amen." The only relationship between the three that eventually
provoked jealousy and suspicion was the one between Elizabeth and her pastor.
Famous for his prominent role in the highly competitive masculine public
sphere and infamous for his neglect of pastoral visiting in the domestic sphere,
Beecher's increasingly frequent calls to the home of Elizabeth, with and without her husband present, departed significantly from his usual pastoral style.
Eventually her welcoming parlor became his frequent haven and private literary salon when he solicited Elizabeth's editorial advice and inspiration for a
novel he had contracted to write. At first, flattered and fulfilled by Beecher's
visits, Elizabeth openly admitted her love for her pastor to her husband but
confessed her confusion over her exact role in the friendship between the three.
"With all the earnestness of my being," she wrote Theodore, "I commit you
both to God's love. He has signally blessed you both, and He will help His
own beloved. Why I so mysteriously was brought in as actor in this friendship,
I know not yet."[31]

By late 1870, however, Theodore came to doubt the quality of Beecher's
love for his wife and, he claimed, extracted a confession of adultery from her.
After Theodore confronted Beecher, however, Beecher confronted Elizabeth
and persuaded her to give him a partial recantation (to be made public only if
someone other than Theordore accused him of adultery). Six months later, after
reading the novel Griffith Gaunt, Elizabeth made another ambiguous confession to Theodore, this time claiming that

Today through the ministry of Catharine Gaunt, a character of fiction, my eyes have been opened for the first time in my experience, so that I see clearly my sin. It was when I knew that I was loved, to suffer it to grow to a passion. A virtuous woman should check instantly an absorbing love. But it appeared to me in such false light. That the love I felt and received could harm no one, not even you, I have believed unfalteringly until four o'clock this afternoon, when the heavenly vision dawned upon me. I see now, as never before, the wrong I have done you, and hasten immediately to ask your pardon, with a penitence so sincere that henceforth (if reason remains) you may trust me implicitly.

Elizabeth's claim to "see clearly," however, failed to help much of the public, or even Beecher and Theodore, to agree on the meaning of her various confessions.[32]

Theodore expressed his confusion by continuing to assert throughout the trial that his wife was a "white-souled" creature who deserved no blame for her adulterous behavior. Beecher, too, tried hard to absolve Elizabeth from blame for her false confessions to her husband. Although two witnesses (Emma Moulton and her husband, Frank, the "mutual friend" who had tried to mediate the dispute) testified that Beecher had confessed to them in explicit terms his adultery with Elizabeth, the pastor stated at the trial that he was unaware of any illegitimate affection between himself and his parishioner. Beecher was "absolutely bewildered" by Theodore's charges, but it seemed to him "that if [Elizabeth] had been led to transfer her affections from her husband by reason of my presence, I could not but feel that I was blameworthy." "I could not conceive," he testified, "of any thing for which a man should blame himself more utterly than to intrude upon a household, and to be the means of breaking it up; that my idea of friendship and love was that it gave strength, and that I had always supposed that my presence in their family was giving strength to all of them. . . . I was amazed and bewildered by it," he repeated. He had always thought of Elizabeth as a "saint-like person": Her confessions could be only the result of someone "bereft of reason." Thus three deeply passionate but confused people came to doubt the quality of their love for each other. All three agreed that the love Elizabeth shared with her pastor—and his love for her—had jeopardized Elizabeth's love for Theodore, Theodore's love for her, Theodore's love for Beecher, and Beecher's love for Theodore. No wonder the press dwelt constantly on themes of confusion and clarification.[33]

The Beecher-Tilton scandal left Americans pondering the nature and quality of the love that the three professed for each other. When Elizabeth denied her earlier confession of adultery and yet initiated a permanent separation from her husband during the Plymouth investigation, the public witnessed the horrific and baffling dissolution of a famous friendship and an ideal marriage by an unholy pastoral relationship. Beecher defended his visits to the Tilton home as part of a reciprocal professional relationship: He sought Elizabeth's womanly counsel while composing his sentimental novel and brought consolation to the grieving mother on the death of one of her young children. When his wife was away, Beecher boarded in the homes of his parishioners. When his parishioners were alone, he provided them companionship. When a distraught Elizabeth reported stories of Theodore's emotional abuse, Beecher counseled her to try a separation from her husband. What remained confusing for the public, however, was that neither Elizabeth nor Theodore accused Beecher of unwanted physical assault. Whatever physical connection had taken place appeared to be between consenting adults, although Elizabeth's claim to adulthood seemed tenuous, given her changeable mind and the regnant notions of women's intellectual and emotional fragility.

Ultimately, the confusion that riveted public attention to the case and resulted in a hung jury stemmed from the bewildering nature of the love all three members of this unhallowed trinity professed for each other. The fraternal love of the two men, the romantic love of the married couple, and the spiritual love of the pastor for the Tilton family all appeared legitimate and unthreatening. Only the love of Henry and Elizabeth for each other defied easy categorization. What masqueraded as a pastoral relationship might too easily be an adulterous one. Only their ambiguous relationship—the reciprocal love between Henry and Elizabeth, the love between a pastor and his female parishioner—threatened the other bonds of friendship, marriage, and spiritual kinship. Henry's love for Elizabeth also seemed to be a betrayal of his love for the rest of his parishioners. The love between Henry and Elizabeth consistently challenged the limits of spiritual, romantic, and physical love; crossed the borders between paternal, fraternal, and marital affection; and hopelessly complicated the participants' and the public's ability to identify the nature of that love. In the press, dozens of graphic images explored the slippery boundaries they transgressed.

The front-page editorial cartoon of the *New York Daily Graphic* of August 20, 1874, toward the end of the very public Plymouth church investigation, mirrored the communal confusion. Titled "The Old Lady in a Fog" (figure 15), the shrouded figure of an elderly woman is led through the dark mist by a group of street urchins holding smoky torches and clamoring to help her with cries of "This Ye're way out!" The small boys are labeled Tilton, Beecher, and the church committee. The "old lady," we must assume, represents the bewildered public searching for an escape from a moral miasma. The Tiltons and Beecher had wandered into a smog of accusation and scandal that now threatened, through the trials, to drag the entire nation into the same quagmire. None of the old woman's "helpers," according to the cartoonist, had proved to be a reliable moral guide out of the mess. Two days later, another front-page editorial cartoon replaced the old lady with a classically dressed female figure as the personification of "Public Opinion" (figure 16). Still confused, she now locates a "way out" through the courts rather than the church. She implores Beecher and Tilton to take their case before the blindfolded "Justice" and to "settle it finally." Clearly, the editorialist and much of the public seemed tired of the sordid story, but despite their distaste they continued to follow the case.

Weeks later, the classical female figure reappeared, this time representing "Religion," with "A Hint to the Plymouth Pastor" (figure 17). She stands between Beecher and the "sacred desk," entreating him for "decency's sake" not to enter again until after the trial. Although Beecher continued to preach from his pulpit at Plymouth church, the cartoonist believed Beecher had, at least temporarily, forfeited his claim to enter its precincts. All these cartoons continue the preoccupation with wandering outside the bounds of acceptable behavior and preventing transgressors from reentering a polite Christian society. In the first, the "public" is led from moral certainty into confusion by the trial protagonists. In the second, the "public" shows a way out of the moral wilderness through the public courts rather than through the private church hearing. In the third, Beecher is barred from his "sacred desk." The images reveal the cultural confusion the infamous three caused by straying back and forth over the boundaries of an acceptable cross-gender relationship.[34]

By the 1870s, new printing technology permitted the press to bombard Americans with hundreds of nearly instantaneous and immediate graphic images of the trial that exploited their anxieties. No longer did readers have to wait weeks after the trial to purchase a pamphlet with a transcript and a few illustrations. They read long excerpts of verbatim testimony in each day's paper. Just as in twentieth-century trials, artists sketched scenes and participants from the trial for duplication in the next edition. Prints taken from photographs of the major participants and facsimiles of key documents provided verisimilitude unavailable before, taking readers as close to the contemporary reality of the trial as the technology of the day allowed. Much of the pictorial coverage of the trial aimed at objectivity. Especially during the church hearing and the interregnum between the church trial and the civil trial, papers such as the *Daily Graphic* reinforced editorial opinions with cartoons that tried to gauge public opinion and push a "public" point of view. They took an impartial outsider's perspective rather than merely defending one of the participants and repeating narrow partisan messages. Many images resembled the political cartoons that commented on city, state, and national politics and vied with them for front-page status. They combined recognizable portraits and caricatures of the participants with classical figures representing virtue, public opinion, justice, and the church to send subtle as well as overt editorial messages. Comics, in contrast, offered humorous comments on subjects immediately or only distantly related to the trial events of the week. For instance, *The Graphic* offered extended comic commentary on testimony by Beecher, Bessie Turner (the young adopted daughter of the Tiltons), and Theodore Tilton, exaggerating and ridiculing the witness or the subject of the testimony. Another comic offers advice to pastors on "How to Make Pastoral Visits and Avoid Slander" (figure 18). In these caricatures, the pastor protects himself by dragging along chaperones on his pastoral visits, making himself unwelcome by wearing muddy boots or blackening his face, or employing bizarre devices to distance himself from the women in his care. The message was, clearly, that pastoral visiting among women was less a serious threat to the republic, the church, or the home and more a threat to the pastor himself and a source of amusement to the public.

Even reproductions of "high art" paintings provided subtle artistic commentary on universal themes portrayed in the trial. In one example, Christ invited those who were without sin to cast the first stone at the adulteress, presumably an invitation to readers to suspend their harsh judgments of the trial's participants (figure 19). Thus, readers of all persuasions viewed the scandal in textual and graphic images from a wide variety of perspectives that increased their choices of interpretive stories beyond the simplistic images of monster or martyr, while feeding their fascination, confusion, anxiety, and outrage.[35]

A few cartoons crossed the boundaries of these genres of illustration, political comment, and humor to reveal the specific confusion about the nature of the love described by Beecher and the Tiltons in their letters and testimony. Two complementary cartoons seriously question the nature of the intimacy but also humorously trivialize the subject and the participants. In the first cartoon, a diminutive Beecher perches on the lap of a maternal-looking Theodore, inverting the relationship as it actually was (figure 20). The younger man becomes the parent, the older one the child. More puzzling is the female figure, perhaps Elizabeth, in the margin: She dances with surprise or joy, apparently delighted or titillated by the men's close relationship. In the other, a petite Elizabeth sits on a paternal Beecher lap, responding to his query about her health that she feels "so-so" (figure 21). This time, a family servant hovers in the background, looking very much like the voyeurs who spied on Kalloch and his alleged paramour. In both scenes, it is the pastoral relationship that fools the eye, appearing alternately as a parental bond and an unnatural affection.[36]

In the end, a hung jury ensured that confusion and controversy prevailed. Beecher's defenders published long defenses in multivolume books, distributed gratis to libraries around the country. On the other hand, *Harper's Weekly*, a Beecher supporter, kept its coverage to a minimum by withholding comment until the end of the civil trial and then publishing thorough but succinct interpretations of the evidence in his favor. *The Daily Graphic* devoted its pages to extensive coverage, some of it quite hostile to Beecher. At the end of the trial, it published a long editorial, arguing for Beecher's guilt while congratulating itself on its singular consistency and impartiality throughout the year of scandal.

Although monsters still appeared in the representations of the Beecher trial, most Americans found it difficult to reconcile the images of the beast with the nation's most beloved preacher. In a *Daily Graphic* comic of May 4, 1875 (figure 22), a devilish spirit makes an appearance, flying toward the reader with a ticket to the trial in his hand. This time, the ghoul represents neither the minister nor his accuser. Perhaps he represents Satan's influence in the proceedings, but any notion of sin seems trivialized in this figure. The ghoul instead seems to represent the spectator, whose fascination with the trial seems diabolically inspired. Of course, this reading also implicitly indicts the observer of the cartoon and the reader of the paper that devoted so much space to coverage of the trial. In fact, it is easy to see the cartoonist mocking his own readers and subtly exposing the hypocrisy in the press as well as in the pulpit. Similarly, the text of a *Harper's Weekly* editorial repeatedly invoked the image of the monster, but ultimately that image described the spectator and skeptic better than Beecher.[37]

The voracious reader of scandal emerged as a more acceptable villain than the minister. The *Harper's Weekly* writer, sympathetic to Beecher, briefly allowed himself to imagine a script wherein Beecher was guilty and a horrid monster indeed appeared. If the preacher had committed the crime of adultery, the writer surmised, he had not momentarily succumbed to a "lapse of virtue" or a "sudden outbreak of hot passion." Instead, he was guilty of the "long elaborate, crafty undermining of the moral character of a trusting woman" and, worse, "the wife of a young man, his disciple, whom he loved with more than the love of an elder brother." Most horrifying of all, in this scenario, was Beecher's refusal to give an immediate and unequivocal denial to the charges: To cover up his seduction constituted a "monstrous perjury" further compounding his sin. If Beecher was guilty, the writer conceded, then he was "an unmatched villain," his conduct displaying a "depravity so exceptional as to sequester him from the human race." But this editor, and no doubt millions of Americans, just could not reconcile the man Beecher with the image of a minister of Satan or a subhuman beast. They could not exile him from humanity as Avery's contemporaries had done. Although the circumstances of the case supported a theory that supposed moral guilt, the editor conceded, it was a "guilt so monstrous, hypocrisy so vast, defiance of Divine Justice and of human decency so insolent" as to be *inconceivable*. Only a truly wicked mind could conjure up such a hideous crime and ascribe it to such an honorable man. Instead, the editor saw Beecher's accusers and critics as the true monsters. To suppose Beecher culpable was "an almost unprecedented moral monstrosity, and adds deeper blackness to the possibilities of human guilt." As in the devilish cartoon, the doubting spectator rather than the alleged adulterer assumed the shape of the fiend. According to the editorialist, only those who upheld Beecher's innocence, interpreting his actions in light of his long and illustrious career and known character, were worthy Christians.[38]

The cartoonist who produced the image of Ephraim Avery as a "minister extraordinary" on a mission to Satan took seriously the charges against the clergyman and pictured the man as an agent of the devil. Given the seriousness of the crimes charged against him, that image made sense to an American public in the 1830s. But by the Beecher trial in the mid-1870s, the minister's crime and his guilt were neither so clear nor so diabolical. Indeed, in many cartoons from the Beecher period, the pastoral relationship is a farce rather than a mythic tragedy. The pastor is a laughable clown making ludicrous attempts to perform the duties of pastoral visiting without incurring the suspicions of a voyeuristic public or the misplaced affections of an addled female clientele. To a nation still repairing itself after a fratricidal war, the pastoral relationship might still appear as a threat to an individual, a family, or a church, but no longer as a serious hazard to the republic or society. Instead, the scandal—as either drama or comedy—served mainly as entertainment. The decades of fear and fascination were, in part, resolved by trivializing what had once seemed a potent political, social, and spiritual danger.

Several factors help explain the shift in the perception of the pastoral relationship from a national threat to a popular joke. First, trials offered graphic evidence of ministers and women gone astray, transgressing the boundaries of a "separate spheres" ideology that was intended to order and regulate relationships between men and women outside the family. But even while trials showed the pastoral relationship as a threat to morality and order, the trial process itself helped to reimpose order and shore up the boundaries of those ideological constructs. As I argue in the next chapter, the subtext of these trials worked effectively to put women and ministers back in their respective gendered spheres. As the greatest number of cartoons from the Beecher period show, the trial successfully constructed a contest or combat between the two male protagonists. "Death Struggle on the Ragged Edge" (figure 23) pits Tilton and Beecher against each other, clad in Roman regalia and suspended over a chasm. More evenly matched physically in the cartoon than they were in real life, the two perform a dangerous duel that must surely spell death and destruction to the loser, as the vultures wait patiently for the outcome. This construction of the trial as a wrestling contest reduced the threat to the institutions of nation, society, and church and confined it instead to the individual men. The trial as manly combat also placed women on the sidelines, banishing them to the periphery of the masculine sphere and diminishing their power in the public realm. In fact, during the Beecher trial, the cause of women's rights was tainted and probably substantially harmed by the close connections between Beecher, Tilton, and such famous suffragists as Susan B. Anthony, Elizabeth Cady Stanton, Victoria Woodhull, and Isabella Beecher Hooker. Anthony made a wise political choice not to issue public statements about her relationship with the Tiltons, but it is characteristic of these trials that they silenced women rather than offering them a forum for righting wrongs. The second factor contributing to the perception of the pastoral relationship as a declining threat, as I argue in Parts III and IV, was the declining importance of the pastoral relationship itself in the real lives of pastors and women. The pastoral relationship between pastors and women, despite its popularity in fiction, was neither so strong nor so dangerous as its contemporaries and subsequent historians have believed. Finally, in some parts of the country, the end of Reconstruction made patrolling the boundaries of race a more pressing concern for the American public. Many Americans constructed new ideals and institutions enforcing racial separation and used vigilante justice and lynching to defend the elusive borders between blacks and whites. Black rapists, not errant clergy, were the greater threat to social stability.[39]

3

Mending Fences; or, What the Public Saw

The highly public trials of clergymen accused of sexual misconduct produced dramatic stories and graphic images of ministers and women straying from their respective gendered spheres. Those images confused, disturbed, and fascinated the nineteenth-century American public. The male and female protagonists wandered, or deliberately crossed, over borders constructed to prevent transgressive behavior. In the course of crossing cultural boundaries that regulated proper masculine and feminine roles and conduct, ministers and women changed from moral exemplars and guardians into deformed characters, unrecognizable within the ideology of separate spheres. The caricatures that emerged from these trials rarely helped contemporary readers to understand the complex individual human characters and situations of the cases. Instead, they effectively undermined and cruelly contradicted the simplistic ideals of gendered separate spheres that intellectuals promulgated to order the relations between men and women in an increasingly urban and industrial society. Thus, these trials appeared as frightening symbolic challenges to social order. More than two dozen trials between 1810 and 1880 captured local and sometimes national attention through the publication of trial pamphlets. Together with the most notorious cases examined in the previous chapter, the trial pamphlets covering these cases produced another set of powerful symbolic images. In addition to displaying dramatic representations of clergy and women breaching gender norms, trials subtly and symbolically reconstructed the broken fences that ought to have separated men and women in the pastoral relationship.

At first glance, the various cases described in nineteenth-century trial pamphlets display few similarities, resisting analysis and meaningful quantification. The publications featured clergy from a variety of denominations. Two Roman Catholic priests appeared, a remarkably small number given the level of anti-Catholic sentiment in the antebellum period. The rest were Protestant clergy from Episcopal, Congregational, Presbyterian, Methodist, Baptist, and Freewill Baptist churches. One man, Robert Matthias, headed his own cult. The variety of offenses ranged from specific criminal charges of murder and rape at one extreme to vague accusations of "imprudence" at the other. Trials took place in a number of venues, sometimes more than one. In criminal courts, public prosecutors brought charges of assault and battery, rape, and murder and argued the victim's case. In civil or tort cases, a plaintiff—usually a father or husband of the alleged victim—charged a minister with seduction or adultery and sought compensatory damages. Clerical peers or laypersons considered a variety of charges in ecclesiastical courts, ministerial associations, or church disciplinary hearings. Cases heard in more than one venue sometimes resulted in contradictory verdicts.[1] (See table 3.1.)

The diversity of clergy, crimes, and courts nevertheless yields striking similarities between cases. A combination of several factors, almost always working together, propelled these cases to the attention of the public. Of course, the clergyman's ascribed status as a minister of God, his presumed moral authority, and often his local or even national prominence prompted immediate attention to his misconduct. But the minister's professional, moral, and social status alone was not sufficient to explain the attention he received. The crime, usually some form of abuse directed against women and linked to sexual behavior, attracted much more attention than, for instance, intemperance, financial mismanagement, or heresy. Yet despite the public fascination with sexual scandal, a united or embarrassed congregation might easily suppress the case. The great majority of clerical sexual misconduct cases undoubtedly remained secret to protect the ministers, the women, and the churches. In short, these public cases represent only a small portion of clerical misconduct but almost certainly resonated with many readers who had personal knowledge of less public cases.[2]

To overcome the institutional and cultural tendencies toward secrecy and to achieve a significant level of publicity, the minister had to enjoy the support of an influential group of fellow clergy or members of his congregation. At the same time, he had to suffer the opposition of an equally vocal and powerful group. These two highly partisan and nearly always male groups constructed the competing melodramatic scenarios that fueled controversy and ensured media attention. Without the partisan politics, the cases drew only local newspaper attention and, perhaps, a public denial or apology from the minister. If the community all agreed on the minister's guilt or innocence, little media attention resulted. If the community publicly split over the issue, the case almost inevitably resulted in an equivocal verdict or a verdict opposed by substantial public opinion, further guaranteeing continuing debate and fascination in the public at large. Thus, the public saw a spectacle not merely because the man was a minister and he engaged in sexual misconduct but because fac-

TABLE 3.1. Cases of Clerical Misconduct in Trial Pamphlets

Date of trial	Name of accused	Crime(s) charged against accused	Venue	Verdict	State	Denomination
1810	William Parkinson	Assault and battery	Criminal	Not guilty	New York	Baptist
1812	David Barclay	Adultery	Ecclesiastic	Not proved	New Jersey	Presbyterian
181?	Ammi Rogers	Seduction and abortion	Criminal	Guilty	Connecticut	Episcopal
1821	William Hogan	Assault	Criminal	Not guilty	Pennsylvania	Roman Catholic
1822	John Maffitt	Immorality	Ecclesiastic	Not guilty	Massachusetts	Methodist
1833	Ephraim Avery	Murder	Criminal and ecclesiastic	Not guilty	Rhode Island	Methodist
1835	Eleazar Sherman	Sodomy	Ecclesiastic	Guilty	Rhode Island	Evangelical Christian
1835	Robert Matthias	Murder Assault	Criminal	Not guilty guilty	New York	Cult leader
1839	Samuel Jarvis	Marital cruelty	State legislature	Not guilty	Connecticut	Episcopal
1842	Romain Weinzoepflen	Rape	Criminal	Guilty but pardoned	Indiana	Roman Catholic
1842	George Washington Van Zandt	Seduction	Civil	Guilty	New York	Episcopal
1844	Joy Hamlet Fairchild	Seduction	Criminal Ecclesiastic	Not guilty Guilty	Massachusetts	Congregational
1844	Benjamin Onderdonk	Impurities	Ecclesiastic	Guilty	New York	Episcopal
1845	John Whittlesey	Impropriety	Ecclesiastic	Not guilty	Connecticut	Methodist
1847	Issachar Grosscup	Seduction	Civil and ecclesiastic	Guilty	New York	Baptist
1847	John Seys	Assault and battery	Criminal	Not guilty	New York	Methodist
1849	George Washington Doane	Fraud	Ecclesiastic	Not guilty	New Jersey	Episcopal
1857	Isaac Kalloch	Adultery	Criminal	Not guilty	Massachusetts	Baptist
1859	Henry Budge	Murder	Criminal	Not guilty	New York	Presbyterian
1859	William Guild	Immorality	Ecclesiastic	Not proved	New Jersey	Presbyterian
1859	Jacob Harden	Murder	Criminal	Guilty	New Jersey	Methodist
1860	William Merrill	Adultery	Ecclesiastic	Guilty	Maine	Freewill Baptist
1870	Lorenzo Dow Huston	Seduction	Ecclesiastic	Not guilty	Maryland	Methodist
1874	John S. Glendenning	Seduction, breach of promise	Ecclesiastic	Not proved	New Jersey	Presbyterian

(continued)

TABLE 3.1. Cases of Clerical Misconduct in Trial Pamphlets (*continued*)

Date of trial	Name of accused	Crime(s) charged against accused	Venue	Verdict	State	Denomination
1875	Henry Ward Beecher	Adultery	Ecclesiastic, civil	Not guilty	New York	Congregational
1878	Herbert Hiram Hayden	Seduction and murder	Criminal	Not guilty	Connecticut	Methodist

Date of trial	Name of Accuser	Libelous Charges	Venue	Settlement	State	Denomination
1819	Alexander Cummings	Immoralities	Civil	Won small award	New York	Evangelical Independent
1822	John Maffitt	Immoralities	Civil	Lost libel case	Massachusetts	Methodist
1838	Moses Thacher	Adultery	Civil	Won small award	Massachusetts	Congregational

tionalism and unresolved conflict generated enough public interest to create a market for publications.[3]

These public spectacles, as we have seen graphically portrayed in the most notorious cases of Avery, Onderdonk, Kalloch, and Beecher, presented melodramatic stories composed by the opposing counsels in each case. Their conventional scripts featured exaggerated stereotypical characters transgressing contemporary gender mores. These melodramas frightened and fascinated because they turned the familiar protagonists in the pastoral relationship into grotesque caricatures "gone astray." Jurors, spectators, and the readers of trial pamphlets struggled to choose between these exaggerated portraits and produced, out of their confusion, a welter of ambiguous and even contradictory verdicts in the courts and in public opinion. Surprisingly, at the same time that trials frightened, disturbed, and confused, they worked to resolve the very dilemmas posed by sex in the pastoral relationship. The conventions of melodrama dictated that trials dispense justice and punish the wicked, but audiences to these trials were frequently disappointed. Instead of watching good triumph over evil, the public saw a more familiar and plausible image of manly combat, a masculine contest that pitted men against men and marginalized women's role in the arena. Political might, rather than right or justice, determined the winner. Trials thus resituated clergy within the masculine public sphere and women within the feminine domestic sphere. These manly contests refocused and reordered public perceptions of the pastoral relationship by mending the fences and reinforcing the fragile boundaries of separate spheres that had failed to prevent the transgressions between clergy and women.

Women effectively endured a course of "feminization" during the trials while ministers enjoyed a process of "masculinization." In the first place, trials effectively discouraged all women, not just the unfortunate victims in a trial, from participating in any intimate relationships with pastors by reminding them of their vulnerability to sexual insult or betrayal. Trials also prohibited women from effective participation in the contest by silencing them in ways that discouraged their entrance into the public arena. While trials made no comfortable room for women in the public sphere, they proved remarkably congenial to the minister. They redeemed him from the stifling feminine domestic sphere and cast him as a man among men. The contest often ended in a draw, the clergyman battered but unvanquished.

In effect if not in law, nineteenth-century American clerics possessed a kind of "benefit of clergy," the legal term for the medieval exemption of clergy from civil or criminal trial and punishment. They reaped the rewards of a profession that still commanded respect and deference, even in an increasingly democratic society. So, even though these cases ranged over seven decades and included a variety of clergy, conduct, and courts, the public continually viewed a subtle reaffirmation of the same gender ideals that clerical misconduct implicitly challenged. At the same time that trials reinforced nineteenth-century feminine values of domesticity and submissiveness in women, they rescued the minister from his precarious position between two gendered spheres and reestablished his hold on the masculine, competitive public sphere. In effect, the trials removed the male and female protagonists from the dangerous no-man's-land between spheres and penned them securely in their proper spheres.

The "Feminization" of Women

Nineteenth-century women, as participants, spectators, and readers, saw trials as painful morality plays that continually reminded them of their vulnerability and powerlessness in the pastoral relationship and in the various judicial systems that should have protected them. The Bible offered pastoral images of both a kindly shepherd and "a wolf in sheep's clothing." Despite the psychological, cultural, and institutional forces that worked together to silence women, their trial testimony gave poignant witness to the distressing disjuncture between the two images of the pastor. In the earliest pamphlet (1811), Eliza Wintringham testified in a criminal case of assault and battery against her pastor, the Rev. Mr. William Parkinson of New York City. During a pastoral call to her home, she alleged the Baptist minister had declared he felt more love for her "than for any in the world." Confused, she reproved him and observed that his conversation was "so unlike a minister of the gospel," thereby revealing her belief that ministers were unusual men who maintained exceptionally high standards of moral conduct. When Parkinson repeated his verbal declarations of love and attempted to "put his hand in my bosom," he tested Wintringham's faith in her pastor as a moral exemplar. "I was off my guard," she said, "for I did not then know of his being such a man." She surrendered her belief in his exceptionalism when she learned that he had preyed on other reputable women in the congregation. Only then was she convinced of his lechery, "of his being such a man." Wintringham, and those who read her story, only reluctantly recognized the predatory man beneath the clerical garb and the threat he posed to trusting women in the pastoral relationship.[4]

Such profound disillusionment illustrates the very high expectations for their pastor's moral superiority that women brought to the pastoral relationship. Those expectations of the pastor's virtue put women, ironically, at greater risk of betrayal. Mary Connell claimed her Catholic priest had attacked her in the rectory. She reportedly exclaimed, "Oh! God! I have heard many things, but I could not believe this of you!" Her outcry oddly implicated both her pastor and her God, the same curious conflation that, as we shall see in part IV, occasionally characterized women's descriptions of pastors in their diaries and letters. At the same time, her statement hinted that she had heard rumors of the man's faults but had repeatedly repressed them. Women attacked by their pastors suffered from cognitive dissonance—the psychological inability to reconcile the difference between their expectations and the actual behavior of their pastors—that often prevented them from resisting the evil they tried to deny. Mrs. Barrows, a Maine housewife, certainly heard her pastor preach on Christian morality numerous times and assumed his own behavior corresponded to the standards he taught. After her seduction by the Freewill Baptist William P. Merrill, she tried to resolve her confusion by asking him "if he believed what he preached." Clearly, the women who were victims of clerical misconduct often lacked a skepticism that might have helped them reconcile a flawed man with a "man of God." However, reading about these cases in pamphlets or in newspapers might have helped some women to see clergymen with less reverential regard. Women could see in these stories that clergy, in all their various roles, exploited feminine vulnerability. As pastors, but also as scholars of scripture, teachers, counselors, and even suitors and husbands, clergymen asserted their authority over women and betrayed their trust with tragic consequences. Exhibit A in these trials was the vulnerability of women to sexually predatory men, even those men assigned to protect them and uphold the highest moral standards.[5]

Women exhibited vulnerability, in part, because ministers drew on a higher authority—the Bible—to help them effect their seductions. According to their victims' statements, pastors devised numerous theological rationalizations for their aberrant sexual behavior. Three decades before the famous Beecher trial exposed the slippery definition of love in the pastoral relationship, the Rev. Joy Fairchild argued with one of his young victims about the subtle differences between evangelical love, marital affection, and carnal lust. He insisted that their own sexual intercourse fell into the former categories rather than the latter. He claimed he "felt no difference towards [her] than towards his lawful wife." In an antinomian inspiration, he declared that "God looked on the laws of our land about marriage as non-essential: that all that God regarded as justifying intercourse was *love* between the parties." The young girl tried to reason from scripture, too, arguing that the Bible had specifically authorized that "every man have his own wife." Fairchild, inspired next by biblical historicism, explained to the young woman that "it was Paul and not God that said so." In short, Fairchild mustered his theological training in defense of his lust. The victim insisted that he "tried to make me think that it was according to the Bible that he should have connexion with me." In similar examples, women eventually came to question their pastor's theological reasoning, but as professional experts in biblical literature and interpretation, pastors asserted their authority over laywomen by justifying their actions in scripture-based arguments. Since theological training remained a male privilege throughout most of the nineteenth-century, women were at a distinct disadvantage in such debates.[6]

Clergy employed their roles as theologians and teachers in the seduction of girls, who showed inordinate trust in their pastors. Ministers crafted a seduction theology that persuaded girls to reluctantly accept sexual behavior that was clearly contrary to most Christian teaching. Seventeen-year-old Mary Driscoll testified that her Methodist pastor, Lorenzo Dow Huston, first introduced her to the topic of sex by unexpectedly speaking to her of prostitution. Surprised at the subject matter and the language he used, the girl claimed "but still I thought it was Dr. Huston and he could not say or do anything that was not right." Once he had begun having regular sexual intercourse with the young woman, he countered her continuing objections by reciting the Old Testament stories of David and Solomon. Huston explained that these Bible heroes taught that God sanctioned, or at least forgave, plural "marriages." Conducting his seductions in the early 1870s, Huston might have drawn on the free-love philosophy that so confused the spectators in Beecher's trial during the middle of the decade. Instead, Huston validated his interpretation of the Bible's views on marriage by allying his biblical models and himself with one of the most maligned religious groups of the nineteenth century, the then-notorious polygamists of the Church of Latter-Day Saints. "Look what good men they were," he told her. "Solomon was just the same as the Mormons are now." "He explained it in such a manner," reported the young Driscoll, "that I thought it was right." Likewise, Rhoda Davidson, a domestic servant in the house of the Boston Congregational clergyman Fairchild, retained a faith in her employer even after he confessed his passion for her and kissed her. "Still, I did not think any evil of Mr. Fairchild," she said, "because I believed he was so good a man. I believed him to be a pious, devoted and exemplary Christian." She based her trust not merely on Fairchild's status as a minister but on his superior education: "His knowledge being greater than hers, she felt a sort of confidence in him." Eventually pregnant with the minister's child, still she thought "that he would live up to what he preached, and would know and act up to what was right in the sight of God." Since cases of assault and rape required that the prosecution establish the use of force, testimony regarding the pastor's persuasive theology certainly served to rationalize the women's apparent lack of resistance to his advances. Of course, girls undoubtedly found it more difficult than older women to challenge male adult authority. But the girls' testimony also suggests that women's vulnerability to sexual attack by pastors increased because of their abiding but misplaced "confidence" in them as moral exemplars. Tragically, young women suffered attack because they listened carefully to their pastor's seduction sermons, trying to adhere to feminine ideals of piety and submissiveness.[7]

Pastors, as teachers of young people, gained access to girls that would have been denied to most other men. Mary Driscoll's mother permitted her daughter to make frequent visits to the parsonage because Dr. Huston had promised to help the girl with her studies and to supervise the young people's activities. The Driscoll girl felt flattered and privileged by Huston's attention. She thought Dr. Huston "wished to talk about religious matters; I was trying to the best of my abilities, at this time, to be a Christian, and therefore was delighted that he took such an interest in me as to take his time to see me." The two had sexual intercourse once or twice a week over an eighteen-month period without arousing her mother's suspicion. In a similar case, the Episcopal rector of a Rochester, New York, church frequently opened his library to the young people of his parish. One mother sent her fourteen-year-old daughter to the pastor's study for a book, only to discover months later that he had "seduced" and impregnated the child on that visit.[8]

Ministers in these seduction cases of young girls betrayed not only their pastoral role but also their paternal role as a stand-in for God the Father. Some served literally, not just metaphorically, as surrogate fathers, with distressing results. Driscoll's mother testified that Dr. Huston had often told her, "You don't know how much I think of this child," and that he was drawn to the child because "she had no father to protect her." To her credit, Mrs. Driscoll, to protect her fatherless daughter, was the only woman to bring a case against a minister. Although girls might naturally look to ministers as surrogate fathers, even adult women such as Mrs. Butler in the Onderdonk case and Mrs. Tilton in the Beecher case viewed the pastors with whom they had grown up as father figures. Mrs. Butler explained her confusion over Bishop Onderdonk's gropings by saying, "His manner had been always affectionate, and I supposed it parental." Such relationships were so close, so trusting in nature, that sexual assaults went beyond conventional notions of immorality and conjured up the horror of incest. No prosecutor boldly named that crime, but the opposing counsel in Beecher's case clearly implied it. Describing the many intimate bonds that connected seducer and seduced, he accused the preacher of "the most infamous charges . . . of having seduced the wife of his life-long friend, and a member of his church—she also a member of his church—a child who had grown up under his eye."[9]

The pastoral relationship between clergy and adult women, rather than the more paternal relationship between clergy and girls, seemed to afford fewer occasions for misconduct. Suspicious witnesses in a number of cases offered vague testimony that the accused pastor frequently had women alone in his study, but these accusations were rarely substantiated by direct testimony from the women involved. Surprisingly, trial testimony rarely revealed women who deliberately placed themselves in jeopardy by seeking out pastors as counselors, advisors, and confessors. Those few who did, however, sometimes found their confidence most unkindly repaid. Emily Barrows's testimony, though heavily expurgated, shows that she solicited advice from her pastor about troubles with her husband. She told the clerical council investigating the case that the Rev. Merrill failed to give her helpful spiritual or practical guidance. "I do not remember of his giving me any religious advice," she explained, "except one time, when I was in his arms, he told me to hug and kiss my husband and to join the church." The testimony in other cases, however, rarely shows women soliciting pastoral contact or deliberately putting themselves at risk in intimate encounters with their pastors. No lawyer advised Emily Barrows in this ministerial hearing, but perhaps lawyers in other cases advised female accusers not to admit that they had initiated contact with their pastors, thereby minimizing the women's responsibility for the affair.[10]

In most trial testimony, distraught women sought advice from clergymen only when the ministers were the "authors of the trouble." Rhoda Davidson consulted her pastor when she learned she was pregnant with his child. He volunteered to support the child if she kept his paternity secret. Roxanna Wheeler complained of the same problem to her pastor, who told her to consult his wife. "He said that his wife had been in the same way twice; that she had a kind of medicine which she used, and got rid of her trouble." Likewise, Dr. Huston assured his young victim that she had nothing to fear from their intercourse. He told her "he had made this subject a particular study" and if ever she "did get in a fix, he would give me a dose of medicine that would set me all right." Trial testimony, when a pregnancy occurred, often included a recipe for an abortifacient. Ephraim Avery, Ammi Rogers, and Herbert Hayden all stood accused of trying to arrange or perform an abortion on their alleged victims. Such testimony elicited gasps of horror from the courtroom audience, aghast at any parallel between the minister and notorious antebellum abortionists such as Madame Restell. However, the testimony raises the suspicion that ministers, even when innocent of illegitimate paternity, consulted with pregnant women and served as sources of information about abortion. This situation, however, would put already vulnerable women in an even more exposed position. Their pastors might realize that the women's sexual virtue was already compromised and extort sexual favors in return for help and silence.[11]

Protestant women might easily avoid seeking personal counsel from their pastors, but Catholic women could not escape the obligation of confessing privately to their priests. Nineteenth-century Protestant Americans, highly suspicious of most things Catholic, perceived the private auricular confession as enforced intimate contact between vulnerable Catholic women and their priests. And priests, deprived of conjugal sex by vows of chastity, displayed unnatural lust in the confessional, according to Protestant critics. Anna Maria Schmoll testified in 1844 that she made a confession to her priest so that she might receive the sacrament of the Eucharist on the following morning. The young woman, recently married to a Lutheran man, feared the priest because he had vehemently opposed the union. She believed he would not absolve her even though she had received a dispensation for the marriage from the bishop. Schmoll told the court that she became alarmed when her confessor, Father Weinzoepflen, repeatedly asked her how many times "her husband had corresponded with her in a month." Three times she refused to reveal the intimate details of her marriage before finally admitting to intercourse "twice or three times a week." The priest then advised her to live peaceably with her husband, even though he claimed "there was little chance for happiness in a family with a Lutheran." Oddly, he swore her to secrecy, since their conversation "did not belong to the confessional." Then, as she began to say her prayers of penance, the priest pulled her roughly from the pew and raped her on the floor of the empty sanctuary.[12]

Schmoll's tearful, tragic testimony so inflamed anti-Catholic fears that it provoked a riot that aborted the first trial. The virulent nativist propaganda stirred up by the case finally necessitated a change of venue. Undoubtedly, the public turmoil helped to convince the Protestant male jurors that their suspicions were justified regarding the secrecy of the Catholic auricular confession and the lechery produced by vows of celibacy. In fact, the prosecution tried to introduce arcane Catholic doctrine and canon law to explain the inherent evil of the Catholic priest as both a man and an institution and to explain why Schmoll could not avoid intimacy with the priest. Exasperated, the judge finally refused to admit any more discussion of Catholic theology. Protestant antipathy to Catholic rituals like the confession helped prosecutors obtain a conviction in this case, but no similar prejudice against clergy and confession applied to Protestant ministers and no similar sympathy to their victims.[13]

Clergymen betrayed their roles as pastors, protectors, and confessors, and they proved equally false in their roles as suitors. The parents of Mary Pomeroy, a young New Jersey woman, permitted their pastor to court their daughter for more than a year, allowing the couple to sit alone late at night in their parlor. Pomeroy accepted presents—even a ring—from the minister but no formal proposal of marriage. When she became pregnant, her pastor denounced her as a loose woman and denied fathering the child. Witnesses claimed the deceived young woman had cried out on her childbed, "I loved him so, he was a minister, and I thought he would not desert me; Oh, God, how could he desert me so!" According to her family, Pomeroy died of a broken heart a few months after the birth of her illegitimate child, abandoned by her lover, her pastor, and her God.[14]

Pastors also failed as ideal husbands, capable of neglect and cruelty. One minister's wife complained that her husband was "cold and inattentive." Others voiced unhappiness with a husband's itinerant schedule or suspicions of his late hours and frequent visits with women. Another resented the duties of the pastor's wife, chafed at entertaining and serving parishioners and clergymen, and received no sympathy from her husband. A few clergymen were accused of murdering unhappy lovers or wives. Louisa Dorland's mother worked hard to see her daughter married off to a young Methodist preacher and pastor. According to the young man's confession, his mother-in-law had framed him, using extortion and the threat of a breach of promise suit to extract a marriage proposal for her daughter. A year after the forced marriage, the unhappy man, plagued with ill health, a contentious congregation, and a complaining wife, determined that poisoning his wife might solve his problems. In another case, the Rev. Henry Budge's unhallowed marriage ended in his wife's highly suspicious suicide. Finally, the married Herbert Hayden, like Ephraim Avery half a century before, escaped conviction on charges that he had murdered the young single pregnant woman he had allegedly seduced. Clearly, women proved highly vulnerable to ministers in all their roles as preachers, pastors, teachers, counselors, suitors, and husbands.[15]

The injury women incurred in these cases went far beyond the loss of modesty or virtue. Betrayal by clergy ultimately threatened the victims' faith and the fate of their souls. Some women appeared to successfully divorce the corrupt clergyman from the church and retain faith in the church and its sacraments. The Butler couple in the Onderdonk case accepted the young man's ordination as valid, even though they believed the bishop's sexual fumbling polluted his hands. Likewise, Maria Schmoll still considered the Eucharist spiritually valid although she received it from her rapist's hands the morning after his attack upon her. Other women, however, admitted to avoiding the offending pastor after his insults. Witnesses at the Rev. Joy Fairchild's trial claimed that one young woman "was not fond of hearing Mr. F[airchild] preach after she lived in his family." Even when she grew deathly ill, she refused to let them send for the minister and requested a deacon instead. Eliza Wintringham told the court that after Mr. Parkinson's offensive behavior, "I began almost to think that there was no truth in religion, and that I must quit the church." Sarah Cornell's family told the jury at the Avery trial that her letters had been "exceedingly religious in tone" until she attended the camp meeting at which they contended she had been seduced by the minister. "I do not enjoy any Religion atall," she wrote. "I have not seen a well or happy day since I left Thompson Campground." Thus, pastors who subjected their parishioners to sexual insult left their victims disillusioned with them as men and also deeply suspicious of the "truth" of religion, a condition that afflicted not merely their bodies but their eternal souls.[16]

Certainly, the cumulative weight of these trials provided abundant evidence of women's vulnerability in intimate pastoral conversation. Some female readers of this testimony must surely have internalized these dangers and realized that illicit sexual attacks might come from the most trusted man in their community. If so, trials reinforced women's belief that they were safe, physically and spiritually, only in the company of men within their own domestic circle— their fathers, husbands, or brothers. In short, trials encouraged women to accept pastors only as public figures, men in the public sphere, and discouraged women from seeking private spiritual and personal guidance in the pastoral relationship. Thus, trials reinforced the segregation of men and women into separate spheres—public for men and private for women—by pointing out the vulnerability of women in relationships with men outside their own families. But trials reinforced separate spheres in another way. Even though women's testimony appears in most trials and affords an intimate view of their pain and suffering, women's voices and their agency, or active participation, were circumscribed and limited in numerous ways. Exhibit B in these trials was women's marginalization—their voicelessness and powerlessness within the church and in the civil and criminal judicial systems.

Besides portraying clergymen as untrustworthy confidants in the private sphere and threats to body and soul, trials reinforced separate spheres by summoning cultural and institutional forces to enforce women's chaste and submissive silence. Their nearly universal response to betrayal by clergy was mute shock and shame. Despite their spiritual doubt and pain, powerful cultural forces prevented them from exposing their deceivers. Their own shame muzzled victims. Even though in sight or hearing of family, they failed to cry out. The women who testified to assaults by Bishop Onderdonk confounded their listeners by claiming his attacks took place in public places where male protectors might easily have seen them. The victim feared public disclosure not only for herself and her family but also for her abuser and his family. One female accuser waited years before making public charges because she dreaded being "dragged into a notoriety painfully distressing to a virtuous and respectable female." The Rev. Fairchild reminded Rhoda Davidson that should she expose him as the father of her child, "it would ruin him for the ministry, and deprive him of the means of doing any thing for me." Fairchild appealed to her own selfish motives, but in fact the young woman was more concerned for him than for herself. "I did not scream," she said, "because there were neighbors so near that they would have heard me, and Mr. Fairchild's character would have been ruined. I had regarded his character as good, and I preferred to suffer what I did, and lose my own character, to save him."[17]

Women also silenced their protests to shield the innocent, rather than themselves. Rhoda Davidson accused Joy Fairchild of fathering her child only after she believed that another clergyman had been accused of the deed. To protect the falsely charged minister, she finally agreed to testify against the guilty one. Sarah Cornell initially refused to tell her physician the name of the father of her child because she worried about harming the man's family. Elizabeth Cram "lost confidence" in her pastor because of his sexual assaults on her but forgave him "for his family's sake." Women preferred mute suffering rather than public exposure of themselves, their families, and their churches to scandal. Not even the most "respectable" women possessed a sense of self-worth strong enough to allow them to openly oppose the power and prestige of their pastors. They internalized cultural ideals that required women to put family and church before their own happiness and that enforced standards of modesty so rigid that a woman risked her character by even speaking of sex, much less "permitting" an assault on her person. Thus, a combination of fear, shame, and altruism imposed by gender ideology made women censor their protests against sexual exploitation by their pastor.[18]

The same cultural ideals that confined women to the domestic sphere severely circumscribed their behavior when, by chance or by force, they appeared in a public judicial venue. Scripture enjoined women to "keep silence" in the church. Custom prohibited women from seeking redress in the courts for seduction or adultery. Only their male protectors—fathers or husbands—

could sue for damages. Custom and law discounted their testimony in judicial forums and disallowed their participation on juries. Both the church and the courts were masculine preserves reflecting masculine values, inhospitable to the voices of women. Even when their complaints of sexual abuse by pastors surfaced, the women's charges entered the public realm where church, criminal, and civil courts continued the process of proscribing their speech. Deep biases against women shaped both institutions. Both treated the problem of sex in the pastoral relationship as a question of the morality of one of the two individuals, often ignoring the inequalities and paradoxes inherent in their association. Both favored men and ministers in a gendered contest that was less a battle between the sexes than combat between men. Men made the rules and performed the dominant roles. In the judicial process, women met constant frustration—prohibited from narrating their stories of victimization and from confronting their oppressors face-to-face. In an adversarial system that ignored moral ambiguity and demanded the declaration of a winner and a loser, women most often lost.[19]

Women suffered a severe disadvantage when they publicly accused their pastors of crimes because they operated within a matrix of religious morality that contradicted some of the tenets of true womanhood. The Bible and other Protestant denominational sources required Christians not merely to control their own behavior and appetites but to monitor and sanction those of the members in their spiritual communities. In most Protestant churches, observing another's transgression required confronting the sinner and encouraging his or her confession, repentance, and reform. Failure to correct sinful behavior invited a public hearing and possible expulsion from many Christian communities. Pastors and laymen, usually deacons, sat on the disciplinary committees that decided these cases. In addition to the general rules of discipline for Christians, pastoral manuals and the "charge to the minister" in installation or ordination sermons set special obligations upon the pastor and his flock. These sources bound the pastor to set a moral example for his congregation. The same sources also compelled the congregation to guard the minister and monitor his morals. *Clerical* sin thus appeared more egregious than *lay* misconduct. Clerical *sexual* sin appeared more hypocritical than other ministerial misconduct. Hence, such behavior should have warranted the most severe discipline. Yet few lay*men* witnessed sexual misdeeds by clergy. By their nature, sexual crimes occurred secretly with the female victim the only witness. Thus, a woman felt religiously bound to confront any sexual misbehavior on the part of her pastor, despite her clearly subordinate position as a woman and layperson. If the transgressor repeated his assaults despite her protests, she was obligated to expose his misconduct to others for reproof and retribution, upon her word only. However, women testified to their own betrayal only at great emotional, social, and spiritual expense and thus rarely complied with these requirements. The cultural forces prescribing silence far outweighed the religious forces demanding disclosure.[20]

If women finally came forward with their testimony, those cultural forces imposed additional constraints on their speech. Whether in church or civil

venues, their words were circumscribed first by the shame and modesty imposed upon them by the gender ideology dispensed from both the pulpit and
through popular culture. Ideals of true womanhood dictated that women be
not only domestic but also pious, chaste, and submissive. As some historians
have noted, these values could conflict, especially in marital relations. A wife
could fulfill the sexual obligations of marriage and maintain her "chastity" or
sexual purity only by remaining passionless in her sexual submission to her
husband. In other words, she could engage in sex with her husband but
couldn't display pleasure beyond happiness with his attentions and satisfaction
in her ability to submit to him. In contrast, she must not remain "passionless"
or submissive under sexual attack by anyone other than her husband, even her
pastor. Despite a cultural ideal that demanded passive submission, she was
obligated to resist a sexual advance—no matter how subtle—immediately, vo-
ciferously, and physically. If she failed to repel the attack, she was culpable. To
protest the insult at a later time, especially in a public forum, contradicted all
the cultural prescriptions for Victorian women. Even as she denounced an
insult to her sexual purity, she injured her reputation as a true woman. Women
had few justifications for speaking in public to "promiscuous" or mixed-gender
assemblies in a culture that prescribed separate gender spheres. For a woman
to speak publicly on sexual topics was especially unthinkable. In short, the act
of publicly charging the minister with a sexual crime fell between the cracks
of Victorian cultural ideals, exposing the accuser as much as, if not more than,
the accused.[21]

A woman who made a public accusation exposed herself and her family
to ignominy, pain, or even dissolution. Eliza Wintringham refused at first to
tell her husband of her pastor's attack because Mr. Wintringham was the pastor's friend. She was afraid "it would break up [my] family." Her apprehension
was justified. In the Schmoll rape case, the victim regretted telling her husband
of the attack. He vowed to kill the priest, and she "begged him not to subject
himself to the gallows." The humiliating ordeal of two trials was not the only
price Schmoll paid for her disclosure. Her physical and mental health deteri-
orated under the strain, her infant died, and her husband finally abandoned
her. And, although the priest was convicted and sent to jail, the governor par-
doned him after only one year, and he resumed his priestly duties. Familial,
judicial, and cultural forces conspired to exacerbate women's suffering if they
told their tales of victimization.[22]

Few women made the decision to go public with their charges. Instead,
they lost control of their secrets and became pawns in a masculine contest.
Eliza Wintringham confided in a female friend, who told her husband, who
informed two other male parishioners, who insisted on confronting the minister. Even when the pastor issued a veiled threat to destroy Wintringham's
family, the male parishioners and her husband proceeded with the charges.
Although Mrs. Wintringham was called the "prosecutrix," the term is a grave
misnomer, implying that Wintringham actively pursued and conducted the
case. Neither Wintringham nor most of the other women claimed or desired
such agency, nor would they be allowed to do so. Like Wintringham, female

accusers found their secrets appropriated and exploited, and themselves marginalized, by a masculine system of justice that set men against men.

Women usually spoke with great reluctance in a hearing or trial, fearing they convicted themselves as well as their attackers. Some female witnesses refused to testify, and the charges had to be dropped. Others appeared but avoided explicit language whenever possible, withstanding tremendous pressure from male interrogators. Rhoda Davidson refused to answer questions about the method of birth control her pastor claimed would prevent pregnancy. "He gave me a reason," she said, "*a plain one*, and one that I do not wish to mention." Pushed by her questioners to be more specific, she insisted, "I cannot very well, but there is a passage in scripture that will explain it." Modesty prevented some women from answering specific questions even when they were not the victims. Ephraim Avery's prosecution was compromised in part because the women who examined Sarah Cornell's corpse would not describe the most graphic details of her condition or speculate whether she had been sexually violated before her death.[23]

The trial process could be extremely hostile to women, preventing them from giving evidence in their own voices and punishing them for offering not only too little information but also too much. Eliza Wintringham's very first sentence of testimony was interrupted by a spirited debate between the prosecution and the defense on the admissibility of the background evidence she attempted to provide. Elizabeth Cram endured ridicule by both the defense counsel and the judge, to the amusement of the entire court, for giving long, detailed answers and being "too talkative," a "failing of her sex." The audience laughed when she wept. At one point in her trial, an exasperated interrogator responded to her testimony with the telling statement, "I don't care what you said." Women who presented consistent stories under various questioners were accused of rehearsing their answers with coaching from their counsel. Those who presented inconsistent stories were accused of lying. Some women felt constrained by the formal method of questioning: They preferred to narrate their stories rather than give short answers to specific questions. They resented the prohibitions against extraneous background information and hearsay evidence, and they chafed especially when prevented from relating conversations between significant players. The only trial pamphlet written by a woman, Catherine Williams's *Fall River Narrative* of the Avery case, claimed to improve on other renditions of the trial by providing just the detailed historical background, character sketches, and re-created dialogues that had been excluded from the trial itself.[24]

The control and devaluation of women's voices in these trials contrasts sharply with the treatment of men in the singular case of Elder Sherman, the only trial pamphlet to report a pastor's homosexual assault. The ministerial consocation hearing the case pointedly excused the young male victims from giving graphic sexual testimony so that they might avoid incriminating themselves. The publisher of the pamphlet further expurgated their testimony. Like women in the other cases, the young men failed to resist the preacher's attacks. But their lawyers explained their acquiescence as a result of their innocence and "ignorance of the extent of evils they would sustain, by indulging in [Sherman's] vices." Despite the victims' failure to testify or to fight off their seducer, clerical peers found the defendant guilty on all charges and deposed him. The judges in this case showed much more sympathy to these male victims than any court displayed toward female victims.[25]

Courts, surprisingly, also proved more protective of male defendants than of female plaintiffs. In a most unusual move during a hearing before several ministers, the Rev. Fairchild's clerical peers allowed him to direct questions to Rhoda Davidson, the young woman who accused him of seducing her and fathering her child. She answered his queries in a remarkably forthright manner, positively rejecting his assertions of innocence. Davidson responded boldly, rather than meekly answering yes or no. She even confronted her pastor, ignoring the conventional rules that prohibited witnesses from asking questions. Fairchild refused to answer her, reminding his fellow ministers, "I am not on the stand as witness." Later, the young woman again directed a question to her pastor, asking pointedly, "Do you mean to deny that you ever had criminal intercourse with me?" Fairchild, compelled to answer such a direct accusation, responded, "I do most distinctly." Disgusted with his hypocrisy, Davidson declared, "I know that you have no apparent accountability to a Supreme Being." Nonplussed, Fairchild retreated in the face of her attack and appealed to the moderator of the hearing for "protection." His fellow clergyman demanded that the young woman apologize for having "overstepped the bounds of propriety." The rest of the court agreed, and the female accuser was promptly chastised and subdued. No other trial pamphlet showed a woman who was permitted to confront her corrupter face-to-face, no other publication displayed a woman's bold indignation at her seducer's perfidy, and no other incident showed more clearly how threatening women's direct testimony might be if unchecked.[26]

Like Fairchild, accused clergymen often needed the protection of the court and the benefit of legal counsel. Ministers arrogantly asserted (and correctly assumed) that their word was worth more than that of their female accusers. The Rev. Parkinson confidently told Eliza Wintringham that should she charge him, "I shall be believed in preference to you, and you will only hurt yourself and your children by making the attempt." Bishop Onderdonk's defenders insisted that accepting the oath of "foolish girls . . . as paramount to the Bishop's [was] almost an insult to that Divine Being, whose high priest the Bishop is." Though a simple denial of the charges usually sufficed, some ministers made the mistake of offering vague confessions when first confronted. Fairchild told his deacons that his kisses with his young servant were only meant to "console and make her contented," and his only object was to "to raise her up, to make her feel herself respected." He was concerned for her *amour propre*, not for his *amour*. After issuing such a feeble justification for his behavior, the accused had to recant or employ the skills of legal counsel to reinterpret his earlier statements.[27]

Similarly, the Rev. George Washington Van Zandt seriously compromised his own defense when initially confronted by his vestry with the seduction of two girls. At first he called the twelve- and fourteen-year-old sisters "strumpets" without denying that he had sexual intercourse with them. Next, he admitted that sexual temptation presented a constant dilemma in his pastoral work, but "knowing his propensities in that area were so strong, he avoided being alone with females of his congregation even for religious purposes." Thus, he confessed that because of his robust sexual appetite he had to forgo any private pastoral mission to women. His vestry, understandably disturbed, noted that his statement contradicted their own observations of his frequent pastoral visits. Finally, Van Zandt offered a very candid solution to the problem of sex in the pastoral relationship. Vows of celibacy offered insufficient protection for either pastor or parishioner. Instead, he modestly proposed that "there should be a law passed that when young men entered the ministry they should be castrated." Van Zandt's lawyers valiantly tried to rescue the immodest rector from himself. They tried to pin paternity of the child on Van Zandt's nephew, a young man conveniently absent in far-off missionary China. But Van Zandt's initial incriminating words to his vestry came back to haunt him and helped convince a jury to award the girls' family compensatory damages. In short, clergymen sometimes displayed uncommon arrogance and stupidity in defending themselves, for which they needed and expected the extraordinary protection of the court. Women rarely received the same consideration.[28]

Readers of these pamphlets derived a most reassuring solution to the tension between women's vulnerabilities and clergymen's conceits: Women were better off at home. They could escape both the assaults and the disillusionment, embarrassment, humiliation, and pain of these public victims by avoiding relationships with men, even kindly and paternal pastors, outside their domestic circle. Women readers and spectators saw in these nineteenth-century versions of morality plays that Everywoman was vulnerable to Hypocrisy and Seduction. Like the fallen women in contemporary sentimental novels, victims could look forward to only infamy and ruin rather than justice. The lesson learned from these trials was that all women needed the protection of male family members because their own ability to defend their chastity was so limited. Finally, if women failed to avoid their pastors' unholy propositions, they learned they had better keep silent. Courts, even the ecclesiastical ones, offered scant protection to women who strayed into the public arena. Thus, at the same time that trials revealed the fragile and flawed boundaries of the regnant gender ideology of separate spheres, they reinforced them by convincing women to remain safely and quietly within the domestic circle.[29]

The "Masculinization" of Ministers

The clerical trials reassured men that ministers were, indeed, men, and privileged men at that, at the same time they reassured women that they were safer at home than at church or in the courts. Just like other men in the public arena, clergy were subject to forces and foes from whom they must defend themselves. They defended themselves, however, within judicial systems—

whether church or civil—that accommodated masculine, not feminine, values as defined by nineteenth-century culture and custom. Clergy thus enjoyed enormous advantages over female and male opponents in cases of sexual misconduct. As we have already seen, the trial process discounted women's testimony and often protected ministers from themselves. But the male venue benefited male ministers in other ways. The minister played his part in the company of other respected male professionals—judges, lawyers, physicians, and other clergymen. In addition, he enjoyed the benefit of a jury of his male peers, who more easily empathized with other men than with women. When new gender ideals of women's moral superiority failed to explain women's behavior and character, male jurors could draw on older gender ideologies that portrayed women as the weaker, more passionate sex. By succumbing to female temptresses and his own robust sexual appetite, the minister ironically gained in masculine stature as he slipped in moral stature. In addition, the masculine judicial system failed to recognize women as persons in their own right, who might sustain injury to themselves (rather than to fathers or husbands) and incur psychological and spiritual injury as well as physical injury. Lastly, ministers gained stature as embattled men manfully resisting unjust conspiracies. Exhibit C in these trials was the minister's masculinity. In the end, clergy often escaped conviction and usually avoided significant punishment. Ultimately, clergy reaped such vital advantages in this masculine contest that they usually received the benefit of doubt of their guilt. In effect, they received a double advantage as men and as ministers. Ministers in a democratic society had to survive without the medieval privilege of benefit of clergy. Yet their elevated social and moral status, whether deserved or not, still usually exempted them from serious punishment.

Trials placed men, especially professionals, at center stage in controlled combat suggestive of the duel. The encounter was not a rational investigation to determine truth and justice but a struggle for honor between male adversaries to determine winners and losers or, preferably, a stalemate. In all the civil and criminal trials and many of the church trials, lawyers battled other lawyers, using words and witnesses as weapons within strictly defined rules of conduct. They engaged in long arguments over the legality of evidence, exchanged witty and sarcastic gibes, or hurled vicious attacks against the character of the opposition. An atmosphere of spectacle emerged when players, whether lawyers or witnesses, drew laughter, applause, jeers, and catcalls from an often enthusiastic and rowdy audience.[30]

The courtroom drama prominently featured the authoritative voices of professional men who, by surrounding and supporting the minister and his adversaries, seconded and legitimated the contest. Attorneys and judges weighed in on fine points of law. Increasingly, physicians and scientists appeared as "expert" witnesses, testifying to the condition of corpses, the size of a fetus or newborn, the probability of suicide, or the possibility of a virgin's conceiving a child during her first sexual intercourse. Bishop Onderdonk's defenders lamented that no medical experts had been called as witnesses in his trial since, they insisted, medical men would have quickly diagnosed the female accusers as "hysterical," thus effectively invalidating the women's testimony. Both sides in these conflicts often brought in other respected clergy to give character references, but in most cases the parties to the dispute relied on secular male professionals to manage, argue, and strengthen their cases. Some historians have noted that during the nineteenth century these experts gradually displaced the clergy as moral authorities in that clergy seemed to take a back seat in these ordeals. But none noticed that clergy still benefited by their association and inclusion in this company of male professional combatants.[31]

An all-male jury or council, charged with determining the most skillful warriors, always judged these contests. Not surprisingly, the men who sat in judgment empathized with the embattled clergyman rather than the accusing female, no matter how virtuous. If she was portrayed as a temptress, the hapless clergyman was as helpless to resist her as Adam was to Eve. In the Parkinson case, the minister's illustrious lawyers employed a score of women who painted a burlesque portrait of the accuser, Eliza Wintringham. One claimed Wintringham was afraid to be "alone in a house with a single man for she had too weak a spot" and that she could not look a man in the eye for fear he could read her sexual desire there. Others said Wintringham had complained that her husband was "incompetent," "insufficient," and "not half enough for her." Still others claimed they heard Wintringham say that if she did not "keep kicking and spurring at him all the time he would never touch her." When Wintringham thought she was pregnant, witnesses reported, she told female acquaintances it "could not be so on account of her husband." Such sexually explicit testimony elicited laughter from the audience but also distanced the male jurors from both Wintringham and her husband. Since the most damning testimony came from members of her own sex, the male jurors were relieved of the discomfiting task of judging Wintringham's sexuality for themselves. They could easily see that in court she appeared attractive and bold, and they accepted the women's portrait of a sexually insatiable vixen. Likewise, her husband attracted no sympathy from the male jurors because he failed to demonstrate his own masculinity by physically satisfying and controlling his wife. On the other hand, jurors easily admired Parkinson as the leader of a large and successful congregation and as a man who had once served as the chaplain of the U.S. Congress. They excused Parkinson's very masculine weakness for succumbing to Wintringham's wiles even as they proved loath to excuse any sexual weakness on her part.[32]

Male jurors accepted Parkinson's version of the relationship because they could still situate the minister within the broad sphere of masculine competitive endeavor even when he forfeited some of his moral authority as a man of God. Mrs. Wintringham, on the other hand, clearly failed to live up to the accepted gender ideals of republican motherhood or the still-emerging ideals of true womanhood. Jurors, instead, understood her alleged behavior within a number of other competing gender stereotypes. In 1811, Parkinson's peers could look backward to earlier notions of sexuality and community discipline. For centuries before the revolutionary era, male authorities such as clergymen constructed women as more emotionally and physically passionate than men, capable of enticing men with bold speech and immodest dress. Women in this older ideology were weaker vessels, physically, intellectually, emotionally, and morally inferior to men. Biblical archetypes for women's sexual behavior bolstered these earlier notions of female inferiority: The seductive Eve led Adam to disobey God's explicit command not to eat the fruit of the Tree of Knowledge and Potiphar's vindictive wife accused Joseph of adultery when he spurned her advances. Additionally, jurors drew on a class ideology that saw working-class women such as Wintringham, a milliner (or later the factory worker Sarah Cornell), as exempt from middle-class feminine norms of passionless purity. Finally, jurors in 1811 were still familiar with earlier forms of local justice, one in which female community members often policed sexual behavior. A notable lack of privacy made sexual matters public knowledge. Neighbors frequently knew very intimate details of each other's marital lives and employed insults and public speech to enforce community standards of sexual morality. Together, these notions of women's sexuality and sexual knowledge convinced Parkinson's male jurors to exonerate him of any sexual transgressions. As ideals of women's superior morality became more accepted over the century, male jurors struggled ever harder to reconcile conflicting images of female sexuality. Even when virtuous middle-class women testified to a minister's sexual attacks, men sitting in judgment more easily commiserated with a sorely tempted man than with his possible temptress.[33]

Within a masculine system of judgment, courts also had difficulty in assessing injury to women in these cases. As evident in the Onderdonk case, some of the clergymen's sexual behavior failed to meet clear definitions of crimes such as assault and rape or tort cases such as seduction or adultery. Parkinson's case certainly fell into that category. Jurors failed to convict clergy for assault and battery when women such as Wintringham offered little or no physical resistance and received no visible or lasting physical injury. Similarly, Wintringham's husband could not sue for compensatory damages to his wife (who was, in law, effectively the same as his own person or his chattel) unless physical evidence of penetration or paternity was proved. Parkinson's prosecutors tried to convince the jury that the clergyman's "assault and battery" was "perpetrating a crime injurious to every married man in the community" and "tending to ruin the peace of Mr. Wintringham, the father of a family, and to break up that family." But for unknown reasons, Mr. Wintringham did not testify in support of his wife and in defense of his family. He appeared only as a woefully pathetic cuckold, not the manfully indignant plaintiff with whom male jurors might identify. Parkinson's defense counsel easily emasculated both the husband and Mrs. Wintringham's male supporters, portraying them as "poor things," the "unsexed" victims of wily and sexually voracious females. Not until late in the nineteenth century did notions of women's selfhood, separate from fathers or husbands, influence court judgments in such cases.[34]

Likewise, until late in the century, male juries had difficulty in calculating the injury that women suffered to their modesty, spirits, and souls. Lawyers probed female accusers with interminable questions designed to reveal the intent of her assailant and the extent of her injury. Had the accused actually touched her naked breast or merely brushed her clothing with his hand? Touched her with the palm or the back of his hand? Rested his hand on her leg or actually lifted her skirts? Was his kiss the "holy kiss" of Christian friendship or the kiss of passion and lust? The Rev. Joy Fairchild's young servant girl insisted his kiss was "any thing but a holy kiss." He had been "intoxicated with passion, as much as the appearance of any man she ever saw indicated that he was intoxicated with liquor." Yet, jurors must have asked themselves how painful or severe an injury was sustained by an "intoxicated kiss" or a fumbling hand on a breast? Not until the end of the next century were conceptions of gender inequity and systematic sexual harassment constructed, tested, and supported in such cases. In nineteenth-century cases, lawyers sometimes tried these arguments but without much success. Parkinson's prosecutors only briefly explored the unequal power relations between male pastor and female parishioner that prevented women from actively resisting and protesting his sexual advances. In the end, courts applied masculine assumptions of injury and damage to these complex human interactions between men and women and found them wanting. If anything, male jurors perceived the possible injury and damage to the clergyman's reputation, stature, and livelihood that attended a conviction and chose to spare him.[35]

The last factor that clinched the clergyman's hold on a masculine identity was his claim that he was a martyr to his church and his public position as the leader of a church. Nearly every trial contained at least a veiled reference to a conspiracy of enemies. Sometimes the conspiracy served as the most explicit element in the defense. Ministers throughout the nineteenth century found themselves caught up in a number of local and national theological and political battles. In the early decades of the century, clergy fought over such highly divisive issues as Masonry, the disestablishment of churches, and the efficacy of evangelical preaching. At mid-century, they clashed over abolitionism, women's rights, and "free love." In a long-running dispute, the Rev. Ammi Rogers blamed his Episcopal hierarchy for framing him with charges of rape as a punishment for his disestablishment views, Masonic membership, and more personal disagreements. All four of the infamous cases detailed in the previous chapter showed clergy claiming conspiracy within and without their own denominations. Father Weinzoepflen earned his governor's pardon when he claimed to be a victim of organized anti-Catholics. In addition to public and clerical conspiracies, clergy confronted divisive congregations split over issues of personality, governance, money, and doctrine. Parkinson alleged that Mrs. Wintringham was merely the pawn of a group of his disgruntled male parishioners. Although many clergy employed this strategy in their defense, few made credible claims that they were indeed the innocent victims of false charges. Only the Rev. Moses Thacher successfully prosecuted his oppressors with charges of slander when he was informally accused of adultery with his parishioner, Jerusha Pond, who testified that Thacher had assaulted her several times. In his defense, Thacher described Pond as a kind of stalker, craving his company and intruding on himself and his family. Several days a week, he claimed, she walked more than six miles from her home to the parsonage and back again. She insisted on nursing the ill pastor and members of his family even when uninvited. Most convincing of all, Thacher produced more than seventy letters from Pond to himself, pathetic confessions of sinfulness and adulation for her pastor. They confirmed his descriptions of her as a woman desperate for his attention. Thacher even candidly confessed that he had committed "adultery in his heart," though not with Pond. He also admitted that some of his actions, such as giving young women rides in his carriage, were subject to misunderstanding. But he insisted he was innocent of any indiscretion or impropriety. A civil jury, a ministerial consociation, and most of his congregation all agreed that a dissident faction within his own church had wrongfully accused him. In most other cases, ministers failed to produce convincing evidence of a conspiracy and relied, instead, on the general benefit of doubt that juries seemed willing, if not eager, to grant to clergymen under fire.[36]

Conspiracies, whether real, fabricated, or imagined, rescued clergymen from the feminine sphere, where, to contemporaries, they appeared to spend too much of their time. The conspiracies situated the man and his profession firmly and comfortably within the public realm, subject to both the hazards and privileges of a competitive masculine sphere. The clergyman's struggle was transformed from a tawdry domestic spat between a minister and petty, spiteful women into a manly combat against potent political and theological enemies. Trials thus strengthened an individual clergyman's claim to masculinity and, perhaps, the claim of the clerical profession as a whole. Trials also conveyed the message to pastors in particular that they should avoid any intimacy, even spiritual intimacy, with women. Just as women took away the lesson that they were better off at home, ministers learned vicariously that they were better off remaining in the public sphere.

"Without Benefit of Clergy"

Courts favored men over women in a variety of ways, but they also favored clergymen over laity. As table 3.1 shows, juries, churches, and ministerial consociations rendered few unequivocal convictions or pronouncements of guilt and, in those few cases, imposed few consequential punishments. Yet few cases ended in forthright exoneration, either, as the public outrage to Avery's acquittal, the hung juries in the Kalloch and Beecher cases, the compromise verdict in the Onderdonk case, and the governor's pardon in the Weinzoepflen case clearly demonstrate. Two courts found in favor of the minister in slander suits but awarded only pennies in damages. Contradictory verdicts emerged in different venues: Joy Fairchild's ministerial peers pronounced him guilty, but a municipal court found him not guilty. Loyal congregations, or factions within those churches, continued to support these men through a number of trials. In one case, a New Jersey presbytery pronounced their fellow minister guilty of a variety of crimes but refused to formally expel him from the denomination. Reasoning that his reputation was so bad that no congregation would call him, they hoped to deter other contentious congregations from bringing frivolous suits against clergy by leaving the man his title if not his dignity or respect. Only two of the published cases between 1811 and 1878 ended in conclusive guilty verdicts against the clergyman, and only one of those two verdicts conclusively ended the clergyman's career. The Rev. Jacob Harden's confession to poisoning his wife left the jury little room for doubt. The minister was executed in 1860. Altogether, less than a third of the trials ended in a guilty verdict of any kind. The major reason for the ambiguity in these decisions was the office of the accused.[37]

The jury in the Parkinson case, as in many others, no doubt felt uncomfortable making moral judgments against a man of the church. Defense counsel in that case argued that the church or, better, God properly decided the question of the minister's moral fitness. Drawing on the principles of the First Amendment, the lawyer insisted that the "arm of civil authority never did, and never can accomplish any good in the regulation of ecclesiastical affairs." The founding fathers, after all, had meant the principle of separation of church and state, frequently tested to this day, to protect the church from the state as much as to protect the state from the church. If the Parkinson jury accepted this argument, they assumed that the minister's actions were morally wrong only because he was a clergyman. The church, therefore, and not the criminal court was the only rightful arbiter in the case.[38]

Doubt effectively protected the minister as surely as secrecy and the trial process. Uncertainty that a man who had been called to be God's representative could be guilty of doing the Devil's work ran deep in a society that valued religion and the church as the source of social and moral order in the republic. Consequently, the clerical office conferred a limited immunity to punishment. In Onderdonk's case, his peers quickly dismissed charges that the bishop had visited a brothel for immoral purposes. His clerical office and station convinced them that "there was consequently room for a charitable hope, that he had never gone to the place from other than pure motives, and for the exercise of his spiritual functions." Clergy asked for, and often received, the benefit of doubt, "the charitable hope" that could not be accorded a layman in the same circumstances.[39]

The controversial issue of clerical privilege in a democratic society arose in several trials. Deferring to the democratic foundations of the American justice system—that no person should be exempt from the law—lawyers on both sides in these cases pleaded with the jury not to show favor to the man because of his office. Then, in case after case, defense lawyers requested the very same deference for the clergyman that they had denied was his due. The plaintiff's counsel frequently asked jurors and peers to understand that the minister deserved special consideration because his office made him more vulnerable to charges of sexual misconduct than an ordinary man. Isaac Kalloch's lawyer asserted that if he "hadn't been a minister he would not have been forced to answer such charges." Only his "sacred position forced him to clear his name." Joy Fairchild argued that it was his professional obligation to fight the charges against him, because resigning his office in the face of malicious accusations set a terrible precedent and encouraged the laity to attack any minister who displeased them. "If clergymen were to run away from every false but specious charge made against them . . . it would take but a very short time to empty all the pulpits, not only in Boston, but everywhere else," he contended. Hence, the beleaguered minister defended not only himself but also his fellow clergy and the church itself. Henry Ward Beecher's lawyer admitted that the church certainly did not "depend on the character or fortunes of any man, however learned, eloquent or devout." He begged the jury to let his client "stand on his own integrity," rather than on his relation to the church. But in the very next sentence, Beecher's attorney conceded that "you can not consider him altogether without reference to that sacred faith of which he has been for a long time one of the most honored ministers, which would acquire lustre in his vindication, and which could not but be deeply wounded in his fall." Thus he argued that extending the clergyman the benefit of doubt spared the church an ignominious injury as well.[40]

The benefit of doubt saddled the council or jury with considering not just the fact of the man's crime but the effect of a conviction on an institution that many of them had some obligation to protect. Conviction was a sharp and double-edged sword. It removed a corrupt church leader, certainly a liability to the church if his reputation was infamous. Yet few accused ministers were so openly notorious that the church automatically suffered from their continuing leadership. If an ecclesiastical body expelled a dissolute cleric, the denomination or parish might be seen as policing itself—purging corruption from the body of the church. But the conviction of a minister by a secular jury ironically condemned the church for knowingly harboring a criminal. And even ecclesiastical discipline failed to cleanse the church of the taint of corruption. The Episcopal bishops learned to their dismay that their suspension of Bishop Onderdonk created only a lengthy embarrassment for them. No wonder that, faced with the trial of Bishop George Doane on charges of financial corruption less than a decade later, they dismissed the charges and excused his problems as fiscal incompetence. If ordinary criminals deserved the benefit of doubt, the Right Rev. Alfred Lee reasoned after Doane's aborted trial, then a bishop certainly deserved at least the same consideration. Besides, Lee argued, Onderdonk's trial had proved the destructive effects of such divisive ordeals on the church.[41]

The conviction of a clergyman risked intangible damage to the church's reputation, but it also risked the very tangible loss of a popular preacher, a valuable fundraiser, or a supportive contingent of parishioners. Joy Fairchild reminded his deacons of his invaluable services to their church. "I have been not merely the *servant* of this people," he admonished, "but their *slave*," and credited himself with raising $6,495.59 for a new meetinghouse. After his expulsion by the ministerial association and acquittal by a municipal court, a good portion of his former congregation left that church and called Fairchild to continue serving them as pastor in a new church. Other congregations welcomed back embattled pastors, deeming the men better for their afflictions. Isaac Kalloch's flock passed a resolution of confidence after his notorious trial, asserting that, despite the hung jury, "he had come out of the fire like pure gold, doubly refined." The only clergyman to lose all—his career and his life— did so because he lacked so many intellectual, financial, social, and institutional resources that he never would be missed. Jacob Harden, an uneducated and inexperienced Methodist preacher who was only nineteen at the time of his wife's murder, was assigned a contentious and impoverished rural church that severely taxed his limited skills of leadership and conciliation. The pathetic young man claimed that the competing demands of his wife and his congregation had sapped his strength and his health, forcing him to take the desperate measure of eliminating his wife. He even claimed that he did not know that poisoning was murder and subject to the death penalty. His confession rings true, lacking any sophistication or artifice, because neither he nor his denomination could afford to hire a lawyer for his defense. The rest of his clerical compatriots drew on far greater resources and suffered far milder fates than Harden. The three other ministers accused of murdering wives or lovers all escaped conviction.[42]

Granting the clergy the benefit of doubt, in effect, conferred a privilege similar to the age-old benefit of clergy, a medieval tradition that counted the clergy too valuable to the church to be sacrificed at the gallows, even if guilty. No clergymen explicitly asked for and received the obsolete privilege, but most benefited from a continuing deference to the clerical office and its perceived worth to the church. In a newly democratic society, requesting such a privilege was anathema, an iniquitous holdover from medieval caste systems. In the Father Weinzoepflen rape case, the prosecution successfully stoked the fires of anti-Catholic prejudice by claiming that the priest was caught while fleeing to his bishop to seek benefit of clergy. Protestant ministers, whether famous or infamous, generally escaped such cultural biases and enjoyed a huge advantage from their intimate association with the church. In not-so-subtle ways, religion itself went on trial with them. If scoundrels and hypocrites found refuge in the church, then the cause of religion was irreparably harmed. Anticlerical writers and freethinkers for centuries employed accusations of clerical immorality to discredit the church and its leaders. Though nineteenth-century ministers in the republic were without benefit of clergy in the medieval sense— they were nominally subject to the same jurisdictions and punishments as their secular peers—they still enjoyed a special immunity that reflected their connection to the church more than their individual reputations or leadership positions. Both church and lay jurors granted accused clergy the benefit of doubt and excused them even in the face of strong evidence, afraid that a guilty verdict would condemn the church and religion along with the man.[43]

Paradoxically, the inordinate respect accorded clergy and the church was a function of the democratic ethos. Americans believed deeply that since a democratic society lacked more oppressive systems of social control, it could survive and prosper only if citizens internalized religious values and morality. Americans deemed clergy and women, supposedly morally superior to their male contemporaries, the persons best able to inculcate those values as moral teachers and guardians. How ironic, then, that women should appear so vulnerable in that relationship and clergy appear so invulnerable. Ironic, too, that clergy accused of moral failure in their relations with women should enjoy a special privilege in a democratic society because that democratic society valued their services so highly as moral teachers and guardians. These trials exposed the flaws in a gender ideology that assigned separate spheres to men and women but then posited clergy and women as moral partners. Trials, however, also resolved this dilemma by sacrificing that putative partnership and reimposing on it the separate gendered spheres that kept men and women apart.

FIGURE 1. "A Present to the Pastor" [by A. Hunt] *New York Daily Graphic*, Jan. 14, 1875. REPRODUCED FROM MICROFILM COPY IN THE YALE UNIVERSITY LIBRARY

FIGURE 2. "The Churches and the Women," *New York Daily Graphic*, Nov. 16, 1874.

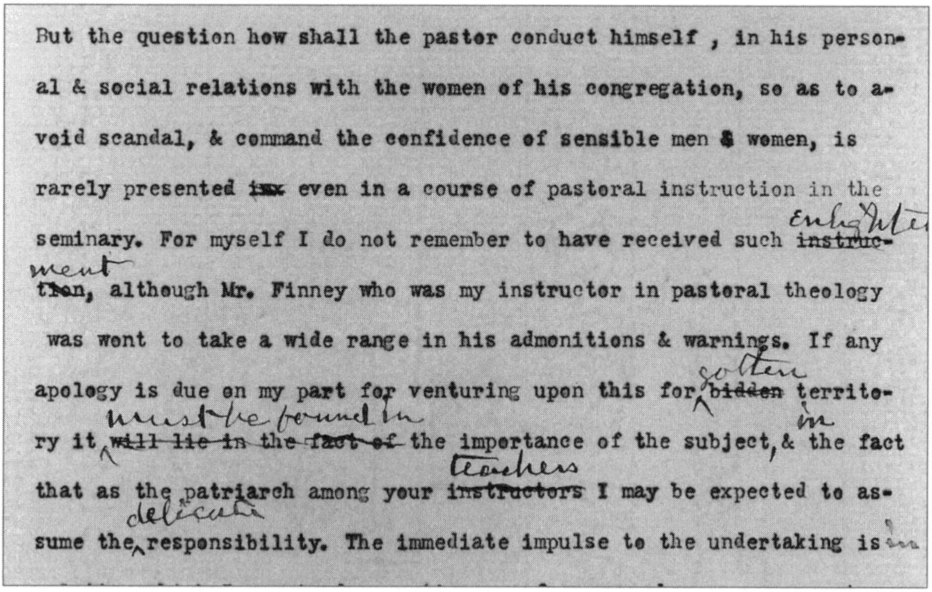

But the question how shall the pastor conduct himself , in his personal & social relations with the women of his congregation, so as to a-
void scandal, & command the confidence of sensible men & women, is
rarely presented ~~in~~ even in a course of pastoral instruction in the
seminary. For myself I do not remember to have received such ~~instruc-~~ *Enlighten-*
ment
~~tion,~~ although Mr. Finney who was my instructor in pastoral theology
was wont to take a wide range in his admonitions & warnings. If any
apology is due on my part for venturing upon this for ~~bidden~~ *gotten* territo-
must be found in
ry it ~~will lie in the fact of~~ the importance of the subject, & the fact *in*
teachers
that as the patriarch among your ~~instructors~~ I may be expected to as-
delicate
sume the responsibility. The immediate impulse to the undertaking is *in*

FIGURE 3. "Suggestions to Theological Students as to the Relations of the Pastor to
the Women of His Church & Congregation (n.d.). COURTESY OBERLIN COLLEGE ARCHIVES

FIGURE 4. Portrait of
Sarah M. Cornell,
frontispiece, *Brief and
Impartial Narrative of the
Life of Sarah Maria
Cornell* (1833). COURTESY
OF BROWN UNIVERSITY
LIBRARY

FIGURE 5. Portrait of the Rev. Ephraim K. Avery, from *The Correct, Full and Impartial Report of the Trial of Rev. Ephraim K. Avery* (1833). COURTESY OF THE AMERICAN ANTIQUARIAN SOCIETY

A Note found in Miss Cornell's Bandbox.

If I should be missing enquire of the Rev Mr Avery of Bristol he will know where I am Dec 20th

S M Cornell

Pendleton's Lithography, Boston.

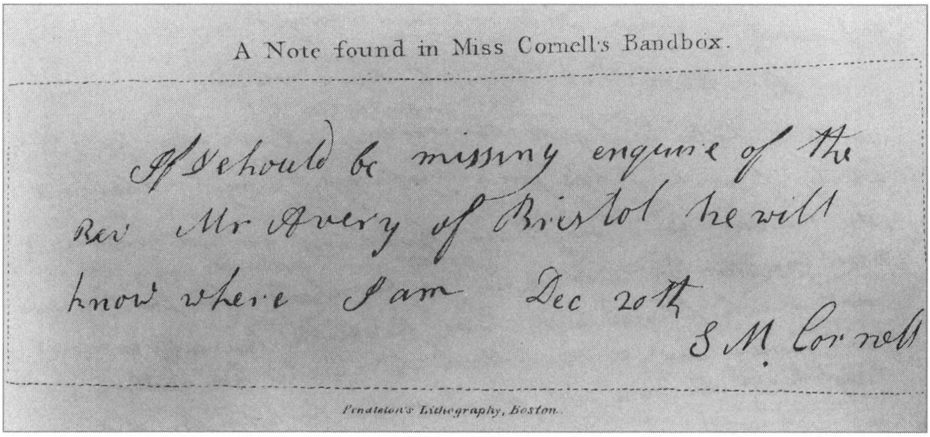

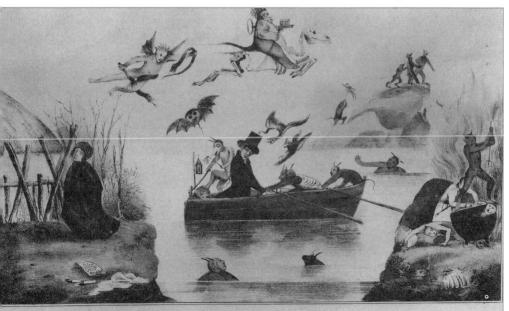

FIGURE 6. "A Note Found in Miss Cornell's Bandbox," from *A Fac-simile of the Letters Produced at the Trial of the Rev. Ephraim K. Avery* (1833). COURTESY OF THE AMERICAN ANTIQUARIAN SOCIETY

FIGURE 7. "A Minister Extraordinary Taking Passage & Bound on a Foreign Mission to the Court of His Satanic Majesty!" (1833). COURTESY OF THE AMERICAN ANTIQUARIAN SOCIETY

LINES

Written on the death of

Sarah M. Cornell.

In times like these, when murderers roam,
And search around for prey,
'Tis a fearful step to leave our home,
Lest dangerous men betray.

This lovely girl in youthful pride,
From virtue's path did stray,
A vile seducer for her guide,
And by him led away.

O little thought the simple girl,
Lured by a villian's smile,
That he from virtue's height could hurl
Her down a stream most vile.

She listened to his artful tongue,
And thought his words were true,
Till Avery from her bosom wrung
What she did after rue.

He forced her to confess a flame
Which his foul breath had fanned,
And there in her vile bed undress
Confessed his love was sham.

Love it was not, but hellish lust,
That urged this monster dire,
On Sarah's head his passion burst
More fierce than flames of fire.

How could she believe this murderous tale,
She knew he would deceive :
That all his promises were frail,
He left a wife to grieve.

His infant children stretched their hands,
Beseeching her to shun
His base unhallowed wicked hands,
Yet still to him she run.

The voice of Heaven was heard around,
The clouds departed from above,
The evening showers had wet the ground,
But she must meet her love.

An inward, warning voice alarmed,
And to her conscience spoke,
Still the virtuous girl unharmed,
Sought nothing to invoke.

She rushed to where her betrayer stayed,
Yet dreaming still of ill,
She found him there, and soon 'twas said,
'Twas heaven's, just Heaven's will.

Her lovely locks with rage he tore,
And strewed the ground with hair,
Then to a stack her form he bore,
And hung the body there.

Cold was the night, and lone the scene,
No friendly aid was nigh,
With Sarah's fate to intervene,
Or heed her dying sigh.

She's gone to regions far away,
Beyond this world of gloom,
To wait until that awful day
When man receives his doom.

The wretch has fled from mortal's doom,
Who done this deed most vile,
But one above can pierce the gloom,
And bring to light his guile.

Ye girls all sound in virgin bloom,
With youth and beauty blest,
Beware the crime for fear the doom,
Of Sarah Maria pierce your breast.

SECOND PART.

Kind Christians all I pray attend,
To these few lines which I have penned,
While I relate the murderous fate
That did await poor Cornell's end.

Miss Sarah Cornell was her name,
Who by deceit was brought to shame,
Your hearts in sympathy must bleed,
When Shepherds murder lambs indeed.

A Reverend Mr. Avery sure,
A preacher of the gospel too,
Stands charged with murder to the test,—
Seduction too, in part confessed.

First inquest he was set at large,
By circumstance from farther charge ;
Soon after that the deed was done,
He ran away the law to shun :

But blood for blood aloud doth cry,
All murderers surely ought to die.
Five hundred dollars of reward
To bring this Avery to the charge.

He soon was taken and with speed,
Was brought to answer for this deed,
Now in Rhode Island bound was he,
In May to receive his destiny.

Methought I heard a spirit say,
" Remember Cornell's end I pray,"
And let no one reflections make,
Upon my friends for my poor sake.

Let woman's weakness plead my cause,
When cruel men break nature's laws.
If man by man was so deceived,
What tongue would not his mercy plead.

Know you but half the artful way
That base betrayer led me astray.
The best may slip, be cautious all,
Depraved is man since Adams' fall.

Ye maidens all both old and young,
Trust not to men's false flattering tongue :
To know a man, pray know his life,—
How few there are deserve a wife.

Though doomed I am to awful end,
I ask the prayers of every friend,
That my poor spirit may be blest,
And with my God in heaven to rest.

Now to conclude this mournful song,
These lines I pray remember long,
Adieu my friends, pray dont repine,
Example's yours, and experience mine.

A man — Mid — Wife.

a newly discovered animal, not known in Buffon's time; for a more full description of this Monster, see, an ingenious book lately published price 3/6 entitled, Man - Midwifery dissected, containing a Variety of well authenticated cases elucidating this animal's Propensity to cruelty & indecency, sold by the publisher, of this Print, who has presented the Author with the Above for a Frontispiece.

FIGURE 11. "Black Onder-donk-en Doughlips" (1845). COURTESY OF THE AMERICAN ANTIQUARIAN SOCIETY

FIGURE 12. Portrait of the Rev. I. S. Kalloch, from *Only Full Report of the Trial of Rev. I. S. Kalloch* (1857). COURTESY OF THE AMERICAN ANTIQUARIAN SOCIETY

FIGURE 13. "Portrait of the Lady in Black," from *Only Full Report of the Trial of Rev. I. S. Kalloch* (1857). COURTESY OF THE AMERICAN ANTIQUARIAN SOCIETY

THE LECTURE ROOM OF THE LECHMERE.

FIGURE 14. "The Lecture Room of the Lechmere," from *Only Full Report of the Trial of Rev. I. S. Kalloch* (1857). COURTESY OF THE AMERICAN ANTIQUARIAN SOCIETY

FIGURE 15. "Old Lady in a Fog," *New York Daily Graphic*, Aug. 20, 1874. REPRODUCED FROM MICROFILM IN THE YALE UNIVERSITY LIBRARY

FIGURE 16. "The Beecher-Tilton Case," *New York Daily Graphic*, Aug. 22, 1874.

right
FIGURE 17. "A Hint to the
Plymouth Pastor," *New York
Daily Graphic*, Oct. 3, 1874.
REPRODUCED FROM MICROFILM IN
THE YALE UNIVERSITY LIBRARY

below
FIGURE 18. "How to Make
Pastoral Visits and Avoid
Slander," *New York Daily
Graphic*, Sept. 14, 1874.
REPRODUCED FROM MICROFILM IN
THE YALE UNIVERSITY LIBRARY

SINE PECCATO EST VESTRUM, PRIMUS
'N ILLAM LAPIDEM MITTAT

"QUI SINE PECCATO."

FIGURE 19. "Qui Sine Peccato," *New York Daily Graphic,* Apr. 3, 1875. REPRODUCED
FROM MICROFILM IN THE YALE UNIVERSITY LIBRARY

FIGURE 20. "Beecher's Experience in Lap-Land," from a scrapbook of clippings of the Beecher-Tilton scandal, vol. I. COURTESY OF THE BROOKLYN COLLECTION, BROOKLYN PUBLIC LIBRARY

Figure 21. "Scene in the Parlor" from a scrapbook of clippings of the Beecher-Tilton scandal, vol. I. COURTESY OF THE BROOKLYN COLLECTION, BROOKLYN PUBLIC LIBRARY

FIGURE 22. "A Sample of Spirits," *New York Daily Graphic,* May 4, 1875. REPRODUCED FROM MICROFILM IN THE YALE UNIVERSITY LIBRARY

FIGURE 23. "Death Struggle on the Ragged Edge," *New York Daily Graphic*, Jan. 11, 1875. REPRODUCED FROM MICROFILM IN THE YALE UNIVERSITY LIBRARYI

PART II

The Pastoral Relationship in the Literary Imagination

4

Paradoxical Pastors; or, What the Novelist Imagined

In the single most important letter submitted as evidence in the Beecher-Tilton trial, Elizabeth Tilton wrote that after reading the novel *Griffith Gaunt* she was able to "see clearly her sin," confess to her husband, and ask his forgiveness. Published in newspapers across the country, the letter's meaning was debated not only by the attorneys in the case but also by the public at large. Whether the sin she confessed constituted adultery may never be clear, but the letter's significance is certain. Elizabeth acknowledged the power of novel reading at the same time that the nationally publicized trial confirmed its importance. The novel had, in effect, performed the role of a personal spiritual pastor, guiding Elizabeth to confront her sinful behavior and to repent. The *Gaunt* novel and the confession it elicited helped to set Elizabeth's life on a tragic course toward separation from her husband. Indirectly, it helped to publicize and politicize the issue of free love. Finally, it led to Elizabeth's public humiliation in a battle between the two men she loved best and who once loved each other. That a novel in the nineteenth century should have such powerful pastoral, personal, political, and public consequences might surprise us in the twenty-first century. But it shouldn't.

Most of us learn in our U.S. history courses that just twenty years before Elizabeth sat down to read the novel that dramatically changed her life, millions of Americans read a novel that helped set the United States on an even more tragic course toward separation and fratricidal war. Harriet Beecher Stowe's famous novel, *Uncle Tom's Cabin* (1852), helped reluctant Northerners acknowledge the terrible sin of slavery and politicize the issue of abolitionism. That novel contributed to the separation of the Confederate States from the Union and to Northerners' resolve to make bloody war on their

Southern brothers. In Ann Douglas's view, sentimental novels such as the one that both Theodore and Elizabeth Tilton read, or the ones that Henry Ward Beecher and his sister Harriet wrote, marked a departure and a declension from the theological sermons and tracts that had occupied the minds and informed the actions of Puritan Americans in previous generations. Douglas faulted sentimentalism for breeding a feminized passivity and consumption of mass culture in readers who vicariously imbibed the emotions of their favorite characters without producing significant new ideas and behavior. Yet, since it might have contradicted her thesis, Douglas did not explore the *actions* readers could have taken as a consequence of their novel reading. Reading mattered to Victorian Americans, perhaps even more than the mass-produced fiction, films, television, art, music, or even advertising matters to present-day Americans. Reading *moved* nineteenth-century Americans emotionally, but it could also move them actively to change their lives in significant ways.[1]

The novel that so dislocated Elizabeth Tilton, her family, her congregation, and the nation was a curious hybrid genre, somewhere between the sentimental novel and the lurid sensational novel that were both so popular throughout much of the nineteenth century. Although the English author, Charles Reade, titled the novel *Griffith Gaunt, or Jealousy*, the central character was really Catherine Gaunt, a woman who struggled to find personal and spiritual satisfaction with a variety of men. The novel described the heroine's relationship with two lovers but also her dependence on and friendship with two very different pastors. Father Francis was a worldly, practical, forthright, middle-aged priest whose wisdom guided Catherine Gaunt as she decided first whether to enter a convent or to marry one of two dueling suitors, then which suitor to marry, and finally how to manage the frightfully jealous husband she eventually chose. To complicate matters, her marriage to Gaunt crossed lines of faith: Catherine was a Catholic and Griffith a Protestant. While Father Francis provided practical wisdom and helped her make decisions in this world, he failed to offer Catherine the spiritual food for which she longed. Instead, Father Leonard, the ascetic and otherworldly young priest who replaced Father Francis, supplied Catherine with abundant spiritual nourishment. Unfortunately, the intimacy with the new priest, especially what she perceived as his growing romantic devotion to her, confused and frightened Catherine. Eventually, Catherine Gaunt feared that she had inspired both physical as well as spiritual passion in the young man and sent him away. But her decision came too late to prevent her suspicious husband from assaulting both pastor and parishioner, fleeing their home, assuming another identity, and marrying another wife. Catherine Gaunt was no passive, submissive, sentimental heroine. Her tempestuous personality put her constantly at odds with herself, her husband, and her faith. Although she possessed the requisite deep piety, it was coupled with a fierce temper and remarkable intellect—she served as her own legal counsel when tried for her husband's murder. The nineteenth-century reader of this novel must surely have wondered how Catherine could ever successfully resolve the serious conflicts in her life, given her inability to submit quietly to the men in her life. But the requisite happy ending owed much to the steadfast Father

Francis, who returned to serve his troubled yet faithful parishioner. With his help, Catherine reconciled with her wayward husband and befriended the wife of his bigamous marriage.

In addition to offering readers an entertaining and incredibly complicated Gothic plot, the novel also provided them with two important imagined models of the pastoral relationship. The avuncular Francis furnished Catherine with the support and practical advice that helped her function as an active Christian within a world of temptation and sin. In contrast, the ethereal Leonard afforded Catherine the spiritual escape from the richly material world she inhabited, but his otherworldly naivety distracted her from her worldly duties and plunged her life into chaos. Although quite different models, each effectual in one way and not in another, both pastors were unusually devoted to their beautiful, pious, mercurial, and spiritually needy parishioner. Indeed, Catherine apparently enjoyed the almost exclusive attention of her pastors. The overdrawn, melodramatic portraits of the pastoral relationship in this novel reinforced the stereotypical perceptions of a close and sometimes dangerously intimate relationship. The lesson the novel taught seemed to be that pastors might be practical advisors or spiritual mentors but expecting both persons in the same man was perhaps unrealistic. Still another message, subtler and more important, emerged from this novel: Not only was the pastoral relationship in dangerous competition with the conjugal relationship but also it was a poor substitute for a solid marriage. The novel suggested that a woman who made a wise choice in a husband, who built a strong marriage with a man of similar faith and piety and who relied on her husband as a spiritual counselor, could probably dispense with a pastor altogether and live safely and comfortably without benefit of clergy.

Unfortunately, discovering and assessing the actions that Americans took in response to individual novels or even to specific genres is extremely difficult. We believe they read them because they bought them in huge numbers and sometimes recorded their reading and reactions. We even speculate, as Ann Douglas did, on their effects on American culture. But few ordinary Americans left records of the consequences of reading as revealing as Elizabeth Tilton's reading of *Griffith Gaunt*. She found her own confused marriage and pastoral relationship reflected in this novel and moved to resolve the tension between them as a result. We can only speculate on the responses of most readers to works that featured this problematic relationship. In this chapter, portraits of the pastoral relationship in a few representative works in each genre reinforce, for the most part, the impression that clergy and women possessed a close bond. They differ from the travelers' accounts and the trial reports in that their portraits included benign as well as malignant pastoral relationships. Sensational novelists cravenly exploited the lurid fears expressed in travelers' accounts and trial reports and imagined truly monstrous pastors who preyed on helpless women. Sentimental novelists, on the other hand, imagined a powerful male pastor who worked in the best interests of the women in his care. Occasionally, however, these novels offered portraits that challenged the notion of a mutual alliance. Some novelists imagined a pastoral relationship that failed, not because it was dangerously close but because it was too distanced by conventions of gender. Thus, readers could find ample fuel for their worst fears, while also discovering a much richer and more complicated portrait of the pastoral relationship in these novels than in the journalistic accounts of the period. Surely these imagined portraits strongly *shaped* the social experience of the pastoral relationship, even if it is difficult to document that influence in individual lives. And, as we shall discover in the unpublished journals and correspondence examined in Part IV, the more complex portraits painted by some novelists in nineteenth-century America actually *reflected* the experience of many ordinary pastors and women more faithfully than the travel accounts or the trial pamphlets.

The Reverend Rake

One of the most enduring characters in nineteenth-century literature, especially in the popular sensational novels of the period, was the "reverend rake," who most closely mirrored the disquieting and frightening image of the pastor as libertine that emerged so powerfully in the perceptions of European travelers and the American audiences for clergymen's trials. Although exaggerated and overdrawn, the caricatures in these novels nevertheless exploited the ambiguity of the pastoral relationship. They played with the disturbing doubt that even respected public men could be deceivers and debauchers. The powerful image of the pastoral relationship as a hidden but pervasive opportunity for sexual misconduct fascinated many nineteenth-century writers and readers, but in the fevered imaginations of novelists such as George Foster, pastors assumed surreal, monstrous shapes that further distorted the public perceptions of a dangerous pastoral relationship. These novels exploited the same fears that pastors crossed gender boundaries to invade domestic space—the homes and bodies of women. The most common prescription for preventing pastoral incursions was to strengthen gender boundaries. The English traveler Frances Trollope called for fathers and husbands to mount a paternal defense of the domestic sphere and protect women from predators in clerical garb. Trials, as we have seen, repaired the damage done by wandering ministers by subtly reinforcing the boundaries between gendered spheres. They enhanced the masculinity of ministers while reimposing restrictive femininity on women. Sensational novels worked in similar ways. They exaggerated the rapacious masculinity of clergymen at the same time that they presented overdrawn pictures of feminine vulnerability. In doing so, they appealed to those who favored the fortification of separate gendered spheres. Most of the writers of these novels, and perhaps most of the readers, were male. Indeed, as historian David Reynolds has pointed out, these works served the contradictory purposes of pornographic titillation and moral reform. By shocking their readers with horrific tales of seduction and corruption, they hoped (or claimed to hope) to inspire moral reform efforts.[2]

The sensational novel exploited the subversive image of the pastoral relationship by reconstructing the minister as a rapacious sexual animal introduced into the domestic sphere as a menacing intruder. The wild popularity of this genre—part sensational exposé, part pornography—belies the marginal place it has occupied in literary history until recently. David Reynolds argued that a "subversive imagination" was central to both the popular literature of the period and the canonized works of the American Renaissance and identified the "reverend rake" as a stock character in both genres. Although much of the work paraded as "exposés" or factual reporting, it was largely fictional in character. And, while it was intended to inspire moral outrage and reform, its lurid prose often obscured and even sabotaged its intentional didactic purpose. For this reason, Reynolds has termed these writers "immoral reformers." One of the first and most popular authors in this genre, the preacher and book peddler Parson Mason Locke Weems, we remember for his imaginative cherry-tree story that exaggerated young George Washington's honesty in order to illustrate the first president's integrity. He also employed fiction to challenge the Puritan ethos that prohibited frank discussion of the violent and erotic by "exaggerating and universalizing the vices he pretended to denounce." In a plot reminiscent of the Greek tragedy of Oedipus, the Devil persuaded a preacher to get drunk, murder his father, and rape his sister. Perhaps some of Weems's many readers understood his literary strategy of exaggeration. Yet even if his audience doubted the truth of his stories, it certainly entertained the fear that they *might* be true. The stories, whether fictional or not, gave explicit expression to the cultural anxiety about the pastoral relationship, one that other literary genres more successfully repressed. Weems, in this anecdote, neatly summarized the primal fears of patricide and incest that gripped nineteenth-century Americans when they contemplated the pastoral relationship. A rogue clergyman threatened to "kill the father" by undermining faith in God and to commit incest by seducing his spiritual sisters and daughters.[3]

Dozens of early pamphlets and novels purported to expose vice-ridden clergymen and their ravaged female victims. *The Confessions of a Magdalene*, the story of a young woman reduced to prostitution after being drugged and seduced by a minister, was a conventional work with stock characters. Undoubtedly, portraying the seducer as a clergyman worked in two ways. Just as in the trials, it highlighted the vulnerability of women, who, literally, could trust no man. Not only might a respected clergyman be her seducer but also he might employ drugs that would render her even more helpless than her gender already made her. At the same time, the novel hoped to expose the venality and corruption of men such as clergy, other professionals, and politicians who occupied respected positions but regularly betrayed the public trust. Especially virulent were the works that advanced a nativist, anti-Catholic agenda. The notorious best-seller *Awful Disclosures at the Hotel Dieu* by Maria Monk convinced many readers that nuns were forced to prostitute themselves to priests and that together the fiendish religious criminals baptized their illegitimate children and then smothered them and buried the corpses in lime pits beneath the convent. The outrage over the report moved a delegation of Protestant ministers to travel to the Montreal convent to investigate. They returned home to denounce Maria Monk as a fraud. Despite their judgment, however, the novel was reprinted several times throughout mid-century. Thus, even though the exposés themselves were exposed as counterfeit, they retained the power of sexual arousal and, for the ill informed, inspired outrage.[4]

George Lippard, perhaps the best-selling author in this genre, produced an infamous combination of Gothic horror and urban exposé of Philadelphia entitled *The Quaker City, or The Monks of Monk Hall.* It sold more copies than any novel before *Uncle Tom's Cabin,* a testament to the significance of this genre in the popular culture. Lippard's clerical character was the Rev. F.A.T. Pyne, a name that conjured up the preacher's grotesque physical appearance and his fire-breathing anti-Papist preaching but also alluded to the stench of hellfire and brimstone emanating from his person. Pyne, like the other socially prominent villains in the novel, conducted his seductions in an old Philadelphia mansion called Monk Hall, an infernal inversion of fraternal organizations such as the Masons that grew more and more popular over the century. Pyne's crime was particularly loathsome not merely because he was a member of this social elite and a clergyman but because his victim was his own adopted daughter. Indeed, the girl may have been his natural daughter as well since the girl's mother had been, years before, a victim of Pyne's lust.[5]

Lippard's portrayal emphasized the potential crime as incest, not merely seduction, which increased its repugnant impact and perverse attraction. What other authors veiled in euphemism, Lippard confronted in all its thrilling horror. The pastor who betrayed his position as the paternal protector, the trusted confidant and counselor to his parochial family, was a more hideous character even than Devil-Bug, the deformed and murderous overseer of the notorious Monk Hall. The accomplice to and facilitator of every seduction, Devil-Bug himself was appalled by Pyne's audacity and questioned him when the girl called the preacher "Father." The accomplice's uncharacteristic apprehensions were not assuaged even when Pyne assured Devil-Bug that he was her father only in the "spiritual sense." Throughout the actual seduction scene, Lippard satirized the sentimental paternal figures of domestic literature. The Rev. Pyne's face displayed the "gloating expression of fatherly affection" as he called to the girl, "Come and kiss your papa, Mabel! It was a good girl, that it was, and it must kiss its papa!" Pyne's seduction was ultimately foiled when the child awoke from her drugged trance and freed herself from the "priestly villain." Pyne's seduction represented not merely the invasion of a forbidden domestic space but, perversely, the violation of his own daughter's virtue. Pyne's lascivious character thus monstrously distorted the clergyman's masculine roles as professional, pastor, and father. His victim was defenseless not only because she was young, innocent, and drugged but also because she was his own daughter. Surely such a grotesque figure provoked humor as much as horror, however. Pyne's caricature is more comic than fearsome. Lippard created a more credible and thus more terrifying preacher for a later work, *The Memoirs of a Preacher.*[6]

Just as Lippard's *Quaker City* exploited contemporary fears of urban corruption and secret societies, his *Memoirs of a Preacher* took advantage of conservative fears that emotional evangelical preachers were more likely bent on seduction than their rational, orthodox clerical brethren. Indeed, the work is a parody of the popular evangelical biographies and autobiographies of the period. This time the main character was terrifying because he was *not* grotesque in appearance. At first glance, he seemed a very handsome and successful evangelist, bringing dozens of tortured souls, mostly female, to Christ. His meetings always attracted overflow crowds. Yet, just like the skeptical travelers, one anonymous onlooker at least was deeply disturbed by the preacher's behavior. The narrator of the scene observed a distraught woman tearfully confessing into the preacher's ear that she had caused her daughter's death by marrying her off to a rich man. The scene of "immovable despair" so moved the bystander that he bent over the two in order to eavesdrop on their intimate conversation, to literally invade the private pastoral space to expose its secrets. But he failed to read the preacher even at such close range. The preacher's reply to the woman's confession, he recorded, was "given in that sweet, calm—almost effeminate voice—and with a constant application of the kerchief in the nostrils." To the onlooker, the preacher's gentle sincerity seemed at odds with the affected manipulation of his handkerchief. Worse yet, his deceptively feminine demeanor seemed at odds with a suppressed violence: He "perceived the Preacher's hand press rather forcibly the delicate hand of [a] young girl." Finally, the preacher's gaze defied definition. When he looked upon the women, it was "so cold, so icy, and yet so full of latent scorn—or was it merely compassion?" In short, the narrator failed to discern the source of the preacher's interest in the women in his audience. Was he there to aid them in their tearful terror of sin or to exploit their feminine emotional weakness to satisfy his own masculine lust and urge for power? The narrator's inability to read the character of the preacher reflected the same "uneasiness and suspicion" that afflicted those who pored over the trial pamphlets as they tried to discern the guilt or innocence of the accused minister.[7]

Nineteenth-century Americans shared the narrator's fascination, frustration, and confusion over his inability to read the character of the preacher, as historians Karen Halttunen and John Kasson have both documented. Millions of Americans increasingly inhabited urban spaces where the anonymity of the population frightened the innocent and protected the criminal. Halttunen argued that middle-class Victorian Americans tried to control the "world of strangers" by constructing and imposing rigid standards of dress and etiquette on themselves and any others who hoped to be identified as respectable. In other words, adhering to middle-class manners marked one not just as a member of an economically successful group but as an adherent of middle-class values of sobriety, industry, and honesty. In a paradoxical fashion, one adopted the artificial modes of behavior of middle-class manners in order to make obvious one's sincerity and distinguish oneself from the charlatan who looked respectable but was in reality a "confidence man" or "painted lady." Lippard's preacher played upon these very fears, exposing the serious flaws in the middle-class identification system by dressing in impeccable clothing and displaying flawless manners yet acting as a deliberate and successful confidence man, mesmerist, and seduction artist. By continually crossing the boundaries between middle-class respectability and criminal impropriety, the preacher assumed the same shape-shifting qualities as the real-life criminal clerics. He was the "oxymoronic oppressor," the last person in the world the reader would ever expect to fear. Lippard thus easily capitalized on the same fear of and fascination with hypocrisy generated by the trials.[8]

"Reverend rakes" is the oxymoronic title adopted by critics to describe the stock characters in the sensational literature, where evil usually triumphed. In a quite different though related genre, the sentimental novel, good inevitably won over evil, yet the clerical characters that regularly and prominently appeared there might also be labeled with oxymoronic titles. At first, the relationships in these novels appear to offer a reassuring and benign model of pastors and women at the opposite end of the spectrum from the disturbing and malignant portraits of the sensational novels. At a second glance, however, a much richer portrait emerges, one sometimes as disquieting as its evil twin. Although benign, the clergymen in these sentimental novels could still be as domineering as any of the predators, and the women as vulnerable and submissive as any of the victims in the sensational novels. In short, the minister emerged as a despot, albeit a benevolent one. On the other hand, the clergyman sometimes appeared ineffective and powerless, while still displaying all the trappings of his office and his manhood. In a radical inversion of the reverend rake and the benevolent despot, the marginal minister possessed the education and intellectual authority that should have given him power in the masculine political sphere. However, the man was essentially impotent in both the public and private spheres. He was a theologian totally dependent upon women for his care. They shepherded him, rather than he them. Despite their quite simplistic characterizations, these two imagined portraits offer important clues to the complicated dynamics of the experienced pastoral relationship.

Sentimental novels, like their sensational contemporaries, suffered from scholarly contempt and neglect until the last few decades of the twentieth century in part because they, too, seemed to embrace melodramatic stereotypes and ignore ambiguity. Their very popularity made them suspect, precursors of the "mass culture" decried by twentieth-century intellectuals and canon constructors. Unlike the authors of most of the trial reports and the sensational fiction and even the authors of pious biographies, memoirs, religious tracts, or the literature later enshrined in the realm of "high culture," women were most often the authors of sentimental works. The "d——d scribbling women" that Nathaniel Hawthorne famously deplored penned novels easily dismissed as women's emotional and didactic fiction, devoid of intellectual rigor and lacking a recognition of moral ambiguity. Recent literary historians and critics have reexamined these previously neglected works, and many have challenged the negative interpretation of the genre offered by Douglas and earlier critics. They argue that nineteenth-century popular literature was less transparent and less stereotypical than it appeared to critics in the past. In the case of the pastoral relationship, a first story or "cover story" might conform to expectations of overdrawn melodramatic caricature, championing the gender ideal of women as pious and pure but still submissive and dependent upon a patriarchal male clergy for spiritual guidance. But a second story or "covert story" told a much more complicated and disturbing story, perhaps even more upsetting than the tales of corruption elaborated in travelers' accounts, trials, and sensational fiction. Sentimental heroines might sometimes find clergymen spiritually, socially, and even physically attractive and engaging, but they also found them spiritually, socially, and even physically inaccessible. Clergy exercised an attraction to women and a power and dominance over them by their superior social status and education, but they also distanced themselves from their female followers by those same qualities. The intrusion of sexuality introduced tension and caution if not distance, although sentimental writers suppressed the overtly erotic language of the sensational fiction. Thus, these novels, previously dismissed as simplistic and overly emotional, nevertheless reflected, even if surreptitiously, many of the cultural tensions and paradoxes reflected in other images of the pastoral relationship. In addition, they offered imaginative renditions of the pastoral relationship that tried to reconcile the tensions as they further challenged assumptions of a close bond and mutual admiration between women and clergy. Two popular works from the 1850s demonstrate the paradoxical qualities of the pastor and his relationship with women.[9]

The Benevolent Despot

Susan Warner's *The Wide, Wide World* (1850) ranked second only to *Uncle Tom's Cabin* as the nineteenth-century's all-time best-selling novel. Like many sentimental heroines, Ellen Montgomery endured a life of trial that nevertheless ended in happiness and triumph. Her principal guide was a dashing and forceful young minister, John Humphreys, to whom she piously submitted in spiritual direction and at last in marriage. While Ellen's submission to God and his representative reinforce the stereotype of women's frailty and dependence, a covert story undermines that easy assumption. Ellen's long and painful search for pastoral care suggests that clerical spiritual counselors were scarce. The successful spiritual guidance she eventually accepted from John Humphreys suggests a number of possibilities that link his role as pastor with his role as suitor. John might be a successful pastor because he was also available as a suitor, or he might be successful as a suitor because he was a pastor. Likewise, Ellen might accept John's spiritual guidance because she could also accept him as a brother and a lover.

Ellen's life of misery owes much to the absence of a strong father figure. Abandoned by a careless father and a dying mother, she often rebelled against her guardian, her fate, and her God. A series of paternal, pastoral gentlemen— living embodiments of a firm, loving, but ultimately distant Father in heaven— occasionally appeared to offer her advice. But Ellen longed for a more consistent source of pastoral guidance. She often visited a local minister who called her "little daughter." But the man was so preoccupied with preparing his sermons that he "generally kept by himself in his study." The aloof older man delegated the bulk of his pastoral duties to his pious young daughter instead. Alice Humphreys, the minister's exemplary daughter, helped Ellen to learn about God, control her temper, and become more submissive. The pious young woman taught the Sabbath school and assisted her father in his pastoral duties—visiting, praying and "preaching" to the women of the parish. Upon receiving a call and a "lecture" from Miss Humphreys, Ellen's feisty aunt noted dryly, "It's a pity you warn't a minister, Miss Alice." Alice Humphreys, like so many angelic characters in sentimental novels, died at a young age, cutting short her unordained ministry. Her father's deep grief isolated him even further from his congregation. Alice's death thus deprived the church and young Ellen of their most effective source of pastoral care.[10]

Alice's gentle educational and spiritual guidance was supplanted by her brother John Humphreys's assertive control. John, usually absent attending seminary, made infrequent but dramatic appearances in young Ellen's life. On one occasion, he rescued Ellen from a tormentor by physically wrestling the man from his horse. He possessed a virile masculinity that was not immediately obvious, however. One character was warned not to take the slight, quiet young man for a coward, for "when he *is* roused he seems to me to have strength enough for twice his bone and muscle." John's masterful manner tamed horses, bullies, and eventually the rebellious young Ellen herself. John tutored Ellen in literature, science, and art but consistently demanded her obedient submission to God and her superiors. John's relentlessly high expectations stood in stark contrast to his late sister's gentle pastoral lessons, but according to the narrator his were more effective. What Alice Humphreys had asked of Ellen, she "*tried* to do; what John told her *was done*."[11]

John Humphreys's character, the Romantic ideal of both the Christian gentleman and the minister, was a potent antidote to the stereotype of the effeminate cleric. Pious, intelligent, and well educated, Humphreys was also gallant and brave. He thus embodied the often contradictory qualities that, as we shall see in the next chapter, the pastoral role demanded. On the other hand, Ellen Montgomery represented the ideal of the Christian woman, belying any images of women usurping the clerical role. As she matured, she grew more childlike, submissive, and dependent on her God and her masculine guides and protectors. Faced with separation from John, whom she called her "brother," she lamented that "no one talks to me as you used to do; and I am all the while afraid that I shall go wrong in something; what shall I do?" On the surface then, the couple conforms, painfully, to nineteenth-century gender ideology. Despite his slight physical appearance, John assumed his role of minister with dash and daring. Ellen, despite her propensity for rebellion, meekly assumed her role as pious, familial parishioner.[12]

Although the characters conform in an exaggerated fashion to gender expectations, the story of Ellen and John's relationship raised the same fearsome specter of sexuality that haunted the more sinister images of the pastoral relationship. Sexual attraction between these two stereotypically gendered characters seemed inevitable and raised questions and inspired fears that Warner failed to resolve, perhaps intentionally, for her readers. Because Ellen was a child and "adopted" member of the Humphreys family, John frequently demanded a kiss from her as his "brother's right." Likewise, instances of physical intimacy delighted the young Ellen. One day when John had failed to give her a welcoming kiss, Ellen became hurt and tearful. But when the young man returned, he grabbed her by the shoulders, kissed her, and demanded to know what was the matter. Though ashamed to admit her resentment and show her tears, Ellen was powerless to resist John's demand that she confess. "Whatever that eye demanded she never knew how to keep back," and she conceded her foolish jealousy. Ellen's passion, whether anger, jealousy, or adolescent sexuality, was under John's control, not hers. In short, John was a mesmerist if not a confidence man.[13]

Several literary historians have noted the inherent sexualized nature of the brother-sister relationship in this novel. As Jane Tompkins argued, the novel's "dramatization of domination and submission . . . is sexualized from the start." Ellen's suffering is both painful and pornographic; by submitting to John's spiritual rule, she unwittingly but willingly submitted to his physical and sexual control as well. Her submission to God was also her submission to John. G. M. Goshgarian has carefully delineated the incestuous eroticism of the siblings' relationship. But no critic has noted that the nineteenth-century minister's familial role—whether acting as father or brother—meant that any romantic or sexual feelings between a pastor and a woman were essentially incestuous and thus highly forbidden. Consequently, the relationship was attractive and repulsive, to writers and to readers, precisely because it tapped such deep taboos. Sentimental writers tamed this sexual tension by reshaping and domesticating it; they transformed the pastoral relationship into a conjugal relationship—the only safe relationship between a man and woman in the nineteenth century.[14]

Nineteenth-century female readers might have come away from Warner's novel with the message that humility and submission would, paradoxically, free women from the enslavement of petty passions and deliver them into a domestic enclosure of peace and happiness. No doubt sharing that new life of passionlessness and restraint with a dashing, indeed passionate, romantic hero complemented the heroine's self-imposed deficits and compensated her to an extent. Reading sentimental novels and vicariously sharing the heroine's passions and her successful repression of those emotions might also have mitigated any reader's restlessness. Warner's didactic purpose, after all, was to uphold and glorify cultural standards of gender behavior, to help women see and model the virtues of true womanhood. The exemplar she held up for men and, in this case, for ministers was one of dominance and control of women, in the women's best interests. Hence, this image reinforced gender stereotypes and upheld masculine privilege and female weakness. Though seemingly more benign, this unbalanced relationship was little different from its malignant counterpart, merely the other side of the coin from those predatory relationships in sensational novels and trial accounts. In the original published version of *Wide, Wide World*, the novel ends with a strong suggestion that Ellen and John will strengthen the bonds that hold them together, but no marriage actually takes place. The sexual tension between the two remains unresolved. But in an unpublished final chapter, Warner married the two and carefully confined Ellen in John's domestic space. As a mere token of respect and freedom, John gave Ellen control of the household finances. But together they both agreed that she would never do anything of which he might disapprove. And should she ever spend unwisely, they both agreed that John would know, whether or not Ellen told him about it. To nineteenth-century audiences, the differences between the reverend rakes' predatory sexuality and John's autocratic control perhaps were more apparent, but it is clear from their preoccupation with pastors' power and women's weakness that the connection between the benign and malignant forms of the relationship was surprisingly close.

The Real, but Illusive, Pastor

While novelists imagined a variety of characters in the pastoral relationship, the pious memoir, an extremely popular genre of the period, imagined the most benign portrait. These memoirs appeared in pamphlets, tracts, and bound volumes throughout the colonial period and maintained their popularity through most of the nineteenth century as well. Although these works were nominally nonfiction, their authors shaped real lives into didactic and sometimes highly dramatic or adventurous stories. Peter Cartwright's rollicking memoir of his preaching exploits in the backcountry represented an unusually adventurous version of a much more staid genre but showed the potential for dramatic imagination the authors could employ. Descendants of the Puritan spiritual autobiography, these works were usually written by clergymen and recorded their work as both pastors and preachers. They drew on a man's practical experiences in the field to describe the rich variety of relationships, personalities, and situations in which the minister might advance his personal ministry to the people under his care. Many devoted considerable space to individual cases—mostly the successful conversions but occasionally the backsliders and the incorrigible sinners. A majority of the pastor's successful cases invariably described pious women whose lives the writer hoped would serve as models to his readers. Another form of the pious memoir, also penned by a clergyman, described the life of a particularly devout woman in his care. In both versions of these memoirs, clerical readers might find admirable models of paternal pastors meeting the spiritual needs of their female parishioners by dispensing sound doctrine and advice. Likewise, female readers might find their own doubts and fears expressed by the women in the pastoral dialogues and the wise counsel offered by a veteran pastor in response. Thus, just as Elizabeth Tilton used a novel as an effective personal pastor, so might a motivated reader of these memoirs vicariously engage in an intimate spiritual conversation with a noted minister.

At first, these memoirs seem to present a pastoral relationship that is at the opposite end of the spectrum from the horrific portraits found in travelers' accounts, trials, and sensational novels. Amid the ubiquitous images of the wolf in sheep's clothing, readers found a model shepherd. The clergymen in these biographies and autobiographies invariably applied gentle reason and pressure to bring wandering sinners into the fold of Christian faith. They provided readers with images of sincere and successful shepherds instead of the monstrous hypocrites or spiritual autocrats of more imaginative genres, but still these portraits bore a striking resemblance to some of their dysfunctional fictional counterparts. The relationship between pastor and female parishioner remained a lopsided one. He possessed all the power by virtue of his office, his education, and his experience. She was often a vulnerable woman too dependent on her pastor for help in achieving spiritual knowledge and accepting divine grace. In some scenarios, the female parishioner was an older woman who resisted forcefully before surrendering to her pastor and Christ. Yet, like their sensational counterparts, the pastor still wielded masculine power and his female parishioner still yielded to it.[15]

The Rev. Ichabod Spencer produced a popular series of pastoral vignettes, ostensibly based on his experiences as a longtime pastor in Brooklyn, that generally offered models of competent spiritual counselors and their tractable female parishioners. Most of the chapters portrayed a pastor and a woman engaged in conversation on spiritual and religious topics. In the happiest stories, an anxious female parishioner relinquished her erroneous notions of doctrine along with her doubts about the validity of her own spiritual experiences. She gratefully accepted her pastor's guidance, his simplification of knotty doctrinal issues, and his interpretations of her own feelings. On the surface, then, Spencer's popular *Sketches* reinforce the notion that pastors catered to, and succeeded with, a largely female constituency. Yet alternative models emerge on closer examination. Despite the overwhelming number of women in these sketches, numbers that match the membership data discovered by historians, Spencer sometimes displayed a disinclination to credit women with the rational, theological minds of men. The minister's note of condescension in these pastoral scripts casts doubt on the level of rapport he achieved with women. Indeed, in one sketch the pastor had largely given up on bringing an especially dissolute woman to Christ. He met with success only after the woman read a particularly moving tract that effectively converted her without his personal intervention. This self-reflexive literary device suggested two possibilities to readers. First, a pastor reading the book might be inspired to distribute copies of Spencer's own sketches as practical surrogate pastoral calls—certainly a clever marketing strategy on Spencer's part if it was done consciously. Second, the piece suggests to female readers that a tract might be just as effective a spiritual counselor as a personal pastor. And, if either party imbibed the cultural fears about the intrusion of sexuality into the pastoral relationship, this sketch offered a safe solution to the dilemma. Again, it is difficult to assess the impact of works like this one. The multiple printings of works such as *Sketches* indicate its popularity. As we shall see in Part III, the diaries of women and clergymen record their reading habits and comment on the power of tracts and books as guides. At least one pastor regularly reported in his diary that women read and were moved by the tracts he left for them.[16]

Another popular form of the pious memoir that appeared throughout the nineteenth-century, the biography of an exemplary woman penned by her pastor, also offered, on the surface, a successful model of the pastoral relationship between minister and women. In the last decade of the eighteenth-century and the first two decades of the nineteenth century, the eminent theologian and Newport pastor, Samuel Hopkins, edited and published the memoirs and letters of two local exemplary women, Sarah Osborn and Susanna Anthony. The two women, in every respect, modeled female piety and respect and appreciation for ministers' lectures and personal attention. As a child, Osborn had displayed an immature wonder and awe in the presence of clergymen. "My very heart would leap with joy, when I could see, or come near enough to touch them." Although this confession appeared to confirm the suspicions of women's exceptional devotion to clergymen, Osborn explained that the response was a function of her youth. "I mention this as a childish notion, that I took pleasure in touching them. I used to go secretly behind them for that purpose," she confided.[17]

The memoirs of Osborn and Anthony portrayed women deeply dependent on their pastor's advice. In adolescence, Osborn and Anthony both reported that they had been moved by the preaching of George Whitefield and Gilbert Tennent, two traveling evangelists of the eighteenth-century revival known as the First Great Awakening. Both young women went out of their way to seek the counsel of the town's elderly pastor, the Rev. Mr. Clap, even though their families regularly attended other churches. Osborn first felt a "grateful love" for the man when he gave her a book of hymns. After listening to Clap preach on one occasion, she felt that he had given voice to her own thoughts. He "told me the very secrets of my heart in his sermon, as plain as I could have told them to him, and indeed more so." In a private interview, she confessed to Clap that she had not attended his church regularly because she felt "too wicked." "But like a tender father to a little child, [he] bid me not grieve" and offered her his unconditional help. "He bid me come to him as often as I had a desire, if it was morning, noon or night, and I should always be welcome." Osborn subsequently visited often with the paternal pastor and eventually joined his church.[18]

While the young women found the elderly Clap a steady source of spiritual guidance, they also formed a deep attachment to a younger man who briefly assisted him. Both had attended the younger pastor at his sickbed and prayed that he might continue his services to themselves and the church. At his death, Susanna lamented, "O how do I now seem to be stripped of my guide, my spiritual counsellor!" Sarah thanked God for "lending worthless me so sweet a pastor, so long," but she mourned that God had "bereaved me of my shepherd." The women's considerable personal affection, dependence, and grief at the young man's death hint at the kind of deep devotion of women to their pastors that so disturbed travelers such as Frances Trollope. Yet their pastor and editor, Samuel Hopkins, accepted such love as sisterly devotion to a fellow Christian. In fact, the women were exemplary precisely because they established close relationships with several other ministers over their lifetimes, men who regularly rendered them valuable spiritual advice. Nineteenth-century readers of these narratives of eighteenth-century women surely reasoned that an intimate spiritual relationship with a supportive pastor was both a prerequisite for conversion and a perquisite of church membership.[19]

Readers who took away an impression of women's deep affection for and dependence on pastors might have missed an important subtext, however. Like a shadow or pentimento beneath this portrait of piety and dependence, a remarkable image of women's spiritual self-sufficiency slowly emerges. Although both women remarked often on the "excellent," "precious," and "dear" sermons they heard, Anthony and Osborn could be critical of a preacher's performance. Anthony, writing to Osborn of a sermon they had both heard, stated, "I cannot think it had any direct tendency, to honor God, or do good to men." On another occasion, Anthony refused to take the personal interpretation of the famous evangelist Gilbert Tennent until she could confirm it by other means. After relating her own spiritual experiences to Tennent, she asked him to review and evaluate them for her using "scripture rules." He gave his opinion, but she resisted his overt direction: "For I was determined to be fully persuaded in my own mind and conscience." Anthony expressed gratitude when her female friends encouraged her spiritual self-reliance, too. They left her, she wrote, "to my own reason, or rather to the word and spirit of God, for direction." This spiritual independence afforded Anthony great personal satisfaction. "For by this mean," she wrote, "I was the better able to see into these matters, and have my judgment established." Clearly, Anthony drew on a much wider range of spiritual resources and guides than pastors and ministers. She acknowledged, but not uncritically, their contributions to her growth in religious knowledge. First and foremost, however, Anthony remained discontented until she had observed and reasoned for herself. This spiritual self-reliance manifested itself in the correspondence between the two women and also, surprisingly, in their actions in the community.[20]

Decades before the "feminization" of the clergy, the church, and theology that Ann Douglas and others claimed to trace, both Anthony and Osborn exerted their spiritual autonomy and leadership and assumed a pastoral role in their own churches and communities. Anthony often led her female society in prayer, but Osborn in effect headed a large church in her own home. She ministered to hundreds of people—young and old, male and female, black and white—over a fifty-year period. Though Osborn worried about overstepping her sphere, Hopkins cautiously observed, she nevertheless received the anxious listeners who flocked to her as a spiritual guide. "They repaired to her as a known pious, benevolent Christian, to whom they could have easy access, that they might enjoy her counsel and prayers." She selected appropriate readings from the scriptures and sometimes read from her own writings. She took the opportunity "to converse with individuals, and sometimes would give a word of advice to them all." Thus, Osborn performed the essential tasks of the pastor—except for public preaching from the pulpit—without the benefit of the education and status a clergyman commanded. Indeed, Hopkins implied, it was her humbler position as a woman that made her accessible to her followers and successful with them. At the same time, of course, he inadvertently admitted that the clergy's elevated status made them less accessible as spiritual advisors.[21]

A century and a half before Anthony and Osborn, the radical and independent-minded Anne Hutchinson was banished from Puritan Boston for conducting prayer meetings in her home, leading religious discussions among both women and men, and openly challenging the teachings of leading ministers. Anthony and Osborn avoided Hutchinson's fate by maintaining deference to preachers and pastors. In fact, Hopkins omitted some aspects of Osborn's life that place her in a considerably less humble position in relation to ministers. First, he failed to record that Osborn carried on a long, friendly, and mutually beneficial correspondence with the Rev. Joseph Fish, a Stonington, Connecticut, pastor. The two exchanged advice on pastoral work, each helping the other. Second, Hopkins declined to relate Osborn's long and frustrating relationship with her alcoholic pastor, in large part the reason that she assumed so many of the pastoral duties of her church. Thus, Hopkins's portrait of these two exemplary women accentuated their piety and dependence on their pastors while suppressing their spiritual autonomy and tremendous leadership abilities, qualities that might have clouded the ideal portrait he tried to create. Although pious memoirs were based in fact, Hopkins's editing reveals the ways in which this genre might construct an imaginary pastoral relationship, one that obscured the elements of equality between men and women and the possibilities of women's challenge or even superiority over their pastors.[22]

This imaginary portrait—that clergymen offered women valuable spiritual guidance—undoubtedly characterized some ordinary and extraordinary pastoral relationships. Women's conversion narratives, a traditional but still popular genre akin to the pious memoir, sometimes made explicit the helpful role of pastors and preachers. Clearly, Osborn herself owed some of her extraordinary success as a religious leader to the advice and encouragement of men such as the Rev. Fish. Historian Catherine Brekus discovered that the even more extraordinary female exhorters and preachers of the colonial and early national period often relied on supportive clergymen. Ann Douglas based much of her thesis on the close pastoral relationship enjoyed by the women writers who broke into the world of publishing with the help of encouraging ministers. Thus the embellished portraits in these memoirs support the notion that women benefited from the careful and benign attentions of clergy, while defusing the sexual tension deliberately constructed in the images of reverend rakes and benevolent despots. On closer examination, however, they reveal a much more interesting and complicated power relationship in which some women questioned clerical advice, sustained a determined effort to reason and interpret their own spiritual experiences, and even assumed religious leadership in the absence of effective pastors. Instead of the powerful male minister and the vulnerable or dependent female parishioner, reverse images of spiritually self-sufficient women and impotent ministers emerged in the novelists' imaginations.[23]

The Marginal Minister

Harriet Beecher Stowe offered both a portrait of spiritually self-sufficient women and a resolution to the problem of sexual tension between clergyman and woman in the pastoral relationship. Instead of marrying the two, she safely separated them. Stowe published the novel *The Minister's Wooing* just nine years after the wildly successful *Wide, Wide World* and her own *Uncle Tom's Cabin*. Stowe's book also featured a sentimental heroine and a clergyman but sent a quite different message to readers. The minister of the title took the name of the famous eighteenth-century theologian, Newport pastor, and author of Sarah Osborn's memoir, the Rev. Samuel Hopkins. Stowe's character, however, shared none of the benevolent despot John Humphreys's romantic qualities and little of the real Hopkins's life except his Calvinist theology. And contrary to the title, the minister did no wooing, nor was he wooed, in the romantic sense. Stowe's heroine, too, bore little resemblance to the rebellious young Ellen Montgomery but a striking similarity to John's departed sister, the saintly Alice Humphreys. Mary Scudder, though a pious, quiet, passive young woman who remains a "true woman" throughout the novel, nevertheless fails to conform to the model of helplessness, vulnerability, and dependence of so many other contemporary heroines. And like the remarkable Sarah Osborn, several women in the novel exercised a powerful spiritual force in their community.

Stowe's characters most closely conform to the exaggerated stereotypes of the emasculated clergyman and the devoted women who usurp his power and religious authority that literary historian Ann Douglas saw in the antebellum pastoral relationship. Although the novel was set in colonial Newport and the historical character lived and worked before the postrevolutionary disestablishment of most American churches, Stowe's imaginary Rhode Island pastor fit the caricature of the disestablished minister described by Douglas. The fictional Hopkins was unmarried and boarded with Mrs. Scudder and her daughter, Mary, whereas the historical Hopkins was the patriarch of a family of eight children. His marital "disestablishment" in the novel signaled his social and political disestablishment as well. Clothed in the attributes of masculinity, especially education and principle, the Hopkins character was nevertheless a man stripped of the power, influence, and manners to compete in the public sphere of men. The fictional Hopkins earned respect from his fellow men for his intellectual command of theology but acquired no authority in the wider sphere of politics and business. "Ministers are the most unfit men in the world to talk on such subjects," declared a rich slave-ship owner whom Hopkins gravely offended with his naivety on the economics and politics of slavery. "It's departing from their sphere," the man of business complained. "They talk about what they don't understand." The offended Mr. Brown accused Hopkins of being a "dreamer . . . an unpractical man." To Hopkins's face, Brown stated, "Your situation prevents your knowing anything of real life." The men of the community dismissed Hopkins for his antislavery arguments: The minister held no power in the pulpit or in the public sphere. But even though the women in the novel admired his principled stand against slavery, the pathetic man held no power in their domestic sphere, either. The women noted his inability to conduct a successful personal ministry. As he "walked manfully out" on his pastoral calls one day, carefully attired in the emblems of refined late eighteenth-century masculinity—coat, wig, cocked hat, and gold-headed cane— Mary's mother looked "regretfully" after him and remarked that "he is *such* a good man!—but he has not the least idea how to get along in the world. He never thinks of anything but what is true; he hasn't a particle of management about him." Stowe thus maintained Hopkin's masculinity as measured by older standards of social status and education but denied him any manly power in either the political masculine sphere or the domestic feminine sphere of nineteenth-century gender ideology.[24]

Stowe recognized, as her character Hopkins did not, how much his masculinity, his profession, his pastorate, and especially his theological study ironically depended on the exertions and efforts of the women who surrounded him. They housed, fed, and clothed him so that he could devote his hours to study and writing. "The Doctor little thought, while he, in common with good ministers generally, gently traduced the Scriptural Martha and insisted on the duty of heavenly abstractedness, how much of his own leisure for spiritual contemplation was due to the Martha-like talents of his hostess." The pastor's ability to spend his time on otherworldly concerns, in other words, depended on the very qualities of mundane attention to duty that he denounced from the pulpit, the duties that preoccupied the women in his household. Thus, he failed to value or appreciate the work of women, an attribute that certainly impeded his own mission to women.[25]

Indeed, Stowe's hero was surprisingly no more successful in his pastoral work with women than with men. His private consultations with the saintly young Mary Scudder merely confused rather than enlightened her. Curiously, her confusion challenged his certitude. Her simple questions and objections, her carefully written treatises, undermined the doctor's own carefully constructed theological understanding. A critical scene in the novel illuminates Hopkins's ineffectiveness in counseling women when a mother, in mourning for her son lost at sea, rejected both the doctor's theology and his personal presence. Inconsolable, the grieving mother refused to accept the Calvinist doctrine that, since her son died unconverted, he had little hope of eternal salvation. When Hopkins paid a visit to the distraught woman, she refused to talk with him. Stowe estranged Hopkins from both his male and his female parishioners. Unable to argue effectively in the male sphere of politics or to comfort in the female sphere, Hopkins faced banishment from both.

The women in the novel, in contrast, proved effective ministers to each other and even to men. Mary Scudder learned, later in the novel, that she had been the instrument of the sailor's conversion when Dr. Hopkins had been

ineffective. With the boy's grieving mother, Mary dutifully attempted to substitute for the doctor by repeating his orthodox pronouncements about God's
will. But the abject woman still refused to accept the same stern Calvinist
pieties, even from the gentle Mary's mouth. Finally, an illiterate black servant
woman, the character with the lowest rank and education and thus the complete opposite of the learned Dr. Hopkins, burst into the room and delivered
her own simple gospel truths about a loving Christ instead of a harsh Father.
She urged the stricken Mrs. Marvyn to "*leave* [her son] in Jesus's hands!" As
"healing sobs" filled the room, the humble servant Candace dispensed her
critique of Hopkins's pastoral practice. "I know our Doctor's a mighty good
man, an' larned,—an' in fair weather I ha'nt no 'bjection to yer hearin' all
about dese yer great an' mighty tings he's got to say," she opined. From her
considerable expertise as a cook and a Christian, Candace recommended a
spiritual diet that omitted the hard teachings of Calvinism. "But, honey, dey
won't do for you now: sick folks mus'n't hab strong meat: an' times like dese,
dar jest a'n't but one ting to come to, an' dat ar's *Jesus.*" Hopkins's "strong
meat" was fine for pulpit teaching or theological pamphlet wars but totally
inappropriate for the pastoral function, Candace insisted. Hopkins's spiritual
impotence in the pastoral role extended even to Mary, his pious acolyte. Mary,
too, grieved for the Marvyn boy, lost at sea. For weeks, the sorrowing young
woman spent nearly all her time in the minister's presence, "but he did not
find any power within himself by which he could approach her."[26]

Hopkins and the women in his household and in his congregation lived
in intimate, daily contact with each other, but he depended on them, not they
on him. They provided his daily sustenance; he provided them with a philanthropic project. Yet the women were profoundly distanced from him because
of his ineffective Calvinist theology, and they worked hard to construct their
own "softer" theology. The push-and-pull of this complex relationship was epitomized in the doctor's relationship with young Mary Scudder. In their private
conversations and daily intercourse with each other, the doctor, at least, could
not escape the intrusion of a sexual attraction. "It is seldom," explained Stowe,
"that man and woman come together in intimate association, unless influences
are at work more subtle and mysterious than the subjects of them dream."
Stowe realized that sexual forces intruded even where least expected, perhaps
even where taboo. "Even in cases where the strongest ruling force of the two
sexes seems out of the question," she warned, "there is still something peculiar
and insidious in their relationship. . . . Grave professors and teachers cannot
give lessons to their female pupils just as they give them to the coarser sex. . . ."
The mysterious and inevitable attraction, which Stowe never explicitly labeled
sexual, alerted readers to the romantic possibilities in the relationship at the
same time that it raised an alarm about the dangers of such intimacy. The only
way to resolve those tensions was to turn the pastoral relationship into a formal
but pale imitation of courtship.[27]

Hopkins and Mary Scudder were never active participants in the "minister's wooing." Both were manipulated by Mary's mother and the other women
who played matchmaker, a device that minimized the sexual tension between

the two. Mary's influence on the doctor was pure and passive: He worshiped her angelic qualities from afar. Stowe never allowed her characters to display any sexual passion. Hopkins's affection remained paternal and "innocent" throughout. Likewise, Mary permitted the betrothal as an act of self-sacrifice, as a duty she owed her mother, her pastor, and her God. One character likened Mary's impending marriage to the minister to entering a convent and a life of celibacy: "the dear little soul has accepted him as the nun accepts the veil; for she only loves him filially and religiously." In the end, Stowe ended this unnatural relationship between pastor and parishioner by invoking a standard plot device: She resurrected Mary's shipwrecked lover. Hopkins then sacrificed his happiness and allowed the two young lovers to marry by absolving Mary from her resolute commitment to marry the pastor.[28]

Although Stowe exploited the tensions associated with the pastoral relationship in nineteenth-century culture, she used it primarily because it afforded an opportunity to criticize the Calvinism of her New England ancestors. At the same time that Herman Melville employed his knowledge of the sea to produce his masterpiece *Moby Dick*, an intriguing combination of sea adventure and metaphysical dissertation, Stowe utilized her knowledge of the pastoral relationship to produce this hybrid of sentimental novel and theological treatise. As the daughter, sister, and wife of pastors, she had studied the relationship for years from a variety of perspectives. She used that knowledge and experience to describe domestic scenes that revealed the anachronism and practical inefficiency of Calvinism in the pastorate and to intersperse them with theological discussions that exposed the doctrinal weaknesses of Calvinism and justified a more liberal and catholic Christianity. She contrasted an impotent masculine, legal, and Calvinist theology that restricted salvation to a ridiculous few with a powerful feminine, emotional, and Arminian theology that offered redemption to all who accepted Christ's love. Although Stowe herself would never have labeled her theology "feminine" or "feminist," she espoused a religious orientation that was distinctly hostile to traditional masculine values of intellectual argumentation and embraced relational, feminine values of sympathy and love. And she did so with confidence. After all, *Uncle Tom's Cabin*, her sentimental appeal for the abolition of slavery, had succeeded in converting more people to antislavery than the legal and rational appeals of men such as Samuel Hopkins. Unfortunately for historians, the impact of Stowe's theology cannot be documented as easily as the impact of her politics. She clearly condemned two images of masculinity—the competitive political and commercial sphere that supported slavery and the intellectual orthodox Calvinism that failed to appreciate feminine relational values. Her female characters appear to love, respect, and revere the clergy while quietly ignoring them, condescending to them, and even contradicting them. Stowe celebrates women without worrying unduly about the marginal minister. Her novel, however, bears a striking resemblance to another contemporary genre—the parsonage novel—that attempted to rescue the minister by exaggerating his plight. The female authors, many of them ministers' wives like Stowe, imagined the minister as an unknowing and unrecognized martyr to Christianity in a callous, competitive religious marketplace.

The Unwitting Martyr

A distinct and highly popular genre during the early 1850s combined the exposé with the sentimental novel to produce the "parsonage novel." In fact, Stowe may have been inspired in her choice of characters and setting by these novels, which advanced a much more modest goal than the moral reform of the cities or the overthrow of Calvinism. They aimed, for the most part, to protest a decline in the respect for the clergy and especially in their remuneration. One of the most prominent and successful authors in this genre, Elizabeth Stuart Phelps, was, like Stowe, married to an Andover seminary professor engaged in the business of training future pastors. Her most successful novel, *The Sunnyside*, published in 1851, was set in a rural parish. A second, *A Peep at "Number Five"; or, a Chapter in the Life of a City Pastor*, published the year after, took place in a city parsonage. Phelps's popularity among female readers and male pastors inspired the publication of several other fictionalized "memoirs" of the pastoral ministry, as well as a body of criticism on the pastorate. While they protested the poor pay and financial hardships of the pastor's family—sometimes in sanguine tones, mostly in maudlin ones—they did so from a uniquely feminine perspective and charged women with a distinctive mission to defend the pastorate.[29]

In these novels, the pastor's wife was the clergyman's chief defender, tireless helpmeet, and fellow sufferer. She sometimes defended her husband in much the same way as the defense lawyers did in the trials of clergymen for sexual misconduct: She painted him as a brave soldier or martyr in Christ's cause or even as a victim in political battles between powerful enemies. But at the same time that she firmly situated him in the competitive masculine sphere, she deplored the values that he assimilated from it. *The Shady Side*, an anonymously authored contribution to this genre, featured a narrator who claimed pastors were especially beleaguered men because they faced more enemies than a layman. Ordinary men, Mrs. Vernon claimed, had one enemy, but the clergyman was "denounced from both extremes." She also feared that the pastor was torn in two by the contradictory values of vocation and ambition. The Rev. Vernon had answered the call and sacrificed an opportunity for wealth and prestige by giving up his study of the law for the study of the ministry. Yet he had also compromised his higher calling by succumbing to the lure of an influential pulpit and a wealthy congregation in an urban rather than a rural parish. In short, the pastor constantly struggled to negotiate a path between contentious parishioners and between unacceptable extremes of self-sacrifice and self-interest.[30]

A rural parish might allow a pastor to be a shepherd to his people, but a city parish subjected its pastor to the worst stresses of an entrepreneurial society. Like some of the travelers' accounts, parsonage novels detected the pressures of the free market rivalry among the voluntary churches. "Competition," Mrs. Vernon complained, "was the order of the day." It "spurred" the pastor through his daily tasks: "darken[ing] those bright morning study hours, [and stealing] away the light of those genial pastoral visits." Worst of all, it tainted his role in the pulpit. He could no longer be content with preaching the simple gospel but must play to a fickle and insatiable audience. "He must come before his people like a stage-player, with clap-trap, and false thunder and lightning, to fill up the house!" In short, the more the pastor shed the traditional masculine values of the father and the shepherd and acquired the new masculine qualities of his male peers in the marketplace, the more he lost the respect of his feminine acolytes: his wife and his female parishioners.[31]

Instead of blaming the pastor's ineffective theology, as Stowe did, the parsonage novelists blamed the parishioners for not appreciating the dual nature and contradictory demands of pastoral work. Neither male nor female parishioners valued the considerable "capital" in education and preparation that went into the production of a sermon. The pastor was torn between his obligations in the pulpit and his duties in the homes of his parishioners. While the Rev. Vernon conscientiously did more than his share of private pastoral visiting, his congregation ignored the way this activity took time away from writing sermons. A lawyer friend who visited the parsonage summed up the dilemma: "I see how it is. You lay down your book, or your pen, and start off to every sick child or whimpering woman that takes a fancy to see the minister. I wouldn't do it. I would cultivate myself for a higher field. The people here don't appreciate such a thinker and writer as you are." In other words, pastoral duties were segregated along gender lines. Too much attention to pastoral visiting in the feminine domestic sphere prevented Vernon from fulfilling his professional potential for success in the masculine public sphere, and vice versa.[32]

In the parsonage novel, the solution to this dilemma was to delegate the visiting and counseling duties of the office to the pastor's wife. She tried to ease the pastor's burdens by assuming his ministry to women, but she, too, was undervalued by the congregants. The city pastor in "Number Five" parsonage avoided women's Sewing Society meetings and sent his wife instead so that he could read his professional journals. One male parishioner insisted that the pastor's wife must do more visiting to "drum up customers." The country pastor in The Sunny Side stayed in his study while his wife handled his business and social calls. "Now I foresee, love," he said to her, "that you will be expected to supply all my deficiencies. You will have to visit, and to be visited, and to attend all sorts of societies." Yet his wife's sacrifices, they both understood, earned her little appreciation and no remuneration. Despite his wife's hard work, expended on his behalf, his congregation failed to value their efforts. "I confess it unmans me," he lamented. "I often lay down my pen and weep." The pen, the minister's potent masculine weapon, fortified by his seminary education, was insufficient to sustain his family. He was neither potent nor patriarchal, but rather a pathetic half-man dependent on his overworked wife.[33]

Split between the masculine duties of the pulpit and the feminine duties of parochial visiting, the pastor, on the advice of his male companion, devalued pastoral work with women and delegated the work to his wife. That work was not necessarily easier for his wife, these pastors' wives and authors insisted. In one novel, the young pastor's wife faced a difficult initiation into her pastoral duties. Embarrassed and inexperienced, she endured the snide and ungenerous remarks of the women who were "testing" her mettle and fitness for the job. Although she found some sympathy from her husband, he, too, disparaged his female parishioners and their benevolent societies, their work, their objectives, and their managerial skills. "Where money is to be appropriated," he told her, "there are many advisers. There will doubtless be as many different 'objects' named as there will be dollars earned." His words of wisdom came from his own experience, he assured her. "I made some acquaintance with such [female] industrial associations while I was in the seminary." His exposure to women's benevolent work as a student failed to teach him to value their efforts or to cultivate their support: He ranked attention to their efforts beneath his duties as a pastor.[34]

The devoted Mrs. Vernon missed the condescension in her own husband's words, but she faulted other clergymen and laymen for their general disparagement of women. She complained that a visiting clergyman "was not slow to declare his supreme indifference to females in general, though quite deferential to me in particular." She especially resented the narrow attention to the church of some of the bustling mill town's leading businessmen. They confined their religion and Christian charity to a few hours on the Sabbath and relegated all other religious observances and benevolence to the pastor and to their wives. They demanded a rousing sermon at the meeting on Sunday, but neglected social prayer meetings and "any personal activities in a religious way entirely eschewed." The secular and spiritual, Mrs. Vernon noted, were "two distinct interests." The busy men "committed the latter, generally, to their pastor: particularly intrusting to their 'better half' the keeping of their conscience and Christian sensibility during business hours, resuming them each Lord's day for purposes of devotion." The criticism of laymen's attitudes toward religion reveals a deep resentment on the part of the pastors' wives who penned these novels. Despite the pastor's efforts to separate himself from the women in the congregation and to appeal to men from the pulpit, he was consistently relegated to the domestic sphere by men in the public sphere. In short, the parsonage novel reveals the female authors' deep ambivalence toward the pastor's peculiar position straddling the masculine and the feminine sphere. They wanted both pastor and laymen to appreciate and value the feminine as well as the masculine aspects of the pastor's duties. Yet pastors consistently chose the masculine sphere of endeavor over the feminine sphere of nurture. Any actual alliance between clergy and women, even between the pastor and his wife, was fragile. Clergy clearly tried to maintain their masculine position as leaders of the church and valiantly resisted the alliance with women imposed on them by the laymen of the church. They resisted so fiercely that they became unwitting martyrs to their masculinity. The Rev. Mr. Vernon died trying to please his male parishioners, not the female ones.[35]

The fragile pastoral relationship with women in these novels still suffered sexual strains but avoided the exaggerated problems of the sensational novel or the trial accounts. For example, as a bachelor, the Rev. Mr. Vernon was the subject of much speculation about his marital prospects. One young woman who "aspired to a parsonage . . . [was] thought to overstep the bounds of maidenly reserve, in her frequent visits to Mr. Vernon's boarding-place." Deprived of the prize she sought, she was "striving to calm a fevered spirit, and struggling for victory over *self* in its most subtle guise." After his marriage, the pastor still suffered girls' teasing until he learned to handle their childish flirting. Another pastor had difficulty in conducting a successful "private conversation" with a shy and embarrassed young woman. Only when her deaf grandfather agreed to serve as a chaperone did the girl feel free to confess to her pastor. "With much paternal feeling," the narrator assured her readers, "[the pastor] gave her such counsel as a young Christian needs." He safely and successfully ministered to an old invalid woman, who "loved her young minister next to her God,—with a love, too, that partook largely of reverence or worship." Another woman expressed her dependence on her pastor, telling him, "I live on your visits." These novelists thus acknowledged the reverence or even sexual attraction of women for clergy that travelers deplored and that other sentimental novelists discreetly exploited. But they tried to persuade readers to avoid imagining pastors as exaggerated stereotypes; no villainous hypocrite, romantic hero, or unworldly saint inhabited these parsonages. "A minister is but a man," Mrs. Phelps reminded her audience. "See that ye bear with his infirmities." She urged male and female readers to see ministers as mere mortals and to neither neglect them nor judge them too harshly.[36]

Thus, the portrait of the pastoral relationship that emerged from a good many of these popular sentimental novels acknowledged that the minister was "but a man," flawed as a pastor, perhaps, but far from predatory with women. They thereby avoided the simplistic caricatures of their sensational counterparts. In these subtler representations, clergy labored manfully, if not always effectively, for the good of their congregations. They deserved understanding and support, but hardly reverence or adulation, from women. Though imagined, these fictional views of the pastoral relationship were more sympathetic and realistic than any of the other popular representations. Clergy might take comfort in the sympathetic portrayals of the pastor; women might resign themselves to their realism. Thus, they offered significant antidotes to the more poisonous portraits by giving both male and female readers models that offered some slim hope for a constructive relationship without raising either positive or negative expectations to unreasonable levels.

Though both sensational and sentimental novelists ruthlessly exploited the cultural fascination with the pastoral relationship, they were not alone. Authors who aspired to a cultural eminence superior to the salacious or the sentimental also found rich material in the same association. The one mid-nineteenth-century American novel enshrined in a literary canon by early-twentieth-century critics and regularly read and studied by students at the turn of the twenty-first century is Nathaniel Hawthorne's *The Scarlet Letter*. Although this enduring work sold only modestly when first published in 1850, it subsequently achieved near mythical status, drawing as it does upon the Puritan roots of American culture. But its historical setting in the colonial period often confuses students, leading them to think it was *written* in the seventeenth rather than the nineteenth century. The novel must, however, be considered as the product of a historical period obsessed about the ways that the pastoral relationship revealed numerous flaws in the cultural fabric.[37]

The Unworthy Saint and the Worthy Sinner

Hawthorne's novel was one of a growing chorus of nineteenth-century critiques of Puritan moral rigidity and hypocrisy, but it also served as a trenchant critique of its contemporary culture as well. More than any other fiction of the time period, Hawthorne's work explicitly explored the moral ambiguities and paradoxes of the cross-gender pastoral relationship and the laws and ideals that governed it. Although the three main characters in the novel—Hester Prynne, her lover and pastor Arthur Dimmesdale, and her avenging husband Roger Chillingworth—all publicly admitted to sin, only Hester reaped spiritual profit. Despite their potential similarities to characters in other works of the period, none of Hawthorne's characters lived up to any of the stereotypes of the more popular works. Although both sensational and sentimental works generated doubt that Puritan theology and morality were still effective standards and means of social control, Hawthorne created characters who challenged not only the traditional theological basis of morality but also its more recent foundation in the gender conventions of the nineteenth century. His choice of characters and his plot closely resemble the exposés of clerical corruption of the period, but Hawthorne more clearly questioned the regnant gender ideology of feminine passionlessness and clerical moral leadership that denied and repressed the "peculiar and insidious" intrusion of sexuality into the pastoral relationship. Hawthorne's historical romance found readers who were simultaneously intrigued by its criticism of Puritan morality and shocked by the apparent triumph of immorality.

Hawthorne defied ideals of feminine piety, purity, domesticity, and submissiveness by creating a female protagonist who was a sexual being, who refused to return to her sadistic husband, and who reinterpreted her sin as virtue. Hester Prynne is an enduring heroine of American literature because she wrested the meaning of the scarlet letter from the patriarchal town fathers and refashioned it to her own feminine (and perhaps feminist) purposes. Her adulterous relationship with Dimmesdale produced the ultimate proof of sin— an illegitimate child. Her sin was symbolized by the mark of shame she was sentenced to wear—a scarlet *A* prominently embroidered on her bodice. Although Hester suffered degradation and especially social isolation as an adulteress, she was never a passive victim of either her seducer or the patriarchal authority that pronounced her punishment. Unlike the lurid novels' porno-graphic scenes of helpless females seduced and raped, *The Scarlet Letter* never explicitly described the sexual relationship between Hester and her pastor. But clearly it was one of mutual affection and sexual passion. Both Hester and her cuckolded husband blamed her waywardness on the lack of affection and phys-ical pleasure in their own marriage. Dimmesdale, as her close spiritual guide and protector during her husband's long absence, usurped the husband's place and sexual privilege with her permission. "What we did had a consecration of its own," she reminded Dimmesdale of their illicit liaison. "We said so to each other!"[38]

Hester's deep humility, compassion, and recognition of sin enabled her to become, in effect, the town's pastor, "so kind to the poor, so helpful to the sick, so comfortable to the afflicted!" Just as she had actively and consciously par-ticipated in her own moral downfall, she purposefully, publicly, and bravely performed penance for her sins. She bore little resemblance to the pale, help-less "heroines" of seduction novels who suffered painful, passive deaths in atonement for their own victimization. She crafted and embellished her badge of shame, turning it into a sacred "symbol of her calling." She became "self-ordained a Sister of Mercy," the scarlet letter worn like the "cross on a nun's bosom." Hester gallantly protected her lover, resisting the authority of the town fathers by refusing to reveal the name of the father of her child.[39]

In contrast to this saintly sinner, Hawthorne's male protagonist was the frail, tortured sufferer, a striking inversion of nineteenth-century gender ste-reotypes in the pastoral relationship. He was neither lecherous nor deliberately deceitful, neither manful nor unmanned. He was, paradoxically, powerful be-cause he was weak. Whereas Hester wore the sign of her sin publicly, even with reverence, Dimmesdale hid his shame behind his clerical bands. Whereas Hester purposefully transformed shame into honor, Dimmesdale publicly but ineffectually confessed his fraud. His truth-telling turned into deceit, and he loathed himself for it. "I, your pastor, whom you so reverence and trust, am utterly a pollution and a lie!" he proclaimed. But the "minister well knew—subtle, but remorseful hypocrite that he was!—the light in which his vague confession would be viewed. . . . He had spoken the very truth, and trans-formed it into the veriest falsehood." Hester provoked public censure amelio-rated by admiration; Dimmesdale earned esteem tarnished by pity. God re-warded Hester with Pearl, a beautiful child. The Devil tormented Dimmesdale. She was strong, he weak; she survived, he expired.[40]

Hawthorne most clearly turns the pastoral relationship upside down in the chapter entitled "The Pastor and His Parishioner." There, Hester displayed the "wondrous strength and generosity of woman's heart" and became the shepherd to her sorry, lost-lamb lover. Although Dimmesdale displayed his "gifts and scholar-like attainments," he had "an apprehensive, a startled, a half-frightened look,—as of a being who felt himself quite astray and at a loss in the pathway of human existence, and . . . only at ease in some seclusion of his own." He kept himself "simple and child-like," without will or voice. Hester, instead, gave him her voice. She bravely "had spoken what he vaguely hinted at, but dared not speak." She reinterpreted their sin as consecrated love and offered Dimmesdale expiation and escape from his passive torment, one he was incapable of envisioning for himself. "Think for me, Hester!" he pleaded. "Thou art strong. Resolve for me!" With an exasperated compassion, Hester commanded him to "Preach! Write! Act! Do anything, save to lie down and die!" Her words urged him to reject the passive female role she herself had discarded and to stand up and be a man.[41]

More than most other writers of his day, Hawthorne made explicit the inadequacy of contemporary gender ideals and traditional Christian morality to explain or regulate the complex relationship between men and women in the pastoral relationship. Both Victorian culture in particular and Christian morality in general valued sexual purity and chastity, denying or denigrating sexual passion or redirecting it into religious passion. For the participants in the pastoral relationship who tried to understand and cope with "something peculiar and insidious" in their association, these values produced confusion rather than confidence. Hawthorne lamented what he believed was the un-yielding condemnation of sexuality in the seventeenth century. But he believed the failure to confront and acknowledge sexual desire in the nineteenth century was worse. The Puritans' standards, while overly severe, were at least straight-forward and consistent. The Victorian standards of his own time, Hawthorne feared, were at best equivocal and, at worst, debased. As if he foresaw the comic interpretations of the Beecher trial, two decades in the future, Hawthorne la-mented that "a penalty which, in our days, would infer a mocking infamy and ridicule, might then [in the colonial period] be invested with almost as stern a dignity as the punishment of death itself." Moral certainty, not moral ambi-guity, lent nobility and purpose to Hester's sentence. The Puritan crowd's def-erential response to her public humiliation "was not without a mixture of awe, such as must always invest the spectacle of guilt and shame in a fellow-creature, before society shall have grown corrupt enough to smile, instead of shuddering, at it." Thus, despite his grim portrait of Puritan morality, Hawthorne saw declension rather than progress in public virtue and ethics. To him, the nineteenth-century Victorian was more hypocritical than the seventeenth-century Puritan.[42]

Hawthorne responded to cultural, religious, and ideological changes that inspired anxiety as much as optimism in nineteenth-century Americans. The evangelical notion that proper Christian nurture and self-discipline could and should replace the external social controls of Puritan orthodoxy had converted many from the older morality. They no longer believed human beings were helpless to effect their own salvation, totally dependent on a stern and often arbitrary Calvinist God. Instead, many evangelicals insisted that humans were capable of choosing salvation. Some radicals even suggested they were capable of perfection. The concept of original sin and infant depravity increasingly gave way to the assumption that children were innocents who should be protected from evil. Finally, some rejected the doctrine that the body was the natural enemy of the spirit and was instead its temple. Such sunny theological shifts inspired a postmillennial confidence in a human ability to bring about the kingdom of God on earth, but it coexisted with a darker lingering faith in the inherent sinfulness of humankind. Hawthorne's ambivalent response to both the old and the new views of human morality reflected a cultural confusion but also a reluctant embrace of ambiguity. He deliberately chose to expose the contradictions in his characters.[43]

Hawthorne understood how difficult it was to recognize sin, whether in the seventeenth century or in the nineteenth century. Puritans easily and regularly condemned wayward behavior as sin, but by the antebellum era in which Hawthorne wrote, that conception began to lose its cultural power. Even though Hawthorne's Puritans assumed Hester's guilt and punished her, they nevertheless failed to recognize their minister's guilt and punish him. When confronted with Dimmesdale's dying confession, the "men of rank and dignity," especially, were "unable to receive the explanation which most readily presented itself, or to imagine any other." They denied the most obvious evidences of Dimmesdale's transgression. Although Puritans were more deeply cognizant of man's innate wickedness than their nineteenth-century descendants, still they effortlessly exempted the clergyman, granting him an unconscious "benefit of clergy." "Mr. Dimmesdale's story," Hawthorne insisted, "was only an instance of that stubborn fidelity with which a man's friends—and especially a clergyman's—will sometimes uphold his character; when proofs, clear as the mid-day sunshine on the scarlet letter, establish him a false and sin-stained creature of the dust." Just as the nineteenth-century juries granted clergy the benefit of doubt, so, too, did Hawthorne's Puritan substitutes. A special privilege was accorded to the clergyman: His role as moral exemplar exempted him from suspicion of wrongdoing, so that a reluctant hypocrite was revered as a saint.[44]

Hawthorne challenged both Calvinist and contemporary evangelical and perfectionist views of sin. He also questioned old as well as new sexual stereotypes. He contested the older myth that women were like Eve, easily tempted and disgraced. But he also rejected the newer feminine ideal of sexual purity. Women might display passion and yet be noble, or commit sin and still be saintly. Hawthorne's recognition of moral ambiguity and declension clearly blamed patriarchy—the ruling male elite who dispensed injustice, punishing the good while exonerating the evil. The only hope he offered was a gender revolution sometime in the future. In the concluding chapter, Hawthorne's heroine returned from a long absence to take up once again her letter and her pastoral mission.

> People brought all their sorrows and perplexities, and besought her counsel. . . . Women, more especially, in the continually recurring trials of wounded, wasted, wronged, misplaced, or erring and sinful passion,—or with the dreary burden of a heart unyielded, because unvalued and unsought,—came to Hester's cottage, demanding why they were so wretched, and what the remedy!

The female characters expressed all the sorrow, anger, resentment, and confusion that women often sought to allay with spiritual explanations. But Hester

did not, as a male pastor might, counsel dutiful submission and cheerful resignation, nor did she merely comfort, nor offer future heavenly rewards for
their suffering. Instead, she proffered a feminist vision of reformed gender
relations on earth. While she "comforted and counseled them, as best she
might," she also prophesied a new dispensation. "She assured them . . . of her
firm belief, that, at some brighter period, when the world should have grown
ripe for it, in Heaven's own time, a new truth would be revealed, in order to
establish the whole relation between man and woman on a surer ground of
happiness." Hawthorne may have believed or wished that such a revolution
would be fostered by women's religious and reform activity, or perhaps by the
nascent women's rights movement developing at the time of his writing the
novel, but he never explored the contemporary aspects of Hester's vision with
his readers.[45]

Popular literature in the antebellum period returned again and again to
the pastoral relationship because, as we saw in the prominent trials of the
period, it embodied the paradoxes of the culture's gender ideology. Separate
spheres demanded that men labor in a public, commercial sphere and women
in the private, domestic sphere. Although Christians traditionally valued the
common good, the new political man and capitalist entrepreneur of the nineteenth century set a higher price on individualism and competition. Clergy
were caught in the middle of this clash between the values of the church and
the values of the masculine public sphere. They seemed to occupy a tenuous
position somewhere between the two gendered spaces, neither comfortable
nor effective in either. Nevertheless, Victorian culture continued to rely, albeit
with less confidence, on religion as the source of moral order and authority.
Men could give attention to the business of the masculine sphere only if they
depended on clergy and women to be the moral guardians of the republic.
Doubt about their ability to perform those roles created the dramatic tension
in imaginative novels as well as in journalistic accounts. Popular literature
continually exposed the weaknesses of that culturally imposed partnership.
Clergymen in these imagined relationships were at best only reluctant associates of women outside their own marriages. Likewise, women were at best
only diffident allies of the clergy and were sometimes critical of the compro-
mises these men made with both the old and the new masculine values. At
worst, the clergyman's potentially virulent sexuality constantly threatened ancient taboos against incest and patricide. But even in the less malignant imagination, both men's and women's sexuality portended "something peculiar and
insidious," a tension that could be resolved only by marrying the two or separating them. Thus, in these novels, the only functional and acceptable pastoral
relationships between clergy and women existed between a pastor and his wife.

How Americans acted on their readings of novels such as these is difficult to
assess. Some men, and the women in their families, undoubtedly participated
in pious and harmonious relationships with pastors. No doubt other men
cheerfully and gratefully delivered wives and daughters into an alliance with
clergy, displaying the same neglect of the church and indifference to religion

that so outraged travelers and the authors of parsonage novels. But some evidence suggests that fathers and husbands responded just as Frances Trollope hoped they would—by vigorously defending the domestic circle from invasion. Whether they read novels or trial accounts or made personal observations of the pastoral relationship, men provoked to rage and jealousy as frightening as any behavior by the fictional Griffith Gaunt may indicate a broader, though hidden, expression of violence and control of women in the pastoral relationship. In one bizarre case, Robert Matthias billed himself as the "Prophet of Truth" and in the 1830s constructed a theology and cult that rested on the premise that clergymen, especially popular evangelical preachers such as the Rev. Charles Finney, had undermined the patriarchal authority in families. These "wicked" men preached to women and encouraged them to usurp the moral authority of the heads of households. In the "Kingdom of Matthias" that this angry man imagined, "All real men will be saved; all mock men will be damned." To Matthias, mock-men were those "who preach to women without their husbands" and "all clergymen, doctors, and lawyers." These wicked men were partnered and damned with "all women who do not keep at home" and "all females who lecture their husbands." "Everything that has the smell of woman will be destroyed," he railed, and "Woman is the capsheaf of the abomination of desolation—full of all deviltry." Not surprisingly, given Matthias's deep animosity toward women, he regularly beat his wife and was convicted of beating his daughter for disobedience. Surprisingly, given his animosity toward clergy and their influence on undermining patriarchal control, Matthias became a surrogate father, pastor, and "prophet" to a large and unruly family. Matthias attracted his neighbors' attention and outrage when a disgruntled male follower reported that his wife had been seduced by the Prophet. Matthias thus fulfilled his own prophecy about the inevitable dangers of the pastoral relationship. His own and his neighbors' rage against clerical sexual plundering are echoed in reports from the famous Methodist circuit rider of the same era. In Peter Cartwright's memoirs, he crowed about his success in attracting women to his meetings and converting them. But Cartwright positively exulted in his physical prowess at turning away the blows of their jealous husbands and fathers. Although we cannot trace the fanatical misogynist teachings and actions of a Matthias or the violent reactions to Cartwright's success among women to the reading of either sensational novels or trial accounts, that literature certainly tapped a malignant level of wrath in American culture against a potentially menacing pastoral relationship.[46]

The message to women and their reactions to reading these novels are even more difficult to trace. Elizabeth Tilton's reading of *Griffith Gaunt* certainly resonated with her own life and had significant consequences for her, her pastor, her family, and her church. But we can only speculate about how she interpreted the novel and the parallels she made with her own life. Surely she saw in the distrustful Griffith Gaunt her own beloved but jealous husband, Theodore, a man she had unwittingly alienated by her close relationship with her pastor, Henry Ward Beecher. But did Elizabeth see Henry as an avuncular friend and counselor like Father Francis, as the piously passionate Father Leonard, or as a confusing combination of the two? How much did she identify with the tempestuous but pious and intelligent Catherine Gaunt? Certainly, this strong female heroine helped Elizabeth take control of her spiritual life and set it in new and disturbing directions. Perhaps other female readers actively responded to novels in a variety of ways. Images of a dangerous liaison in the pastoral relationship might have inspired some women to withdraw in fear and avoid close contact with a potential pastoral predator. Images of women dependent on effective clergymen might have inspired some women to hope for and expect the same strong relationship with their own pastors. A woman who internalized the desire for a fulfilling and intimate spiritual experience with a minister or personal religious guidance from a pastor might be inspired to search for one, but she ultimately would be forced to woo one into marriage to avoid any scandal. Perhaps women experienced disappointment with pastors who failed to offer the helpful advice and comfort to them that women sometimes received in novels. Perhaps women who read novels that described or offered criticisms of clergy, whether subtle or explicit, gained cultural permission to question or condemn the efforts of those disappointing clerics. Finally, strong heroines may have inspired some women readers to seek spiritual counseling from other women or to take control of their own spiritual lives. The complexities revealed in these fictional works shaped perceptions as well as actions toward the pastoral relationship. Evidence of the way that people responded to the tensions revealed in both the perceived and the imagined relationship emerges in the ideal images of the pastoral relationship, those constructed by a variety of pastors, theologians, and seminary professors. The ideal images described in the next chapter manfully but ineffectually tried to address and reconcile the tensions exposed in perceived and imagined relationships. In the lived experience of ordinary pastors and ordinary female parishioners described in Part IV, however, these tensions consistently elicited the very complex attitudes revealed in these novels.

PART III

The Pastoral
Relationship as Ideal

5

Forbidden and Forgotten Territory; or, Where the Pastor Feared to Tread

The anonymous clergyman who reviewed a few of the parsonage novels in a contemporary religious journal liked them very much. He applauded the authors—the "pastors' wives"—for their efforts to reform attitudes toward the ministry and to increase the pay and respect for the clergy. But where the women's novels pointed to the interpersonal tensions between pastor and parishioner, the reviewer listed the political, social, and economic changes that had produced tension and declension in the ministry. Indeed, he seemed to regret the novelists' dismal portraits of the pastorate because he feared they might dissuade qualified candidates from answering the call to the ministry. His critique of the parsonage novels echoed the tone of crisis that pervaded ministerial rhetoric through much of the first half of the nineteenth century. For decades, the clergy had perceived a decline in the status of the minister and cited a wide range of factors. Disestablishment was partly to blame, but so was a decline in the quality of young candidates and a deficiency in their education. The response to this perceived crisis was slow but steady. Beginning with the founding of Andover Seminary in Massachusetts in 1808, the orthodox clergy of New England revolutionized the selection, support, and training of new ministers. Other denominations followed suit until even those denominations such as Baptists and Methodists that emphasized piety over intellect were establishing theological seminaries to train their clergy. The men who founded and taught in these new institutions produced a number of publications that reveal the crises they hoped to address by preparing young men to better assume their professional duties as preachers and pastors.[1]

In 1848, the Rev. Enoch Pond, a professor at Bangor Seminary in Maine, published a manual intended to guide young pastors through the course of their duties. He warned students that the ministry had undergone a "very manifest" change since the colonial period. In the past, he claimed, "ministers possessed more of what may be termed *authority* among a people." They kept their parishioners "at a greater distance" and "associated less with them." Their manners, costume, and, indeed, "their whole appearance were calculated to inspire a degree of veneration bordering upon fear." A minister thus served as a venerable patriarch to his people, the visible presence of an awesome God. But in the nineteenth century, Pond submitted, the minister's influence with his people no longer rested on reverence, veneration, and fear but rather on affection, love, and familiarity. Pastor and people now "live together, on terms of intimacy and equality. They associate freely and without restraint. They confer together on topics of general interest, and, as occasion offers, afford mutual assistance and advice." In short, the relationship between pastor and parishioner was no longer paternal and deferential but fraternal and egalitarian. The minister, no longer a stern gatekeeper and lawgiver, must now serve as a confidant, a loving friend, and a counselor. He not only gave advice to his parishioners but also gratefully received it from them. Pond refrained from passing judgment on this striking new development, acknowledging only that some thought the influence of "a pious, intelligent, familiar, devoted *friend*" may be of "greater value" than the stern, distant power of an authority figure. He did not positively urge his students to embrace this new democratic model of the pastoral ministry. In fact, he displayed palpable ambivalence when he allowed that "every wise minister will accommodate himself to it, as well as he can."[2]

The orthodox clergy from the formerly established churches of New England recognized that the traditional reverence for the minister, if indeed it had ever existed, could never be renewed or reinstated. At the same time, they conceded that the new democratic ethos might hold some benefits for the pastor and his mission. So, while they aimed for balance between the extremes of formal detachment and informal familiarity, most wanted to restore some power and prestige to the office by strengthening the qualifications and training of new ministers coming into the field. They accomplished this through a process of professionalization, training young men in theological seminaries and developing other educational and publishing organizations to enhance the power and status of the clergy. By mid-century, evangelical denominations as well as orthodox ones accepted the new model of ministerial preparation and founded their own institutions. The clergymen who created these seminaries remade the ministry in the process of remaking the training of ministerial candidates. They constructed a new paradigm, upholding some traditional values but, less obviously, embracing the emerging ideologies of gender. The new ideal clergyman earned respect by conforming to new ideals of manhood. No longer the stern patriarch nor the kindly father, the ideal pastor in the nineteenth century was to be an enterprising competitor in the masculine public sphere. He must be an expert manager who carefully cultivated and grew his flock, diagnosed and treated their individual spiritual ills, and skillfully guided them through this world to the next. In short, he was a man accepted and respected, by his clients and other professional men, for his professional knowledge and skills. Seminary professors built a new curriculum that upgraded a student's preparation in classical languages, controversial theology, and rhetoric, all subjects that enhanced the minister's expertise and professional credentials, thus reinforcing his masculinity as well. At the same time, the curriculum drastically downgraded the traditional attention to practical pastoral duties and experience in them. That work detracted from the minister's masculinity within the new ideology of separate gendered spheres.

In the new system, professors taught pastoral work in lectures or manuals, rather than in the field, by trying to define the essential qualifications and duties of the ideal pastor. Most often, they failed to offer clear directions for the job and succeeded, instead, in painting pastoral obligations as particularly "onerous." Indeed, the image that emerged from the manuals deviated significantly from the ideal of a confident, efficient, well-respected shepherd in a pleasant pasture. More often, the image resembled a cautious man carefully picking his way through forbidding territory, trying to lead his unruly flock along a narrow treacherous mountain defile between a huge variety of dangerous and unacceptable extremes: immovable walls of rock on one side and deep chasms on the other. Manual writers posted dozens of warnings and admonitions along the precipitous route, but the negative proscriptions far exceeded the positive practical directives that might help novice pastors navigate the rocky path. In addition to warnings, writers provided detailed lists of the kinds of parishioners the pastor could expect to find in his flock and the special concerns each group posed for him. Oddly, the female portion of his flock, his largest constituency, received the least attention. When writers occasionally offered directions about tending the women in the flock, they sent contradictory messages that simultaneously counseled the pastor to seek out women and to keep his distance. The special needs and dangers of shepherding females were best met, according to an overwhelming consensus of writers, by entrusting the female portion of the flock to a carefully chosen, capable wife. In short, the clergy tried to "accommodate" to the new democratic ethos by transcending it. By professionalizing, they hoped to reimpose some distance between clergy and laity and to enhance the status of the clergyman as a minister and as a man. But in doing so, they ignored and failed to resolve the most significant contradictions in the theology and practice of pastoral work: the minister's mission to women, the greatest portion of his flock.

The Professional Pastor

When Enoch Pond perceived "manifest" change in the clergy, he was not alone. Others, too, observed a decreased distance between clergy and parishioners, but not all hoped to "accommodate" it as best they could. Some viewed the change as declension rather than progress. In the 1840s, a number of prominent Northern leaders of the clergy, both orthodox and evangelical, agreed that a fundamental decline in status and respect for the ministry had taken place over the preceding century, but they had difficulty identifying the exact sources of that change. Gardiner Spring, the influential pastor of Brick Presbyterian Church of New York City, believed that competition and dissension among clergy was one cause. "Unhallowed divisions" among ministers, public disputes over doctrine and politics, "speaking ill" of each other, and competition for funds for various reform projects alienated and disappointed the laity. On the other hand, Spring also claimed that a proliferation of Sabbath schools, many taught by young women, had "severed the relationship between pastor and children." He also blamed "spurious religious excitement," revivals, and the birth of many new sects for producing a crop of poor and uneducated clergymen who debased the ministry. Yet even those who were well educated in the new seminaries, Spring claimed, received too little practical training in the pastoral work that might earn them the respect and affection of their parishioners. In short, Spring revealed real confusion not only about the sources of disrespect but also about the fundamental question of whether the pastoral relationship had become too close or too distant. Where Spring tended to blame social and institutional change for the declining status of the ministry, Enoch Pond blamed individual ministers. They indulged in too frequent fluctuations in religious opinions and thus revealed a lack of theological certitude and authority that cast doubt on the reliability of religious truth. Many ministers suffered from "mental indolence" and, Pond lamented, had "no heart" for "*study—severe study*, for even a reasonable amount of time." Finally, a number of cases of immorality and "criminal indiscretion" had tainted the entire ministry. Thus, Spring and Pond both had difficulty pointing to the exact cause of the decline in respect for clergy and, hence, could propose few specific recommendations for addressing it.[3]

In addition to blaming both societal change and individual ministers' shortcomings, clergy believed parishioners deserved censure. The clerical office, Spring asserted, deserved respect even if its occupant did not. Laity ought to ignore the fallible medium and pay attention to the message of the gospel no matter what their opinion of the man who delivered it. In a society where a growing majority could read and had access to Bibles, tracts, newspapers, pamphlets, and novels, laypeople confirmed the adage that a little knowledge is a dangerous thing. Based on their own readings and interpretations of scripture and philosophy, laypeople disregarded, rejected, or impugned the religious truth offered by those with superior learning. Enoch Pond argued that since the public was no longer obligated to support the established minister, they had become discriminating and finical consumers of the Word, showing little patience for "a dull, worldly, uninteresting preacher." Heman Humphrey, president of Amherst College, agreed that the laity demanded novelty. "This is a bustling and *hearing* rather than a *thinking* age," he lamented. To "hear, hear, hear, seems to be the all important concern." Humphrey doubted this development was a "healthy appetite" for the gospel, but instead a "morbid craving for excitement." Listeners suffered from "itching ears," the scriptural reference writers employed when disparaging a congregation's desire for variety in

preachers or modes of preaching. Finally, parishioners demanded tangible results from pastors, who needed to show rising membership rolls and increasing coffers to earn respect. As Pond admitted, in a free republican country, all
men must be the "makers of their own fortunes." A meritocracy had replaced
the traditional deferential society, and even ministers had to work hard to earn
respect.[4]

For the most part, these clergymen did not indulge in a traditional jeremiad
or lament for a declension in religious piety, although their complaints were
certainly not new. Precedents for these protests regarding a reduced distance
between clergy and laity abound in the Reformed tradition. Since breaking
away from the Catholic Church, Protestants had nurtured an anticlerical element that sometimes backfired on their own clergy. They consistently valued
a direct personal relationship between an individual and his or her God, insisting that a priestly intermediary was unnecessary. In addition to the inherent
anticlericalism of Protestantism, the clergy contended with a persistent challenge to their authority from the laity. Most American churches were in practice, if not in theory, congregational. In other words, the majority of American
pastors answered most immediately to their followers rather than to a clerical
hierarchy. Even in those denominations that had a hierarchical polity—Episcopalians, Methodists, and Catholics, for instance—clergy were often isolated
from each other and their superiors in rural and frontier churches and, sometimes, even in urban parishes.[5]

Despite these endemic threats to the status of the clergy, historians have
generally agreed that real change overwhelmed the ministry in the first half of
the nineteenth century. They support the observations of nineteenth-century
clergy that the effects of disestablishment, the proliferation of new sects, the
waves of revivals, and the democratic egalitarianism and anticlericalism manifest in American culture and society all reduced the authority and prestige of
clergy. But historian Daniel Calhoun also pointed to causes that contemporary
clergy never considered. He blamed the economic degeneration of rural New
England for causing a decline in "permanency" in the ministry. After the Revolution, he found, fewer and fewer clergymen served out their lives in the same
parish because those churches failed to provide adequate financial support.
Calhoun discovered an ideological change, too. He claimed careerism in the
clergy had "downgraded" lifetime service to a small pastorate. Only young
pastors just out of seminary and aging, unsuccessful, or mediocre preachers
were willing to fill poor rural or urban pulpits. The well-educated, dynamic,
and ambitious seminary graduate pursued one of the more lucrative and powerful positions created by the professionalization of the ministry.[6]

Clergy from orthodox and formerly established denominations—those
who suffered most acutely from the forces of social leveling—were first to
respond to change by shoring up their sources of authority. They could do little
to affect broad political, economic, and social transformations, but they could
reform and strengthen religious institutions and regulate membership in the
ministry. Over the first half of the nineteenth century, clergy in the Northeast
initiated and maintained a massive organizing effort to improve the selection,

support, education, and placement of new pastors, as well as the continuing education and support of seasoned clergy. If the laity were better educated, reasoned William Cogswell, then the education of clergymen must be "proportionably extended" or, "instead of being suitably estimated, they will be undervalued." Insisting on the merits of an educated clergy, a centuries-old Reformed tenet, clergy funded large charitable organizations such as the American Education Society to support the education of indigent but worthy ministerial students. They established formal seminaries, separate from the undergraduate colleges, to prepare graduates for the ministry. They supported a religious press that produced an ever-increasing volume of tracts, sermons, and journals for lay and clerical readers. Finally, they founded a wide variety of organizations, many national in scope, that pursued benevolent and reform activities. These impressive and prestigious organizations certainly improved the caliber and status of clergy as a whole, but they had the unintended effect of attracting the best and brightest graduates away from the traditional local pastoral ministry.[7]

The new system of preparing ministers differed dramatically from the old, but not coincidentally it mirrored the changes in gender roles and ideals. In the colonial period, the patriarch of the preindustrial family served as a model for masculinity for almost all men—fathers, pastors, governors, and kings. A good man was a good father: the benevolent ruler of his household, a nurturer and provider, as well as a lawgiver and judge. The colonial pastor and ministerial training conformed to this familial model. A responsible clergyman took likely boys into the parsonage with his family. The young candidates rarely chose themselves. God called them, but he worked through local pastors, sponsors, and relatives who selected appropriate young men to train. Pious parents might even tithe a son to the church. Usually from families of "the better sort," these students received tutoring from their local pastor before entering a preparatory school and then college. After an undergraduate education, the young man returned to his mentor or another settled pastor for an apprenticeship period of six months to a few years; the training period varied widely.[8]

During this stage of the training, the minister prescribed a course of reading in theology and examined his pupils daily on their understanding and facility in explication and argument. More important, each student prepared and delivered sermons in his mentor's pulpit, soliciting the criticism of both pastor and parishioners. As an observer and assistant, the young man accompanied the minister on his pastoral rounds, gaining valuable practical experience in comforting the sick and afflicted, catechizing the children, awakening slumbering sinners, and supporting the faithful saints. His training consisted of much observation and participation in the pastoral relationship and considerable interaction with the various constituencies of the parish in a closely supervised environment. A successful candidate earned a license to preach from the local ministerial consociation and, after a probationary period of preaching, might be called to a pastorate and ordained by the same council. The entire process was personal, intimate, and familial. The student acquired a good deal of practical training in the paternal pastor's household, where he usually boarded.

He practiced good manners under the careful tutelage of the minister and his wife and sometimes secured a helpmeet by marrying their daughter. If he studied under a much older man, he might succeed his mentor in his pastorate. When he accepted a call from a congregation, the commitment between pastor and people, like a marriage vow, was often considered permanent.[9]

The paternal model of masculinity served as the paradigm for educating the ministry until its power faded with the growing democratization, urbanization, and industrialization of the nineteenth century. The ideal of separate gendered spheres gradually supplanted familial ideology. As democratic governments extended suffrage to most men and production moved out of the home and into the marketplace, men increasingly defined themselves not merely as fathers in the domestic sphere but as active participants in the political and economic public sphere. The preparation of ministers changed at the same time and in similar ways. Embracing new masculine ideals of enterprise and competition in the masculine sphere, clergy gradually moved the preparation of ministers from the parsonage to the seminary.[10]

Seminaries accepted and trained a more mature, self-directed student, who studied a revised curriculum and assimilated a new ideal of the ministry that contrasted sharply with the older model and more closely conformed to the new model of masculinity. Unlike the young boy chosen for his piety and intellectual promise, the nineteenth-century seminarian was a self-selected young adult. Historian David Allmendinger argued that declining economic opportunities for young men in rural New England, coupled with the emergence of more local colleges—closer and cheaper than the traditional Harvard and Yale—produced a bumper crop of young men who purposefully chose a career in the ministry for social and economic upward mobility. Lacking the financial support of parents or local patrons, these young men subsidized their schooling in a variety of ways. They could delay matriculation for several years to work and save money for tuition, take off for a term or two to teach school, or apply for funding from agencies such as the American Education Society.[11]

The new generation of students, older and more highly motivated, chafed under the strict paternal supervision of the college and forced school officials to accommodate them. The college's familial model, long institutionalized in the policy of in loco parentis, was suspended during much of this period. Colleges loosened the rules and allowed students to board in town. They adapted term calendars to make it easier for students to teach school. Since the new students, as Gardiner Spring had noted, came from an uncertain or middling social background, colleges eliminated the traditional ranking of students by the social prominence of their families and replaced it with simple alphabetical listings or merit rankings. All these changes contributed to a liberalization and democratization of the student population that persisted until the end of the nineteenth century, when colleges reinstated stricter supervision of undergraduates.[12]

These self-selected and self-sufficient young men, when they entered the new graduate theological seminaries, encountered a rigorous curriculum that emphasized intellectual preparation in biblical scholarship and interpretation, theological controversy, and the practical skill of public speaking. In the standard three-year program first developed at Andover and replicated by succeeding schools of various denominations, seminarians usually spent the first year studying Hebrew and Greek languages and literature. During the second year, they mastered systematic (often termed more appropriately controversial, dogmatic, or polemical) theology. In the third year, they reviewed ecclesiastical history and polity and immersed themselves in the study of sacred rhetoric or homiletics—the composition and delivery of sermons that demonstrated the student's command of the content of the theological curriculum. Almost as an afterthought, the last term sometimes included a series of lectures in pastoral theology—the practical application of theology to the mundane duties of the settled pastor. Unlike the old parsonage schools, seminaries could not easily offer supervised field experience in pastoral visiting. So, the new emphasis on a rigorous academic curriculum came at the expense of pastoral theology and the practical pastoral skills of care, nurture, and personal instruction. The overwhelming thrust of the curriculum aimed to make the student an able combatant in the public debates over interpretation, doctrine, and methods—skills that clearly marked the minister as masculine under the new ideals of manhood. The nurturing parental qualities required of a patient shepherd of his flock, though formerly within the paternal model of masculinity and developed in the parsonage school, now fell out of the seminary curriculum and into the feminine realm of domesticity.[13]

A typical seminary student tried to complete all three years of the curriculum before he applied for a license to preach, but financial exigencies might shorten his course of study to one or two terms. He acquired his first practical pastoral experience by taking a short stint as a missionary or temporary "supply" preacher before seeking his own pastorate and ordination. The most ambitious seminary student looked forward to utilizing his specialized academic training in a distinguished career in a prominent urban pulpit, as a missionary at home or abroad, as a professor in a college or seminary, or as the administrator of a benevolent or reform organization. These prestigious appointments depended on his writing, speaking, and organizational abilities and required him to have little experience or skill in pastoral work. Less promising or enterprising students looked for permanent pastorates in a small parish, posts that demanded more personal interaction with the congregation and consequently suffered from a lack of prestige and status when compared with the new professional opportunities open to the best students. As historian Donald Scott noted, pastoral work was "subtly downgraded" by the professionalization of the ministry.[14]

The professionalization of the ministry succeeded in raising the status of seminary-trained ministers at the same time that it profoundly undermined the pastor's relationship to his parishioners. The image of the pastor as a patriarchal figure who watchfully tended his family and his flock, and who many times literally inherited his position and authority, no longer fit cultural models of masculinity. The pastor who fit the new model of masculinity earned his position and authority as an educated professional: a competitive, ambitious soldier and entrepreneur who aggressively fought for a market share of adherents. Though clergymen of the time (and historians since) chronicled and explained the changes in the preparation of the clergy, none of them noticed that the concurrent shift in gender ideology helped to legitimize the minister as a new man. The professional model of the ministry located the minister more firmly in the masculine public sphere and less precariously in the feminine domestic sphere. It may have helped some pastors earn respect, attract members, and raise funds for churches and organizations, but it also alienated him from the traditional pastoral face-to-face relationships with his largely female constituency. So, even as Pond lamented the new intimacy and equality in the pastoral relationship, the seminary curriculum worked to reimpose distance and hierarchy.[15]

That newly reconstituted distance probably comforted the orthodox clergy, whose approach to religion was "head-centered" or intellectual and who led the way in professionalizing the ministry. But by mid-century, evangelical or "heart-centered" Christian denominations such as the Baptists and Methodists also increasingly adopted the same new masculine model. Though evangelicals had long denigrated the orthodox, educated clergy as insufficiently pious and espoused a more democratic ministry, they reluctantly endeavored to raise the educational status of their own clergy to more effectively compete for prestige with their theological opponents. In 1845, George Ide argued for the founding of a Baptist seminary by summoning up both the military and the entrepreneurial models of masculinity. He hoped to prepare men for competition in the religious marketplace by demanding a ministry of "such vigour and such resources, that it can grapple with the most astute and polished minds, and become by its lofty standing and its masterly power, the object of veneration instead of scorn or pity." The seminary would emulate a military academy and provide the church with "commanders" who would "arrange and concentrate her forces, and conduct them on, conquering and to conquer, to her ultimate and universal dominion." A minister, Ide insisted, "must show qualities of business, energy, [and] performance" to be effective. Yet Ide still mourned for a warmer, more egalitarian pastoral model. "One plain, unlettered preacher, with his warm heart and glowing utterance, his practical habits, and his intuitive perception of human passions and prejudices, will achieve more for the advancement of Zion, than an army of these slow, torpid bookworms, with the starch of the college yet stiff upon them, with their heads of knowledge and souls of ice, their frigid manners, and their sluggish delivery that lulls like an opiate." He conceded that an increasingly literate public demanded a highly educated man. A character of "unquestioned rectitude" was no longer sufficient qualification for the ministry: Men must be of "elevated intellectual character," too. Thus, the evangelical Ide displayed the same deep ambivalence to the new professional model that, from the other end of the theological spectrum, his orthodox contemporary Pond had displayed to the too-intimate and democratic relationship.[16]

Clearly, theological differences deeply affected attitudes toward pastoral work. While orthodox clergy worried about, and worked to counter, the lowered status of the ministry, evangelical clergy worried about the opposite problem. They feared sacrificing intimacy even as they yielded to the principle of a professional clergy. For example, Archibald Alexander, an "old school" Calvinist and one of the early educators at Princeton Theological Seminary, communicated a much different message to his students from that of Charles Finney, his "new school" Arminian counterpart at Oberlin College's Theological Department. Though both men agreed on the necessity of revivals and conversion and numerous other details of pastoral work, they disagreed fundamentally on the power of the individual pastor to effect religious change. Alexander assured his students that a lack of visible results from their pastoral work was no reason for anxiety. "No faithful sermon is probably altogether unfruitful," he taught. "But if a minister should labor unsuccessfully yet his labors will be acceptable to God." According to Alexander, no minister controlled the working of the Holy Spirit. His own converts, Alexander assured his students, sometimes took months or years to reach conviction of their salvation. On the other hand, Finney argued that he owed his phenomenal success at producing immediate conversions to his urgent and very personal demands on behalf of the Holy Spirit. "We told [the people] the Spirit was striving with them to induce them *now* to give him their hearts, *now* to believe, and to enter *at once* upon a life of submission and devotion to Christ. . . ." The two men also differed on the efficacy of the laity in pastoral duties. Alexander urged pastors to carefully distinguish between the pastor and his duties and the laity and their duties. Ideal pastors, according to Alexander, reserved preaching to themselves and never allowed lay persons to "preach or expound." Laity might "ask questions for information" but should not be permitted to tell their experiences in public prayer meetings. In contrast, Finney encouraged laity—both men and women—to speak in prayer meetings. He also strove to create an intimate physical and spiritual bond between himself and inquirers, even in large meetings filled with strangers. He went from one person to the next, putting his hand on a shoulder and entreating each individual until he or she believed. He "spoke to each one in a low voice so as not to be heard by others than those in the immediate vicinity," offering intensely personal counsel even in a crowded, public setting. Where orthodox Presbyterian Alexander urged a hands-off approach that largely left the process of conversion between the individual and the Spirit, evangelical Presbyterian Finney urged a hands-on approach that made the minister a forceful and active intermediary between the individual and the Spirit.[17]

Thus, even though seminaries of all denominational stripes downplayed the teaching and practice of pastoral theology, evangelicals labored under a greater imperative to develop an effective personal pastoral ministry. This tension between the ideal of a respected, educated professional debater and the alternative ideal of a sincere and intimate counselor did not escape early seminary educators, who realized that their students frequently lived up to stereotypical characteristics. Seminary-trained ministers, their professors complained, were pretentious and contentious—too eager to display their learning and engage in arcane doctrinal battle and too reluctant to condescend to the

level of their parishioners. Even when seminary professors attempted to address this problem by calling for a greater emphasis on pastoral manners and
methods in the curriculum, they failed to attract the experienced and successful
pastors who could teach the appropriate courses. Over the nineteenth century,
these institutions increasingly hired their own graduates as professors, and
many of these men had gained little practical experience in a pastorate. Finney
himself embodied this paradox. He was a most vocal critic of seminary
education and had pointedly refused offers to attend Princeton and Auburn
seminaries when he had trained for the ministry. Yet he served as a founder
and long-tenured professor at Oberlin College. To keep teachers practiced in
pastoral work, he insisted that professors, including himself, maintain pastoral
ties with a congregation in addition to their teaching duties. But Finney's own
peripatetic routine of regular evangelistic tours through the United States and
Britain frequently took him from his teaching responsibilities at the college
and his pastoral duties in the parish. In short, he hardly set the best example
of pastoral commitment to a congregation.[18]

Of course, no nineteenth-century clergymen argued that professionalization was necessary or desirable because it distanced the minister from feminine duties and resituated him more firmly in the masculine sphere. Nevertheless, the professionalization of the clergy coincided with the development
of more rigid definitions of separate sexual spheres in antebellum American
culture. Practical pastoral theology suffered neglect within the seminary in part
because the culture redefined the values of care and nurture as exclusively
feminine. Overlooking or dismissing pastoral work had the unintended effect
of producing a group of men often ill equipped to garner the respect, admiration, and permanent devotion of a congregation—exactly the situation the
seminary had tried to remedy. But with little practical training, little supervision
from an experienced mentor, and few of the social skills of a genteel family
background, a crop of sincere and determined, but nervous, self-conscious,
and insecure candidates entered a competitive religious marketplace still seeking guidance in pastoral theology. What direction they found was not reassuring. In the absence of supervised field experience, they turned to the manuals
and lectures of their professors. There, young men who answered a call to the
ministry could find a list of the qualifications for and duties of the office by
which they could measure themselves and their mettle before entering the
field. They also discovered writers who unanimously described the field as filled
with tension and danger.

The Ideal Pastor

"The duties of the ministry are onerous, I had almost said *overwhelming*,
at the best," admitted Enoch Pond in his *Lectures on Pastoral Duties* in 1848.
Perhaps the very difficulties of conducting pastoral work, especially work outside the pulpit, explains the difficulty of teaching the subject from the lecture
rostrum. Yet no matter how neglected, devalued, and inconsistent with the

values of the new professional ministry, personal pastoral work remained intrinsic to the office. Conscientious students took a lecture course, purchased or consulted manuals in the library, met and discussed the topic informally with other students, or debated pastoral issues in their rhetorical societies. They learned that the pastor served as the guardian of his flock, carefully prevented any sheep from straying, and defended them from attack. They learned that the pastor, too, was susceptible to wandering or vulnerable to attack, even from members of his flock. The conscientious shepherd who emerged from these sources cautiously negotiated a path between dangerous extremes. Nineteenth-century pastoral manual writers drew on the wisdom of Christ and the "pastoral epistles" of Paul in the Bible, as well as on a long line of Reformed writers, but found it extremely difficult to provide clear, unambiguous, straightforward guidance to an anxious new pastor. Instead, they sketched out three often overlapping roles a pastor should play. In the first role, he taught indirectly, by example. In the second, he publicly, directly, and collectively instructed his congregation from the pulpit. In the third role, he privately tutored his parishioners as families and as individuals.[19]

All writers agreed that the chief qualifications for an exemplary pastor ought to be piety and intellect, two qualities often in conflict. Tilting too much toward the heart or the head upset an uneasy balance. The ideal pastor also needed a vocation, a divine call to the ministry that was not merely a career ambition. Finally, an upright moral character was essential, but on its own insufficient. The *appearance* of good morals was deemed as important as the maintenance of good morals. "There is no preaching like a holy life," argued Gardiner Spring. All disciples of Christ, but especially his ministers, ought to be "living epistles, known and read of all men." The minister's life served as an immediate text for his flock to "read," one that illustrated the scriptures and supported his teachings. Spring admitted that ministers should not and could not be perfect. In fact, Satan, the "great Adversary," singled out ministers as special victims, sending them greater temptations than "ordinary Christians." Yet even a minister who resisted sin and led a blameless life still suffered by misreadings of that life. He could inadvertently give the appearance of wickedness when he was innocent, or he might "speak like an angel" and be thoroughly corrupt. William Cogswell, the president of the American Education Society, contended that a minister's piety, his "holiness to the Lord," ought to be so clearly visible, "so legibly inscribed upon the visage which [God] has given you, that 'he may run that reads it.' " In short, the minister must not only *be* good; he must also clearly *seem* to be good. "Abstain from all appearance of evil," wrote the apostle Paul and all subsequent pastoral writers. Though a pastor could possess a fervent piety and cheerfully obey God's law, still his life and actions would be constantly read and frequently misread by his parishioners.[20]

This preoccupation with the appearance of good character led pastoral advisors to devote much discussion to a pastor's ideal *manner*—his temperament and the way he conducted his life and work—but also to his *manners*—the polite social conventions that rendered a pastor acceptable to all ranks of society. Good manners resembled neither the artificial, insincere affectations of the aristocracy nor the obsequiousness of the servile. "Meekness, gentleness, purity, and benevolence" were manly Christian principles, not signs of weakness. These qualities of piety counterbalanced and compensated for the intellectual weapons the pastor was taught to employ in the pulpit. Manners were the subtle instruments he used in the "hand-to-hand" combat of personal conversation when "carnal weapons" proved ineffective, driving away the opponent instead of subduing him or her into conversion.[21]

The ideal pastor never demeaned himself by falling into the extremes of human emotion and vanity. All levity, jesting, groveling, lightness, volatility, pettiness, and meanness were forbidden. At the same time, he never gave the appearance of perfection, arrogance, dourness, or professionalism that signaled a superior or holier-than-thou attitude. He lowered himself into the "world which lieth in wickedness" but only in order to live and work effectively in it. Never "suppose that what is called a knowledge of the world," warned Samuel Miller, "necessarily implies *conformity to it*." The ideal pastor rose above the world, periodically, for prayer and introspection. But he condescended to employ worldly measures to accomplish God's mission. Worldly manners were the tools he used to self-consciously create the text of his life. He presented a self that was sincere and trustworthy, authoritative yet approachable, in order to sell his product—religious truth. Manners allowed him to influence rather than dictate, persuade rather than confront, seduce rather than conquer. In these manuals, gentle manners were often presented as more effective than the forensic warfare of the pulpit. Historian Ann Douglas deplored this apparent substitution, labeling such tactics "feminine": the devious, manipulative, and underhanded methods reserved for the nineteenth-century domestic matron without access to real power and the use of legal and rational strategies. Yet the minister who used these strategies actually emulated an assertive masculine—not a passive feminine—model. He imitated the commercial model of aggressive salesmanship, the methods of self-presentation practiced by the new nineteenth-century entrepreneur and the self-made man. How ironic, then, that seminary training neglected practical guidance in just the kind of manners and methods these manual writers advocated.[22]

The ideal pastor, while carefully constructing his life as a text, also performed the roles of public educator and personal counselor. In both roles, writers instructed him to "feed the flock"—to determine the needs of his parishioners and supply those needs. Preaching the Word from the pulpit in weekly sermons was widely accepted as the most efficient and effective means of fulfilling this obligation. In the first half of the nineteenth century, many preachers still delivered two or three lengthy lectures each Sabbath. Though preaching was only one component of pastoral theology, it usually took precedence over all other pastoral duties because it most clearly depended on the knowledge and skills developed by the seminary curriculum in biblical scholarship, doctrinal theology, and rhetorical eloquence. For novice pastors, the preparation of sermons required a huge investment in time, energy, study, and writing. The young man might rise to great heights in the intellectual quality of his argument and his citations, yet still fail abysmally with a dull, "insensate," and pedantic delivery. Advisors suggested that a modulated tone and pitch enhanced the delivery and effectiveness of the sermon. Avoiding a too hard or too soft tone was essential, too, warned William Sprague. Zealous young pastors tended to be too harsh, "severe and objurgatory." Instead, the preacher "should make it manifest to his hearers that he preaches [leading truths], not because he delights to render [his congregation] unhappy, but because he desires their salvation." The ideal pastor never avoided harsh truths, but he made sure that when he preached them, his parishioners knew it was only for their own good. "When he is dealing the heaviest blows upon their consciences, the spirit of christian kindness should still breathe in his manner," cautioned Sprague. Gardiner Spring agreed that a kinder, gentler approach was more effective than a blunt one. The pastor shunned "representing in all their terrors the torments of the damned." Instead, he "alludes to them, he affectionately affirms them; but he knows too much of the terrors of the Lord, to dwell upon the fearful theme." Still, the ideal pastor remained constantly aware that he served God first, not his people, so he avoided courting popularity by softening his theology too much.[23]

Maintaining the appearance of impeccable character and treading a narrow path between extremes in the pulpit only partially fulfilled a pastor's obligations. He also seized every opportunity to fashion a more personal instruction in prayer meetings, Bible study classes, and set visits to families. He gave personalized instruction in impromptu visits to and from parishioners; in visits to the sick, the dying, and the bereaved; and in funeral ceremonies. On these occasions, too, the ideal pastor deftly sidestepped disaster. He held meetings neither too frequently nor too infrequently, although writers suggested no ideal number. He neither dominated the meetings nor allowed his parishioners to monopolize the discussion. He invited laypersons to help but did not depend on them too much. He neither ignored the anxious nor hurried them too much. In short, the ideal pastor must constantly evaluate his performance and its effectiveness while trying to avoid any undue influence from his parishioners. No amount of advice could either relieve him of the awesome responsibility for the souls in his care or reassure him of the best way to lead each one to salvation.[24]

The ideal pastor crafted an individualized instruction for each parishioner by emulating the methods of the medical profession. He became a "physician of souls," an expert diagnostician who treated the specific spiritual ills of each person. Most writers hoped that the ideal pastor could visit each family in his care at least once or twice a year and to speak to each family member privately whenever possible. Writers catalogued the various social and spiritual estates the pastor must be prepared to meet and treat. *No one* should be excluded: "the young and old; parents and children; masters and servants; those who are in communion with the church and those who are not." Distinguishing between various social estates generally meant identifying the different needs of the rich and the poor. Pastors must "ascend in order to reach those who are above them; they must descend to those who are below them." Most especially, they must take care not to erect a "wall of separation" between themselves and any class of men. The ideal pastor encouraged benevolence and charity in the rich but avoided spending too much time with them. "It has an ill aspect, indeed," admonished Samuel Miller, "when a minister of the gospel is found begging for his own emolument, or even indirectly endeavouring to attract presents to himself." He spent his time more profitably with the poor, being careful to "lay . . . aside every thing like an air of haughtiness or superiority." Similarly, every age group deserved attention, although each posed special risks. A minister ought to spend much time with children in Bible schools, Sunday schools, and individual catechism, but he could also meet with disaster there. A minister might "so demean himself towards children as to become the [object] of their aversion and dread. They will fear him, and flee from him; or if compelled to remain where he is, his presence will impose a severe and unnatural restraint," cautioned Enoch Pond. The old, especially widows, deserved the pastor's special sympathy and often charity. But "ancients," too, posed a danger: They resisted change. Worse, cantankerous old skeptics tempted rash young pastors into inappropriate confrontational disputes.[25]

The list of *social* conditions a pastor must serve, however, was not as long and complicated as the list of *spiritual* conditions to which he must attend. In his first sermon to his new pastorate in New Haven in 1825, Leonard Bacon informed his listeners of the daunting challenges that awaited him:

> I must adapt myself to every variety of moral character. The objector must be met wisely, and in the spirit of meekness. The open trans-gressor must be reproved. The careless must be addressed. The trembling sinner must be led to him who is the sinner's friend. . . . The wandering Christian must be sought out and brought to the fold of Christ. The doubting Christian must be instructed patiently and diligently till all his scruples are removed. The selfish Christian must be excited to deeds of benevolence. The indolent Christian must be roused. The active Christian must be urged to a more en-tire devotedness.

The pastor acquired knowledge of his parishioners' inner spiritual condition by thoughtful inquiry, not by "mere worldly acquaintance." He must diligently avoid visits that consisted merely of chats about gardening, the weather, travel, or politics.[26]

Sprague sympathized with the difficulty a pastor faced in turning the conversation to the more serious subject of salvation. He was "often embarrassed in his attempts to learn the spiritual condition of his flock. On every other subject but that which interests them most, he finds a cordial welcome to their houses, and a ready access to their hearts; but there is a barrier which he often seeks in vain to remove." The ideal pastor strove to remove any barriers with a scrupulous examination into and assessment of the patient's spiritual health, "as a physician inquires of symptoms." Still, a pastor erred if he employed an insistent probing or applied unpleasant truths. If his parishioner was sick, he risked aggravating the illness. A sickbed quickly became a deathbed, which posed a different set of dangers. The ideal pastor avoided giving the deathly ill a hope of salvation without sufficient evidence. He must also beware of declaring the dying "lost" and exacerbating the distress of family members. Most of all, he should avoid any unnecessary meddling, such as "tampering with the mind of the patient, in reference to the disposition of his property." In short, the pastor must carefully wield a delicate scalpel rather than a dull knife when performing exploratory surgery on the afflicted souls in his flock.[27]

Despite his best efforts, the ideal pastor expected few rewards for his superhuman efforts in this life. Best friends betrayed his confidences; parishioners proved contentious and tight-fisted; fellow clergymen imposed on his hospitality; even perfect strangers "lay a snare for your politeness." Only fervent piety sustained the ideal pastor through this "awful and difficult," "arduous," "onerous," and "overwhelming" work. Without piety, everything must be "forced and heavy, if not positively irksome," exhorted Samuel Miller. Without piety, "what shall rouse him to action when neither honour, nor pleasure, nor profit invites; but when all worldly motives conspire to discourage and impede him?" he implored. Only on judgment day would the pastor's successful labors earn honors or his unsuccessful efforts merit condemnation. In sum, writers presented pastoral work as a grim undertaking. The ideal pastor warily trod a path between unacceptable extremes of piety and intellect, of being good and appearing good, of artlessness and artifice. He carried the burden of serving two masters simultaneously—his very demanding God and his very needy parishioners—expertly balancing the conflicting demands of rich and poor, saved and lost. The faithful shepherd drove on tirelessly, always assessing and modifying his course, while never quite sure he was on the right track.[28]

The Ideal Pastor to Women

Given their prominent majority in most congregations, women as a social constituency in the church ought to have attracted the attention of the ideal pastor and the seminary professors who constructed that ideal. But late in the nineteenth century, Professor James H. Fairchild addressed a lecture to the students in the Oberlin Theological Department on a topic he felt had been ignored for far too long. Looking back over a tenure of six decades or more, Fairchild could not recall receiving "enlightenment" on the subject of women in the pastoral relationship during his own student days between 1838 and 1841 as he sat in Charles Finney's pastoral theology lectures. The elderly Fairchild approached his topic for the day with some trepidation but believed it too important to ignore any longer. He assumed that, as "patriarch" of the faculty, he could assume the "delicate responsibility" without apology. In the draft of the talk he prepared for his students, he referred to "the relations of the pastor to the women of his church and congregation" as "forbidden territory." Sometime later, he amended the sentence by crossing out the word *forbidden* and replacing it with *forgotten*. Obviously perplexed about why women had been neglected in the field of pastoral theology, Fairchild wavered between two possible explanations: Either a strong social taboo or a collective amnesia prevented professors from discussing the subject with their students. Whatever the source, Fairchild's confusion accurately reflected the attitude of nineteenth-century theological educators toward his lecture topic. Despite Gardiner Spring's warning that pastors "ought to be careful how they erect a wall of separation between themselves and any man, or any class of man [sic]," a massive curtain wall of cultural convention separated the ideal pastor from his large female constituency. The seminary curriculum consistently avoided and ignored pastoral work in general, but the pastoral relation with women was set off as particularly hazardous "territory," a dangerous and uncharted province for even the most conscientious pastor.[29]

Clergy ignored women as a constituency in large part because they took them for granted. Women were generally viewed as the part of the flock that required the least attention—they followed no matter what the quality of attention they received from their shepherd. Writers included women in the lists of social estates to which pastors should attend but rarely gave them special mention or elaborated on their special needs. Language conventions of the day certainly explain the oversight to some extent. Nineteenth-century writers habitually employed the masculine pronoun to refer to all human beings. Only Archibald Alexander, in referring to his series of pastoral tracts subtitled the "Poor Man's Guide and Friend," reminded readers that "when I say that this little book is for the poor *man*, I do not mean to pass by the woman: no; I consider her as perhaps more likely to profit by what I may write than the other sex." Writers also ignored women because they affirmed a sexual equality in Christian teaching. In the same introduction, Alexander explained that "In Christ there is neither male nor female," the tenet of an equality of believers set forth in Galatians 3:28. Alexander's clarification reveals that two contradictory reasons justified ignoring women. One assumed women's spiritual superiority over men; the other presupposed their equality. First, women were *different* from men because they displayed a greater understanding and appreciation for Christian teaching; hence, they required less attention from a pastor than men did. Men were less susceptible to preaching and so demanded the greater effort. Second, women were *equal* to men in the eyes of God; hence, women required no special consideration. Since God made no distinctions between the sexes, neither should his servant. Similar contradictions emerged in social reality. The institutional church regularly denied both the assumption of superiority and the promise of equality to women by prohibiting female church members from voting or serving as deacons or ordained pastors, or even from speaking in church or prayer meetings attended by both sexes. Women were a pious silent majority, "forgotten" because their pastors assumed their loyal following.[30]

Pastoral theology never confronted this subtle discrimination between the sexes and its inconsistency with Christian teaching. Only one popular manual devoted more than a paragraph or two to women. The rest curiously ignored women, despite a growing body of sermons that described an enhanced role for them as Christian mothers and teachers. None of the manuals mentioned the growing presence of women in benevolent and moral reform organizations or in political movements such as antislavery or women's rights. None even confronted the controversial issue of women's public praying and preaching, which consumed many pages in professional journals and pamphlets. Thus, the principal paradox in pastoral theology regarding women was the implicit promise of Christian equality, or even superiority, in the spiritual realm and its frequently explicit denial in the churches.[31]

Only Samuel Miller, a colleague of Archibald Alexander at Princeton Seminary, devoted several pages to the subject of women when he wrote one of the first and most widely recommended pastoral manuals of the antebellum period. Miller opened by stating what seemed obvious to contemporaries, although it was rarely acknowledged in this literature: "a clergyman will, of course, have much and constant occasion to be in the company of females." His statement implied that the clerical profession in the nineteenth century occupied a peculiar status, affording ministers entrance into a female society usually reserved for men only as family members. No other calling, with the exception of the growing medical profession, regularly brought men into intimate contact with women outside their families. But while Miller recognized the opportunity for clergy and women to share a physical space, at the same time he sensed a disturbing social and intellectual distance between them. He felt obliged to admonish young men to cease uttering any "contemptuous expressions concerning the female sex." He demanded that ministers absolutely refrain from misogynist remarks and jokes. "No truly wise man" indulged in such talk, for to do so was "to depreciate, in the view of many, a most precious part of the church of Christ." Miller's injunction suggests a sizable resistance: Some wise men, at least, regularly indulged in such talk, believed it did not disparage women, and remained unconvinced that women constituted "a most precious part" of the church. In short, clergy might "forget" women because they held women in contempt.[32]

The ideal pastor refrained from denigrating and ignoring the female portion of the church primarily to protect his reputation and his effectiveness. If he spoke ill of the other sex, he proved that he knew only "the most worthless portion of the female sex" or that he had suffered "ill treatment" from women. The ideal pastor realized that times had changed, Miller warned, and "pious females take a far more active part in promoting the spread of the gospel, than was common half a century ago." The ideal pastor cultivated women as an important spiritual resource. "Many things may be accomplished by [women's] pious agency, which could scarcely be attained in any other way," he asserted, suggesting that females had an important and perhaps exclusive role in the church, one that men, including ministers, could not perform. Cultivating women, Miller argued, not only augmented a pastor's efficiency but also enhanced his reputation. To "conciliate the esteem, and to acquire and maintain the unlimited confidence of his female parishioners, and of other persons of worth of that sex," was to possess "one of the most valuable pledges of permanent popularity, [and enjoy] advantages for doing good of the richest kind."

In other words, to "forget" women hurt the pastor, if not the women in his congregation.[33]

Although Professor Miller wrote in the 1830s, he shared a similar confusion and ambivalence about gender issues with Professor Fairchild at the century's end. "The female part of every congregation have, in general, an influence, which, while it cannot be defined, cannot, at the same time, be resisted," he maintained. Miller easily judged women's influence powerful and irresistible; he had much more difficulty in defining women's influence or even declaring it unambiguously benign. He temporized, reassuring readers that "for the most part" it was "as just in its ultimate award, as it is sovereign in its sway." Miller's ambivalent view of women's influence undoubtedly reflected his conservative theology and that of his peers at Princeton. In other publications regarding women, Miller stressed the traditional scriptural views of women as silent, obedient disciples whose religious duties should be confined to the private sphere of the family. Women might engage in benevolent—though not reform—activities only if they directed them at poor women and children. God, Miller argued, had raised "everlasting barriers" between the sexes: Any "masculine" religious role for women defied scripture and divine authority. So, although Miller recognized a female influence for good, he denied women a larger sphere. While his ideal pastor worked to encourage and cultivate women's influence, he also struggled to define and confine it. While he labored to dismantle the social barriers that prevented him from extending his mission to all members of his flock, he worked to maintain those barriers in the case of women.[34]

Miller's advice regarding women's intellect was just as contradictory as his views on their influence. He assured his readers that women were fully capable of understanding theology but then denied them access to theological debate. He warned pastors never to underestimate the rational capabilities of women: They possessed as much "native intellectual *soundness* and *justness* of mind" as men and could converse on all serious and religious subjects. A pastor performed a major disservice to his female parishioners if he believed them capable only of trivial and light-hearted talk. But, as with all parishioners, a mission to women posed special risks. Combat with women in theological debate was especially dangerous. "In acuteness, wit, sprightliness, and delicate raillery, [women] often prove powerful opponents," warned Miller, "while the hands of a male adversary are, in a great measure, tied, so that he cannot wield with unrestrained freedom many of those weapons which he might properly, and with great effect, employ against an adversary of his own sex." The seminary-trained minister, when engaged in serious religious discussion with women, was deprived of much of the intellectual and rhetorical arsenal he had assembled for use in theological dissertation. He was disarmed, especially vulnerable. Controversial theology—the cornerstone of the seminary curriculum—served no appropriate purpose in the minister's mission to women, his largest constituency. Clergy, in their own self-interest, were "forbidden" to engage in theological debate with women.[35]

Similar contradictions abound in this pastoral literature, even when educators devoted only a few lines to the pastoral mission to women. At times, they urged the ideal pastor to seek women's company for his own benefit. "Their presence has a tendency to restrain from improprieties of conduct, to soften the manners and to promote good moral sentiments and feelings," William Cogswell maintained. "Their delicacy and refinement are adapted to check the boisterous passions and to tame the brutal." In other words, the pastor, but not the women, reaped advantages from their mutual association. An even stronger message, however, warned the pastor not to waste time at ladies' tea parties or to allow women to impose on his kindness while traveling. Writers enjoined the pastor to "exercise great delicacy," "scrupulous delicacy," or even "perfect delicacy" with women—all warnings that females required deft and careful handling. Methodist manuals, including one from the African Methodist Episcopal Church, offered the tersest and bluntest advice: "Speak sparingly, and cautiously, with women." Thus, writers presented women as rational, refined, and virtuous but also as trivial, tiresome, and treacherous. A pastor might cultivate women to acquire better manners, but he risked losing their influence if he had not already acquired the cultivated manners necessary to treat them with the utmost prudence.[36]

Women constituted "forbidden" territory primarily because pastoral writers believed that sexuality posed the most significant danger in the pastoral relationship. Any appearance of sexual impropriety was as serious as an actual offense, they insisted. "More than all," warned Enoch Pond, "let [the pastor] indulge in too great liberties with the other sex, so that respectable females shall be afraid of him, and others shall laugh at him," and his character would be destroyed. "The injury will be done before he is aware of it, and when done, it can never be retrieved." Only Samuel Miller, however, carefully delineated the offensive and suspicious behavior to avoid.

> Everything that approaches to fondling with females; frequently taking hold of their hands; leaning on, or over their persons; saluting them; retiring much with them into private apartments; often taking solitary walks with them; corresponding with them by letter, &c.— are all practices of which clergymen, young or old, ought to be extremely cautious, and more especially in respect to married females. In a word, in all your associations with the other sex, let your delicacy be of the most scrupulous kind. Shun not only the reality, but even the appearance of evil.

While Miller, alone of all these writers, offered such precise directions, neither he nor any other author acknowledged that the specific advice regarding women contradicted the general pastoral advice to "associate freely and without restraint" with one's parishioners. Miller recognized the irony, however, that the clergyman's reputation for moral purity actually made him more vulnerable to temptation. "Remember that the very confidence, with respect to purity, which is commonly placed in a clergyman's character, while it is, in some respects, highly advantageous, may become a snare to him in a variety of ways easily conceivable." Miller neglected to again list the "variety of ways" the pastor might fall into a trap and this time left his readers to imagine them. His circumspection illustrates the process by which the discussion of women in the pastoral relation was "forbidden" and "forgotten." For fear of addressing frankly the sexual hazards of ministering to women, educators employed discreet euphemisms that conveyed the gravity of the threat without directly confronting it and resolving the inherent paradoxes in a mission to women.[37]

Perhaps lecturers in pastoral theology, addressing their students in a hall or classroom, managed to give them more explicit advice and even engage them in specific discussions of a ministry to women. However, Archibald Alexander's lecture notes contained no specific references to women. He made vague references to the "difficulties of the Pastoral Office" and especially to the problem the pastor faced in "ordering his conduct and conversation aright." He signaled the importance of the subject indirectly by declaring "a minister needs nothing more than prudence." But he failed to offer more specific advice. "A thousand things must be regulated by prudence concerning wh[ich] no rules can be given." It was impossible to be precise, he insisted, since "the propriety of a thing often depends on *time, place, company*, etc." Without clearly defining the boundaries for his students, Alexander contended that "A minister should never approach the . . . limit of propriety." Any mistakes the pastor made might stain the "white garment" of his reputation. Once contracted, those stains were "hard to be obliterated." Perhaps in the act of delivering this lecture Alexander overcame his reluctance to be explicit and gave his students some specific examples or illustrations of his concerns. Yet even though he never labeled women as archetypal Eves or as evil or wanton temptresses, Alexander left his students pondering just how they might successfully negotiate the perilous territory of a mission to women.[38]

One of Charles Finney's students recorded his professor's more explicit advice. Like Miller, Finney urged his audience to give up any preconceived notions of women's inferiority. "Banish the thought that ladies have nothing but trifling subjects of conversations," he ordered. But much of his advice warned the young men to avoid "flattery," "deceptions in conversations," or any behavior such as "giving significant eyes" or "peculiar intimacies with one person in the presence of others." Anything that resembled flirtation constituted risky behavior. In the majority of advice, meager and vague as it often was, the hazards of a mission to women outweighed the benefits to the pastor.[39]

No authors or lecturers ever described the particular needs of women or the benefits women might derive from a specific pastoral mission to them. Samuel Miller briefly included new mothers in a discussion of the peculiar needs of sick persons. Women in that condition, he assured his readers, were "in a state of greater tenderness of moral feeling, more ready to listen to serious remarks, and more deeply sensible of parental responsibility than usual." Miller offered no specific advice on what exactly the pastor should offer women at this significant time in their lives but assured the pastor he was likely to meet a more vulnerable and receptive female than he might at other times. But her condition was a threat as well as an opportunity: The ideal pastor visited the new mother only "as soon as propriety admitted."[40]

When Oberlin Professor James Fairchild wrote at the end of the century, he better recognized and articulated what women want than any other educator of his time, but he firmly insisted that directing a special mission to women was a huge mistake. He admitted that women had "a growing activity & influence" in the church but admonished the pastor never to give in to "the majority" by "mould[ing]" his public ministrations to them. A pastor risked losing control of himself and his church by associating with its women. "There is some danger," Fairchild warned, "that his preaching may become unduly emotional or esthetic" and the "virile presentation of the truth" neglected. In fact, Fairchild claimed the "effeminate presentation of the Gospel" was both cause and consequence of the absence of men in a congregation. While women might gather for benevolent work, prayer, or "peculiar" spiritual interests, the pastor must take care he was not "captured" or made a "pet" by these female groups. Although most women were discreet and moral, Fairchild assured his students, some required too much of his time for their individual problems and gossip. Some intelligent and agreeable woman in his congregation might make an excellent "confidential friend & counsellor" to the pastor, Fairchild conceded, or some attentive female listener might pose useful questions to him regarding one of his sermons. Yet he firmly reiterated that, regarding women, "there is one safe position & only one, that is to leave it off before it be meddled with." Fairchild argued that human history, both ancient and modern, offered too many examples when "religion & the lust mingled strangely with each other." While he acknowledged that religion and sex might work beneficially together in some cases, the combustible combination never worked in the best interests of the pastor. The ideal pastor scrupulously shunned any personal conversation or correspondence with women while still appearing to be warm and friendly; he displayed strict propriety without advertising priggishness. "Stiffness & prudishness spring from such a consciousness [of well-ordered conduct], while ease & freedom of deportment, & of intercourse must be spontaneous & instinctive." Thus, Fairchild's advice, though much more explicit than that of previous generations, contained the same bewildering and contradictory messages regarding a pastor's mission to women.[41]

The cumulative effect of advice regarding women was to induce confusion and anxiety even more acute than any a pastor faced in his relations with his male parishioners. The warnings to avoid women were inhibiting at their best and impractical at their worst. Where manuals sometimes provided specific scripts for catechism or helpful prescriptions for conversing with particular social or spiritual estates, they offered only vague proscriptions and warnings regarding relations with women. Most disturbing of all, the advice regarding women contradicted much of the general pastoral advice that counseled pastors to cultivate a confidential acquaintance with his congregants. Manuals clearly implied that any intimacy with women would likely be misread by either the immediate participants—the women he counseled—or by the community at large. The ideal pastor kept women at a distance, treated them with extreme care and caution, benefited from their positive moral influence when possible, and employed their gifts as best he could without encouraging them to move beyond their sphere. He always considered his own welfare before that of his female constituents. He walked a narrow path of self-control, mindful of his own self-interest. He dared not risk his own reputation in selfless service to his female parishioners.

The Pastor's (Dis)staff

Writers and lecturers, despite giving scant attention to the problem of women in the pastoral relationship, achieved consensus by offering one viable solution to the dilemma. Instead of risking his vocation in a mission to women, the prudent pastor delegated the work to other women. Samuel Miller advocated enlisting "the aid of those 'mothers of Israel,' whose piety, experience, and influence render them capable of eminent usefulness among anxious inquirers of their own sex." In this way, the ideal pastor recognized the goodness and power of his female followers and escaped the dangers of a personal ministry to them. But most pastoral advisors offered even better advice. The ideal pastor enlisted the permanent aid of a competent wife and helpmeet who not only maintained his home and offered him personal and spiritual support but also conducted the pastoral work to women in the parish. As with every other decision, a young man could make a fateful misstep. A wife "could make or mar" a minister's career: His choice of spouse ranked as the most significant decision he made after accepting a call to the ministry.[42]

Despite the significant risks to his career of a bad marriage, no prudent pastor remained celibate. "An unmarried Minister," Charles Finney warned his students, presented a "peculiar temptation to the other sex." Celibacy, he added, was a "source of temptation" to the minister, too. "Nature demands it [marriage and sexual relations]," he asserted, "and we men have a right to expect it." Enoch Pond agreed, citing the celibacy of Catholic priests as a "source of intolerable corruption in that church, and of untold abominations and miseries in the world." Although nineteenth-century writers lacked a vocabulary to describe homosexuality, Pond perhaps alluded to homosexual proclivities in unmarried clergy when he argued that those who don't marry "come to be distinguished by peculiarities; and by *such* peculiarities as, in a minister of Christ, would serve to render him less agreeable, and might even go to impair his usefulness." Only itinerant preachers escaped the marriage mandate. For everyone else, marriage miraculously eliminated the problem of sexual temptation in the pastoral relationship and ironically allowed the pastor more intimate access to his female followers. As Samuel Miller assured his readers, the married minister's "female parish[i]oners will have more confidence in him, and feel more freedom in approaching him."[43]

Marriage strengthened both the man and his ministry. Matrimonial experience lent authority to his teaching and counseling of men and women by helping him "enter into the feelings and wants" of his parishioners on the subject. Marriage also gave the ideal pastor the opportunity to play an exemplary role as husband and father. In fact, intoned Miller, he "ought to make a point of being *the best husband in his parish*." But in this role, too, the ideal pastor avoided extremes. He was neither "austere, tyrannical, and unkind" nor overly solicitous; he avoided "undue fondness and even caresses before company . . . [or] punctilious and extreme attention, which is really a kind of overacting." In sum, marriage ideally afforded the minister the experience and education in treating women that he missed in his seminary education.[44]

Courting a wife, however, was no easy task. The young pastor could mistakenly and disastrously excite expectations of matrimony where no such intention existed. Since ministers were such "prizes" in the marriage market, writers cautioned, extreme prudence must govern his relations with all young unmarried women. Physical distance did not protect him, because even "epistolary correspondence" could be misconstrued as wooing. Explicit denials of matrimonial intentions could not protect him, since "effusions of refined sentiment; and 'epithets of *brother* and *sister*,' " all wore "the aspect of what is commonly styled 'courtship.' " Writers discouraged even the most casual friendships with females. Courtship must be not just exceptionally deliberate and forthright but timely as well. The most cautious seminarian could make a mistake in timing and marry before "he should need a wife." Or, if he delayed courtship too long, he deprived himself of his necessary "help-meet." "Marriage & permanent settlement," Alexander advised, "ought therefore to coincide as near as possible."[45]

A pastor selected a likely matrimonial candidate with the most exceptional care. "When a man is tied up to a bad wife and cannot be divorced he had better keep out of the ministry," declared Finney. A man who hooked up with "a gay flatterer," warned Alexander, was "like a man who was running a race for his life, voluntarily clogging himself with a dead weight which he must drag after him every step of the way." Since an unsatisfactory marriage unfitted a man for the ministry as surely as a lack of piety or an immoral character, Charles Finney's student carefully transcribed his professor's list of the "indispensable or important qualifications of a wife" by which a young man might measure his prospective bride. He began with good health and a "thorough and extensive education," qualities that, like "conversational powers," "discretion," "gifted in prayer," and "a leader of her sex," would be professional assets to the pastor. Although the attribute "prepossessing appearance" appeared twice on the young man's list, so did more traditional domestic capital, such as "good housekeeper," "economy," and "good judgment in the qualities of articles bought." The pastor who ignored such qualifications and followed his heart rather than his head risked gaining a hindrance rather than a helpmeet. Letting charity or patience inform his choice was also foolish. "I will not suppose you capable of being so insane as to wed a known valetudinarian [invalid]," Miller wrote contemptuously, "in other words, voluntarily to connect yourself with an *incumbrance*, rather than a *help*, for life."[46]

The ideal pastor's wife performed a dizzying array of duties. Of course, she undertook the "principal management" of the home, to free her husband to concentrate on his study and sermon preparation. Finney's student noted that she ministered personally to her husband, providing him with the "sympathy and council" a minister needed. Samuel Miller expected her to "aid him in the conflicts of the spiritual life . . . stimulate him in devotion when he is languid; . . . sympathize with him when he is dejected, and comfortless." In short, she served as consummate pastor to the pastor. The ideal pastor's wife offered her husband professional advice, "counsel[ing] and excit[ing] him in the delicate and arduous duties of his office," Miller assured his readers. Her support resembled the essential work of the female camp follower, who cleaned, clothed, fed, and nursed her soldier husband in a military campaign. Bishop William Meade reminded the seminary student that as a "good soldier of Christ," he endured hardness to "follow his great Captain from land to land." But his wife signed on for combat duty, too. She must be prepared to follow him "to camp and field, whether the war be in our own or other lands." Meade deemed the wife's duties so important that, alone among his seminary cohorts, he espoused a "private form of ordination, by which those who are disposed to become helpmeets to the minister, might try themselves, and see whether they are prepared for the undertaking." But no certificate of competency guaranteed a young man that his wife was prepared for her awesome professional duties.[47]

The pastor's wife's duties took her into the field to serve not only her husband but also his constituents. As an exemplary wife, she was frugal, plain, discreet, and pious, avoiding levity, gossip, indiscretion, and stylish clothes for her own soul's sake and her husband's reputation. She supplemented her teaching by example with active instruction and counseling, however. She served as his crucial public relations expert, his deputy pastor in the parish, and his liaison to his female constituency. According to Samuel Miller, she must be

> *above all*, a happy medium of intercourse, and pledge of confidence, between you, and the other pious females of your congregation. I have often known the pious wives of clergymen exert an influence so manifest, so extensive, and so happy, within the pastoral charges of their husbands, that, in some cases, there were those who felt constrained to doubt whether the pastors or their companions, were, all things considered, the more useful.

Miller envisioned a pastor's wife who served not merely as her husband's assistant but as his surrogate, an authorized independent agent in the mission to women. She accompanied him on his rounds or visited parishioners on her own, "as much as her family, health and degree of leisure would permit." She concentrated on the females, but, like her husband, she gave due attention to the poor as well as the wealthy. In addition, Miller believed she should serve a prominent leadership role and "appear foremost among the sisters of the church, in every pious benevolent and laudable undertaking in which they engage." Thus, the pastor's wife not only shouldered the domestic management of her home, in order to free him for his study, but she also undertook the pastoral work to the overwhelming majority of her husband's church members because he was unfit to do it. As we shall see in the next chapter, it was no wonder the selection of a wife caused so much anxiety in young ministers.[48]

In sum, the ideal pastor of the nineteenth century no longer performed a paternal role to achieve status and respect as a man among men. Instead, he worked very hard to achieve a masculine status within shifting norms of masculinity by re-creating the pastor as a dedicated, well-educated, professional manager of the flock. He distanced himself from the feminine sphere by downgrading pastoral work in the domestic sphere and privileging scholarship, debate, and rhetoric within the public sphere. Pastoral work in general represented a slippery course strewn with unseen obstacles and crisscrossed with passages that led him away from the intended goal of guiding his flock to salvation. Governing the female portion of his flock posed the most significant danger. Caught on a narrow ledge—pushed to offer women intimate spiritual counsel to fulfill his mission to God but at any moment liable to slip into the moral abyss of sexual temptation—the prudent pastor cast off the most "precious portion" of the flock. So, "forbidden" to mingle among women in the private pastoral sphere, even the ideal pastor consequently discovered that women were easily "forgotten." Though forbidden and forgotten in private, still women remained a charge upon ministers in the public pastoral sphere. He occasionally addressed women from the pulpit, along with the rest of his flock. But to bridge the considerable physical and cultural rift between them, the ideal pastor employed an ideal pastor's wife as his go-between—his "happy medium of intercourse." He handed over the personal pastoring of women, so essential to the evangelical mission, to a carefully chosen surrogate, though one without the professional credentials he prized in himself. Thus, the idealized image of the pastor that seminary professors constructed for their readers evaded and failed to resolve the inherent threat and tension of sexuality in the pastoral relationship. Delegating the pastoral responsibility for women to the pastor's wife placed a huge burden on her without formally training her for the job, rewarding her efforts, or recognizing her within the formal institution of the church. In short, she reaped none of the dividends of the professionalizing process in the ministry because that process so clearly defined the job as masculine and thus off-limits to women. Yet the pastor did not escape a heavy burden: He must carefully choose his wife and helpmeet or risk losing his professional usefulness. If a wife could "make or mar" his career, then all his training, status, and efforts in the public sphere were jeopardized by his poor marital choice.

The ideal pastoral relationship envisioned by theology professors bore some striking similarities to the perceived relationship depicted by travelers and pamphleteers, as well as the imagined relationships painted by novelists. Although sexual threat and temptation never surfaced quite as explicitly in the idealized version as it had in the perceived relationship, it nonetheless dictated the terms of the relationship and haunted even the most perfect visions. In the idealized as well as in the imagined relationship, the only woman who might legitimately benefit from a pastor's attention was his wife. Still, no manual even hinted at the pastor's spiritual obligations to that wife. Clerical writers forgot her needs, too. Women both inside and outside the marital relationship were without a clearly defined pastoral relationship. Only other women, it seemed, served as suitable pastors for women. The ideal image of the pastoral relationship, like the perceived and imagined images, was a fictional one. However, it hints at an alternate reality by suggesting that clergy and women were profoundly distanced from each other rather than drawn together in a mutually beneficial relationship. The two were properly separated by "barriers" that a pastor worked to uphold rather than remove. The ideal relationship suggests that a newly professionalizing clergy defined itself as masculine within the newly prescribed ideals of manhood, erecting another "wall of separation" between public pastoral work and women's private sphere. Professionalizing clergy cautioned against any partnership with women outside their own marriages and relinquished any specific mission to women to their wives. In short, the idealized image constructed by prominent clergymen raises the suspicion that no alliance, either easy or uneasy, existed between clergy and women. To test that assumption requires examining the intimate, private, unpublished records of both pastors and women. There we discover that, indeed, cultural conventions of gender did more to separate clergy and women than they did to bring them together. The relationship as experienced and described by its participants bears little resemblance to the popular perceptions or imaginative renditions of the pastoral relationship as a close, even too close, alliance between clergy and women. It bears a more immediate correspondence to the estranged relationship that emerged in some of the novels and most of the pastoral manuals.

PART IV

The Pastoral Relationship in Experience

6

The Unsteady Shepherd; or, What the Pastor Experienced

In 1825, the Rev. Leonard Bacon gave an inaugural sermon to his new congregation at First Church in New Haven, Connecticut. He took as his text 2 Corinthians 2:16: "Who is sufficient for these things?" In this humble introductory sermon, Bacon revealed the anxieties and self-doubts that must have plagued many new pastors in the first half of the nineteenth century. Bacon went on to serve the influential church for the rest of his long life, but at the beginning of his career he sounded a note of dismay rather than confidence and triumph. He reminded his audience of his own human fallibility while still asserting his role as an "ambassador of Christ." He claimed that his words from the pulpit were less his own and more Christ's and asked his audience to listen "as though God did beseech you." By doing so, Bacon denied that he crafted his words, drawing on his study of classical languages, his theological training, and his practice in homiletics. As the next verse in the scripture reminded him and his listeners, pastors "are not, like so many, peddlers of God's word; but as men of sincerity, as commissioned by God, in the sight of God we speak in Christ." In effect, Bacon called on God as the traditional, most powerful source of authority and respect, ignoring his careful training and success in seminary and rejecting the entrepreneurial model of masculinity that had probably helped him obtain such a prestigious parish. As he first took up the shepherd's crook to assume the role of pastor, Bacon stripped himself of any personal honors or accountability and donned instead the more traditional, comforting, and protective mantle of God's authority.[1]

Bacon made certain that his new congregation understood the onerous duties that his new position entailed. He acknowledged that both the dictates of pastoral theology and the desires of his parishioners forced him to spend time in work that was generally less valued than his more public responsibilities. "Your feelings and mine, and the business of my office demand that I should cultivate a personal friendship with you all," he averred. But then he reminded the audience that while his private pastoral chores "may be less important than some other official duties," they were not therefore "less oppressive" a responsibility. He listed the various constituencies he must faithfully serve and the enemies for which he must be wary. These "wolves in sheep's clothing," some of them the "scandalous" members of his own congregation, might easily become dangerous "partizans" who could "intimidate the church, and trample her order in the dust." In short, Bacon declared to his congregation that he assumed the role of shepherd to a diverse and potentially unruly flock who threatened to overwhelm his human abilities to represent his God. Carefully lowering their expectations for his success, he implied that no man, much less a novice such as himself, was adequate or competent for such a daunting task.[2]

Bacon employed accepted conventions in his inaugural sermon, so it was no more or less pessimistic or modest than those of his peers. A new minister saw no value in portraying the duties as simple to perform or any advantage in appearing arrogant or cocksure about his ability to carry out those duties. Instead, the sermon took the form of an urgent plea on the part of the young pastor for the respect, love, cooperation, and support of his new congregation. The formulaic humility of this genre was not insincere or affected, however; it reflected the genuine uneasiness that young men felt at the prospect of taking charge of a parish. To displace some of that anxiety, Bacon charged his church members with much of the responsibility for his success. They must, he admonished them, support him spiritually as well as financially. They should not make unrealistic demands on their new servant. Despite their desire to cultivate his friendship, he warned them not to "lead him into temptation" by inviting him to mere social occasions and amusements. To respect the "official sanctity of his character," his parishioners should restrict their encounters with him to a strictly pastoral nature. The defensive tone of his lecture signaled not only his trepidation at fulfilling his duties but also his belief that his congregation must bear a good deal of the responsibility for his success or failure.[3]

Bacon shared his feelings of inadequacy, and the subsequent necessity of drawing on God's authority and his congregation's cooperation, in a public forum and in a conventional format, but dozens of fledgling pastors disclosed the same apprehensions in their private notebooks, journals, and correspondence. Twenty-five seminary students, preachers, and pastors provide an intimate glimpse into the pastoral relationship from the perspective of its clerical participants. Their experiences reveal a high degree of tension, anxiety, and conflict—a consequence of the social leveling described and decried by the leaders in their profession. However, these private sources reveal that the frustration of pastoral work was most acute when these men recorded their personal dialogues with the women they attempted to serve. New pastors, especially, document disturbing encounters with women that challenged their assumptions about the other sex, as well as their confidence in their ability to serve women. As a consequence, young pastors took very seriously the advice to delegate much of their pastoral work to competent wives. Yet their search for a suitable candidate proved a most unsettling undertaking, too.

Taking Up the Shepherd's Duties

Even though theological seminaries offered little formal practical training in pastoral fieldwork, the conscientious theological student prepared for his future duties by engaging in a variety of activities that were pastoral in nature. During the school year and through the long recesses between terms, seminarians regularly taught secular and Sabbath schools, distributed tracts, supplied vacant pulpits or impoverished churches on a temporary basis, or served as missionaries to urban neighborhoods and prisons. Both students and educators acknowledged that these activities allowed students to gain practical experience, but in many if not most cases, financial compensation, rather than educational experience, motivated students to accept such work. In addition to fieldwork of various kinds, students practiced pastoral manners and methods in their personal relationships. Seminarians took the opportunity to counsel each other on professional and spiritual matters, but they also used their social visits and personal correspondence with friends and family to engage in "religious conversation." They inquired into religious feelings, debated theological issues, and counseled, consoled, and admonished acquaintances within the fairly narrow confines of the family and the all-male seminary. When they ventured beyond these rather exclusive groups by distributing tracts, supplying vacant churches, or finally accepting their own pastorates, young pastors felt ill prepared and ill-at-ease performing pastoral work.[4]

Journals and diaries of seminary students and young pastors resonate with the tensions produced by the paradoxes of pastoral theology. They realized that their formal course work was insufficient preparation for their future duties. On the first page of the journal that young George Moore kept during his theological studies at Harvard Divinity School, he pledged to use its pages as a record of his spiritual introspection (a measure of his piety) and for discussion of topics from his lecture courses (a measure of his intellect). But he also promised to faithfully record the practical wisdom he acquired through his observations and accumulated "knowledge of men and things" (a measure of his manners and methods). These journals served the students as handy references to their spiritual and professional growth. They serve historians as a measure of the effects of social and institutional change on the relations between pastor and people and, more especially, between pastor and women.[5]

Based on their private records, the lists of qualifications for the pastoral office and the contradictory advice dispensed from the seminary lectern and the pastoral manual took a heavy psychological toll on conscientious young seminarians. Serious evangelical students, as well as their orthodox and liberal cohorts, all subjected themselves to regular spiritual self-examination, diligently probing their feelings and motivations for any lack of piety or attention to God's will. They also scrutinized their own conduct and that of their peers for evidence of good moral character and seemly manners. Isaac Bird, a theological student at Yale and at Andover in its first decade, chastised himself in his diary for weeks after his public profession of faith. Although his self-criticism was a requisite ritual for all heirs of Puritanism, Bird's journal reveals the additional burden he suffered by trying to avoid the extremes of either levity or sobriety. In the first weeks of entries, Bird lamented his "criminal propensity to relaxation" and his "want of habitual soberness," even though some of the college students had taunted sober-minded Christians like himself with the nicknames "informers [and] blue skins, etc." Bird's inclination to "sinful levity," he confessed repeatedly, interfered with his commitment to pray and to record his spiritual self-examinations in his journal. He also flogged himself for his reluctance to speak of religion to others.[6]

Bird's struggle to maintain an appropriate gravity and seriousness must have been excessive, however. His diary entries betray an abrupt reversal after a few weeks. Suddenly, Bird worried that he had "acquired habits of reserved gloominess & melancholy to a degree of which I am told I am not conscious." In a discussion with fellow students, he discovered that they viewed his immoderate solemnity as bad manners—a detriment rather than an asset in his religious conversations. He admitted to himself that he, too, had been put off by "Christians too tasteless & forbidding." He resolved, after "mature deliberation," to "pay more attention to this subject . . . hoping that I shall also take effectual care not to run into the *contrary extreme*." He promised to "conform to the world" only to the extent that he could be "influential in the cause of my dishonored Redeemer." Bird's uncertainty and confusion clearly showed the strains of living *in* the world but not *of* it, of maintaining the strictest Christian dignity and moral standards while remaining accessible to those he strove to instruct and influence. Obviously, moderation and balance proved elusive goals for earnest young men such as Bird. They spent their time in painful self-scrutiny, constantly concerned with the appearance of their temperament and conduct and worried that losing their equilibrium seriously hindered their ability to do God's work in the pastoral relation.[7]

Bird's anxiety about his effectiveness extended beyond serious concerns over his piety or lack of it to apprehension about the more mundane but equally important matter of his manners and propriety. He constantly sought guidance on these subjects in his everyday relations rather than in lecture courses or textbooks. He lamented that his piety and his attention to his studies had left him "in almost utter seclusion from polished society ever since the beginning of my collegiate life," and therefore he was not "in manners as I ought to be." He tried to take cues from his professors in their casual relations, observing that Dr. Timothy Dwight "converse[d] as familiarly as a boy at table, & thinks it wrong when refreshing the body to weary the mind with philosophical reasoning & research." As a result of this and similar observations, he concluded that religious conversation must be governed by social circumstances. At times, light conversation might be acceptable, perhaps even preferable, he admitted.

But he returned to his commitment that it was "best, without a doubt, for christians to converse on religion whenever it can be done with propriety."[8]

Determining the best times to stress religious concerns and the best times to ignore them posed constant problems for Bird. Once he had been short of cash and, in return for his room and board, he had given his hosts a copy of the popular novel *Charlotte Temple*. Later, however, he expressed doubts that his decision to pass on this tragic story of a fallen woman had been proper. He would have "felt better," he confessed, "had the book been of another kind." Yet even his doubts raised concerns, and he worried that "I may hereafter call this superstition." His constant anxiety about propriety left him "rather inclined to assist & instruct the necessitous and ignorant, than to be influential in the more polished circles of life." Frustrated by his attempts to prepare himself for all social situations, Bird scaled down his ambitions for a pastorate among the genteel and wealthy.

Bird suffered even in speaking of religion with friends and family, which only increased his confusion over the proper timing and manners of religious conversation. His journals during college and seminary give numerous examples of practical pastoral experience within already intimate relationships, but even in these familiar and familial conversations Bird met unexpected resistance to his earnest inquiries. He spent one Sabbath with an aunt and uncle very "unprofitably," he glumly reported. His uncle argued with him on the doctrines of the "fall, the trinity, holiness of sabbath, moses' history, propriety of vocal prayer, etc." He resolved to be more "carefull where I . . . spend the Sabbath." If he still found himself confronted with such vociferous challenges to his orthodoxy, Bird promised to "be more silent if I can not converse profitably on religion, or read the Bible more which can not be construed in a bad sense." Bird retreated to the passive reading of scripture when he realized that his scholarship in orthodox theology did not serve him well in intimate conversation and that a pitched battle with his uncle was an unpleasant spectacle. On a visit to his aged grandmother, Bird again met embarrassment and disappointment. Although the older woman had professed her faith many years before, Bird questioned her piety because she never discussed religion, even with him. Fearing he might not have another opportunity to check her spiritual readiness for death, he inquired whether she was "anxious to be gone." As an Andover Calvinist, Bird hoped to hear her give a cheerful, affirmative response. "Why no," she replied ("with some Spirit," noted her grandson). "I like to live as well as other people." Her reluctance to speak with him about her future prospects left Bird in some doubt about her claim to salvation, but he decided to discreetly drop the conversation.[9]

The confusion, anxiety, and doubt Bird experienced were common among earnest young seminarians. Their apprehensions multiplied when they took their ministry beyond the seminary or family circle. "Who is sufficient for these things?" Paul asked the Corinthians, and no young man volunteered himself as adequate to the task. Before delivering his first sermon as a student at Rochester Theological Seminary, Edward Gurney felt confident of his intellectual preparation but woefully inadequate in piety and appropriate manner. "My head may with study prepare sermons but they will want soul and pungency," he complained. "I am yet in spiritual babyhood." Young Lyman Beecher chafed under the scrutiny of his prospective parishioners, afraid they would misjudge his character and talents. "The people watch me as narrowly as a mouse is watched by a cat," he protested. One year into his first pastorate, Jonathan Lee could still lament his "unworthiness & insufficiency." Novice pastors experienced acute anxiety in taking up the shepherd's duties.[10]

Even a successful graduate of a prestigious seminary suffered extended bouts of inadequacy and reconsidered his commitment to pastoral work. Charles Hodge, an early student and protégé of Samuel Miller and Archibald Alexander at Princeton Seminary, chastised himself for numerous faults in his early pastoral work. While supplying a number of vacant pulpits, he discovered with dismay that he had carelessly preached the same sermon twice in a row to a congregation. After five months of preaching, he dispiritedly noted "no visible fruit resulting from my labours." The young man complained that "it is painful to preach Sabbath after Sabbath & I see no solitary instance of seriousness & conversion." Yet despite his frustrations with preaching, he found personal conversation even more distressing. Supplying two separate pulpits on the same day, he had to spend several hours dining and riding with one of the parishioners. Like young Bird, Hodge reported, "This method of spending the Sabbath I find very unprofitable. . . . I have neither talent nor piety to give a spiritual & devout character to conversation & hence other subjects than piety become the matters of conversation." Also like Bird, Hodge's uncomfortable experiences as a fledgling pastor probably convinced him to turn his career in a different direction. He first took a teaching post, where his intellect compensated for his deficient pastoral skills. Soon after, he joined the faculty at Princeton Seminary, where, in spite of his dearth of pastoral experience, he enjoyed a long and distinguished tenure. Although he undertook pastoral work in Princeton, he failed to craft a specific message to his various constituencies or to condescend to his intellectual inferiors. He drew criticism for preaching the same sermons to parishioners, seminary students, and professors, all as if they were "learned theologians."[11]

Pastoral work for some young pastors proved truly unpleasant and hazardous, not merely discomfiting. Ephraim Abbot, one of Andover's first graduates, supplied a number of vacant pulpits in rural New Hampshire and Maine after completing his seminary courses. He wrote one discouraged letter to his fiancée, describing his rude reception. "My conduct so far as I know is as agreeable to my profession as it was in the eastern country, but I am very differently received, & very differently treated," he complained. Perhaps Abbott's frontier parishioners misread his cultivated manners and erudition as arrogance. "My sentiments are misrepresented, & in many respects I have been calumniated," he moaned, and "some lie about me & one person has said all manner of evil against me to my face." Although he endured very personal attacks, he claimed his maltreatment hurt him only because his divine mission suffered. "If I know my own heart things grieve me only as they tend in some instances to deprive me of hearers & probably to lessen my influence." Abbott discovered little to fault in himself. Instead, he was "greatly distressed for the stupidity, the infidelity, the avariciousness, & the corruption of the people." His "treatment," he insisted, differed greatly from "what my conduct and the sentiments of my heart merit." In the most frightening incident, Abbott reported being called a "liar, & a thief, & a villain going into all the poor houses after old negros, squaws, & old dirty women." Thus, his mission to condescend to the most marginal people—women of color and of poverty—raised the most vocal and physical opposition. When he found his horse's mane shorn one morning, Abbott suspected his attacker's violent anticlerical speech had escalated to vandalism.[12]

Such open hostility finally prompted Abbott to make some adjustments to improve his effectiveness. His church members claimed they preferred that he preach from a written discourse, but one day he was forced to preach without any notes. He remarked with pleasure that the Baptists, among others, admired his effort. "Considerably encouraged," Abbott decided to renew his exertions, concentrating on a less formal approach and individual pastoral discussions. "They need much instruction, & many are desirous to have me visit and converse with them on serious subjects," he happily reported. After a prayer meeting, he spoke with several of his parishioners, and "from what I perceive by the best observations I can make[,] *conversation* is more likely to be blessed than preaching." Abbott learned from painful practical experience to rely on personal dialogue, not the learned discourse he had mastered in the seminary, as the most effective means of religious communication. "The great body of the people here are very ignorant of the nature of religion," he concluded, "and a man must speak very plain & very definite in order to convey any correct ideas concerning it." Abbott's people thus forced him to significantly change the methods and manners he had taken from the seminary. Rather than retreat back to the seminary as Charles Hodge did, Abbott salvaged his mission to the rural poor by giving up polished theological discourses and resorting to plain speech delivered in intimate conversation.[13]

The anxiety and tension these novice pastors endured stemmed in large part from their lack of experience, but the contradictions in the status and concept of pastoral theology increased their reluctance to undertake the work and their trepidation while performing it. Students and graduates quickly discovered that pastoral work was fraught with discomfort and danger. That negative attitude, coupled with their inexperience, produced unhappy encounters with family, friends, and parishioners that, in turn, increased their anxiety. Some, like Bird and Hodge, took an alternative career path to avoid pastoral work altogether or to serve different constituencies. Others, like Abbott, learned from painful experience that an effective pastor might see positive results and achieve conversions by dividing his flock into smaller, more intimate groups for private pastoral counseling instead of employing his intellectual skills in the pulpit, the method most emphasized in the seminary curriculum. In short, pastoral work required canny social skills and an uncanny ability to maintain one's balance and equilibrium while negotiating a treacherous path between unacceptable extremes, talents that few young men acquired in seminary. The perils of pastoral work were only exacerbated when the pastor attempted to minister to women.

Guiding the Female Portion of the Flock

Young men reeled from shock and dismay when they encountered women who failed to meet their expectations of piety and submissiveness, as dictated by cultural ideals of womanhood. Just as young Isaac Bird felt disappointment at his grandmother's quick dismissal of his earnest inquiries about her spiritual preparation for death, he experienced a keen distress in personal interviews with women outside his family. On his vacations from Andover Seminary, Bird spent many weeks visiting and distributing tracts among Boston's poor and recorded the most singular impressions in the journal he kept of his missionary work. Appalled by the filthy houses and muddy streets, Bird was especially disturbed by the "women (chiefly black) frequent in streets talking loudly, impudently, romping with men &c." The women's behavior offended Bird, but their rejection of his evangelical message proved even more upsetting. In the "female compartment" of the prison, the women laughed at his missionary efforts. In a bawdy house, one young prostitute at first impressed him as "intelligent." She responded "with much spirit" to his urgent questioning, assuring him that her profession was "not from choice" but forced on her. But his initial positive reaction changed when she showed him her Bible "with a great deal of self-complacency." Worried that she misunderstood the gravity of her spiritual health, Bird "endeavoured to warn her faithfully." But the young man was stunned by her parting words to him: "I think *my* chance for heaven as good as *yours*." No pastoral manual had specifically cautioned Bird that women as independent and corrupt as this one might cavalierly resist his message. On the other hand, no manual warned him that some women might appear dangerously dependent upon him. An exceptionally warm reception unsettled him as much as a cool one. Visiting a sick young woman and her sister, Bird noted with satisfaction their candor and tears. But when he and a fellow seminary student turned to leave, the girls "reached their hands & clung as if they felt themselves sinking & we could deliver them." The two men maintained their equilibrium only by hurriedly disentangling themselves from the frantic grasp of the desperate women, so fearful of dying without hope of salvation. The men left agitated and bewildered, with no assurance that they had brought either comfort or adequate warning to the women. In both these instances, Bird recorded what appeared to be a hopeful and positive reception that rather quickly turned into a disappointing and disturbing interview.[14]

Bird never singled out women as the most troublesome portion of his pastoral mission, yet his diary entries recording meetings with them register a distinct tone of shock and confusion. Though Bird never explicitly cited gender difference as a problem in the pastoral relationship, other entries suggest he worried about his own masculinity and the manliness of his profession. Bird's older brother Henry was an intransigent skeptic, inaccessible to Isaac's evangelistic efforts. Obviously, Bird had disturbing and unsuccessful encounters with men as well as women, but his brother's irreligion bothered Bird most when the older man insultingly questioned his manhood. Henry seemed "grossly hardened in sin," wrote Bird, and "says religion *unmans* a person. . . ." Martial metaphors, however, helped Bird recover his masculine identity. A fellow seminarian one day likened their urgent mission to a military campaign, a "simile" Bird admired as "very striking." "He compared us to a collection of rulers in time of war met to reproach themselves & each other for failure in duty when the enemy were in the very act of sacking the city & house in which they were holding consultation." Military imagery also structured Bird's vision of God's kingdom. After observing an impressive militia muster, Bird wrote that the "grand performance" reminded him of the "order in heaven." "Military order with all its melancholy associations is so grand & beautiful, what will be the grandeur & beauty of order in heaven?" he wondered. Thus Bird, uneasy in his relations with women and threatened by accusations that religion emasculated him, found reassurance of his masculinity by envisioning himself as a commander, his pastoral work as a campaign, and his ultimate goal of salvation as a military victory.[15]

Bird's journal reveals the extent to which the minister's work was often conducted in a female world and yet deeply threatened by that association with women. Bird began his career in the early nineteenth century but in an urban setting that already showed evidence of the demographic changes that much of the rest of the country would eventually experience during the remainder of the century. In the rural past, a pastor might make calls in households where men, women, children, and servants lived and worked together. But as urbanization and industrialization developed over the century, production increasingly moved out of the household and into the public workplace. Unless the pastor held a rural or frontier pastorate, his daytime rounds of visiting took him increasingly into the private domestic sphere where women, children, and mostly female servants resided and worked. He might make visits to specific shops, factories, or offices to converse with men in the workplace, but these sites afforded an uncongenial atmosphere for religious dialogue. So, in addition to his home visits, a nineteenth-century pastor called meetings for prayer or inquiry in which he could conduct more intimate discussions with participants, but again he discovered an overwhelmingly female audience. Only in unusual seasons of revival, in a specific call to a male constituency, or in evening lectures on more secular topics did men constitute a significant portion of his listeners. Thus, a dutiful pastor could not and did not ignore or avoid women, but he experienced and maintained a wary distance from them, nonetheless. With women, he felt ill-at-ease, ill prepared, and "insufficient" for the task of ministering to them.

The anxiety Bird endured echoed in the private writing of other novice pastors throughout the first half of the century. In 1844, Unitarian George Moore recounted a disturbing "adventure" that helped establish a wariness of women that plagued his pastoral career. After delivering a guest sermon in Nashua, New Hampshire, Moore received an invitation from one of his female listeners. As he was "taken by surprize, [and] . . . knew not what to say to her," he followed her home with some embarrassment. She showed him her books, but when she began to play "dance tunes" on her music box and offered him a refreshment of tea, he balked, wondering, "Who and what can this be?" He decided to retreat in haste, not merely because of her forward behavior but because she was "exceedingly nervous, and an exceedingly ugly spinster." On returning to the village, he discovered her reputation as a "weak sister" who habitually bothered visiting clergymen.[16]

Women too eager to entertain clergy actually repulsed them. Charles Swan Walker, another graduate of Andover, recalled his early pastoral work, when "all sorts" greeted him on his rounds. The most peculiar seemed to be women. He vividly remembered a visit to a woman who had introduced herself as "Amy . . . the prophet of the Lord," who spoke in tongues and kept writings in an unknown language. She assured Walker that she knew "a great deal more about religious things than you do." A poor widow who should have attracted the special concern of her local pastor, Amy despised the man. She told Walker, "Young man, I like you. That preacher down in the village is an obstinate sinner. He put me . . . out of the sanctuary and would not let me prophecy." Like Moore, Walker "beat a hasty retreat." Like Moore, he shared his disquieting interview with another man and learned of the woman's dubious reputation as a spiritualist. Though "sane on every other topic, on religion she rode her hobby to the limit," he recorded. Also like Moore, Walker covered his fright and embarrassment with a cynical amusement. These encounters with women who showed a special interest in the clergyman but failed to live up to pious stereotypes drove ministers away rather than attracting their special concern. Neither of these two men reciprocated the women's attentions by showing any spiritual interest or helping to free them from their delusions.[17]

These two men showed a subtle contempt for women, finding their behavior and activities merely "amusing," but others exhibited a genuine concern for including women in their mission. Still, even a conscientious pastor such as Edward Whiting Gilman, a former student at Yale Divinity and Union Theological Seminary, met with frustration in serving the women in his Lockport, New York, Congregational church in the 1850s. Gilman seemed to take women's inquiries and conversation seriously but was repeatedly disappointed in his ability to influence them. A call on one sick woman found her "indifferent respecting the matter of the greatest moment & unmoved by all that I could say." Another sick woman, this one younger, was equally distressing to him. "She told me that her former interview with me did her no good . . . that she felt worse after it and was assured that it was not best for her to speak with me about religion." Gilman dutifully examined his manner and method but could not determine his own responsibility for the miserable conversation. "Perhaps it was my manner of speaking with her," he reflected, "perhaps the subject matter." Despite such dispiriting setbacks, Gilman persisted in his pastoral work with women. During discussions with one anxious young woman, he "feared I could say nothing more to her, but yet have found words, and trust not in vain." Gilman did not avoid women—visits to them clearly made up the bulk of his personal pastoral work. But the conversations he recorded with women reveal a man who struggled to communicate effectively with them.[18]

Gilman included in his journal an extended report of two pastoral conversations that dramatically demonstrates the condescension he displayed to women and the respect that, in contrast, he accorded men in similar situations. Despite the insistence of professors and manual writers that women were as capable of rational theological discussion as men were, examples show that ministers perceived women as more emotional and irrational—more resistant to their careful religious arguments—than their male peers. Gilman was "surprised" and perturbed to find on a visit to one of his female parishioners that she not only attended Roman Catholic services and participated in their devotions but also defended Catholics as slandered and persecuted people. Worried and upset by this development, he returned a few days later to confirm his negative interpretation of her actions and her words and found his "worst apprehensions were true." The woman's manner toward him had "wonderfully and painfully changed," he reported with dismay. "Her language was full of sneers at my remarks: she was quick & snappish—extremely sensitive and unwilling to hear reason." To his credit, Gilman stayed to engage her in further conversation but made no progress. "No talking of mine seemed to have the least good effect," he protested. When he suggested to her that she had "dust thrown in her eyes," she "took umbrage." When he tried to "explain and illustrate" her errors, "she took offense at that." Gilman primarily registered the woman's emotional responses, but in places he also recorded her opposing arguments. When he listed the "corruptions of the Romanism," she countered that there were "wicked people in any denomination." When he accused the Catholics of using an inferior translation of the scriptures, she asked him "why Protestants had altered the Bible" from the Catholic version. In fact, Gilman had no logical answers to her objections. The woman based her arguments not on scriptural expertise but on her firsthand observations. She carefully weighed the positive aspects of the Catholic service and the negative aspects of the irrational prejudice of nativists, and found the latter less convincing. Yet Gilman could neither acknowledge her reasoning nor effectively counter it. Nor could he see that some of his arguments were particularly offensive to her as a woman. When he "reminded her of Eve's self confidence in temptation . . . she was piqued that she should be likened to Eve." When all of Gilman's arguments failed, he tried to appeal to her feminine sympathy. But this tactic misfired, too. "If I spoke of my pain at her position," he moaned, "there was no Christian response."[19]

In his diary entry reporting the grievous interview, Gilman pondered the reasons for the woman's defection from his church but not the reasons for his own ineffectiveness. The "peculiarity" of her suspected apostasy puzzled him because it lacked those familiar evangelical signposts for which he customarily looked. He discerned no "single element of religious conviction" about her change of mind, "no intellectual process of enquiry and discovery." He ascribed her bizarre behavior to an irrational and emotional mind, something he expected from women. He speculated that her defection was a consequence of romantic desire: She hoped to marry a Roman Catholic widower of her acquaintance. On the other hand, he also blamed her for "a spirit of independent self-will" that he found both unexpected and unacceptable in a woman. To Gilman, the woman was either deluded or perverse. In his view, her religious opinions could never be the consequence of thoughtful persuasion or sincere conviction. Even if Gilman correctly assessed the woman's motivation, however, he showed no sympathy for her. In the end, he felt only his own personal defeat and humiliation.[20]

In the same long and painful journal entry, Gilman recorded an interview with a man that provides a striking contrast to the one with his female parishioner. While the man, too, appeared sympathetic to Catholicism, his case, Gilman insisted, was "entirely different." The man was "tolerably well informed; cool, close, and in some measure unstable in his plans." Gilman saw an opportunity to lead him away from the dangers of Catholicism and pursued the discussion. He liked the man's character, especially since he had once studied for the ministry. But unlike his bewildering and agitated dispute with the woman, Gilman conducted an amicable debate with the man about Catholic doctrine. He could disagree with the man but still admire and respect his adversary's theological learning and reasoning.[21]

Gilman's relations with women were marred by his feelings of inadequacy and his disregard for female reasoning, but gender difference and sexual tension also interfered with his ability to serve women. Young women, especially, had difficulty in speaking with him. One admitted to him that she felt "rather embarrassed & restrained" in his presence, so he finally recommended that she instead talk with a pious young female friend. Similarly, another woman told him she "dreaded" to see him. Again, he hoped she would be able to "converse fully and freely with her sisters" in order to overcome her difficulties. Still another young woman suffered terrible agitation after her visits with him. "To-day she hardly wanted to talk with me," he worried, "yet would not let me go." She finally admitted to Gilman that she had quit going to prayer meetings "on account of remarks from the other girls" who had "misconstrued" her motives and "accused her of caring more for the minister than for religion." Gilman stayed to pray and talk with the girl "for some time," undoubtedly adding fuel to the gossip surrounding their relationship.[22]

These troubled pastoral encounters with women seriously undermine the assumption that clergy and women shared a mutually beneficial relationship or even an "uneasy alliance." Though women made up the majority of church members, church attenders, and recipients of pastoral visits, the evidence does not support historian E. Brooks Holifield's argument that "early nineteenth-century pastoral care was designed for an institution filled with women." Holifield examined Samuel Miller's pastoral manual and its chapter on women and then generalized from that source that teachers of pastoral theology took a "special interest in the spirituality of women." Holifield surmised that "an adept physician of the soul would need to understand and work with women." But pastors from across the denominational spectrum fell far short of that goal. They left seminary training without receiving much instruction regarding women or developing "a special interest in the spirituality of women" and, hence, failed to "understand and work with women" in their pastorates. Instead, they imbibed the regnant gender ideology that taught them women were domestic, pure, pious, and submissive. Truly pious women owed their male superiors—fathers, husbands, and clergymen—deference and subservience. When women failed to live up to those ideals, whether they boldly disagreed and argued with pastors or just quietly resisted a minister's message, pastors registered dismay, shock, and confusion. In seminary, young clergymen learned to juggle opposing ideals, one that claimed women should keep silent and the other that the pastoral visit should be characterized by "free conversation," candor, and confidentiality. In practical experience, however, they learned that women's speech threatened masculine clerical authority, whether uttered in public or in private. Young ministers like Isaac Bird, engaged in the business of disseminating God's Word, were shocked and "struck dumb," robbed of their ability to speak by women's words. In spite of their careful theological training and their study of classical languages, theological dissertation, and homiletics, pastors too often found themselves in a painfully vulnerable and defenseless posture in dialogue with women.[23]

When women proved corrupt and belligerent or seemed illogical, emotional, and unreasonable, when women suffered constraint and embarrassment with clergy, or when women and clergy generated gossip regarding a romantic attachment, the prudent pastor turned away. He "beat a hasty retreat," dismissed the woman, or referred her to a female friend. But he also took the repeated advice of his teachers and mentors: He searched for a suitable wife to assume his pastoral mission to women. But just as the advisors predicted, young men agonized over the quest for a qualified pastoral helpmeet. Their wariness of women in the pastoral relationship also haunted their search for a fit wife.

Searching for a (Dis)staff to Lean Upon

Theology students and young pastors assimilated the injunctions to marry, giving marriage and the choice of a spouse the most serious consideration. The subject filled their diaries and letters, clear evidence of their concern and the pressure applied by educators, family, and friends. The process proved to be just as unsettling as any other aspect of pastoral work with women, however. Elam J. Comings, taking notes in Charles Finney's pastoral theology class at Oberlin, wrote, "Avoid anxiety about [marriage]," suggesting students suffered much trepidation. Malcolm Douglass, an Episcopalian student at General Theological Seminary, received numerous warnings and recommendations about matrimony in his correspondence with his father. Douglass assured his father that he took the subject seriously and even passed on the paternal advice to his roommates. The elder Douglass urged the young men to be cautious and deliberate about marriage, and they all concurred. "They thought the advice there given very sound and sensible," Malcolm reported, and "as neither of them are ensnared as yet," they would "act upon the hint and let the subject rest for a while." In fact, the young men had internalized the grim warnings and "come to the conclusion that if a Minister had not a wife fit to be a minister's wife he had better have none at all." Malcolm himself despaired of finding a "fit" wife and wrote, "I might as well vow a life of celibacy at once." He wanted to make it clear to his father that he did not "underrate the sex," however. "I think it [the female sex] is—i.e. some individuals of it, are about as near angels as our human nature can well be," he asserted. "But they are precious few of them, and those who are not, are not angels by a long shot." The contempt and suspicion that so many men held for women impeded their search for a suitable partner in their vocation. Douglass displayed both his scholarly learning and the scriptural sources of an antipathy to women by reminding his father that St. Paul had recognized the infirmities of the female sex in his instructions to the elders and deacons of the early Christian church. In the original Greek text, he confidently informed his father, Paul had used the word *diabolous* in referring to women, "from which I will leave you to draw your own inferences." Young Douglass, an adherent of the high-church party in the Episcopal seminary, affirmed a traditional Christian view of women as sources of evil and found celibacy more acceptable than some of his low-church evangelical brothers. Still, Douglass shared his caution toward women with young men across the entire range of theological differences.[24]

Ferdinand Clarke, a student at Princeton Theological Seminary, shared Douglass's wariness toward marriage but could not choose celibacy without giving up his calling as a foreign missionary. During his first year at seminary, Clarke wrote to his sister to solicit her suggestions for possible candidates and complain that his social circle at Princeton was too small to afford any prospects. "If you come across any young lady in your tours who wished to go on a Foreign Mission just notify me," he requested, "not that it is the only qualification but that it must be fundamental." Clarke's commitment to missionary work abroad meant that he must reject any woman who objected to his calling. "She must be a christian . . . intelligent," he reminded her, insisting on her fitness for the job of a missionary's wife. But then he added "not homely" as a final qualification, an admission that worldly qualities were still an important concern for this deeply pious young man. He confessed the job of finding a wife would be difficult since "I have never yet seen the lady to whom I had the most distant desire to pass the special addresses." By his graduation in 1836, Clarke was desperate: His application for a missionary position in China depended on his finding a suitable helpmeet. "The Board say I must marry and give to that object my entire time," he lamented to a classmate. "I do not like it; I want time . . . for other things." Both Douglass and Clarke exhibited serious apprehensions about marriage. Douglass realized the risks of a poor choice, despaired of finding a good one, and leaned toward a celibate life. Clarke, too, found no likely candidates but was forced to marry to fulfill his vocation in the foreign missions. The reluctance the two young men experienced demonstrates the enormous personal and cultural forces that repelled young seminarians from marriage and the opposite sex. Conversely, the sig-

nificance of the topic in their letters illustrates the equally compelling professional and even physical forces that pushed them toward marriage.[25]

Despite the general aversion to women, the considerable professional risks
of marriage, and the imperative to marry only when ready to assume a pastorate, some pious young men succumbed to romantic or "carnal" lures and wed
contrary to their elders' advice. Frederick Gallagher, a student at Lane Seminary
in Ohio, defied the conventional counsel and married while still in school,
explicitly disregarding the well-meaning warning of a faculty wife who tried to
dissuade him from a mixed marriage. "I learned to my grief," the older woman
wrote him, "that the lady on whom you have apparently set your heart is—
shall I speak that fatal word—a *Methodist!*" Certain that the prudent young
man would reject a woman of that denomination, his self-appointed advisor
concluded, "For how can you, an aristocratic Presbyterian wed a lowly, meek
Methodist?" Gallagher persevered in his choice of companion, however. He
married before finishing his third year in seminary and, after graduation, took
his modest Methodist wife off to a successful Presbyterian pastorate.[26]

Edward Gurney, a devout young man at Rochester Theological Seminary,
suffered a more strained conflict than Gallagher, painfully recognizing that his
physical desire for women conflicted with his spiritual calling to the ministry.
"Still harrassed by temptation and an unusual proneness to carnal sensual
thought," the tormented man repeatedly confessed to his diary. The subject
loomed so large in his thoughts that he preached his very first sermon from
Romans 8:7, "the carnal mind is enmity against God." He struggled for months
with the question of his physical longings and the requirements of his calling
before coming to the conclusion that marriage might relieve the tension. On
vacation from course work, he took the time to "consider . . . a most important
question pertaining to my future upon the proper decision of which hangs the
bliss or bane of all my happiness in a great degree as a minister of Jesus Christ."
He had long hesitated to confront the issue for fear of acting "prematurely."
"Knowing the powerful influence which a bosom companion must have not
only on the ministers happiness but success in life," Gurney sought divine
guidance. "With two exceptions," he admitted, "my first starting in the divine
life & my call to the ministry, this is the most serious question that ever came
before my mind for consideration."[27]

Gurney's deliberate steps in choosing a wife mirrored both his evangelical
conversion experience and his decision to enter the ministry. He subjected first
himself and then the object of his matrimonial intentions to a detailed examination of their respective motives and commitment. In his journal, Gurney
freely admitted that the young woman was his choice in "judgment as well as
my religious feelings." But although his reason and spiritual insight confirmed
his selection, "my worldliness would have sought another," he confessed. God's
choice prevailed, but not without considerable reluctance on Gurney's part. He
desired to "be submissive to the guidings of his Spirit" but found "nothing but
a worldly heart that does not fall in with the choice." The young woman clearly
fulfilled the professional requirements of the position but failed to satisfy the
physical desire he sought to alleviate. A number of other young women vied

for his attentions and affections, but only one met the most important criteria. "I am false to that highest prize if I sacrafice usefulness on the altar of world- liness," he wrote with resignation. Instead, he arrived at his choice by asking *"which* (one of many) *will add the most to my usefulness as a minister of Jesus Christ."* Gurney struggled to maintain the uneasy balance between his profes- sional needs and his physical desires.[28]

Gurney's matrimonial calculations and correspondence, carefully recorded in his diary, reveal his deep ambivalence about the courtship. He wrote his prospective wife to demand that she search her soul for the true source of her willingness to marry him. "If it is a mere attachment to me (essential as this is) that would lead you to give me your heart & hand, without having consid- ered, prayerfully considered your fitness & duty in reference to the work of which you as well as I must labor," he warned her, "I say if such is the case, it were better p[er]haps had we never seen each other." Gurney tried to reassure her that "I trust such is not the case." He confessed that he shared the hesi- tation she might be feeling: "my worldly heart shrink[s] back from lifes conflict, from the self-denyal, the responsibility of the ministry." But the ministry was such a "glorious privaledge that angels well may envy." Gurney's proposal was candid if not romantic. He tried to convince his matrimonial candidate that their higher calling would compensate for any lack of worldly love or physical desire: "Hearts united by such a tie cannot but be happy." Clearly, Gurney asked the young woman to consider their marriage primarily as a spiritual and professional partnership rather than as a romantic union.[29]

The young woman responded to Gurney's proposal of marriage with all the self-doubt and anxiety of a true evangelical, addressing precisely the issue he regarded as most important. Although she had "considered prayerfully," she still entertained one "chief trouble," admitting she was "afraid I am not qual- ified for the station a ministers wife has to occupy." She assured him that the Lord had called her to be useful and hoped that the two of them would be "guided by the Divine Spirit in this matter." Gurney accepted the sincerity of her vocation and tried again to reassure her that their mutual calling would eventually beget both a spiritual and worldly union. "In religion as in every thing else we shall assimilate to each other," he promised her. But Gurney could only imagine their marital relationship as a reflection of a pastoral re- lationship. "I shall be as you are & you as I am—like wife like minister—like minister like wife—like pastor like people—like people like pastor." Just as pastor and people grow in grace and learn to love each other, he surmised, so do a husband and wife. Perhaps his simile reassured his bride-to-be that at least Christian love and affection would grace their marriage, even if a physical attraction and romantic love did not. In any case, he confirmed that a spiritual and personal intimacy characterized both the ideal pastoral marriage and the ideal pastoral relationship.[30]

The case of George Moore, a Unitarian student at Harvard Divinity School, inadvertently reveals how a novice pastor's primary commitment to his voca- tion and apparent indifference to romantic affection seriously impaired both his personal life and his professional life. After a lengthy courtship and engagement to a likely young woman named Elizabeth, Moore recorded the painful news that his fiancée had canceled their wedding plans because of the "want of affectionate tenderness in my nature, which was necessary to her happiness." Just as Edward Gurney had promised his fiancée that their love would grow out of their shared Christian commitment, so did Moore's fiancée entertain hopes that his reserve "would upon intimate acquaintance only become the more open and frank." Her hopes remained unrealized, however. "She now feels," he wrote sadly, "that this reserve is a part of my nature, and that it cannot be changed—and that my disposition cannot be changed, so that she never can understand me." For Moore's intended bride, the prospects for future usefulness as a pastor's wife did not outweigh the probable lack of physical and emotional warmth and intimacy in their marriage.[31]

Moore agonized over the reasons for his fiancée's defection and the implications for his personal life as well as his professional life. He accepted Elizabeth's decision as God's providence and did little to examine his own actions or understand the woman's needs and desires. Instead, he found fault with her, projecting his own reticence onto her behavior. He believed she "herself did not manifest those tender attentions that I would be glad to receive from so loved an object, and this very feeling in me has sometimes put me under restraint when with her—so that perhaps what she thinks she has observed in me is only the reflection of herself." In addition, Moore explained his self-restraint as a fear that he might insult the pious young woman. He assumed that "she did not require these manifestations of affection that some might, but that they would be rather offensive to her." Thus, the mutual reserve that pastoral manual writers insisted was so necessary in courtship between a minister and a woman actually destroyed Moore's chances for the intimacy he craved. Finally, he blamed the young woman for misreading his actions, another problem of which pastoral writers warned him. Once he had cut short a vacation visit to her, in "haste to resume the studies of my class." But Elizabeth had not appreciated his commitment to the seminary over her. He had "supposed she would regard it as a sacrifice and only love me the more for it," but instead she had resented his conscientious attention to duty instead of to her. He rationalized his inability to share his feelings with her, assuming that "my actions would certainly speak out my regret at leaving her more than any words could." Only weeks later did Moore admit to himself that he had taken Elizabeth for granted and might have worked harder to retain her affections. After much petulant self-pity and reflection on the failed courtship, Moore unexpectedly changed his career course: He took a private vow of celibacy and planned a missionary career on the Illinois frontier.[32]

Moore's painful problems in communicating and empathizing with women in his private life paralleled those he experienced in his pastoral career. As a divinity student, he rarely addressed the topic of women in his journals, but when he did it was with a note of disdain. He confirmed his allegiance to the ideology of separate spheres and his opposition to talk of women's rights by agreeing with Horace Mann who wrote that a woman's "striving to raise herself to equality with man is degrading. Her sphere is as high as man's, if not higher." "If she would but see her sphere in proper light," he remonstrated, "she would stop complaining about being degraded by man." Even though Moore subscribed to a liberal Christian doctrine that espoused spiritual equality and salvation for all, he resisted applying such radical tenets to a temporal society. And even though historian Ann Douglas discovered an "uneasy alliance" between liberal clergymen and women, Moore made no special effort to cultivate a spiritual or social association with women. While still in school, he attended a meeting of a "Ladies Society" and recorded it as a social affair rather than a benevolent mission. "It was a rather amusing assemblage," he confessed, "if one were inclined to make sport of it." Although the experience impressed him as "pleasant," Moore tried to remind himself that such duties were not trivial but constituted a necessary part of pastoral work. "It is well for one occasionally to meet a multitude and exchange a passing salutation," he rationalized about his attendance. Moore revealed at best an indifference to women and at worst a quiet contempt for them and a dismissal of their work. His seminary education had instilled in him some sense of duty to women but one that was limited to promulgating the concept of separate spheres and maintaining a polite, if bemused, acquaintance with them and their activities.[33]

Even after Moore accepted his first pastorate on the eastern bank of the Mississippi River, his uncomfortable and distant relations with women interfered with his ability to feel successful in his pastoral work. He assumed their presence but had difficulty in understanding and reaching out to them. Moore took a special pride in his sermons and the intellectual culture he brought from Cambridge, Massachusetts, to his frontier parish, but he often expressed disappointment in his work, especially with women. When he attempted to write a series of sermons on biblical women and their role in Christianity, he suffered an unusual writer's block and failed to complete the series. Though Moore accepted five times as many women as men into his church and recorded visits to many families, he never explicitly acknowledged women as the most significant segment of his parishioners.[34]

Moore's diary recorded a good number of visits to women, but only his conversations with men received any detailed attention. When he mentioned visits with women, he usually registered the benefit to himself rather than to the women he served. The women acted as mirrors for Moore, reflecting and magnifying his good work back to him. For example, he was "grateful" to a woman who complimented his sermons just when he had despaired of their effectiveness. In a visit to a dying thirteen-year-old girl, Moore tried to converse with her, but she was too sick to speak beyond a brief whisper. Still, Moore spoke to the desperately ill child for quite some time, "a rambling talk about death, and the importance of [Christian] faith." Moore had no idea whether his speech comforted the girl but assumed from her placid countenance that she was at peace. "For myself I enjoyed it very much," he wrote cheerfully, "and I hope I comforted her. I prayed with her—And I know not when I have enjoyed an hour of greater satisfaction to myself than this." In a similar visit to a "feeble old lady," Moore conducted another one-sided religious conversation for nearly an hour. She "seemed pleased and edified," he noted hopefully. But Moore confessed that he had trouble judging his "effect" on the sick and helpless, although the "effect on myself is very good. In my conversations I am often surprised at the ease and fluency with wh[ich] I talk. I say many things that I have never thought of before—that seem to be suggested at the moment—that come fresh from the fountain of truth." The weakest and most pious females proved to be his best-loved parishioners, but mainly because they served as his sounding board, helping him to hear his own voice if not theirs. He never recorded a mutual exchange of ideas or even a question-and-answer dialogue with these women. Yet, as quiet, docile, and apparently receptive listeners, they bestowed an invaluable gift on their pastor: He received a feeling of contentment, satisfaction, and fulfillment, whether or not he had successfully met their spiritual needs.[35]

Only the most vulnerable and defenseless women received Moore's attention and approbation. For the most part, they elicited his pity, sympathy, and spiritual instruction, although he occasionally reported extending them some temporal help as well. Stronger or more self-sufficient women, however, elicited his disappointment and annoyance. Several times Moore noted visits to Mrs. Case, a poor woman who attended his services regularly, even though she was a member of an Episcopal church. Moore admired her perseverance and faith through innumerable hardships: Two of her children died, and her husband remained back in New York, imprisoned at Sing-Sing. "Nothing but true faith could have sustained her in those trials," he marveled. Once again, Moore recorded the benefit he received from visiting Mrs. Case. "I feel grateful that I am permitted to witness such spectacles, which angels would be glad to behold. It does me good," he wrote with satisfaction. Nowhere, however, does Moore record any benefit he might have brought to Mrs. Case. His unbounded admiration for the afflicted woman's "true faith" quickly turned to dismay, however, when he learned that she had sought spiritual comfort in the Church of Latter-Day Saints. Most especially, he lamented the fact that Mrs. Case had never consulted him or any of her pious friends on her momentous decision to take up with the Mormons. When he challenged her judgment and attempted to dissuade her, she asserted, "I take no counsel of flesh and blood, but of my Father in heaven." This statement Moore dismissed as the "reply of fanaticism." "She has a mind easily biassed," he now reasoned, and he revised his earlier perceptions of her fortitude, faith, common sense, and intelligence. As before, Moore never assessed his own responsibility for Mrs. Case's conversion to the Mormon church and never asked himself whether he had taken the poor woman for granted. Likewise, he never recorded any temporal or spiritual help he had offered the woman that might have prevented her defection to Mormonism. No doubt one of the attractions of Mormonism for Mrs. Case was its strong patriarchal structure, one that may have provided her the male protection and support she so obviously and painfully lacked within her family and her church. Moore quit visiting Mrs. Case, but on her death over a year later, he attended the funeral service presided over by a Mormon elder. She "remained a good and true Christian," he charitably admitted then, despite her deluded profession of Mormonism.[36]

Moore initially experienced success in attracting members to his new church but could not sustain his early achievements. The problems Moore encountered with women undoubtedly contributed to his increasing discouragement in the ministry. He began to question his effectiveness and, in the fourth year of his pastorate, looked inward for the source of his inadequacy. At that time, he concluded that some of his failure might be caused by his "living more in the intellect than in the affections." "A minister," he reflected, "can never succeed in his sacred office in making men [sic] Christians unless he has a large heart. He may dazzle by his intellect, and convince by his arguments, but he cannot deeply affect the hearts of men unless his own heart is softened, subdued, affectionate." Moore eventually traced the failure of his ministry to the very same factors that his disappointed fiancée had blamed for the failure of their engagement. He had left Harvard Divinity School with the qualities most valued by his profession—the ability to engage in theological debate with scholarly erudition. But he had never developed the personal and empathetic manners and methods in his pastoral work that might have complemented his preaching and ensured his success.[37]

Although Moore chastised himself for failing with "men," the generic term he used for the people in his congregation, he sought the solution to his pastoral problems in marriage. "Perhaps my greatest want, at the present time," he determined, "is a companion for life." A wife, he reasoned, might help him develop the empathy and affection that would strengthen his pastoral mission. "If I had such an one, a meet one," he reflected, "I can readily conceive how my affections would grow, and thus how my usefulness would be extended." Moore hoped a wife might ameliorate both his personal loneliness and professional inadequacies, serving him as a confessor and pastoral advisor. "Oh, that I had some one," he mourned, "at such a time as this—when I feel that I have failed in my duty—to whom I could open my heart, and from whom I might receive sympathy! I have no one unto whom I ever venture to speak of my Services in the church—no one in whom I have full confidence." Although Moore craved a connection with a woman, his cold and aloof manner still inhibited his search for the "meet" one. "I have at times lifted the veil, and permitted some to obtain a glimpse of my heart," he confessed, "but not to enter the holy of holies." Abdicating responsibility for resolving his pastoral problems, Moore remained strangely passive and continued to rely on providence to supply an answer. "I pray heaven that such an one may be sent erelong—a friend unto whom I can open my heart of hearts."[38]

Moore claimed he wanted a wife to help him develop his affections because his cold intellectualism failed to serve the "men" in his congregation. It seems more likely, however, that the women in his congregation, just like his fiancée, found his impersonal manner ineffective in his pastoral work. Moore desired a wife not merely to help him be more effective but also to serve him as his own personal, sympathetic, and tender pastor, to give him the affection he failed to give others. Moore's liberal Unitarian theology—just the "feminized" or softened doctrine that Ann Douglas claimed appealed most to women— was no guarantee of success by itself. He still lacked an empathy and special concern for women that might have helped him deliver a more effective message to the majority of his church. The personal qualities that crippled his pastorate—his inexperience, loneliness, emotional reserve, and self-centeredness—were not his alone. He shared them with other young men in the ministry, regardless of their denomination. Moore and other pastors specifically sought a distaff partner to serve as his shepherd's staff, the necessary support in his pastoral duties. At the least, she would perform the essentially feminine task of caring for and nurturing him and helping him to develop the necessary feminine empathy to effectively reach the female portion of his flock. At best, however, she would also undertake the same mission as himself: the pastoral care of his congregation, especially its female majority.

Although young and inexperienced pastors recorded painful encounters with women in their ministry and actively sought or prayed for a female helpmeet, more experienced pastors rarely divulged the problems of gender difference in the pastorate. They rarely included the same lengthy and reflective entries found in the records of novice pastors; at most, they merely recorded the names and dates of pastoral visits. When veteran pastors provided more information, terse remarks usually sufficed. Occasionally, they recorded hope for an anxious potential convert or joy for a new admission, and, as usual, most of these were women. Yet between these brief but positive entries appeared those that registered annoyance, frustration, and discontent in the relation between the pastor and the women in his congregation. Elisha Cleaveland, pastor of a New Haven church, recorded an unsatisfactory conversation with a woman who claimed she no longer attended his services "because the church did not call on her while she was confined with lameness." Cleaveland took no responsibility for the pastoral oversight. Instead, he pointed out to the woman her "pride & wickedness" and argued with her over the doctrines of the Methodist church, to which she had turned because of his neglect. Elias Nason's pastoral records generally described pleasant relationships with his female parishioners, but he registered annoyance and pain when one of them treated him "cooly and cavalierly." Clearly, even the most successful veteran pastor failed to please all his female parishioners.[39]

Likewise, neither marriage nor experience protected veteran clergymen from imputations of sexual indiscretion. Of course, young bachelor George Moore was alarmed to learn that a young woman had been punished with excommunication from her church because Moore had served as her escort on a brief journey. But Elisha Cleaveland, who sometimes made pastoral calls with his wife and young child in tow, did not escape rumors and angry charges, either. An enraged man accused Cleaveland of showing a "peculiar interest" in his unmarried sister, a charge the minister emphatically denied. Instead, Cleaveland blamed another woman for the spurious charges, claiming "Mrs. F.," the author of the rumor, had falsely impugned his character. Even the well-known evangelists Asahel Nettleton, a lifelong bachelor, and Charles Finney, married to a woman very helpful to his mission, endured unsubstantiated charges of sexual impropriety.[40]

No wonder, then, that Finney emphasized the necessity of marriage for his theology students. His own experiences as a pastor taught him that a close, even physically intimate relationship with both men and women encouraged them to confess their wickedness and accept God's grace and to undergo a more forceful and immediate conversion. But Finney also knew through personal experience that a wife might extend and strengthen a pastor's influence among women by serving as his surrogate pastor. On his evangelical campaigns in the United States and Great Britain, Elizabeth Finney led women's prayer groups and anxious meetings that attracted hundreds of mostly female listeners. She served as his intermediary and relieved him of some of the burden and danger of the personal counsel to women he had offered in the past. Elizabeth also assisted her husband by providing him with personal and professional advice. To his credit, Finney's seminary at Oberlin allowed women to enroll not just in college courses but in theology classes as well so that they might be better qualified for the work of a Sunday school teacher, pastor's wife, or missionary. But Finney and most of his clerical peers refused to consider the ordination of women as pastors in their own right.[41]

Pastoral manuals warned of conflicts with parishioners, and the journals of pastors in the field reveal that they experienced a variety of problems in their work. Just as the manuals warned, the journals demonstrate that the most acute hazards of pastoral work came in working with women. Ministers' journals confirm that women made up the majority of their church members and that the majority of pastoral visits were to women. However, no evidence in these case studies shows that any clergyman developed a special interest in women and their spiritual needs. Instead, the private records of pastors' experiences reveal a relationship at odds with perceptions of either an uneasy alliance or a too-intimate association between clergy and women. In some cases, clergy were deeply troubled by their ineffective proselytizing and dismissed as irrational those women who argued with them. Likewise, clergy quickly retreated from women they considered threatening or corrupt. Similarly, they maintained a safe distance from women, especially the young, who seemed uncomfortable with the sexual tension between them, urging them to seek pastoral counseling from their sisters. Finally, they felt comfortable and successful only with the weakest, most passive, and vulnerable women in their care. To maintain his shaky equilibrium, the unsteady pastor maintained a wary distance from the female portion of his flock. He might safely take charge of the weakest and most vulnerable women, but to be safe, he found a "fit" wife, culled the females from his flock, and turned them over to his distaff partner. In sum, the nineteenth-century clergy's mission to women, viewed from the perspective of novice and veteran pastors alike, seems more distant, troubled, and ineffective than the contemporary and historiographical perceptions of dangerous intimacy. The view from the women's perspective, as we shall see in the next chapter, only reinforces that contrasting portrait of the pastoral relationship.

7

Sheep without a Shepherd; or, What Women Experienced

In 1852, Abigail Price addressed the Syracuse National Woman's Rights Convention in a pointed protest against the clergy. She objected not merely to the fact that the profession excluded women but, more particularly, to the male clergy's inherent inability to serve women's spiritual needs. Speaking to the relatively few proponents of women's rights only four years after the Declaration of Sentiments issued at Seneca Falls, New York, Price's angry attack on the clergy's ineffectual mission to women was radical and unusual for its time. Yet she grounded her arguments for women's dissatisfaction with the church on traditional masculine sources of authority— theology, natural law, and political philosophy. All churches, she asserted, prohibited women's exercise of their God-given rights. She drew on both Old and New Testament sources to show how the Christian church denied the sexual equality promised by scripture. She argued that Christ had "mingled" both the natural masculine *and* feminine elements of humanity in his person and that his church ought to strive to do the same. Women suffered because the male leaders of the churches, both clergy and laity, denied them any legal representation and also because, most unfairly, the Christian clergy ignored and denigrated the very source of their most obvious support. "The poor young men that she [the Christian woman] often educates by toil early and late," Price protested, referring to women's charitable efforts to support indigent seminarians, "teach her, when properly prepared, that this absurd tyranny [of men over women in the church] is supported by the word of God!" Price believed the clergy cruelly betrayed women in the church.[1]

Price objected to the unfulfilled promise of gender equality in the church and the male monopoly of the clergy on the grounds that men and women differed because of their varied experiences, not because of any essentialist biological distinctions. "Every class of society, and especially each sex need religious teachers of their own class and sex," she argued, "having the same experience, the same hopes, aims and relations." Mere "intellectual instruction" failed to satisfy the needs of all human minds, she asserted. Individuals required the "strength imparted by an earnest sympathy born of a like experience."

> In order rightly to appreciate the wants of others, we must know and realize the trials of their situation, the struggles they may encounter, the burthens, the toils, the temptations that beset their different relations. These should be apprehended to some extent, and the more the better by the person qualified to speak to the spiritual wants of all. Each relation, therefore, needs its teacher—its peculiar ministry.

A man ministering to women could hardly compensate for his lack of feminine experience with his education. In fact, it might handicap him even more. "No one can demonstrate by college lore the weight of a mother's responsibility," she declared. "No man, not even the kindest father" could understand a mother's anxieties and fears. "Man may prepare sound and logical discourses; he may clearly define the mother's duty; he may talk eloquently about her responsibility," she contended, but still a mother would hear the "good instruction" and think to herself, "*You* cannot *know* of what you are talking." Rather than the "power of mind," pastors required "the zeal and inspiration of the inner life; the unction of love and faith and courage produced by a struggle amid life's realities." No college-educated scholar and theologian could match the sense and sensibility of a woman, Price implied, because women, and especially mothers, lived closer to and better understood the real issues of spiritual life. Women, she also hinted, might not be better teachers merely for other women but for men as well. "Not the dreamer," she insisted, "but the toiler can best affect the lives of others through their hearts." In short, Price believed the male clergy failed to give women—the overwhelming majority of their churches—the spiritual support and guidance they deserved. Women were, to extend the metaphor, sheep without an appropriate shepherd. They required shepherds of their own sex.[2]

Price's unrestrained indignation at the clergy's ingratitude, effrontery, perfidy, and incompetence regarding women in the church, while an admittedly radical position, expressed a general discontent and dissatisfaction among the silent majority of her sisters in the church. While Price articulately drew on the clergy's own intellectual resources of theology and philosophy to justify women's claims to equality, she also tapped into a huge reservoir of women's largely unvoiced discontent by appealing to their unmet need for clerical empathy and guidance. Many of Price's contemporaries feared and believed that the clergy catered to women and that women responded with inordinate adulation. Price, in contrast, argued that the clergyman's emphasis on scholarship and his experience as a man—not a woman—distanced him from the concerns of real people, but especially from the lives of women, his largest constituency. Women's private records and correspondence, like those of contemporary pastors, support Price's contention that distance rather than dangerous intimacy generally characterized the pastoral relationship between clergy and women. A broad range of ordinary women expressed a dissatisfaction with preachers and pastors uncannily similar to that of Abigail Price. They suffered from a distressing distance between themselves and their pastors based on a number of spiritual, social, and cultural factors that the women themselves could not always identify. In the case studies offered here, one woman saw her pastors as nearly divine and infallible, as difficult to approach as a stern and transcendent Calvinist God. Other women, however, generally viewed the pastor as a man—a fallible creature subject to human foibles like themselves. These women thus saw ministers as merely human, closer to themselves than a socially and spiritually transcendent divine, yet many continued to experience distance between themselves and their pastors. Instead, they saw ministers as men with masculine shortcomings who shared few of their feminine concerns. Some also experienced gender difference as the distraction of romantic or sexual attraction. A disturbing element of the pastoral relationship that could be both appealing and uncomfortable at the same time, the confusion between sensual love and spiritual love marked only a very few of the women in this sample. Instead, a frustration and failure based on distance rather than affinity characterized many of these relationships. Whether speaking from the pulpit to a collective and diverse audience or meeting his parishioners face-to-face in small groups or as individuals, ministers often failed to offer women the spiritual nourishment and guidance they sought from their teachers.[3]

Seeing God in the Pulpit

Of the more than thirty women included in this study, only one viewed her pastor with the uncritical adulation so often depicted and feared by her nineteenth-century contemporaries. Sally Bliss, as her surname so aptly suggests, experienced real, though sometimes painful, pleasure and satisfaction under the preaching of many pastors over her long life. Bliss experienced conversion during a revival led by the Rev. Asahel Nettleton sometime before she began her spiritual diary in 1823 as a mature woman of thirty-one. She rarely recorded the minutiae of her everyday life or her personal relationships with family and friends in the small volume she kept for the next fifty years. A barely literate woman, she nevertheless regularly registered commentary on the preaching she attended during numerous religious meetings—Sabbath sermons, anxious meetings, revivals, and lectures by visiting speakers. Although other women in this study reported they heard a "good sermon" on occasion, Bliss did so much more frequently. Much less often, she provided some details of her response to a particularly moving lecture. In the first year of entries, she admitted to her diary that "the preaching was more close then I could bare but it was the truth but my stubborn heart is so hard but it is easy for God to forgive if I could but come to him." Her use of the word *but* four times in this one tortured sentence reveals her confusion and inner conflict. The preaching was "more close" than she could "bare," her misspelling of this last word perhaps a clue that the preacher had achieved an uncomfortable intimacy with her soul. Bliss failed to respond, however, by drawing closer to her God. Despite the minister's offer of God's forgiveness, her stubborn heart refused to "come to him." Given the orthodox Calvinism that Bliss espoused, the sermon's painful "truth" was what she needed if not what she wanted; her failure to respond was no shortcoming on the part of the preacher but instead the fault of her own stubborn heart.[4]

Bliss recorded joy when preachers pleased her, sorrow and regret when her favorite pastors were absent, dismissed, or died. The only overt criticism she ever expressed came after a visiting preacher replaced her own. "Mr. Brown being sick Mr. Gillet did preach the second of Kings 8 11 A good sermon but A poor voice." When her pastor returned to the pulpit six weeks later, she rejoiced, "O how good it was to hear his voice once more." Bliss lamented the preacher's physical defect—a poor voice—because it failed as the medium for the solemn and important message of God's Word. She expected and frequently heard God's voice speaking directly to her through his ministers. "It appeared to me," she wrote, "that the spirit of god attended Mr. Foots prayer or that the holy gost did help him to pray I hope I shall live more faithful for I believe that those men were sent her[e] by God." Bliss understood the role of the pastor as a literal messenger from God, the physical medium through which God spoke. When she learned that her "beloved pastor" Mr. Brown was leaving the church, she felt bereft. "I think if he should go the people will be in A poor state Oh the gloom that is on my mind." Without a shepherd, Bliss felt spiritually lost.[5]

Her pastor's absence signaled God's absence to Bliss. "I feel as if [Mr. Brown] was gone from us here and if God does not appear for us soon we shall sink," she mourned. She blamed both herself and her fellow parishioners for God's leaving. "But if all the church are as unfaithfull as I am no wonder if God should give us up." When the church elders finally dismissed Mr. Brown, Bliss sharpened her grief and her censure. "I think it is woe to him by whom this took place," she wrote with reproach. "If the church did but know their condition they were left in it appears to me they would repent and be humble left without A minister." Clearly, Bliss took the pastor's side in the dispute with his male congregants and viewed their rejection of a good preacher as a rejection of God himself. When several new candidates preached, Bliss admired their sermons and marveled at God's mercy to her and her sinful church. "Oh what A wonder that God should send such a man here for we are so wiked A people and have abused so much good preaching," she remarked after one man's sermon. "It appears to me that God has sent that Godly man to this place," she asserted after another. She waited for God's permanent presence to return, praying, "How it doth fill me with wonder to think that the doors have once more been opened at the house of God Oh God do appear for us."[6]

Sally Bliss's relationship with her pastor mirrored her relationship with her God. She loved both with a mixture of awe and fear and from a distance she found difficult to close. She identified her pastor so nearly with her God that she personalized the deity in the man: He was "a Godly man." For Bliss, the minister served as an ambassador of Christ who, as his personal emissary, deserved obedience from the congregation. She feared that an angry God intervened directly to punish their disobedience and watched for signs of divinity in the pulpit. Just as she experienced difficulty in coming to her God, she experienced a similar social and spiritual distance from her pastor. She never recorded a personal conversation *with* any of her pastors, although she did record a meeting with one of the male elders *about* the pastor.

This curious absence of reports of pastoral visits suggests that Bliss found sources of more intimate spiritual counsel elsewhere. Perhaps she and other women collectively received attention from their pastor or from each other in the female prayer meeting she reported attending, although she never commented on his presence there. In the only reference to individual spiritual guidance, Bliss noted gratefully, "Mrs. Mather was here what good advice she gave me I hope I shall live more faithful then I have done I hope I shall not fear to speak for christ." Even in periods of deepest distress, when she struggled to accept her childlessness and even contemplated suicide because of it, or later when her husband died, she apparently never sought or benefited from her pastor's counsel. Thus, despite her epithets of "beloved pastor" and her frequent commendations for "good sermons," Sally Bliss's spiritual diary gives no evidence of a close relationship between her and her pastor or of a pastor's special ministry to women.[7]

Certainly Bliss's orthodox Calvinism, with its conception of a distant and often angry God, might have contributed to a distant relationship with her pastor. Indeed, historians have argued that women in the nineteenth century increasingly rejected orthodox Calvinism because of its harsh legality and instead embraced more evangelical and liberal creeds that emphasized God's love and mercy over his judgment. Likewise, Bliss may have adhered to older, hierarchical social norms that demanded deference from social inferiors to superiors; she probably resisted the democratizing and leveling social forces that would permit her to more easily approach a minister for individual spiritual support. In addition, although she never articulated gender difference as a problem, Bliss may have been reluctant to bring such peculiarly feminine problems as childlessness and widowhood to her male pastor. Perhaps, like Abigail Price a generation later, she despaired that he could understand her hopelessness.

The case of Sally Bliss provides a useful foil for understanding women's perspective on the pastoral relationship. Most other women in this study revealed little of the reverence and awe she exhibited toward her pastors. Perhaps more heavily influenced by the democratizing forces of evangelical religious movements or of Jacksonian politics, other women, unlike Bliss, saw their pastors as *men* rather than as godlike divines. They responded to preachers and pastors as *men* not only in the sense of being human or "other" than God but also in the sense of being male or "other" than themselves. This conscious-ness of pastors as *men* had the paradoxical effect of allowing women to feel at the same time both closer to and more distant from their pastors. By recog-nizing their shared humanity, women experienced a social and spiritual equal-ity with pastors that offered them the potential for a closer, more intimate relationship yet also allowed them the opportunity to evaluate and criticize those pastors. Still, despite this apparent reduction in the social distance be-tween women and pastors, women could not ignore the separation imposed by gender difference and gender ideals. By recognizing, however dimly, their pastors' masculine identity, women experienced a social distance that inhibited or prohibited the formation of more constructive spiritual relationships with male clergy. Sally Bliss might have fulfilled the role of ideal female parish-ioner—granting her pastor unconditional reverence and attention while mak-ing few if any demands on him for individual attention—yet few other women in this study did so. Most exhibited a critical view of clergy that more nearly resembled Abigail Price's resentment. Few ministers, according to these same women, fulfilled the role of ideal pastor by offering the collective and individ-ualized ministry to women that pastoral manuals had hoped to inculcate.

Seeing Mortal Men in the Pulpit

Whether girls or mature matrons, women failed to exhibit the reverence for their pastors that Sally Bliss did, even when they admired his sermons. Positive appraisals of pastors appear scattered throughout women's writings, yet even their compliments imply that negative evaluations might have been made instead. Schoolgirls often dutifully reported "excellent sermons" and the benefits they offered. After hearing "two very interesting sermons today," young Hannah Cabot in the 1830s wrote, "Oh Mother if I do not come back to you a better person, it will be my own fault, for everything here tends to produce that effect." Cabot, like Bliss, credited the minister for an effective sermon while holding herself responsible for becoming "a better person." Yet she terms the sermons merely "interesting," rather than "more close" than she could bear. They lack the palpable power of God's presence that Bliss experi-enced under her pastor's preaching. Similarly, young Helen Hart told her diary that she looked forward to hearing "some good preaching" on a trip to visit relatives, implying that good preaching made a change from her usual fare. Though both girls praised the preachers, they assumed the role of competent judges in evaluating a sermon. They knew the difference between good and poor preaching. Not all shepherds were equally fit representatives of God. While they might admire a preacher, they did not revere him.[8]

Despite their youth, even schoolgirls failed to view preachers with awe or esteem. Young Ann Stoddard, a Freewill Baptist in rural Vermont in 1866, admired good preaching. "Elder Heath preached very good," she noted, "a number of very good exhortations." She especially liked a relative's efforts, judging "Uncles preaching the best." But Stoddard's admiration for good preaching fell far short of veneration for those who delivered it. When her grandfather and Uncle Moses took off for the yearly Baptist meeting, Stoddard recorded with relief, "I was Heartily glad to see their back sides." Another girl expressed scorn for her nominal spiritual leaders. "Lissie Weld's brother preached," wrote twelve-year-old Elizabeth Dana. "I do not like him very much." She preferred Mr. Mills, wishing "we could have him oftener he makes such nice sermons." These young girls, as family members and acquaintances of the clergymen they heard, may have experienced a familiarity that bred contempt. But the reduced social distance that allowed these girls to privately express their irreverence for clergymen also characterized relationships between women and pastors outside family and friendships.[9]

Women's ability to see preachers and pastors as mortals, creatures with human limitations similar to their own, did not necessarily imply criticism. Indeed, it almost certainly had some positive implications for the pastoral relationship. Women could view clergymen as exceptional human beings who, through their own extraordinary efforts rather than divine intervention, more nearly lived up to Christian ideals than their fellow men. As potential spiritual peers, women could strive to emulate clergymen as spiritual exemplars. Two young women, Frances Kingman and Frances Quick, viewed preachers and pastors as role models for their own work as schoolteachers. Unlike Sally Bliss, however, they ascribed a good sermon—or "interesting discourse," as Kingman often termed it—to the preacher's method rather than to heavenly inspiration. Kingman recorded admiration for a Mr. Smith on several occasions, remarking that "the manner in which he treated his subject was truly calculated to make us feel our weakness & sufficiency, & to feel more deeply the power and greatness of him who governs all things." Kingman took away the same orthodox theology from this lesson—the portrait of an omnipotent God—as Bliss did from her preachers, but Kingman acknowledged that the power of the Word was "calculated," a direct result of the preacher's "manner" rather than the presence of the "holy gost." She credited the man's talent and expertise in shaping and presenting the Word, rather than the power of God or of the Word itself.[10]

Women expressed admiration for a pastor even when they understood that his own humble efforts and not God's immediate intervention produced an eloquent and effective sermon. Frances Quick recognized the skill and labor required to produce a good sermon and expected and hoped to feel God's presence, even if it was only a rhetorical illusion. She admired one preacher, she reported, who "spoke solemnly *as if* the word was hid in his heart, and God's commission was in his heart, and the great work and eternity was before him." Even though she doubted that this minister actually harbored the spirit within him, she liked to "hear a minister speak *as if* the word within him was a fire in his bones, compelling outward manifestation of the inward stirring of the soul." In other words, Quick hoped that the minister's manner, if properly cultivated, or "calculated" as Kingman had put it, would produce at least an impression of God's inspiration.[11]

Frances Quick recognized her pastor's ability to sound inspired and also his capacity to teach effectively. She gratefully admired a sermon that "unravelled some confused thought which I have had with regard to the truth." She liked the "system" her pastor introduced in prayer meetings: He assigned a topic for discussion and directed participants' attention to "one object of thought." Her training in pedagogy at the normal school in Framingham, Massachusetts, taught Quick to recognize and appreciate the pastor's teaching methods. Quick admired her minister's manner as well as his method, recognizing that they combined to make him an unusually effective pastor. After a visit from Mr. Allen and his wife, Quick noted her pleasure "with their free sociality; certainly a most desirable quality in the pastoral labors." By recognizing that his manner and method, not God, accounted for his efficacy, she could take them as a model for her own teaching.[12]

Although Quick and other women recorded observations and positive responses to their pastors' manners and methods, acknowledging the constructed nature of God's word rather than its revelation, they responded most appreciatively to a sermon's substance—its doctrine and interpretation of scripture. Yet just as women realized that the "manner" of delivery was a product of the man, they also recognized the "man-made" quality of theology. They approved of a preacher's sermon only if his views accorded with their own views. Sarah Dana greatly admired Horace Bushnell for his "sober" and "rational" style of preaching, but what Dana most liked was the substance of Bushnell's sermon rather than its delivery. "His ideas on the cultivation of the powers," she affirmed, "coincided with my own." Significantly, young Dana approved of Bushnell's sermon not because he had taught her something new but because he had reinforced opinions she had already developed for herself. Sarah Dana's comments reveal a young woman confident not only of her ability to appraise the clergy but also of her ability to make judgments about theology and philosophy independent of a pastor's teaching. She employed her own intellectual criteria in assessing the content of a sermon. She also tried to assess a sermon's effect on listeners other than herself. Dana claimed that "the principal fault" of a Mr. Peabody's preaching was that "he speaks to the mass not to individuals." She condemned the substance of his sermon precisely because he discounted the ability of individuals to come to differing interpretations and hold differing theological tenets. "He endeavours to make his congregation feel that they are a poor, persecuted people, pointed out by all as heretics, merely because they are not a *set of blind bigots*—and he succeeds," she protested. She tried to "select . . . the evangelical parts" from his sermon but derived very little "individual profit" from the experience. Dana accepted little responsibility for the failure of the sermon—the preacher himself was to blame. She also reveals that she experienced a frustrating distance between herself and her teacher. When a preacher's theology did not accord with her own, she failed to feel that he was communicating to her as an individual.[13]

Women who judged a sermon by the conformity of the preacher's theology to their own saw a man constructing his own interpretation of scripture from the pulpit. That perception allowed women to choose from among a variety of doctrines the ones that "coincided" with their own views. Frances Quick admired "pungent, positive sermons" delivered with "solemn, weighty and beautiful speech," but she also demanded "sound doctrine." Quick, like Dana, judged that doctrine by its "correspondence in my own thoughts."[14] Both Dana and Quick conducted a quest for ideas that "coincided" with their own in a competitive religious atmosphere, one that fostered tremendous expansion of well-established denominations and also creativity and growth in numerous new sects. Though Quick favored an orthodox evangelicalism and Dana a latitudinarian theology—the liberal view that some historians have argued appealed to women more than orthodoxy—both searched for "correspondence" with their own thoughts because they listened to preachers espousing dozens of different doctrines. Even loyalty to or membership in one congregation, parish, or denomination did not confine women to the preaching of one man or one theology. Women regularly visited other churches in their own towns or away from home. At the same time, they heard lectures and sermons from preachers visiting their own churches. This pluralist religious atmosphere encouraged the independence of religious thought revealed in women's writing and encouraged their critical appraisal of competing doctrinal interpretations served up by various preachers. But in many ways, it also discouraged women who listened to what sometimes seemed like endless theological posturing and wrangling. The same religious competition that fostered the growth of theological seminaries and, within those institutions, the emphasis on controversial theology, contributed to the discontent that many women expressed about the clergy in their private diaries and correspondence.[15]

Because women failed to see God attending and inspiring the preacher's efforts and instead saw a man contending with other men in a competitive religious arena, women could criticize preachers for what they saw as a variety of faults. Too much or too little emotion, too much or too little learning, and too much or too little Calvinist orthodoxy all earned women's opprobrium. Although few of their criticisms reached the sophisticated level of feminist protest espoused by Abigail Price, many of their complaints targeted not just human failings but peculiarly masculine rather than feminine cultural vices. At times, their criticisms sounded inconsistent. Sarah Dana pronounced one preacher too "enthusiastic, 'raptur'ous & gesticulating" for her taste. Yet, while she faulted one preacher for his ebullience, she found another woefully lacking in passion. Of a Dr. Taylor, she asserted, "I cannot *like* the man however great his talents who has so much the appearance of display & preparedness of *mind* with so little heart . . . he is not the preacher suited to my own feelings."[16]

Clearly, Dana sought emotional moderation, but more important she and other women frequently objected to a preacher's intellectual pretentiousness. Dana condemned Mr. Samuel Osgood Wright for "quite a flouncy & somewhat egotistical discourse." When the minister had informed his audience of his "intention to go to Africa—that these walls would hear his voice no more &c.," he inspired her disgust rather than her admiration. Sarah Wetmore similarly discounted the efforts of a Mr. Danforth. She could summon only faint praise, remarking that "he labors as well as he knows how . . . he is sincere in his masters cause I believe." Wetmore believed that though the man was diligent and honest, he spoiled his preaching with his pompous speech. She complained that he "thinks much of his elegant sentences and well rounded periods—in giving out his appointments this afternoon for the week—he says—'on Thursday evening there will be simultaneous meetings in various parts of the Town.'" Her disdain for the man, his manner, and apparently his use of words with multiple syllables prevented her from according him the respect he should have enjoyed. "I try," she wrote, "but cannot treat him with anything more than cool civility." Rarely did women complain that a sermon was too intellectually challenging. But Angeline Morehouse admitted that one Sunday her pastor's "exposition . . . was too abstruse for me—it tired me to think about it." She, too, blamed the preacher and not herself. Instead of properly explicating the text, he merely "replied in passages of scripture similar to the text," she protested. Although carried away by his own presentation, he failed to bring his listeners with him. "He was much elated with his subject—& used some strong language," but the sermon's force was lost on Morehouse. These women, like the radical feminist Abigail Price, sometimes judged learning in preachers a disability rather than an asset and consciously distanced themselves from these men. As literate women, they understood the conventions of sermon writing and delivery but seemed to resent the manner in which these men flaunted their literary or seminary education, privileges not generally available to women of the time. They at least dimly acknowledged and resented the cultural barriers that gave the clergy a masculine monopoly on higher learning, even though their protests lacked a consciously feminist voice such as Price's.[17]

At the same time that they resented men for their educational advantages, women might easily resent ignorant or uneducated men who still earned authority, respect, and popularity by their membership in an exclusively male clerical fraternity. Sarah Wetmore heard the popular evangelist John Maffitt and could "unhesitatingly say his manner is pleasing." However, his sermons suffered from a "redundancy of metaphor." She suspected he lacked education and preparation: He was not a "man of many literary acquirements." Perhaps more damning, she believed he "did not read his Bible with sufficient care." Maffitt's popularity astonished Wetmore, who never considered that the simplicity of his words probably accounted for some of the large crowds he attracted. Alternatively, she failed to consider that God's presence may have attended Maffitt's efforts and explained his extraordinary success. Likewise, Wetmore never specifically noted that Maffit's good looks and virile masculinity, a source of controversy and litigation during his career, accounted for his "pleasing manner" and celebrity. Instead, she merely distanced herself from both the man and his admirers, counting herself a capable judge of Maffit's less than perfect preaching. She clearly saw a flawed and uninspired man struggling to deliver God's Word.[18]

Seeing a modestly endowed man in a position of religious authority allowed women to doubt not just the ability but the character of the man dispensing God's Word. Both implicitly and explicitly, women accused preachers of hypocrisy—of not living up to the principles they preached. Frances Quick was so acutely aware of a man, not God, in the pulpit that she frequently questioned his character and fitness for his position. Her distrust distracted and disappointed her. "I have thought often, when listening to some sermon, what is the character of him who delivers it?" She wondered, "Does his life correspond with his precepts?" Abigail Sewall, a middle-aged Maine farmwife, suffered similar doubts but expressed them in more pointed fashion. "There is more care in the preachers to secure the dollar," she grumbled, "than save the souls of their hearers." By accusing preachers of materialism, Sewall identified a value inconsistent with Christian teaching and thus a hypocritical position for a preacher. But she also pointed to another masculine privilege. Just as education was a privilege reserved mostly for men, so, too, was the accumulation of wealth. Since most women lacked access to wealth or the means to acquire it (other than marriage), they may have resented a male preacher's inordinate interest in money and his ability to accumulate it. The wife of a struggling farmer, Sewall certainly waged a lifelong struggle against poverty. In fact, she worked hard to encourage her daughter to get an education and to support herself rather than depend on a husband, advice the young woman followed. Finally, Sewall's contempt for some clergymen pointed out yet another peculiarly masculine shortcoming—lust. Drawing on denominational prejudices and perhaps perceptions from popular culture or her own experience, she implored her sister to "only think what lots of old Methodist ministers have run away with other men's wives." In the nineteenth century, the prevailing gender ideology labeled women as naturally chaste and pure. Men, more lustful by nature, required mothers to teach them sexual virtue and wives to help them maintain it. Like the exaggerated display of learning that some women accused preachers of exhibiting, the exaggerated pursuit of wealth or women constituted another subtle feminist condemnation of the clergy.[19]

Flawed manners, methods, and messages elicited criticism that betrays some of women's resentment of the male clergy. But the contentious spirit that too often accompanied interpretations and explanations of doctrine particularly offended women. These complaints constituted still another subtle feminist protest that linked women's perceptions of ministers as both men and males. The ability to see a man dispensing his own, sometimes flawed, interpretation from the pulpit allowed women to reject clerical teaching and propound dissenting views in the privacy of their diaries or their correspondence. Women chastised ministers for making very narrow interpretations, paying too much attention to fine points of doctrine, or fostering too much discord and debate among Christians. Abigail Sewall, especially, filled her letters to her sister with indictments of "such small stuff as we have to call preaching." She was not "very fond of going to hear such sectarian stuff as we have dealt out to us by such narrow contracted souls as pretend to labor in holy things when in fact they are only trying to build up their own creeds." Although Sewall occasionally looked forward to hearing a good sermon, she was often disappointed. A Baptist who preached at her church gave a "good free sermon, but in the afternoon he fixed in so much Calvanism that it spoiled it all." Another minister promised a "lecture to prove the immortality of the soul" but failed to deliver more than a brief introduction to the subject and left Sewall dissatisfied. Unlike other women who chastised themselves for inattention or a "hard heart," Sewall placed the blame for her dissatisfaction squarely on the men in the pulpit. She rarely heard "such preaching as I like" or, as she put it, "preaching of the right stamp." Good preaching emphasized the "doctrine of the final triumph of the Redeemer's kingdom . . . a subject all engrossing and interesting, and dear to the heart of every true christian and philanthropist." Sewall subscribed to the principles laid out in the Sermon on the Mount, which she believed contained all that was true Christianity. Everything else was "man-made doctrine," a reflection not of divine inspiration but of confused human minds. She deemed a number of preachers not merely hypocritical but foolish or wrong. She belittled their intellectual abilities, staying home one day from church "partly because the minister is such a numbhead." She disparaged another preacher, contemptuously noting his feeble attempts to "fire off his little big gun." Once again, Sewall's criticism identified another masculine shortcoming—competitiveness and combativeness. Her condemnation of the minister's impotent belligerence constituted one subtler but effective feminine (if not feminist) critique of his preaching.[20]

A faithful Calvinist, Frances Quick occupied the other end of the theological spectrum from Abby Sewall, who eventually espoused spiritualism. Nevertheless, both condemned preachers, rather than themselves, for their failure to derive spiritual benefit from sermons. Quick, as a schoolteacher, had admired some men's methods, but she easily found fault with them, too. She judged some sermons "indifferent" and others "inappropriate and unsatisfying." As an orthodox believer, she chafed at ambiguity in a sermon. Some preachers failed to say enough or so qualified their statements that they left listeners to "draw double inferences," she complained. In some instances, she disagreed with a preacher's tenets rather than his presentation. After one preacher delivered a sermon on "Ministering Angels," she objected in the privacy of her diary to his argument. "I doubt the *constant* ministry of angels on this earth," she wrote, and asserted instead that "the Holy Spirit is our helper here." Yet, despite disagreeing with preachers in private, Quick, like Sewall, objected to public theological disputes in the pulpit. She considered quarreling over doctrine and disputing heretics to be futile efforts, ineffective in bringing outsiders into the fold. Both Roman Catholics on the one hand and Unitarians on the other, she believed, would yield more quickly to passive example than to aggressive attack. "Living Christlike before such ones and praying for them will be more effectual than hosts of arguments or doctrinal conversation," she averred. Quick viewed with reproach the argumentative quality of many sermons, products of both the religious competition and the theological education of the era. Too much of the time, she heard not God's pure message but men's confusing debates from the pulpit. After listening to a Mr. Bodwell rail against the Unitarians, she faulted him for "get[ting] so nervously vehement, that, although he says [many] forcible and right things, he becomes too much of a man, and loses his ministerial tone and spirit." Quick did not blame his character: He was "a good man, healthfully pious, earnest for the truth." Still, his delivery left her uninspired because he himself lacked, not just inspiration, but the *appearance* of inspiration. "His sermons are rarely suggestive or permanent in their impressions to me," she protested. "I do not feel, either, as if he appeared before us with a message from God." Instead, Quick believed the man's contentious manner, rather than the Spirit, informed the lecture. "He appears too often to feel that he is going to accomplish God's work by mere force of language," she wrote, lamenting his bellicose tone. The man failed not just because he did not "appear" godly but because, as "too much of a man," his human failings were so unlike the passive spiritual role that her culture dictated for women.[21]

Thus, much of the criticism leveled at these men implicitly indicted masculine assertions of superiority. Women's irritation with vain and pretentious preachers signaled resentment of the minister's special entitlement to a superior education. Women's denunciation of the preacher's limited intellectual abilities affirmed their own intelligence. Women's objection to contentious, argumentative theological disputes registered their alienation from theological discourse. Denied the opportunity to participate, they denigrated theology as "man-made" doctrines. While some historians have suggested that criticism of preachers served a dramatic and entertainment function, that interpretation trivializes women's sincere dissatisfaction. Instead, understanding their complaints as implicit critiques of gender roles and ideology lends them more legitimacy. Late-twentieth-century feminist theories of gender difference in men's and women's moral development seem more helpful in comprehending women's perspective on the clergy. According to Carol Gilligan, men favor a morality based on legal and rational precepts. The clergy's preoccupation with theological dispute suggests not only that they lived in a period of tremendous religious competition and diversity but also that they viewed the law—in this case, sets of doctrines composed in precise language—as the foundation of religious and spiritual values. Defining, refining, and distinguishing between tenets helped clergymen establish not only their doctrinal positions but also their masculine identity. Disputational sermons appealed (and perhaps were calculated to appeal) to a male audience increasingly engaged in and distracted by ideological arguments in the political as well as the religious sphere. And these sermons drew on the masculine skills of rhetoric and scholarship emphasized in the seminary curriculum of the nineteenth century. Gilligan's theory posits that, conversely, women's moral development rests on relational foundations rather than abstract principles of right and wrong. Certainly nineteenth-century clergymen emphasized women's moral suasion through relationships. They taught women that their moral power was based on their "influence," their ability to set examples and teach gentle lessons of humility and submission rather than argue and dictate. Thus, an irritated and alienated female audience complained of pretension and contention in protest against a preacher's legal mode of instruction and his lack of exemplary piety. When Frances Quick accused a preacher of being "too much of a man," she certainly referred not merely to his too human shortcomings but to his too masculine weaknesses as well.[22]

Though women frequently offered critical comments, they occasionally questioned the propriety of criticizing the preacher. Sarah Dana, after one negative evaluation of a preacher, confided to her diary, "Perhaps I have done wrong in saying all that I have for this day but I wish to compare my present views with future experience." Frances Quick explained, "I have sometimes doubted as to the propriety of criticising the teacher, rather than the things he taught, but I can not listen to the words of truth with the same deep feeling, when I feel that there is no correspondence in the life and the language." Her disappointment in a preacher was similar to what she experienced when she discovered that the author of an admired and edifying book was "a better writer than he is a man." The message, like the man, was flawed: "His thoughts may still be beautiful, but they have lost their power and attraction for me," she insisted.[23] Such comments show that women believed themselves qualified and justified in making critical and negative judgments about preachers and thus saw themselves as closer to these men in social, educational, and spiritual development than Sally Bliss felt toward her pastors. But any social or spiritual equality women felt with their pastors was often diminished by their disapproval of those spiritual leaders. Disdain and scorn reimposed a distance in their relationship, a distance caused by women's recognition that clergy, as males, held a different set of cultural values and experienced cultural privileges denied them as women. Women's perceptions of clergy as masculine beings and not just kindred human beings, although muted in comparison to Abigail Price's feminist objections, appeared in subtle forms in their complaints about preachers. But in some of their comments on preaching and in more intimate face-to-face encounters with pastors and preachers, the recognition of gender difference and a consequential distance between them emerges even more distinctly.

Seeing Males in the Pulpit

Early feminist Abigail Price argued that no matter how learned or sympathetic the man, "he cannot *know*" or understand women's spiritual needs and concerns. Most women failed to articulate gender difference as clearly as she did—their criticisms are implicit rather than explicit. But in numerous comments women revealed a perception of the minister as "other" than themselves, not because of his office, his vocation, his moral character, his education, or his social status but because of his gender. In a variety of ways, they revealed their unspoken recognition of a difference and a problem. For instance, Frances Kingman, after listening to a sermon by a young man about to leave for a foreign mission, manifested both admiration and regret at not being able to do the same. "I love to see young men do thus, & would almost wish that I could do likewise," she wrote wistfully. Then, with resignation, her next line read, "But . . . may I ever be ready to do with my might, what my hands find to do, leaving the future with Him who careth for all his creatures." She accepted the limited sphere of usefulness that she believed God had assigned to her, but not without regret. The ellipsis in her statement is significant. Kingman suffered dissatisfaction with the cultural norms that prohibited her from following in the young man's footsteps. When she paused after the word *but*, her repressed disappointment and even anger almost emerged, but she recovered herself and resigned her fate to God. Because she cut off her protest in mid-sentence, she never made the explicit connection between the gender norms that constricted the evangelistic and missionary efforts of women but not of men.[24]

Other women similarly chafed at gender ideology and its inequities that a masculine clergy dispensed from the pulpit. Martha Barrett listened to a Congregational minister lecture on the topic of women and gave a qualified approval. "Quite good," she pronounced the sermon and then added, "But I don't see so much to admire in him as many do." "He lauded woman highly," she explained, "but she must be in her sphere, and all that." Clearly annoyed by the contradictory message that praised women for their piety and virtue and then confined them to the narrow domestic sphere, Barrett's complaint never reached the level of feminist protest. Likewise, Frances Quick responded to two sermons on sex roles that reveal an awareness of her pastor's masculine perspective on social and religious issues and her qualified disagreement with him. After hearing a sermon on "woman's mission," Quick, like Barrett, at first registered approval. "There is so much truth in what Mr. Stearns said to-day of woman's mission. His view seems to be just the right one." In this statement, she implied that she had heard others speak on the same topic and felt their views were not "just the right one." But in the few sermons on the topic that rated comment in women's private writings, their ambivalence to the minister's message is palpable. Quick reported that Mr. Stearns informed his audience it was better for woman to "exercise the influence God has given her over the heart, mind and will of all mankind in the most lovely and becoming manner, than to speak about woman's rights, or to step out of her heaven-ordained sphere." The man clearly subscribed to the prevailing gender norms. He hoped to reinforce them from the pulpit and, in 1855, to counter the destructive influence of women's rights advocates such as Abigail Price. Yet Quick disagreed with the minister's injunction against women's right to speak and expand their influence. "I am glad these rights have been talked of, nevertheless," she asserted and then, retreating to a more conventional position, she continued, "for I think that many true women, after seeing a few [experiments] tried, will rejoice more heartily in the lot to which God has appointed them, and be more awake to its high and holy requirements." Like Kingman and Barrett, Quick caught herself before she voiced more explicit opposition to the minister's words. She disagreed with the preacher, claiming that a discussion of women's rights was appropriate and even that women's experimentation in different roles was beneficial. But she retreated, after her interjection, to a defense of the lot God had appointed for women. While her conception of women's roles was certainly broader than that of the preacher, she stopped far short of Abigail Price's feminist outrage at male ministers who employed God to defend "the absurd tyranny" of men over women.[25]

The companion lecture on the proper roles of young men that Quick heard, however, elicited a more vehement disagreement. The preacher again advanced the prevalent ideology that young men should be trained to take leadership roles in politics, industry, and religion. But Quick's assessment of young men's ability to do good in their wider sphere was far less optimistic than her pastor's. "If I judge rightly," she asserted, "a very large proportion of the present generation of young men are forward and perverse. I do not know whether they will compare favorably or otherwise with the young of the other sex." In her opinion but not that of her pastor, young men could easily fail to do as well as young women in "filling the places which they should fill in society." Furthermore, Quick was "often disgusted with the self-conceit and want of principle which I see in young men." Instead, she hoped that "young men of the future" might be better trained by the proper "influence" of mothers, teachers, and ministers. "I cannot keep back a feeling of pity and charity towards them," she admitted. "I know that there is much done for young men, but there is a great deal more to be done."[26]

Though Quick seemingly disagreed with her pastor over the potential value of young women's and young men's Christian influence in the world—judging girls more capable of good than boys—she unconsciously collaborated in the notion that women needed less attention from their pastors and teachers than the other sex. She had great difficulty in accepting this preacher's blatant dismissal of "woman's rights" and his favorable assessment of the younger male generation. She saw herself and other pious, able, and willing young women unfairly relegated to an inferior position in society and in the church, beneath even the young men who so "disgusted her." Quick and others found it difficult to reconcile the ministers "lauding" women for their moral superiority when those same men sanctioned such a constricted sphere for women's influence.

Seeing (or Missing) Men as Pastors

Though women might object to a preacher's masculine perspective on "women's mission" in the privacy of their diaries, their opportunities to counter a pastor's arguments or even converse with him in person appear rare indeed. In comparison with their reports of sermons and lectures, women recorded so few personal encounters with ministers that one suspects they occurred very infrequently. As in Sally Bliss's diary, which contained no mention of a pastoral visit or conversation despite her affection and reverence for her pastors, women's private writings speak most eloquently of the distance between women and pastors by their silence on the subject. Yet those few references that do appear reveal more of women's disappointment and disagreement with pastors and further expose the obstacles that gender difference imposed on their relationships.

The pastor's role as a shepherd to his flock took place on two social and spatial levels. When he preached, dispensing guidance to a collective audience, the social and physical distance between him and his parishioners was the distance between pulpit above and pews below. The minister's elevated social status and his often elevated physical position in the pulpit lent a remoteness, a critical distance, to the man and his message. That physical distance, if not the social differences, permitted women more freedom to object to his teachings than they might have enjoyed in more intimate conversation. Conversely, the distance between pulpit and pew probably comforted many ministers, protecting them from some of the criticism and demands of parishioners. When diarist Sarah Dana complained that a preacher spoke "to the mass and not to individuals," she recognized the problem of distance in the relationship between preacher and parishioner. Though many women sensed the distance and sometimes resented it, few found it possible to reduce that social and physical gap between them, either in writing or in speaking.

The pastoral manuals reviewed in a previous chapter encouraged ministers to reinforce their weekly teaching from the pulpit with pastoral visits in which they could better assess and address the individual spiritual needs of their parishioners. At a reduced physical and perhaps social distance, the experts claimed, his message acquired a more immediate and personal quality that increased its force and effectiveness. But ministers' private journals and correspondence sometimes exposed painful conversations between women and pastors that proved unsatisfactory to both parties. Similarly, women's private writings about pastoral conversations show that they, too, suffered misunderstanding and dissatisfaction in these encounters and suggest they received little spiritual benefit from their clergy. Although most diaries never record a pastoral visit or speak to the absence of pastoral guidance in oblique ways, a few poignantly remarked on the absence or failure of a pastor in a time of spiritual need.

Of all the visits a pastor could be expected to make, those to the sick, dying, or bereaved were most urgent and obligatory. Yet pastors seemed to fail women in just those circumstances. Elizabeth Dana, deeply distressed by a beloved cousin's death, devoted twelve pages of her diary to an account of the young man's character, the events surrounding his death and funeral, and the depths of her own grief. Four days after the death and one day before the funeral, she reported that her pastor, a Mr. Stickney, had paid a brief condolence call on "Mother & me." Although both mother and daughter recalled many of the boy's good qualities, Elizabeth noted, "I was sorry that I could not get [Mr. Stickney] to talk more about Frank." The two recorded disappointment rather than comfort in the pastor's call. A week later, the two women attended services in the parish of the boy's family, hoping to have a conversation with the pastor of that church. Again, they came away dispirited. "We wanted to ask [Mr. Williams] about Frank's family," Dana mourned, "but didn't dare to." Neither Dana nor her mother could bring herself to close the social and physical gap between pastor and laywoman even at a time of acute grief. Similarly, Sarah Wetmore lamented the absence of her regular pastor as she nursed her dying mother. "Peculiar circumstances prevented my Pastors visits," she wrote with deep regret, "and tho' in the place where I first professed my faith in My Redeemer— yet I felt like a stranger." Like Bliss, she felt like a sheep without a spiritual shepherd.[27]

Louisa Hughes experienced a similar spiritual loneliness during her husband's long terminal illness and the many months of mourning after his death. A regular Episcopalian churchgoer and a self-proclaimed "friend" of her pastor, Mr. Harwood, Hughes nevertheless felt desolate and disconsolate during this period, bereft of support from her pastor and church. She recorded only one visit from Harwood during the year of dying and grieving. The pastor had called, but Hughes turned him away because her husband was too sick to speak with him. Why did the pastor not stay and speak with her or return another time? Perhaps Hughes relied on her husband for both temporal and spiritual support. When he died, she felt forsaken, "like a frail boat in mid ocean with the dear pilot lost and I alone to weather the storms and the whirlwind and to protect my children as I can." Her grief and loss were so painful that she was prevented from seeking solace in the church without her husband beside her. After seven months of grieving, she returned to church for the first time only on the momentous occasion of President Lincoln's assassination. "I dared not go even had I the strength, for fear of being overcome in church as I sat where we had sat for years together, & he my loved husband not there, & all the memories of life rushing back upon me," she explained to her diary. Although Louisa Hughes had earlier described her support for Mr. Harwood's call to the church and her pleasure at his leading their parish—surely the pastor played a role in her life—his absence from the pages of her diary during her long affliction belies her statements of affection for him. He certainly never stepped in to replace her husband as her "pilot," suggesting that his role was a minor and perhaps ineffectual one at best.[28]

Hughes later recorded another painful period in her life that reveals some deep ambivalence toward pastoral advice. After her husband's death, her grown son inflicted much spiritual misery on her by bringing legal claims against his father's estate. Hughes wisely turned to a family friend, the executor of the estate, for legal advice but apparently sought no help from her pastor, even though she blamed the whole incident on her spiritual failure to accept God's will. In fact, she viewed her son's disgraceful behavior as the result of her own resistance to pastoral advice in the past. She guiltily recalled in her diary the story of a woman who, tending a desperately ill child, had rejected her pastor's advice to resign herself to God's will. Her rejection of her pastor and her God had cost the poor woman the soul of her child, who had grown up "the curse of his mother, and died dishonoured & infamous." Hughes recognized in this story her own similar opposition to God's will. "This is the lesson I am to learn," she chastised herself. "I read this new this terrible affliction, this ingratitude of my Son this criminal unkindness as the voice from Heaven to me, because I found it so hard to [give] up my treasures to Him," she wrote, referring to her difficulty in accepting the deaths of several children. Perhaps Hughes's own anguished rebellion against God and her perceived estrangement from him prevented her from either seeking or accepting her pastor's counsel in her "new affliction," as well as during her husband's death. In any case, her pastor seems strangely absent from the pages of her diary during these critical periods in her spiritual life. In all the cases just described, the pastor, either by his presence or by his absence, failed to provide women with the spiritual support they sorely needed in times of intense pain and grief.[29]

With the best of intentions, ministers engaged women in conversation and offered personal counseling that, because of misunderstandings, fell far short of helpful advice. Women usually gave clergy the benefit of doubt and appreciated their earnest sincerity, if not the quality of the advice. Hannah Cabot's diary contained a detailed account of a conversation she had with the eminent Dr. William Ellery Channing, the dean of Boston Unitarianism and pastor of Federal Street Church. The remarkable record of the encounter reveals the gap that separated even well-meaning pastors from earnest young women. Cabot was pleased and flattered by Channing's attention to her, even though he consistently failed to comprehend her problems or to empathize with her. She had long regarded the man with a mixture of love and awe but not because she identified him as godly. She developed a filial love for him over her childhood years when she spent several summers as a guest of Channing's daughter Mary in Newport, Rhode Island. Her awe stemmed from her admiration for his great "mental powers." She marveled that as a parent Dr. Channing took "a great deal of pains to direct [Mary's] energies & thoughts to their proper objects, & [kept] her so continually interested in some of the great questions of our being, that she [had] no time for frivolous or useless thoughts." She was grateful that Channing included her in the family lessons. Yet while she admired his attention to the young people and his continuous efforts to direct their minds to "higher things" and "great principles," she was not always comfortable with him. "Dr. C talks & reads with us very interestingly but still there is always a sort of constraint." Cabot attributed her discomfort to her inability to "feel perfectly at home, with people who live so differently from us."[30]

The young woman happily overcame her restraint with Channing one day during her nineteenth year, when the pastor invited her to accompany him on a long carriage ride. He engaged her in a lengthy discussion of several topics, and Cabot was so impressed by the event that she hurried back to her room to record it as accurately as possible. Cabot's report reveals the awkward gap between the two. Despite the man's obvious interest in the edification of young people, he demonstrated very little empathy with or understanding of them, especially the women. Throughout the discussion, Cabot challenged his judgment of her and her female friends. When Channing observed that Cabot did not suffer much from bashfulness, she responded, "I do suffer from it however." When he hinted that the young people suffered few afflictions and led a "very bright and easy existence," she countered, "We have a great deal of trouble." When Cabot described some of those problems, he belittled them. "He seemed to think that after all I was remarkably happy in my home & asked if ennui was one of my troubles," she reported, and "I told him 'never.'" Asked if she suffered much from the "jealousies and quarrels" of companions, Cabot archly told him that they were "above that." Although Cabot was pleased and flattered by Channing's attention, she clearly thought he misjudged and misunderstood the girls' problems.[31]

Young Cabot ascribed Channing's inability to understand the young women not to the difference in their ages but to the difference in their gender. "He asked if he had heard all of our troubles," she noted, but "I told him he did not comprehend them." Channing tried to relate the girls' experience to his own unhappy childhood, but Cabot refused to compare the two. She argued "that women suffer much more than men from the delicacy of their feelings," but then admitted that "such sufferings seem to be less calculated to do good." Again, Channing disagreed with her, countering that all suffering was beneficial. He offered Cabot his standard prescription for what he saw as the common ills of young women. "It is a misfortune which you ladies particularly labour under," he told her, "that your reading for instance is so light, that you so seldom read anything wh[ich] you are obliged to stop & strive to understand." Again, Cabot discounted his negative assessment of the girls' reading by rising to his intellectual challenge. She asked Channing to judge which was the best exercise for the mind, those "little questions concerning their relations & duties to others or the great principles of philosophy & morality." Perhaps unconsciously, Cabot asked Channing to choose between the relational feminine values of self-sacrifice and the rational masculine values of intellect and the law that Carol Gilligan identified. Channing took the middle ground, admitting that both were necessary. But just as soon as he had conceded that both feminine and masculine notions of virtue were equally valuable, he undercut the dignity and seriousness he accorded her question by asking Cabot if her friend Anna was "a good deal interested in Mr. Bartol [a minister]." Cabot protected her friend and avoided his question about the girl's personal affections by replying that "the whole parish liked him quite well." Once again, she tried to shift the conversation away from his condescending interest in the girls' personal lives to "higher things." Perhaps referring to Ralph Waldo Emerson's notion of self-culture as well as Channing's pronouncements to young people, she wondered if "self-improvement is not the highest object, that [instead] we owe something to others." In a gently assertive manner, Cabot again juxtaposed masculine individualist and feminine relational moral values. She questioned Channing's incessant efforts to educate the young people on philosophical principles and reiterated the importance of personal and social obligations.[32]

Cabot's diary entry never remarked on the various disagreements the two discovered in their long and intimate conversation. Instead, she counted herself pleased with the encounter, satisfied that she had made valuable contributions to the discussion, and gratified that this prominent intellectual man had attended to her. She congratulated herself on "outgrow[ing] a good deal of my foolish fear of him." She liked that, when she offered an explanation for his daughter Mary's loneliness, "he seemed to take my word for it." Finally, she wrote appreciatively, "he spoke very openly to me of [his children] & made me feel that he loved & trusted me as a friend & and I had a delightful ride." Nowhere in her comments does Cabot explicitly reject Channing's judgment and advice. Only the description of their conversation discloses her disagreement. At the end of the entry, she repressed her objections and resolved once again "to act upon his noble principles."[33]

Channing, despite the hours he spent talking with young people, displayed no special empathy for Cabot and her friends, no sympathy for her "troubles" as a young woman, and no personal insight into her mental, moral or spiritual character. He offered her no specific personal advice but instead dispensed his usual wisdom about self-culture, with the additional admonition that young women were particularly needy in this respect. Still, Cabot dutifully and gratefully accepted his instruction, in part because of her respect for his intellect and also because of his friendly pastoral manner. Though they disagreed on many points, his mere willingness to listen to her views earned him her confidence and admiration. Few women gave evidence of experiencing this level of intimacy, this give-and-take, or even this level of satisfaction in an encounter with a pastor. A preacher in the pulpit earned the most positive comments from women when his ideas coincided with their own. A pastor in a more intimate setting earned the most positive comments for his friendly and candid manner, whether or not his personal message corresponded with the ideas of his female clients.

Only one remarkable account of a face-to-face conversation between a young woman and a pastor gives a glimpse of the anger some women undoubtedly experienced in disagreements with their pastors. The account shows that some women overcame the disadvantages of their status to articulate their objections to an older professional man. Young Emma Brown recounted a conversation with the esteemed Charles Finney, the president of Oberlin College, where she became a student in 1860. Seventeen-year-old Brown, the daughter of a successful dressmaker in Washington, D.C., acquired a good education and taught school before she entered Oberlin, but she was one of only a small number of African American women enrolled at the college. While Finney favored abolition and headed the first integrated college, he was too moderate in his antislavery views for Brown. She wrote to her friend Emily Howland, a white Quaker abolitionist who served as her mentor, that she had attended a prayer meeting with Mrs. Finney when Dr. Finney called Brown into his office, where "we talked about religion of course." But when the conversation shifted to politics and reform, Finney made some very derogatory remarks about antislavery radicals such as Theodore Parker, John Brown, Wendell Phillips, and William Garrison. "I wish I could tell you all the absurd arguments he used to convince me that this was true," she confided to her friend. But Emma Brown, unlike so many of her white sisters, did not hold her tongue. "I dared to argue with him," she announced proudly. "I never would have commenced such a conversation with the President of the Institution," she modestly averred, "but as he forced it upon me I would defend those noble men." Their conversation continued until they were called to chapel by the bell. He invited her to go to church, which she "dared not refuse." But the disagreement continued into the prayer service. Finney invited the congregation to pray "for a young lady with whom he had conversed that afternoon who was in an awful state." Finney's exasperation with the young woman's courageous impudence compelled him to share their conversation with the congregation. "Then he told what I said," she reported with chagrin.

"Imagine my unpleasant feelings," she begged her friend, but then admitted that she found humor in the whole affair. "There seemed something so ludicrous in it that I could not restrain my laughter," she admitted, and then vowed, "I shall not visit over there again very soon."[34]

Brown saw not just a man but a man who failed to live up to the ideals of Christian equality he preached from the pulpit. In her personal conversation with him, he revealed the angry and irrational side that rarely emerged in public. He also exposed the limits of many Northern whites' antislavery beliefs. Despite its stand for abolition and integration, the college admitted many white students whose racist attitudes and behavior made Emma Brown's stay there a social challenge as well as an intellectual one. Brown's courage in confronting Finney shows the grit and intelligence required by blacks to gain admittance to a white school and succeed there. Despite her age, her sex, and her color, she dared to defend those men who embodied her own ideals to Finney's face and not just in the privacy of a journal or letter. Brown's noteworthy audacity shows that some women, at least, could drop their deference, even to eminent clergymen, to express their deeply held convictions. Her humorous response to his breach of confidence shows that she could rise above the embarrassing encounter and put the incident in perspective. She could physically and psychically distance herself from the man who served as her pastor.[35]

These few accounts of pastoral conversations record more examples of disagreement and disappointment than of satisfaction and comfort. Only Frances Quick recorded admiration for her pastor and his wife and their "free sociality" in her report of a call they paid to her. Just as she recognized the constructed quality of a good sermon, she realized the minister's manner was key to his success as a teacher. "Free intercourse," she observed, "makes people understand each other better and renders them more accessible to the good influences which a pastor hopes to throw around his people." Mr. and Mrs. Allen's sincerity, Quick judged, inspired a remarkable reciprocal candor in those they visited. "I have been astonished," she marveled, "at the revelations of character people will unconsciously make to those who meet them unrestrainedly." The Allens possessed "rare gifts" that rendered them "capable of making another reveal thus unconsciously the salient features of his character." Quick seemed to view both the pastor and his wife as equally adept in eliciting conversation and perhaps confession. They worked as a team of proto-psychoanalysts, helping clients to "unconsciously" divulge the "salient features" of a personality. Quick immediately applied the primary lesson of the interview to her own teaching. "I feel that this is one thing that I must earnestly labor for, that I may bring my self in direct contact with my pupils, and exert over them an active influence for good." In her role as a teacher, Quick recognized her pastor as a spiritual and social exemplar and also as a peer role model. She rated his performance and evaluated his effectiveness, giving him high marks and recommending his techniques for herself and other pastors and teachers.[36]

Curiously, Quick's record of this pastoral call is the only formal set visit that appears in any of the diaries or correspondence in this study. Quick obviously judged the interview a successful one, although she revealed no details of the substance of the conversation or of its spiritual benefits to herself. She also failed to note whether she was the beneficiary of the pastor's skillful probing or merely an observer. The pastor (or maybe his wife deserved more credit) apparently succeeded in getting his parishioner to bare his (Quick used the generic masculine possessive) or her soul and presumably strip away some of the social impediments to honest spiritual conversation. If so, this spiritual counselor achieved the kind of religious intimacy that pastoral manuals lauded as a benefit of the personal pastoral visit. Clearly, Quick valued that intimacy as a necessary component in the teaching process. Why, then, did she omit any further discussion of her personal spiritual dividends from this interview? The interview may have proved too intimate even to confide to her diary. Yet, since Quick's diary was a reflective one—purposefully recording her progress as a teacher, as a Christian, and as a Christian teacher—her omission suggests something quite different. She observed and admired the pastor's interaction with others rather than actively participating in the interchange. She profited pedagogically if not spiritually.[37]

Thus, even the positive remarks of women regarding face-to-face encounters with pastors raise the suspicion that women did not regularly enjoy spiritual benefits at the feet of their spiritual leaders. Few women recorded specific instances of either experiencing or particularly benefiting from a pastor's personal ministry to them. Distance, both physical and spiritual or psychological, more often characterized the pastoral relationship. Ironically, however, when women did experience and appreciate an intimate conversation with a pastor, the difference in gender, and the intrusion of romantic or sexual attraction it sometimes introduced, either changed the nature of their relationship or reinforced the necessity of distance.

Frances Kingman, the conscientious schoolteacher, experienced shame and embarrassment instead of support at the hands of one pastor who proffered friendly advice. A regular visitor to her boarding house, the Rev. Mr. Holmes engaged its residents in mostly social conversation. On one occasion, Kingman reported that "he urged me much to purchase *a gold watch*." The minister was peculiarly insistent, contending that her position as a lady with a $500 salary demanded that she have a gold watch, not a silver one. "He urged the matter," she recalled, "until it was painful to me & I determined, as soon as I was alone with him, to tell him why I was thus economical." Kingman later explained to Holmes that her salary went to pay off her father's debts, an obligation she cheerfully but discreetly met. The pastor's lighthearted teasing had threatened to expose her father's pecuniary difficulties and left her distressed and embarrassed rather than amused or flattered.[38]

Yet despite the pastor's casual and inept advice, Kingman eventually succumbed to his "fatherly" attentions. Conversely, the minister so much admired her filial piety and sense of Christian obligation that he not only admitted his grievous error but also began an awkward courtship. The Rev. Mr. Holmes, a widower with grown children and old enough to be her father, undoubtedly found Kingman's devotion to her aged father appealing. For her part, Kingman appreciated his paternal spiritual (if not temporal) guidance and looked to him for pastoral care. "I had ever been disposed to regard him as a sort of spiritual father to whom I loved to look for sympathy & instruction," she admitted to a friend. But the pastoral bond almost inevitably led to a romantic affection and the couple's engagement. Kingman explained that "the strong confidence, respect & esteem with which I then regarded him has ripened into another sentiment & I have been led to forget that we were born in different centuries." Kingman accepted the evolution of their feelings from pastoral association to romantic love as a natural process of maturation, a "ripening" of their relationship. So natural was the course of that change that it easily overcame a substantial difference in their ages. Thus, ironically, she came to understand his powerful attraction as a man because of his alienating and inappropriate remarks as a pastor.[39]

The peculiar push-and-pull in the relationship between women and pastors was exaggerated when they closed the distance between pulpit and pew. From a safe distance, women might sometimes admit a personal attraction to a clergyman. Orthodox Calvinist Frances Quick made a visit to a Catholic seminary and exclaimed to her mother in a letter that one of the priests "made quite an imposing appearance in his cornered cap, and flowing gown." The man's exotic vestments certainly impressed her, but she also admitted that "he had such a noble, benevolent good humored countenance, that I almost fell in love with him." Although the man professed an alien faith despised by her own church and unnatural vows of celibacy, the young woman discovered herself charmed by his presence. Indeed, his exotic appearance, faith, and vows provided both the source of her attraction to him and sufficient social distance between them to allow Quick to safely indulge a romantic fantasy and confess it to her mother.[40]

When the distance between clergy and women closed, young women might still express a similar attraction to clergymen, but in covert ways. Elizabeth Dana recorded a strange dream in which her sister was called out of a religious service by the young assistant minister, who "offered himself." In the dream, the sister accepted his offer. The next morning, the two young women took the dream quite seriously, discussing the propriety and practicality of the marriage proposal. The girls thought the circumstances of the proposal "peculiar" and the young man's ability to support her unlikely, and they questioned her fitness as a clergyman's wife. Elizabeth's dream may have been a symptom of her own repressed sexual desires and attraction to the young man. Her comments suggest that the relationship between women, especially young women, and pastors was never quite free of the implicit intrusion of sexual attraction. But nineteenth-century women suppressed their own sexuality to conform to numerous cultural sources that dictated women's purity and chastity. The women represented here were not unusual in avoiding explicit sexual language, at least in terms that contemporary historians can interpret, even when they discussed husbands and beaux in their diaries. Yet their candid comments regarding a personal attraction to a minister stand in striking contrast to their muted discussions of lovers. Why did women feel free to confess their "love" for clergymen when they were otherwise so discreet? The inclusion of the minister in a metaphorical Christian "family" and his assumed position as a moral paragon perhaps allowed women to make declarations of "love" without threatening their own morality.[41]

Women who actually married ministers sometimes confused romantic love and spiritual love and conflated their love for God and his representative in ways similar to Sally Bliss's visions of God in the pulpit. Frances Kingman and Frances Quick, the two schoolteachers who so appreciatively admired their pastors' manners and methods and who so clearly saw a man and not God in the pulpit, nevertheless both took pastors as husbands. Yet quite unlike Sally Bliss, these two women both worried about separating their love for God and their love for their husbands and pastors, suffering serious spiritual distress because of their devotion to their husbands. Frances Quick admitted that she derived little spiritual benefit from a communion service when her husband was absent. She missed his presence but also "felt sad to see another officiating, at the altar, when I have learned to associate him with that sacred place." Frances Kingman Holmes expressed concern that her love for her husband had displaced love that she properly owed to God. "My happiness is almost *centred in one earthly object*," she worried. "I think *too much* of *him*—because it allows not of thought *enough* for God & things divine." So even though marriage vows sanctioned their love for their pastors, their tendency to conflate their spiritual, pastoral, and marital relationships still proved troubling to them.[42]

No set of sources better illustrates the simultaneous attraction and revulsion between women and pastors than the correspondence of women with the Rev. Mr. Asahel Nettleton. A respected itinerant revivalist who traveled in New England, the southern states, and England during the 1820s and 1830s, Nettleton used methods that rigorously avoided the emotional extremism of many contemporary evangelists. He stressed instead a rational yet still very personal and systematic pastoral approach of "home visitation, personal conference, inquiry meetings, and follow-up instruction." At the founding of the Theological Institute of Connecticut in 1833, Nettleton declined to fill the newly created chair of pastoral theology because of his chronic ill health. So notwithstanding the fact that he never held a settled pastorate, he earned acclaim as an effective preacher and pastor. And despite stressing a rational approach to conversion, his preaching and pastoring engendered deep and conflicting emotions in many of the women to whom he ministered.[43]

Nettleton's appeal to women can be measured to some degree by the number of women who wrote to petition him to come to their homes and communities. Most of his invitations to preach came from fellow clergymen, but he received several requests directly from women. Some emphasized the social and physical advantages, others the spiritual benefits, to him and to them of a sojourn in their communities. Through a female friend, Nettleton learned that a Mrs. Lyman "wants *you* to come there and make your home her house—& she will supply your every necessity as long as you will stay with her." Many offered to nurse him as well as provide food and shelter. "Let us have the pleasure of taking care of you and enjoying your society," one group of women implored him. Another group assured him that they continued to "enjoy the presence of god . . . but still need your advice for we are young and unexperienced as to spiritual things." Anxious to obtain his personal, individualized attention, they wrote in a schoolgirl scrawl, "we hope we shall . . . receive your advise by writing to each of us if not hearing it from your lips we wish to be remembered in your prayers and we have not forgotten you." By making their requests in writing and through a friend or as a group, these women were able to request intimacy with Nettleton but from a safe physical and social distance. For others, closing the gap between themselves and Nettleton was a more difficult process.[44]

As much as they craved his presence, women worried he would misunderstand their longing. Because his leave-takings from a community generated so much painful emotion, he often left town unannounced. One woman described the suffering of her female friends after his departure but was concerned that Nettleton would dismiss their emotionalism as "female weakness." She assured him that it was not just his person but his pastoral manner and message they missed. "Oh what would we not give to hear again the sound of your voice from the sacred desk, & to hear those precious little *fire-side* sermons which we used to take so much delight in." Although they appreciated his preaching, the women wanted him to know that their intimate sessions by the hearth were most "precious." Yet while Ann Waddell desperately wanted Nettleton to understand the depth of their affection for him, she still feared he would misunderstand and dismiss their sorrow as nothing more than "female weakness." Waddell overcame some of her feminine fears by addressing Nettleton in the first person plural rather than singular, a representative of all the women in her community. Her concern is a symptom of women's vulnerability in the pastoral relationship. While they anxiously sought his personal advice as a minister, they feared his misunderstanding and disapproval because he was a man and they were women.[45]

As individuals rather than as members of a group, women displayed even more misgivings about approaching him, whether in writing or in person. Mary Anne Mew communicated her hesitation to write by asking him to "excuse the liberty I take in addressing you." She apologized for not speaking when they met in person, but explained that "my tongue cleaved to my mouth." Still, his "entreating manner to all sinners" had encouraged her to write. Her question to him followed the classic evangelical catechism: "What must I do to be saved?" She knew the answer was "Believe in the Lord Jesus Christ," but this simple prescription was insufficient: She desired more specific and personal advice from Nettleton. She remained, however, extremely uncomfortable in seeking his counsel, even in writing, and justified her petition by employing a medical analogy. "Now whilst I am writing I feel as if I was doing wrong," she confessed. But, she explained, "We tell our *bodily* Physician all our feelings my excuse for so troubling you as I wish you kindly and beneficially to prescribe for one who has 'no health in her.' " Humbly, she begged him to read her missive only "at leisure" and to "condescend" to answer her question by letter.[46]

Mew's humility and restraint were, of course, among the values ascribed to and prescribed for women in the nineteenth century. Women were expected to address men in a submissive manner. When Elizabeth Cook wrote that she "could not think of intruding upon your valuable time," she displayed that appropriate modesty. But some of Nettleton's female correspondents go far beyond these simple conventions to worry more about imprudence than impudence. The fear and anxiety these women experienced in their correspondence with Nettleton stemmed from their subordinate positions as sinners, as laity, and as women. Sarah Lee's letter illustrates the painful simultaneous attraction and aversion these women suffered. She "relucted" to bother him with her request to be "one of the happy circle" gathered around him. On the other hand, she felt compelled to approach him; she "still felt so strong an inclination to state to you my case I beg your prayers for me as I know not how well to suppress." Ironically, she overcame with great difficulty the social subservience she felt she owed him because of the shame and remorse she felt as a humble sinner. In that pitiful position, she believed Nettleton alone could offer her help. But Lee's letter also hints that her identity as a poor sinner and a layperson was made worse by her being a woman. "Since I began to write I have been led to ask myself why do thus trouble Mr. Nettleton," she worried; "your soul is of no more worth than others." But Lee also "feared there was an impropriety in my writing." "I have given you . . . but a faint view of my dreadful situation, nor *could* words express it," she assured him. "Be so kind sir," she begged him, "as not to expose this." She signed off as his "anxious and distressed friend," describing not just her spiritual torment as a lowly sinner seeking guidance but her social anguish as a woman confiding in a strange man. Surely her fear of appearing indiscreet prompted her to add, "you will oblige me in consigning this to the flames." She worried not only about her soul but also about her own and his reputation for chastity.[47]

These sources show that women approached Nettleton with reluctance because he was a preeminent evangelist, busy with his hectic preaching schedule and correspondence and not merely with the care of a small parish. But they also hesitated because, as women, they feared he viewed their concerns as trivial, mere "female weakness." In addition, they desired closing the physical and social gap between them as advantageous to their spiritual health but feared that intimacy might be hazardous from a cultural perspective. Nineteenth-century mores strictly regulated cross-gender relations outside the family. Pastoral manuals discouraged even epistolary relationships between clergy and women. The same gender ideology of separate spheres that labeled pastor and female parishioner as spiritual allies separated them because of the risk of sexual transgression. In short, these women respected and feared the cultural boundaries of separate spheres that divided them from their spiritual guides. Although Nettleton extended the offer of an intimate pastoral relationship to women in his revival sermons and his hearthside homilies, they felt uneasy and embarrassed in accepting it, despite its strong appeal.[48]

Seeing the "Charm" of the Pastoral Relationship

One of Nettleton's female correspondents hoped that his offer of a personal ministry to her signaled something even more intimate than a spiritual relationship. Her letters reveal, however, the psychological cost of her attempts to see Nettleton as someone other than her spiritual shepherd. Sarah Wetmore's letters to Nettleton between 1821 and 1823 contained much more than the comments on preachers that have already been cited here. In these letters, Wetmore displayed little of the humility and modesty of his other correspondents. She never viewed him as a transcendent minor divinity and rarely as a busy revivalist, but most often as a personal friend. Her letters to Nettleton thus afford a rare glimpse of the intimacy and also the exposure to emotional injury and misunderstanding that women risked within the pastoral relationship. This case, while isolated and probably atypical of most women's experience, may be just one example of a common dilemma. When the social, physical, and spiritual distance between a woman and a clergyman was drastically reduced, the consequences could be just as painful and distressing as that resulting from the enforced distance that many women seem to have experienced.

Wetmore usually approached Nettleton in her letters as a social equal as well as spiritual guide, as a man as well as a minister of the gospel. Her correspondence with him outwardly wore the garb of "Christian friendship" but inwardly bore the marks of a romance. She consistently confused and conflated the spiritual and the temporal in much the same way as the women married to pastors. In an early letter, she asserted her belief, which she knew Nettleton supported, that spiritual blessings were essential to happiness and that humans were helpless without God. In the same sentence, however, she admitted that God was not enough: Nettleton's presence, too, was necessary to her happiness. In requesting his return to her town, she asserted that "many temporal blessings," not just spiritual ones, "will increase our enjoyment." By employing the plural possessive *our*, she communicated her concern for the well-being of the whole community and not merely for herself. Yet she quickly shifted to the first personal singular and issued a very personal plea for Nettleton's physical presence. "Your return . . . will add *very very* much to my happiness," she assured him. In addition, she reminded him that "your parting words at Lenox afforded me much comfort." Her emphatic closing words indicated her very personal request for his return. "Good-by for a *little while*. I shall anticipate your return and *do not O do not* disappoint me," she begged.[49]

In a subsequent letter, Wetmore pleaded again for his return; but in his absence, she begged also for his prayers. The petulant tone of that request, however, showed little of the humility displayed in other women's letters to him. "You wish my prayers," she reminded him, and promised that she had tried to make them. "Tho I may never have had the spirit of prayer yet you are often remembered in suplication," she wrote, implying that although her attempts at prayer may have been feeble and ineffectual, he was frequently the subject of those entreaties. In the next sentence, however, she sought reciprocal prayers from him. "And now will you not sometimes remember me too," she beseeched him, "perhaps no one needs them more than I do." Reminding him of previous requests and his failure to respond to them, she wrote with resentment, "perhaps I am one of those unhappy ones—that everyone forgets when they go to their Heavenly Father." Wetmore assumed a position of social and spiritual equality with Nettleton quite unlike the humility of his other female correspondents. She made bold requests on her own behalf without the humility and embarrassment the others displayed. Wetmore asked Nettleton to trade prayers with her as favors or tokens of affection rather than as mutual concern for their souls or his ministry. She counted reciprocal prayers as a sign not just of Christian friendship but of personal affection and concern as well.[50]

On occasion, Wetmore exhibited some shame or guilt over her affection for Nettleton: She termed it "selfishness." By doing so, she labeled her implicit romantic desire for him a "sin" without confessing it more explicitly. "If it did not seem so much like selfishness," she admitted, "I would urge you to come to Fairfield immediately and let me nurse you." With little trace of humility or shame, she assured him that "I feel as if no one could take as good care of you as I can." She ineffectively disguised an earthly affection for him as a need for personal spiritual direction. Instead of calling their time together spiritually rewarding, she wrote, "I have often told you I counted them the pleasantest hours of my life." She recalled the revival he led, remembering the "breathless anxiety" she felt for the "conversion of my dear friends." But in her catalogue of memorable spiritual experiences during that period, she moves from the collective to individual and very personal events. "Those interesting meetings, those times of prayer and praise, those precious communion seasons, those social interviews—those delightful conversations," she remembered with special fondness. But one event in particular impressed her most forcibly. "When the clock strikes eleven," she reminded him, "there is still such a pleasing association of ideas—that I almost forget where I am." Perhaps Wetmore referred to an especially emotional point during the revival, or perhaps even to a personal conversion experience. But her recollections of these events, as they move from the collective to increasingly more intimate personal encounters between them, suggest that their "parting visit" held romantic as well spiritual significance for her.[51]

Wetmore's candor with Nettleton as well as her affection for him sometimes troubled and discomfited her. Her honesty attests to both the intimacy of their relationship and the conflict that intimacy generated. Though rarely humble, she occasionally feared she was imprudent. Unlike the women who "relucted" even to write to Nettleton, Wetmore was frustrated by the impersonal quality of their correspondence. She ardently desired a face-to-face relationship, rather than their epistolary one. She worried about his reaction to her letters because she could not read it in his face. "When you was here," she recalled, "I used to express to you my thoughts just as they arose in my mind and often did I find a corresponding one in yours." Like the women who enjoyed preaching when it "coincided" with their own theology, Wetmore sought evidence of "corresponding thoughts" in Nettleton's face rather than his words. She experienced frustration and doubt when it failed to emerge in their letters to each other. She acknowledged that the personal rapport she felt with him was unusual as well as highly desirable. "There are those who have *listened* to all that I might have to say—but seldom have I known *that* pleasure when thought meets thought," she confessed. Yet while she desperately sought to re-create that intimacy in their letters, it still troubled her. "This was such a luxury," she admitted, "that I know I indulged myself beyond what propriety would sanction or female decorum would authorize." Wetmore worried, like others, that the candor she so appreciated in Nettleton's pastoral manner ineluctably led to imprudence and impropriety because of their gender difference and potential sexual attraction.[52]

On the one hand, the mutual affection and candor that Wetmore believed the two shared allowed her to speak freely and even to offer him pointed advice. On the other hand, that affection and candor prompted her to project her confused desires onto other young females to whom he ministered. She inadvertently communicated her own passionate responses to him in her fears that the intimacy of his ministry to women posed a serious danger to him. "I have some advise—*important advise* to give you," she wrote emphatically. And to reassure him that her concern was not purely "selfish," she added, "It may make you a better minister." She tried again to get him to come speak to her in person, asserting that the "delicate nature" of her concern could not be communicated in a letter. While Wetmore worried he would dismiss her worry as foolish, she convinced herself it was "unpardonable to withhold an opinion however trivial in itself—when I have before given it so much importance." The urgent question that so distressed her was: "*Is it best to increase the number of your intimate female friends?*"[53]

Wetmore struggled to articulate her anxiety over his relationships with other women as a concern for his professional efficacy and his reputation while repressing her own sexual longing and jealousy. But to describe the source of her worry for him, she was forced to describe the source of her own personal attraction for him. "Perhaps you may not be sensible of the charm that is attach'd to the still silence, may I say the secrecy of your friendship," she labored to explain. "Let me assure you that no lady possessing the least degree of sensibility, can remain unaffected when you honor her with these tokens of your regard." Whether she intended it or not, she confessed that she herself had succumbed to the "charm" of his intimate pastoral manner. She also confessed that she had considered whether he should marry and had decided she opposed it. But that opposition, she now realized, was also "selfishness . . . for I felt that in such a case the fredom of my correspondence with you would be interrupted." This admission surely betrayed her romantic affection for him. If she had merely worried about his reputation, rather than the intimacy of their own relationship, she would have encouraged his marriage. Protestant wisdom had long held that clerical vows of celibacy encouraged rather than prevented sexual misconduct and slander. Protestants defended clerical marriage because it permitted pastors and women to engage more freely in spiritual conversation. But Wetmore could only reluctantly "consent" to his marriage "if it was for your happiness." Desperately, she repeated her request that he "come and tell me more . . . on this subject."

Wetmore's torment reveals the vulnerability of young women in the pastoral relationship. As she tried to express it, the "secrecy" or intimacy of their relationship, even the Christian friendship of a "sister" and "brother," had an irresistible "charm," an allure that sensitive women might easily misunderstand as romantic rather than pastoral in nature. The consequences of that misunderstanding might easily injure the minister, Wetmore contended. She neglected to explain the potential injury to the women as well. Like the pastors who wrote manuals, Wetmore advised marriage, rather than a less intimate pastoral manner, as a solution to the problem. Her boldness in broaching the subject to him, in confessing the "charm" of his manner, and in proffering her personal advice to him all attest to the intimacy he had encouraged in their relationship.

Wetmore's concern for Nettleton and her prescription of marriage were clearly based on her perception that he not only encouraged but also enjoyed a number of "intimate female friends." Perhaps she hoped her candid letter would prompt him to make *her* a proposal of marriage. At any rate, her letter at last betrays the same fear displayed by others—that he would dismiss her worries as foolish and feminine. "But what do I write!" she burst out. She feared she had forfeited both the "title of friend & sister" and his "esteem." She imagined his scornful reply to her letter, "foolish girl indeed—does she pretend to direct my conduct toward her sex—I who have been ten years in the ministry and certainly know better than she can, what is consistent with propriety[?]" Wetmore assured herself that even if he misunderstood or dismissed her, "Our Father in Heaven knows better my feelings than I can express to you." But that knowledge did not protect her from the misunderstanding of others. "I am unwilling the world or any part of it should know what I write to you," she admitted. After reading over her letter, she declared herself "heartily ashamed of it." "Oh what would the world say if they knew what I had written you," she wrote with deep misgivings. "Burn my letters in pitty to me burn them." Nevertheless, her fear, love, and jealousy overcame her apprehensions and shame, and she posted the letter anyway.

But her anguish and vulnerability to Nettleton's charms and her awareness of the intrusion of sexual desire into the pastoral relationship, while less explicit than her concern for making him a "better minister," clearly emerge in these letters. They expose both the dangers and the distress of gender difference between pastor and female parishioner. It is difficult to imagine a fellow clergyman or male friend writing to Nettleton on the same subject with the same emotional burdens.

Nettleton replied to Wetmore's tortured letter in a manner that aptly demonstrates the appeal of his personal pastoral methods. First, he encouraged Wetmore to offer him advice, which, he assured her, "I esteem . . . as an act of friendship." He thus reestablished an equality and intimacy between them that at least in part erased the superiority and authority he might have held over her. Next, he excused her boldness, stating that "less fear of giving offence, & still greater plainness of speech might give still [higher] proof of christian friendship." Rather than chastise her for overstepping the bounds of propriety, he sanctioned her frankness and candor. Instead of calling her "foolish girl" and widening the gap between them, he tried to close it by offering her a story he hoped would address her fears indirectly and gently defend his ministry to women. "Since writing the last sentence," he wrote, "I have been interrupted by a poor sinner who called to see me in deep distress." The immediacy of the story—it occurred just as he was writing to Wetmore—conveys an intimacy, authenticity, and personal quality that increased the story's power. His visitor, he explained, was "a young woman of pleasing appearance & manners—she came alone, & had no other errand than—What must I do to be saved?" In one short sentence, Nettleton introduced the very person Wetmore most feared—a sensitive and attractive young woman who arrived at his doorstep without chaperone or guile. But he assured Wetmore that the woman had spiritual wants and nothing more. "We will not exclude her from our company our friendship or prayers, will we?" he gently chided her. Again, he raised Wetmore to his level, asking her to put herself in his place and decide whether she would turn away a young woman in distress. He then recounted the scriptural text and the homely anecdote of another young woman that he had offered to the visitor in their discussion, in the same way he recounted his story to Wetmore. Some hours after the interview, he told Wetmore, he received word that his comely visitor had "found the saviour."[54]

In short, Nettleton's story succinctly and delicately made his point. If he had turned the young woman away from his door and denied her his personal spiritual counsel, her soul would have been lost. He confessed to Wetmore that he had wept for joy at the news and begged her to keep his confidence. Once again, he exposed his own emotional weakness and entrusted her with his heart. He deftly created a sense of mutual confidence between pastor and laywoman, but just as expertly he kept the discussion on a very professional level. Not once in the letter does he acknowledge that Wetmore is any more deserving of his personal or pastoral attention than any other young woman. He certainly never replied directly to her advice that he marry. All of his strategies reduced the social distance between them, simulating a dialogue between peers rather than a morality lecture from a superior to an inferior. Simultaneously, he struggled to keep the discussion on a professional and spiritual level. Without ever encouraging any romantic attachment to him, however, his closing might easily have been misunderstood as personal rather than pastoral by any "lady possessing the least degree of sensibility." "I write," he reminded her, "because I cannot bear to be forgotten."[55]

This letter apparently ended the couple's correspondence. Twenty years later, however, Wetmore received a request from Nettleton to return his letters to her, ostensibly for his use in composing a memoir of the revivals of 1821 and 1822. She responded in one last letter that shows that the pain of their failed relationship, from her perspective, remained fresh decades later. Once again, she termed her confused emotions of love, longing, loneliness, and resentment toward Nettleton as "selfishness" and struggled to suppress them. "Reading over your letter before sending it—my selfishness overcame my better feelings," she admitted. Resentfully, she reminded him of a journal she had made for him, "in which you never wrote a page." Her memories of their days together remained vivid, she assured him, and she hesitated to return his letter since he must certainly remember "every circumstance related in [it]." Years of loneliness and hard work in raising a family had left her feeling "like a stranger in a strange land." Reading over letters from earlier friends, his among them, made up one of her few pleasures. They "afforded a rich repast," she assured him, and asked, "How could I part with any of these testimonies of friendship, without some effort, will you forgive me?" Clearly she resented that her affection for him had never been returned after that letter. The conflict she suffered in deciding to return the letter offered poignant testimony to the place Nettleton occupied in her otherwise lonely life. She looked back on their friendship with a terrible longing and also deep bitterness. No one else since then had offered her the candid intimacy he had. Perhaps no one else had caused her such pain, either.[56]

Wetmore was undoubtedly unusual but probably not singular. Most young women never had the opportunity to develop such an open and intimate friendship with an eligible young preacher. Obviously, those women who married preachers probably experienced a happier resolution to that friendship. And perhaps married women could enjoy the spiritual attentions of a pastor without as readily succumbing to his personal "charm." Yet the trials of several ministers showed that married women were not emotionally or physically immune to a pastor's intimate ministry. Wetmore's case was extreme in degree but not in kind. Pastoral manuals warned young men of the dangers of a ministry to women often enough to make us believe that it was a real threat. Young women falling in love with their pastors probably occurred just frequently enough to fuel the rumors of sexual indiscretion that haunted many clergymen. In fact, at least twice in his career, the never-married Nettleton suffered charges of sexual immorality, although Sarah Wetmore was not involved in any of those known cases. Neither charge was substantiated, and Nettleton enjoyed the full confidence of his clerical consociation in Connecticut. Yet his effort to retrieve his letter to her may have been an attempt to protect himself from further charges.[57]

Without doubt, cases like Sarah Wetmore's helped to create and sustain the destructive image of idolatrous young women and their "popular" preachers. Historians must look beyond the highly notorious cases that support that image and probe more deeply into the private relationships of pastors and women. This study goes far to undermine the image of women and pastors as either uncomplicated allies or partners in dangerous liaisons. It suggests that women and male pastors experienced distance more often than dangerous intimacy. They were divided by nineteenth-century constructions of gender rather than united by them. The private sources show women without benefit of clergy, without the spiritual shepherd they expected to lead them.

Epilogue

Separating the Ewes from the Rams; or, Seeing through a New Lens

Readers should now have a quite different perspective on the pastoral relationship in nineteenth-century American culture. They have, I hope, acquired a new lens that permits them to see it in new ways. Revisit, for example, figure 14: the print of the "reading room" at the Lechmere Hotel in the Kalloch case. To nineteenth-century viewers, it offered a titillating glimpse of the minister and woman in a domestic space. He prepares for his lecture while she primps before the mirror. Beneath the bed and above the transom, three voyeurs transform the apparently innocent scene into a lurid nest of adultery. However, viewing that image through a new lens offers additional and unintended insight into the antebellum pastoral relationship. Kalloch's relaxed self-confidence, elegant clothing, and self-absorption in his studies all impress the viewer with his professionalism and high social status. Although he occupies the same space as the woman, he pays no attention to her. His back is turned toward her as he concentrates on his masculine business— the intellectual task of preparing his lecture for the evening. The woman's pose is less easily interpreted, however. Nineteenth-century readers familiar with other trials might see the woman as a temptress, vainly primping before her own image in the mirror, hoping to entice Kalloch's attention. Readers familiar with travelers' accounts, those that detected a too-reverent female gaze on the man in the pulpit, might see the woman as an adoring disciple, casting an indirect but worshipful glance at Kalloch in secret. But after one reads the private records of both pastors and women presented in Part IV of this volume, an alternative interpretation of this graphic image emerges, one that may better explain the pastoral relationship as it was experienced in nineteenth-century America.[1]

In the alternative scenario, the minister still ignores his parishioner, but the woman engages in neither narcissism nor idolatry. Instead, she is engrossed in reflective soul-searching, questioning what exactly her pastor has to offer her either spiritually or physically. Viewed as an estranged couple, with backs turned toward each other, instead of an amorous one, the image aptly illustrates the pastoral relationship as nineteenth-century ministers and women experienced it. Contemporary viewers, culturally conditioned to see mutual admiration in the pastoral relationship, probably failed to perceive the subtext of mutual rejection that emerges from this striking image. But, as we saw in Part IV, this may be the most telling image of the pastoral relationship. Pastor and female parishioner neither enjoyed nor sought a mutually satisfying spiritual relationship. Instead, both endured the intrusive gaze of a suspicious public who saw them, with or without hard evidence, straying beyond their respective spheres and caught in compromising surroundings. Separate-spheres ideology is the powerful, but ultimately inadequate, conceptualization of gender relations that allowed nineteenth-century Americans to interpret this image as that of a too-intimate pastoral relationship. Only by examining the relationship from the inside out can we see through a new lens. Although both pastor and female parishioner occupied the same space, whether public or private, we can see them distanced rather than allied by separate spheres.

"Feminization" is the powerful, but ultimately inadequate, paradigm that has distorted the historian's view of the relationship and produced a similar interpretation of that image. Historians saw individual churches as "feminized" because women dominated the membership of most congregations. Even though men retained firm control of leadership positions, the institutional church looked "feminized" because women took on more active roles in religiously inspired benevolent and reform organizations. Clergy, too, looked "feminized" because they lost status and authority and served a largely female clientele. Because Calvinist orthodoxy lost ground to a sentimental evangelicalism in many pulpits, theology appeared to become "feminized," too. And finally, when sentimental novels rather than theological treatises dominated the popular press, American culture seemed to succumb to "feminization" as well. Historians took at face value the portraits of clergy under the influence of women and of women under the influence of clergy that were painted by travel writers such as Frances Trollope and Harriet Martineau and exposed by sensational trials. Male clerical leaders and religion itself seemed to have shifted from the masculine public sphere of logic and law to the feminine domestic sphere of sentiment.

"Feminization," however, fails to explain the much more complex portrait of pastoral relationships that emerges from a closer look at the perspectives of travel writers and sensational trial publications and also from an examination of a variety of fictional genres, pastoral manuals, and the private writings of pastors and women. In that more complex portrait, the clergy consistently resisted the shifting gender ideology of separate spheres that seemed to press them into a feminine domestic sphere. Instead, they bowed to those same cultural pressures by redefining the ministry as a masculine enterprise. As patriarchal and familial models lost their power to define masculine authority, the clergy adopted new professional and entrepreneurial models of masculinity for their work. The ministry pioneered the professionalization of American culture, a process that sometimes subtly, sometimes self-consciously, excluded "feminine" values in its practice and women as practitioners. The clergy's wholesale acceptance and promulgation of separate-spheres ideology gives evidence of their commitment to maintaining gender distinctions and situating themselves firmly within the masculine sphere. As historian Nancy Cott observed about all middle-class American men during this period, domestic ideology was "a means to underline and shore up manhood (by differentiating it from womanhood) at a time when the traditional concomitants and supports of manhood . . . were being undermined and transformed."[2]

The feminization paradigm fails to explain not only the ways the clergy distanced themselves from the feminine sphere but also the ways that women distanced themselves from masculine clerical leadership. Though they sat mute under the teaching of a male minister on many Sabbaths, they often expressed dissatisfaction and disillusionment in their criticisms of the man, his manner, and his lessons. Few women left the church entirely, few tried to make it more accepting of women's participation, and fewer still tried to remake it as a feminine institution. Still, Abigail Price's call to make women legitimate pastors in the church might be seen as a moderate reform, given the unspoken alternatives. Instead, women's religious lives frequently centered on family and, more particularly, on a "female world" of prayer groups, private conversation, correspondence, and reading. Women young and old sought out each other as friends and teachers for spiritual guidance. Mothers both advised daughters and depended on them for advice in return. Fathers, husbands, and brothers, rather than pastors, provided masculine, yet familial spiritual support for a number of women. Many women relied on tracts, printed sermons, missionary biographies, and sentimental novels for inspiration and models for their spiritual lives. Few, surprisingly, reported specifically consulting the Bible for religious instruction, even though they confidently quoted and interpreted scripture. Many trusted themselves as advisors by confiding to their diaries and reflecting there on their experiences. The only partnerships between clergymen and women that emerged from the private writings of this sample of women were those contained within the family and marriage. In short, this evidence shows that women who regularly attended church and supported religion relied hardly at all on their male clerical leaders for personal spiritual counsel. Rather, they accommodated themselves to an imperfect masculine institution rather than publicly protest or reform that institution.[3]

Clergymen and women, for the most part, maintained a discreet distance. An "uneasy truce" may be a better characterization of the relationship between the two groups than the "uneasy alliance" posited by historian Ann Douglas. While men headed churches with large female memberships, clergymen and women were estranged by gender differences. How can historians acknowledge the power of these gender differences within the pastoral relationship without falling back on essentialist explanations of sexual difference or, on the other hand, retreating to the position that separate spheres was not only an ideology but also a reality? Perhaps a better way to conceptualize the relationship between clergymen and women is to adapt theories first proposed by sociologists of religion decades ago but largely ignored by historians of religion. Historians of religion for too long produced denominational histories, the stories of particular traditions that focused on theology, church leadership, and organized institutions. These histories, however, often ignored the broad spectrum of religious experience that existed both inside and outside the established and organized churches in modern societies. Sociologists, on the other hand, recognized that an "extra-ecclesial" religious experience belonged to the laity rather than religious elites. They termed the very different experiences of those two groups the "Little Tradition" and the "Great Tradition," respectively.[4]

In the past few decades, historians have discovered the rich sources of religious symbolism and social movement that popular religion supplied throughout American history. Peter Williams, for example, traced the diverse popular religious movements from the colonial era to the late twentieth century, arguing that culture, race, and class often separated a "folk" tradition from an "ecclesial" tradition. But Williams failed to note that gender, too, was a factor. Because institutional church leaders generally excluded women from their ranks, women must necessarily fall into a category that corresponds to a "little" or "extra-ecclesial" tradition, related to but separate from the "great" tradition. To understand the geographical, social, cultural, and psychological space that separated the man in the pulpit from the women in the pews is to begin to understand the way the two groups experienced religion differently in the same institution. Despite all the threats to their status as men and public leaders, nineteenth-century clergymen continued to participate in a "great" tradition that was almost wholly masculine.[5]

Heirs of centuries of organized Christianity, the clergy carried on a tradition of elite masculine leadership in institutional religion at the same time that they helped to create a new "professional" identity for themselves. They still relied on theological and doctrinal (or rational and legal) definitions of religion to distinguish one denomination from another. They continued to perform in the public sphere, using the pulpit and the religious press to disseminate the gospel and debate doctrine. In the nineteenth century, clergy added to their masculine power by administering increasingly larger educational, benevolent, reform, and missionary organizations. In both Catholic and Protestant Christianity, the masculine "great" tradition had embraced an expansive mission, looking outward to the frontier and overseas to promote church growth. More than ever before, church leaders measured the success of their efforts in numbers of missions and converts. Although uneducated sectarians might appear to be outside this "great" tradition, these mostly male leaders still drew on an apostolic tradition to legitimate their authority. Male church leaders expressed distress at their loss of social and civic status, at the competition for public moral authority from other professionals, and at the flight of male members from the church, but they suffered few direct threats from women to their ownership of church authority. Their efforts to defend doctrinal positions against proliferating sects, to oppose papist invaders, and to vigorously promote "separate spheres" for men and women should be seen as a zealous defense of a distinctly masculine great tradition. Whatever concessions they might have made to women—whether modifications of manners, methods, "measures," or doctrine—they made them reluctantly and sparingly.

A clerical defense of that tradition continued in a more self-consciously masculine vein in the decades after the Civil War. A persistent call for a "manly" Chritianity constituted one assertion of masculine power in the churches. Another, from the most conservative wing of the church, was the fundamentalist rejection of modernism by a careful, intellectual rationalization of traditional Calvinist orthodoxy. Still another, from the liberal side, was a vigorous Social Gospel that required men to take seriously their Christian principles in the public sphere and use their economic and political power to reform society. At the same time, theological seminaries discovered a new, more "masculine" rationale for pastoral work. Professional and masculine "social science" methods, drawn from the new academic disciplines of psychology, sociology, and anthropology, gradually replaced traditional but outmoded patriarchal models for pastoral work. All these postbellum movements represented not a "remasculinization" of Christianity, as historian David Hackett called it, but the continuation of a process of redefining the masculinity of the ministry begun at the beginning of the century.[6]

Women filled the pews and dominated the membership lists of Christian churches but almost never participated on an equal basis in that "masculine" tradition of leadership. They took part, instead, in a "feminine" tradition of religious experience that coexisted more or less peacefully with the "great" or "masculine" tradition. Religion for most women was not a creed, a charismatic leader, an institution, or a geographic place. For some, at least, religion was an individual spiritual orientation to God, one that varied considerably from one woman to the next. Women did not share a "natural" inclination to one theology or another. They embraced and rejected a wide range of doctrines dispensed by spokesmen for various religious viewpoints and felt confident in judging the truth, effectiveness, manner, and authority of the preacher. Most often, they sought a preacher who confirmed their own interpretations or doctrinal positions. While certainly limited, the spiritual autonomy expressed by these women suggests a degree of independence in spiritual matters rarely acknowledged by their own cultural peers or by historians since. Rather than thoughtless sheep following an unreliable bellwether, women appeared to be autonomous seekers for truth in a variety of people and sources within and without the institutional churches.

The case of one extraordinary woman may represent to some extent the experience of many of her more ordinary sisters who expressed frustration with male church leaders. Lucy Mack Smith, the mother of the founder and prophet of the Mormon church, exhibited in the extreme the kind of spiritual autonomy displayed by other women of her time. She was frequently disappointed in her search for pastoral guidance. On visiting one Deacon Davies, she complained that he was overly concerned with her physical condition and gave her not "one word in relation to Christ or godliness," an approach that "sickened and disgusted" her. She returned home very sorrowful and disillusioned. This incident launched her on a purposeful search for spiritual truth. Although she visited numerous churches and listened to many preachers over several years, she sometimes felt the preacher "neither understood nor appreciated the subject upon which he spoke." Finally, she found a minister who would baptize her but "leave me free in regard to joining any religious denomination." She found a permanent spiritual home only when her son, Joseph Smith, began his prophetic revelations and offered her a uniquely familial church. That church attracted many women after Lucy Mack Smith, perhaps in part because it included all men as clergy, not just an elite. The roles of father, husband, and son were inseparable from the roles of priest and religious leader. Women might more easily seek spiritual guidance from a man who was a family member than from a professional outside the family. Perhaps more benefited from the kind of spiritual partnership that women married to clergymen seemed to have enjoyed. And, ironically, the decision to reinforce patriarchy in Mormon families through polygamous marriage offered women a larger and more immediate sisterhood from which to draw spiritual support and sustenance than those who lived in monogamous relationships.[7]

Religion as a social orientation, not just a theological or institutional orientation, constituted an important part of the feminine or "little" tradition. The church for many women was a community of family and friends but not one necessarily gathered in the same building every Sabbath. As historian Joan Gundersen demonstrated in her study of eighteenth-century Anglicans, women participated in what she called a "non-institutional" church long before the more formal organizations of the nineteenth century attracted active women to the church. This familial and communal aspect of the church continued to be a source of support for many women, whether or not they engaged in more formal associations. Women's private sources show they relied for spiritual counsel not just on immediate family and friends but on relatives and acquaintances near and far. They discoursed on religion, not in the "great" tradition of the pulpit or the press but in the "little" tradition of personal conversation, small group discussion, and private correspondence or personal diaries. The "great" tradition, of course, made room for some women's communities within the institutional church, most notably in the case of Catholic nuns. For centuries, these women structured their spiritual communities and provided pastoral care to the young, the poor, the sick, and the members of their own sex. Some Lutheran denominations, too, supported similar religious communities of deaconesses. Most nineteenth-century Protestant women's organizations, however, continued this tradition in a less formal way, helping destitute seminarians, supporting pastors at home and missionaries abroad, clothing, feeding, and rehabilitating the poor and vice-ridden, and educating children—all activities firmly within cultural definitions of the feminine. For the most part, however, a feminine tradition of religious participation has been characterized by voluntary work in the broadly defined domestic sphere, only marginally within the "great" tradition.[8]

Explaining the separate religious experiences of clergymen and women by labeling them dominant, great, or masculine traditions and subordinate, little, or feminine traditions is useful only to an extent because it obscures the way the two traditions sometimes overlapped and the huge variations that existed in both categories. But these two categories help to correct the "peculiar and insidious" vision of a church, a clergy, and a theology that were feminized, hybridized, or transformed in some fundamental way during the nineteenth century. Because contemporary ideals of gender roles labeled as deviant any behavior that did not conform to distinct constructs of sexual difference, no truly androgynous model of the Christian gained much favor then or now. Despite long-held Christian ideals of spiritual equality and new liberal ideals of natural and women's rights, most men and women in the church chose to maintain their separate religious traditions because those old roles conformed to newly constructed ideals of gender difference and separation.

Still, shifting notions of appropriate gender roles for men and women fueled women's discontent with their subordinate position in the church. Pastors as *patriarchs* commanded respect and allegiance from women. Pastors as *professionals* had to earn respect from women who saw themselves as moral and sometimes educational peers. In a newly competitive religious market-place, many women for the first time in history could freely choose their pastors from among a number of men. They could criticize and even reject preachers if they wished. They could conceive new pastoral roles for women in their imaginative literature. A very few could challenge men's exclusive right to church leadership.

Understanding that women and clergy in the church were estranged rather than allied helps explain the slow progress of women toward spiritual and social equality in the nineteenth-century churches. Female evangelists had roamed the countryside in the eighteenth and early nineteenth centuries, but a backlash against women preachers by mid-century ensured that only a few women earned ordination by its end. At the same time that Abigail Price demanded female spiritual leadership at the Syracuse Woman's Rights Convention in 1852, Antoinette Brown Blackwell attended Charles Finney's pastoral theology lectures at Oberlin College but only briefly served as a pastor, ordained by her congregation. In the last few decades of the century, a small but significant number of women penetrated the ranks of male clergy in the liberal Congregationalist and Unitarian denominations. So, few women gained recognition for their spiritual leadership in the dominant churches. More explicit expressions of nineteenth-century women's discontent with the male monopoly on the clerical profession can be found outside the religious mainstream, however.[9]

Women's religious movements often, and of necessity, constituted themselves as "extra-ecclesial," anticlerical, and anti-institutional. As early as 1776, Mother Ann Lee declared her independence from both clergy and erotic desire. Her Shaker movement eliminated the office of the clergy and, to eliminate the threat of sexuality in any religious relationships, demanded celibacy of all adherents. After her death, some Shakers even admitted that Ann Lee had embodied Christ in her female body. Yet despite such radical concepts of androgynous and asexual spirituality, Shaker communities grew steadily through the mid-nineteenth century. Other expressions of women's discontent with the masculine great tradition can be discovered in the parachurch of nineteenth-century spiritualism. Female preachers' voices may have been largely silenced by mid-century, but female spiritualists took their places. They challenged male clerical authority by speaking publicly before mixed audiences, through "spiritual voices" if not their own. Spiritualists resisted organizing formal churches and remained anti-institutional and often explicitly anticlerical throughout the nineteenth century. Abigail Sewall, whose private correspondence cited in the last chapter showed her deep disgust with preachers and the institutional church, eventually embraced spiritualism. Within its loose theology, she discovered the doctrine she most favored. And among her deceased female family members and friends, she discovered the pastors from whom she derived the most benefit.[10]

Perhaps the most powerful female religious leader of the nineteenth century, if not in American history thus far, established a church quite explicitly opposed to the exclusively male professionalized ministry of her day. Mary Baker Eddy, founder of the highly successful Church of Christ, Scientist, worked hard to eliminate those aspects of the masculine church that most disappointed women. She banished the contentious preacher from the pulpit and replaced him with a rotating reader who used her prescribed texts and interpretations. In the first years, a man usually served as reader, but in later years the congregation elected both a male and female reader to share the duties. These readers never interpreted scripture, however. Eddy tried to eliminate theological controversy by providing her adherents with her own definitive interpretation of scripture. The Bible and her publication *Science and Health with Key to the Scriptures*, she declared, would "henceforth be the Pastor of the Mother Church." "Personal preaching," Eddy maintained, "has more or less of human views grafted into it. Whereas the pure Word contains only the living, health-giving Truth." With an "impersonal" pastor—her own writings as well as the Bible—Eddy hoped to remove the masculine taint of ambition from the office of the reader, too. No special theological training was required. For each week of the year, she provided texts and interpretation so that followers could rely on reading and hearing a consistent and undisputed theology. Thus, Eddy deposed the masculine professional preacher—too contentious and pretentious for many women—and replaced him with lay members of the congregation.[11]

As Eddy eliminated the professional preacher, however, she elevated personal pastoral work to professional status. "A real scientific Healer," she wrote, "is the highest position attainable in this sphere of being. Its altitude is far above a Teacher or preacher; it includes all that is divinely high and holy." Eddy created a rank of counselors, called practitioners, to serve as these "scientific Healers." Many, though not all, were women schooled at her Massachusetts Metaphysical College to provide care and spiritual advice to their clients. Her followers, therefore, no longer depended on unreliable professional male pastors or physicians to heal their spiritual and physical pain. Eddy herself re-corded decades of illness and spiritual distress that these men had failed to cure. Now, her adherents could call on women knowledgeable in the art and science of imparting physical and spiritual health.[12]

Eddy's distrust of the institutional church and its leaders, both firmly within the masculine great tradition, ran deep. Like "primitive" Christian movements before and after her time, she tried to strip away the layers of accumulated cultural and institutional practice and ritual. She centered her church on the Word, not man, and on "spiritualized thought," not "personal preaching." Yet ironically, as she fought to eliminate these "man-made" ele-ments of the Christian church, she succumbed to them. Her own growing institutional church suffered from the very problems she tried to avoid. To control the orthodoxy of her interpretations of scripture, she institutionalized them in numerous publications, her school, and the organization of the mother church. She became embroiled in endless disputes and litigation with followers who disagreed with her. Her work was constantly revised and attacked from within and without her church, despite her best efforts to eliminate controversy. Her schools and her press battled to maintain the "purity" of her vision. She resisted having her followers call her Mother and make her an icon of the church, but many idolized her. In other words, Eddy's struggle to create a religion free of the problems of the masculine tradition, in the end, embodied them all.

Women's struggle within and against the masculine tradition continued throughout the twentieth century. By its end, dozens of denominations or-dained more and more women, and many theological seminaries reported that women made up a majority of students, yet denominational leadership re-mained largely a masculine prerogative. In fact, recent studies show that the ministry continued to view pastoral work as feminine—women's work, not men's. Catholic nuns have been allowed to assume the title of pastor but not priest. Even in denominations that welcomed women as clergy, those women most often assumed assistant roles to male head pastors and primarily per-formed duties as personal pastors and religious educators rather than as administrators and preachers. Male clergy still dominated the professional leadership of most denominations and seminaries and, like their nineteenth-century brethren, largely delegated personal spiritual counseling to women. So, even though women have made great strides in gaining some equality within the ranks of the clergy, women and men remain divided within those ranks. But, at least, women have come to claim official roles as pastors and perhaps to shape the ministry in ways more beneficial to women.[13]

In the twentieth century, as in the nineteenth, women may still have re-mained within the institutional church without much personal spiritual benefit from male clergy. But cultural perceptions of the pastoral relationship changed significantly, again in large part because of changing gender ideologies. The second wave of feminism that emerged in the last half of the twentieth century, like its first-wave counterpart in the nineteenth, called for gender equality at the same time that it exposed the historical sources of gender difference, the problems caused by the culturally constructed notions of gender difference, and the possible advantages of reforming culture and society in a more feminist (feminine) cast. A push for gender equality in late-twentieth-century feminism called for more women entering the ranks of previously exclusive male professions, such as the clergy, but also in all other masculine occupations from firefighters to construction workers. Gender egalitarianism also implied that neither men nor women could or should claim moral superiority over the other. Finally, it tried to erase a long-held double standard that punished women more severely than men for sexual promiscuity and generally assumed that both adult men and adult women were responsible for policing their own moral behavior, especially sexual behavior. In short, ideals of gender equality changed some of the dynamics of the pastoral relationship. The culture no longer linked women and ministers as allies with the special burden of public guardianship of morality. No cultural spotlight shone on them, magnifying and distorting their behavior, no matter how innocent. In a world of gender equality, women might more easily choose among men and women as pastors and spiritual leaders or counselors without suffering either the great chasm of gender difference in that relationship or the stress of erotic attraction. Because women in a culture of gender equality are neither more nor less moral than men, they are neither more nor less vulnerable than are men in sexual relationships. So, while scandals involving prominent clergymen still routinely made headlines and scandals involving less celebrated pastors still caused confusion and conflict in local congregations, they tended to generate cynicism and humor rather than horror and fascination. As the impeachment of President Clinton demonstrated, however, Americans were deeply divided over the issue of holding public leaders accountable for their sexual behavior and, indeed, what was morally acceptable sexual behavior.

Over the last four decades of the twentieth century, both the sexual revolution and the civil rights movement (for racial minorities, women, alternative sexualities, and the disabled, among others) created a culture at war with itself. Among a secular and liberal Christian portion of the population, newly constructed gender norms relaxed prohibitions against consensual and extramarital sex among heterosexual adults. Among these progressive groups, interracial and homosexual couples enjoyed less stigma as well. These still marginalized couples sometimes found male and female clergy to sanction their unions. This liberal segment of the culture also increasingly accepted adolescent sexuality as normative and attempted to manage it through sex education that insisted on mutual consent while minimizing pregnancy and sexually transmitted disease. This group defended abortion as a woman's right, defined the term "family" in a variety of forms, and promoted multicultural tolerance and understanding. Among American Catholics, for the most part more conservative than the liberal Protestants, many laypersons and even clergy went against a conservative church hierarchy and reduced social prohibitions against birth control, divorce, and remarriage but generally not toward abortion.

On the other hand, a powerful religious right (made up primarily of conservative evangelicals and fundamentalists among others) tried to resist these cultural changes and reinforce crumbling barriers against all but heterosexual marital intercourse. These "pro-family" groups mounted the barricades to defend strictures against extramarital, homosexual, and sometimes interracial sex. They enforced traditional gender roles by opposing abortion, usually defined a family as nuclear and male-dominated, and denied adolescent sexuality by preaching sexual abstinence.

If these two groups converged at all, it was in trying to maintain the line against irresponsible or unwanted adolescent and, especially, child sex. Politically, they agreed to send young welfare mothers to school or to work and to deny them extended benefits for additional illegitimate children. Curiously, a double standard still prevailed as both the cultural and political left and right generally agreed to punish young women much more harshly and regularly than young men for illicit and irresponsible sexual activity. But as an ideology of gender equality insisted that women assume roles as equally responsible, independent, and autonomous adults, only children now enjoyed the protection (and limitations imposed on their behavior) once reserved for both women and children. Letting women through the gate, however, made maintaining the barrier against children more difficult to patrol.

While they disagreed about the reasons, both groups agreed that prohibiting sex between adults and children was an almost unquestionable boundary to preserve. The left generally opposed sexual relationships in all unequal power relationships. Thus sexual harassment in the workplace or in a professional relationship was increasingly policed to promote gender equality in the face of continuing masculine dominance of work and other relationships. It labeled sexual activity between any professional—clergy, doctors, therapists, lawyers, and educators—and a female or dependent client inappropriate and exploitative. And, since children obviously suffered an unequal power relationship with adults, they could never engage in consensual sex with adults. Conservative groups usually condemned child sex on traditional moral grounds prohibiting any extramarital sex (while still sanctioning marriage and marital sex between young adults). Both groups also generally opposed violence in sexual relationships. They also often objected to an increasingly sexualized culture that used media images of sex and violence to sell a wide variety of goods and entertainment to these same young people.[14]

So any transgression of the boundary between adult consensual sex and sex between children and adults made visible some contradictory cultural values and fragile cultural prohibitions against sex and violence among children. It also exposed a slippery boundary between childhood and adulthood. As male children took up arms in schools and on streets, an alarmed public increasingly chose to treat them judicially as adults. As male and female children joined violent gangs and prepubescent female children affected the sexually provocative dress of their media role models, schools tried to discourage sex and violence with uniforms or dress codes and conflict management courses. Despite some deep contradictions in their approaches, then, both sides in the culture wars generally united to oppose sex and violence among younger and younger children. Not surprisingly, then, Protestant clerics who transgressed porous and poorly maintained boundaries between marital and extramarital sexual activities or those Catholic priests who merely broke their vows of celibacy and engaged in heterosexual intercourse earned relatively little media attention and public opprobrium. True horror was reserved for those who made the increasingly eroding boundaries against homosexuality and, especially, taboos against child sexuality all too apparent.[15]

Shifting notions of gender ideology still affect the pastoral relationship, however. While twentieth-century feminists insisted on principles of gender equality, they also explored the sources and consequences of gender difference. Recognizing the historical inequality of power between men and women exposed the political, social, and physical vulnerability of women to abuse by men in all their relationships. Feminists have thus tried to legislate gender equality but paradoxically have called for more legal protection of women against such abuse. Thus, cases of sexual misconduct in the pastoral relationship are sometimes culturally and legally recast as cases of sexual harassment and abuse of power rather than cases of moral and sexual indiscretion. The recent emphasis on gender differences, even by some feminists, sometimes recalls nineteenth-century ideals, however. Many feminists have called for reforms in education, medicine, politics, law, and business that reflect more "feminine" or feminist values that might be termed democratic, cooperative, exemplary, and nurturing over and against more "masculine" values that are elitist, competitive, aggressive, and scientific or professional. In short, American men and women entered the twenty-first century still viewing and experiencing their pastoral relationships, as well as other personal and professional relationships, distorted and divided by shifting cultural constructions of gender.

Appendix

Historiographical Essay: Counting Sheep; or, What the Historian Did

This study examined the nineteenth-century pastoral relationship from a wide variety of perspectives: from the distanced viewpoint of European travelers to the most intimate perspective of participants. Historians, obviously, hold even more distanced perceptions of that relationship. They approach the pastoral relationship not only from a different time but also from a different culture with different interests in religion, social change, and questions of power and agency shaped by gender, race, and class. In addition, historians apply multiple methodologies, from literary analysis to quantification, to a wide variety of sources—the ephemera, artifacts, and documents that have survived—in order to piece together a picture of the past. Viewing the relationship from a distance may be a challenge, but it also has advantages. The historian can take the long view: examining the subject in its political, economic, and social contexts to understand the broad forces that shaped individual and institutional change. Historians traditionally examined subjects from the top down, analyzing and interpreting the writings of political and intellectual leaders. In the United States, this elite was usually limited to men of European heritage. Since the middle of the last century, however, historians have attempted to view history from the bottom up by investigating the private and published writing, data, and objects left behind by those beneath the elite stratum—the lower classes, women, and racial or ethnic minorities. Historians also sometimes attempt a close-up view of a subject, taking an individual or a community as a case study to determine how representative (or anomalous) it is of the larger society.

Although the pastoral relationship between clergy and women has rarely claimed much of the political historian's attention, studies in church history, literary history, and women's history have sometimes briefly brought the topic into focus and offered arguments, speculation, and assumptions about it. By looking at the historical context of the pastoral relationship, historians saw that increasing democratization, industrialization, and urbanization wrought important changes in nineteenth-century American churches, in the leadership of those churches, and in their membership. Perhaps the most striking and puzzling discovery historians made about churches came, in effect, by counting sheep. By carefully computing the membership of voluntary churches, historians discovered a growing church membership despite the disestablishment of churches in the early republic. In addition, historians discovered that church membership during this period nearly always included a much larger number of women than men, although the revivals of the Second Great Awakening at least temporarily redressed some of the gender imbalance. Whatever the angle of their perspective, historians disagreed about the meaning and significance of these numbers. Yet nearly all agreed or assumed that the numerical supremacy of women in the churches signaled a close relationship between church leaders and their largely female membership.

An Overview; or, the Historical Context of the
Pastoral Relationship

From a distance, historians saw that tremendous political, economic, and social change marked the nineteenth century. The political ideal of equality first voiced during the American Revolution generated broader political participation and increasingly fierce partisanship over the century. The hierarchical political structure of the colonial period, where each man knew his place and deferred to his betters—the wealthier and the more educated—gradually gave way to political ideals of equality. The new nation was an experiment in republican government that generally restricted the vote to stakeholders, the male citizens who owned taxable property. But over the century, both federal and state governments gradually extended the franchise. During the Jacksonian era of the 1820s and 1830s, most white men, even those without substantial property, gained the right to vote. After the Civil War, the Sixteenth Amendment granted all men, including ex-slaves, voting privileges, although few governments protected that right during the first hundred years. By mid-century, women had begun to demand the right to vote as well but failed to gain suffrage at the national level until 1920. In theory at least, any man, even a poor boy born in a log cabin, might grow up to be president in this new political system based on merit and achievement rather than on status or heritage. Where local colonial governments had tried to honor values of consensus, the new nation quickly departed from these values and witnessed the rise of political parties that fostered heated electoral contests and a partisan press. Conflict, not consensus, appeared to be a fixture of American politics when, at mid-century, divisive sectionalism tore the nation apart in the bloodbath of the Civil War.[1]

Late-twentieth-century historians also saw that, despite the painful and limited progress toward political ideals of equality, industrialization produced increasing economic diversity and inequality that exacerbated the conflict in the political realm. Industrialization slowly transformed a nation of farmers into a nation of artisans, entrepreneurs, and wageworkers. The early republic wore an overwhelmingly rural and agricultural face. Trade was generally local, although commercial products such as cotton, fish, and timber reached national and international markets. Thomas Jefferson's pastoral dream of a nation of self-sufficient yeomen, however, quickly evaporated as native-born and immigrant alike left farms and joined the ranks of wage laborers, artisans, merchants, and professionals in small towns and growing cities that became hubs of regional, national, and international commerce. Roads, canals, and then railroads connected the markets of a nation that more than doubled in size over the century. The industrial revolution replaced the production from homes and small mills with mass-produced goods such as the textiles issuing from both small and large factories. Although disparities in wealth and class increased dramatically and steadily over the century, the nineteenth-century American publishing industry reached a largely literate public, affording the nation a shared print culture. The press was increasingly produced by (and reflected and shaped the concerns of) a commercial, technologically progressive, urban society, even though a majority of Americans lived in rural areas up until the 1920 census. Thus, Americans were both divided and united by economic change.[2]

Historians saw that, in the midst of democratization and largely because of industrialization, America developed an urban society quite different in its diversity and anonymity from the village community. The increasing inequality of wealth, plus the expanding immigrant population from Western (and much later in the century, Eastern) Europe, made an already diverse population even more so. Slavery was gradually phased out after the American Revolution in the states north of the Mason-Dixon line and left small but growing communities of free African Americans in small towns and cities who competed for mostly low-wage jobs with the recent immigrants. Face-to-face encounters with familiar community members still marked small town life or even neighborhoods in large cities, but for many Americans the city introduced the social freedom and anarchy of anonymity. A newcomer with an unfortunate past could hope to escape it in the city. On the other hand, a person without history and without family could not easily establish his character or trustworthiness. As a consequence, Americans—especially the growing middle class—developed manners and rituals that would help them identify the honest, reliable, and well educated among the many diverse strangers.[3]

These political, economic, social, and cultural changes produced churches that differed dramatically from their colonial forebears. Historians saw a dramatic "democratization" of American religion during the nineteenth century that produced a wide range of religious organizations competing in a voluntary religious marketplace. Throughout the colonial period, the established Protestant churches—Congregational Puritans in New England, Presbyterians and Dutch Reformed in the middle colonies, Church of England in the south— endured challenges from separatists and sects as diverse as Quakers, Baptists, and Shakers. Even Catholics and Jews supported small but growing congregations through much of the colonial era. The founding fathers reflected their uneasy relationship with religion in the First Amendment to the new Constitution. It prohibited Congress from making any law "respecting the establishment of religion," protecting the new republic from the undue influence or intolerance of a powerful state church. But at the same time, the framers of the new government counted the churches as important sources of moral education in a free society. So the same amendment that forbade the establishment of religion also carefully protected churches by forbidding Congress from making any law "prohibiting the free exercise" of religion. After the revolution, the new states gradually disestablished their churches: Massachusetts, in 1832, was the last state to remove tax support for its Congregational churches. To the surprise of most contemporaries, religious interest thrived, even in the absence of state support.[4]

A series of revivals over the first three decades of the nineteenth century gathered ever more adherents into increasingly diverse voluntary churches— some organized, formal denominations and others small sects or short-lived movements. Historians have variously termed this period the Second Great Awakening, a "hothouse" of religious enthusiasm, a "democratization" of American Christianity, and a nation "awash in a sea of faith." The spectrum of theological difference widened from a fairly narrow Calvinist orthodoxy to the heterodoxy of the Spirtualists and Transcendentalists at one end and the Millerites and Mormons on the other. Some churches resisted the increasing individualism and materialism of American culture while others accommodated it.

Churches reflected the growing economic and social diversity of America. The wealthy funded the construction of elaborate neo-Gothic cathedrals in the big cities, while the poor congregated in their homes, in cramped meetinghouses, or in fields. Denominations like the Episcopalians increasingly appealed to wealthier congregants as movements like the Methodists attracted the financially insecure. African Americans and European immigrants founded their own separate churches. By the middle decades of the century, formerly small groups had reached dominant positions: Methodists grew larger than any other Protestant denomination, and Catholics were the single largest denomination in the United States. Yet this consolidation masked the continuing proliferation of new and old churches that drew Americans to worship throughout the nineteenth century. Although church growth was one measure of religiosity, Americans also demonstrated faith and energy in a huge number of benevolent and reform activities, ranging from temperance, moral reform, and abolition in the first half of the century to domestic and foreign missions and the YMCA in the second half. In short, American churches mirrored the democratic divisiveness, the spirit of growth and progress, and the social and economic diversity of the larger society.[5]

The leveling effects of disestablishment and the competition from the profusion of sects had a profound effect on clergy, who, historians argued, responded by professionalizing. In the first decades of the new century, the clergy lost their protected status as public servants and competed with less educated preachers for pulpits and adherents in a fierce religious marketplace. The conservative and educated elite clergy, trained and ordained by their peers, denounced their democratic rivals as dangerous, uneducated, rabble-rousing enthusiasts. The evangelical upstarts, sometimes illiterates drawing on their own spiritual experiences rather than on theological training, accused the orthodox clergy of lacking inspiration. Yet despite the divisiveness, most orthodox and evangelical clergy over the century developed a method of professional education, systematically training young men in theological seminaries and licensing or ordaining them through denominational organizations. Clergy traded a traditional paternal persona for a professional one, providing a model of training that served, later, for doctors, lawyers, educators, and others with whom they would compete for moral and civic authority in a democratic society. Since the advent of feminist scholarship in the last few decades of the twentieth century, some historians have understood those changes as not only reflections of political and social change but also as part of a profound change in gender roles.[6]

Historians saw that the roles, ideals, and experiences of women and men shifted under the influence of dramatic political, economic, and social change. In the colonial period, the ideal woman worked hard in the home—alongside husbands, fathers, and brothers as well as mothers, sisters, and servants—to produce the food and clothing and maintain the shelter for her family. Although men and women worked at different tasks, they generally shared the same domestic space. Men who worked as artisans and farmers rarely left home—they shared a workspace with women. They also shared with women the task of rearing, teaching, and disciplining children and servants. The husband was the head of the household, but his wife was his helpmeet. A woman was considered the weaker vessel: physically, emotionally, intellectually, and morally inferior to men. As a consequence, she had little autonomy in law. She was termed a *femme covert*—"covered" or cared for by her father when unmarried and by her husband when married. A married woman became one with her husband: Her assets, wages, and even her children belonged to him. This colonial ideal was breached in practice because some women—especially in the absence of husbands—exercised a good deal of autonomy by running households, farms, and businesses. Gender ideology—the way men and women ought to be and to act—during the colonial period was based on a familial and hierarchical model. That ideology changed, however, with the political rhetoric of democratic equality, the economic impact of industrialization, and the social force of increasing class distinctions.[7]

The democratic republic, in which more and more citizens assumed civic responsibility, assigned women the new and important role of "republican mother." As such, they shouldered the responsibility for raising moral, productive young men as future citizens of the republic. Thoughtful leaders called for better education for women to help them perform this important civic duty. The newly industrializing society likewise shaped new roles for men (and sometimes women) by increasingly sending them to work outside the home. They tended shops and offices, ran machines and supervised workers in factories, constructed canals, or sailed ships in a "public sphere" of commerce and industry that took them from home during the day or for weeks and months at a time. Women might, from choice or necessity, follow men into the shops and factories, but the new ideal for middle-class women was to remain in the "domestic sphere," tending to her children and supervising servants to maintain the home. Over the century, the middle-class woman less frequently produced household goods herself and more often purchased food and clothing produced outside her home. Ideally, as a "true woman," she displayed the virtues of piety, sexual purity, submissiveness to the male head of household, and domesticity. Compared with her colonial female ancestors, the ideal woman in the first half of the nineteenth century was no more autonomous in law, but she did assume more domestic responsibility since her husband often worked elsewhere. In contrast, her middle-class husband participated in the competitive public sphere of politics and commerce. He was not expected to uphold the same standards of piety and purity or to participate in the rearing of the children to the same extent as his colonial male ancestors. Thus, true women gained in moral stature what they apparently lost in economic productivity. Instead of man's moral inferior, true woman was his exemplar and guardian. Of course, many poor and working women had difficulty emulating true women, but like their more privileged sisters, even factory girls strove to live up to these ideals. Historians noted that the cultural and psychological advantages the true woman enjoyed over her colonial ancestors were mixed, however, and have debated whether nineteenth-century women were better off than their colonial sisters under the new dispensation of separate spheres ideology.[8]

Historians saw some positive effects for women in the new ideals and roles assigned to them, despite the fact that they more strictly segregated women in the domestic sphere from men in the public sphere. Because good republican mothers undertook the moral education of young children and exemplary true women displayed moral superiority over men, women might be expected to extend their moral "influence"—the only power they might properly exert outside the home—to take on more public roles of moral stewardship. Historians discovered that women increasingly replaced men as teachers of the young during this period. They noted that women collectively raised money (their "mites") to support young seminarians, missionaries at home and abroad, temperance, moral reform, and abolition. In the new voluntary churches, women still usually outnumbered men by two to one, just as in most colonial churches. But women seemed to work harder than in the past to bring in male family members, to support revival efforts, and to participate in praying, exhorting, and even preaching in public. In fact, historians saw that women's religious roles often justified their active participation in the supposedly public sphere.[9]

The historian's broad view of political, economic, social, and religious change in nineteenth-century America yielded important insights about the effects of such changes on the pastoral relationship. Because the churches and the clergy were charged with upholding the morality of the republic and women were charged with upholding the morality of the family, historians posited a close relationship, even an alliance, between the two groups of moral guardians. Statistics seemed to confirm that bond. By distinguishing between men and women in the various flocks, historians documented that the vast majority of church members—from 55 to 75 percent or more by various counts—were women. These startling numbers prompted historians to look for, speculate upon, and make assumptions about the reasons for women's stronger, and men's lesser, attraction to the churches. They have explored the problem from the top down, from the bottom up, from the outside in, from one side of the relationship or from the other, from a telescopic view of the big picture, and from the microscopic view of individual relationships. In short, historians have looked at a huge variety of external evidence and external forces and come up with an amazing variety of explanations for women's impressive presence in the churches.

Unfortunately, counting female sheep has lulled historians into a fitful consensus. The power of those numbers confirmed historians in their assumption that an affinity developed between the two principal parties within the church—the clergy and their overwhelmingly female congregants. They have, sometimes reluctantly, agreed that women's presence signaled a "feminization" of, variously, the church, the clergy, theology, religion in general, and even the American culture as a whole, while disagreeing about whether that process was ultimately good or bad, "progress" or "declension," liberating or accommodating. Thus, in the view of many historians, changing gender roles and demographic evidence combined to produce a theory of feminization that has become an encompassing, enduring, powerful, and, at the same time, controversial explanation for both the causes and consequences of the phenomenon of female majorities in American churches.

The social historians, who looked at the churches from the perspective of women, found allies even among more traditional historians of political, intellectual, and religious history, who viewed the churches from the perspective of its leadership. They generally saw the decades surrounding the Revolutionary War as a period of religious "declension." Declining church membership seemed to reflect the deism and even religious infidelity of many of the founding fathers. In addition, the forces of liberalism and religious tolerance divorced the church from the state, making churches dependent on voluntary rather than government support. For some historians, this was an inevitable process of modernization—moving away from a communal and hierarchical vision of state and church to an individualistic and democratic model of state and church. In other words, declension for many intellectual historians was a positive move away from a medieval and European orientation to religion and toward a modern and American one, from a superstitious, religious worldview to a rational, secular one. These historians, for the most part, viewed this declension from a masculine and secular perspective. They failed to note that while men's participation in the churches was dropping, women's membership remained constant or grew during this same period. So, any positive effects of "declension" applied to men, not women. The view from the top down, although still from a masculine perspective, also produced a nearly opposite interpretation of the period from the beginning of the nineteenth century forward.[10]

A later generation of intellectual historians noted that in the Second Great Awakening of the first three decades of the new century, a revival of an emotional or "heart-centered" evangelical theology gradually displaced the "head-centered" rational theology of orthodox Calvinism. Calvinism had emphasized the strict and omnipotent judgment of a wrathful God over helpless and sinful human beings. Evangelical Christianity increasingly emphasized a loving God who forgave any sinners who chose repentance and might even help them achieve salvation, if not perfectionism. Some historians saw this change as a different kind of declension. They saw falling standards for admission to the church and salvation and a decline from Calvinism to an Arminian heresy. The means of salvation slipped from the hands of God into the hands of humans. The intellectual rigor of orthodoxy and the "hard" doctrines of salvation confined to the elect gave way to the "soft" tenets of a universal salvation available to all who chose to embrace it. Even worse, some historians noted that this change coincided with the higher percentages of women as church members. They noted that Calvinist doctrines such as infant damnation, which they surmised were especially repugnant to women, fell from the doctrinal vocabulary of many denominations. But whether the "softening" of theology was a cause or an effect of the increasing numbers of women and the decreasing numbers of men still puzzled historians. Did clergy react to the increasing numbers of women by tailoring a theology to feminine values, or were women attracted to preachers who espoused a more liberal theology?[11]

Only one historian produced a monograph that explored the pastoral relationship between clergy and women in much depth, and her nightmarish interpretation has influenced perceptions on the topic for more than two decades. Ann Douglas's study of the pastoral relationship examined the lives and literary works of thirty women and thirty clergymen, most of them well educated and liberal in their politics and theology. From this sample, Douglas argued that clergy, as well as church and theology, became "feminized." Douglas saw that "disestablishment" and marginalization affected both clergy and women. The two groups both lost important and recognizable roles in the masculine sphere of politics and economics. The nineteenth-century clergy, especially those who surrendered the "hard" Calvinist orthodoxy for the "soft" sentimentalism of Unitarian and Universalist theology, lost their intellectual power and authority as moral guardians and as men. By writing sentimental novels instead of theological dissertations, they exchanged "fiction" for "dogma." They lost their manhood with their orthodoxy, Douglas contended, becoming "emasculated," enfeebled, and ultimately displaced by women. Women, too, lost economic power when they surrendered their household production to men and machines. To compensate, they tried to assume moral authority, also through the production of sentimental literature. "Ministers and mothers," in Douglas's view, were thrown together in an "uneasy alliance." Ministers became more like women; women became more like ministers. Through their production of a sentimental literature that held up passivity rather than agency as a virtue, the two groups could exercise only a limited "influence" rather than real power in American culture.[12]

Douglas saw few redeeming qualities in this mostly literary alliance. She conceded that, on occasion, it allowed "lady and clergyman" to "cross cruel lines laid down by sexual stereotyping." Women could be aggressive and angry in the right cause; ministers could be gentle, even nurturing, in their pastoral role. But for the most part, Douglas took a dim view of women's ministerial role and clergymen's maternal role, as well as the "parasitic interaction between ministerial and feminine egos." The minister was "cut off from his masculine heritage" and pushed into a feminine sphere. He competed with women for "possession of sacred territory." Ministers even displayed hostility to women as they came to resent the "too cramped common space" they shared with women. Within this confined space, however, the "bonds of nineteenth-century liberal clergymen with their female parishioners were apt to be close ones which formed early, and held." Indeed, women exercised "genuine control, no matter how limited, over their ministers," Douglas insisted. While Douglas devoted a few chapters to analysis of this putative bond between women and clergy, her real purpose was to explain the decline of Calvinist theology and the rise of sentimental literature. Douglas argued that the "feminization" of the clergy accompanied a feminization of theology and literary culture. The hard, rational doctrines of Calvinism—that a stern and judgmental God chose only an elect for salvation and damned all others, including infants—gave way to a sentimental belief that a kind and forgiving God saved everyone, no matter how sinful. Clergy dispensed this theology from the pulpit, but women popularized it in their highly popular sentimental novels. Together, they "feminized" American culture. Douglas's indictment of the pastoral relationship between clergy and women was a condescending judgment of a small, elite group that served her larger indictment of sentimental literature and American culture. Nevertheless, her negative assessment of the pastoral relationship shaped historians' perceptions in powerful ways.[13]

In contrast to Douglas, historians who looked at the female majorities in the churches from the perspective of the pew (a mostly feminine perspective) instead of from the pulpit tended to take a more positive and progressive view of women's presence and influence in religion. To be sure, some of these social historians and historians of women have noted the ways that the church and Christian theology frequently served as a conservative force for the social control, limitation, and even oppression of women. However, many also have noted the ways that religion helped women accommodate to their unstable, changing, and restricted roles within a modernizing society. Some historians of women have even suggested that the church had a liberating effect for women. For example, the inherent egalitarianism of Christ's teachings, the ways that piety elevated women over men, and the dignity and autonomy the church granted to women in their roles as wives and mothers all potentially worked in women's favor. So did the church and benevolent activities that gave women an important social and political role acceptable within their designated domestic sphere. These historians have noted women's agency in bringing themselves and their families to conversion, as well as their increasing use of religious authority to assert demands for emancipation and suffrage for slaves and for themselves. In other words, religion helped women cope with unsettling change in the first half of the nineteenth century, but it also gave them a source of authority and a scope for their individual and collective agency. From the perspective of the pew, the feminization of the church and theology looked like a generally positive step up from the superstitious and oppressive misogyny of Puritanism to the validation of female agency in evangelical and liberal Protestantism.[14]

A few historians of this period have focused on the pastoral relationship by examining one of several public trials of ministers for sexual misconduct. They looked at a particular pastor and his relationships with women and discovered exactly what nineteenth-century observers did—a very dangerous and dysfunctional relationship. What distinguished the historians' view from the contemporaries' view, in general, was the historical consciousness they could bring to the topic. Although they looked at one man and his pastorate under a microscope, they also stood back and looked at the man in his broader historical context and tried to explain the cultural and historical forces that shaped his behavior and the publicity that attended it. So, for instance, David Kasserman explained the Ephraim Avery trial as symptomatic of the growing pains of industrialization. The trial illustrated the growing class divisions between traditional wives and mothers and female factory workers, as well as the conflict between bourgeois factory owners on one hand and "enthusiastic" Methodist clergy on the other. Similarly, students of the Henry Ward Beecher trial tended to condemn the man as an example of Gilded Age cultural excess and hypocrisy. For the most part, however, historians treated these cases as isolated and unusual events, rather than as part of a recurrent cultural preoccupation with the pastoral relationship during the nineteenth century.[15]

Despite their many disagreements, nearly all historians agreed with Douglas that female majorities signaled a "feminized" church that was more attractive to women than to men. Some confirmed that female majorities marked a feminized theology and a somewhat emasculated clergy, arguing only that it began earlier, ended earlier, or that its effects were more positive than Douglas described. Not even historians of masculinity have challenged her perception of the clergy. Anthony Rotundo noted that "the minister's tasks placed him at a great distance from the men who subjected themselves to the daily pressures of the market." In addition, he speculated that the public perception of ministers matched Douglas's view: The "daily association of the clergy with women and with the traits and cultural spaces allotted to women must surely have had an impact on the popular view of their profession." Similarly, the historian of religion E. Brooks Holifield looked at pastoral advice literature and argued that nineteenth-century stereotypes about feminine domesticity and piety "shaped clerical conceptions of pastoral labor" and, indeed, that "early nineteenth-century pastoral care was designed for an institution filled with women." Thus, no matter what their orientation was, few historians have questioned the assumption that, in a "feminized" church, clergy adopted a position and crafted a message peculiarly attractive to women and that, as a result, women developed close relationships, whether productive or dangerous, with their pastors. Only a few hints of dissent appeared. Jane Pease and William Pease agreed that preachers "vying for followers played on women's special susceptibilities . . . with special appeals to women's emotions." But they also uncovered examples of tension between women in benevolent groups and the ministers who tried to control their activities. In addition, Margaret Thompson studied Catholic nuns and sisters in nineteenth-century America and characterized the relationship between this select group of women and their pastors and clerical supervisors as one marked chiefly by "conflict." But since few American historians consider Catholicism as equal to Calvinism in its cultural influence and intellectual rigor, or Catholic women religious as counterparts of middle-class Protestant laywomen, no historian has yet discovered a similar process of "feminization" in nineteenth-century Catholicism.[16]

From the broad view, from the top looking down, from the bottom looking up, or from the outside looking in, the consensus around the feminization theory of women's influence on the church fails to satisfy, to result in true consensus, or to bring fresh understanding of the pastoral relationship. Historians have failed to open their eyes and look specifically at the pastoral relationship from the inside out—from the perspective of the participants in this most personal relationship—and to test the assumption that women and clergy enjoyed a close, perhaps dangerously close, relationship. They have failed to look at the private writings of ordinary pastors and their female congregants and specifically at personal pastoral relationships in order to test the validity of this assumption of a "peculiar" or "uneasy" or "unnatural" alliance. Likewise, none probed the causes, the meaning, and the persistence of the overwhelmingly negative cultural image of a close bond in the pastoral relationship.

My work has addressed those shortcomings by examining the sources and meanings of the negative images of the pastoral relationship from the perspective of travelers, journalists, and novelists. Novelists imagined a much wider spectrum of possible pastoral relationships than most literary historians have heretofore acknowledged. Clearly, some reflected heroic ideals while others articulated the worst nightmares of their readers. Despite the critics of sentimental literature, however, few offered simplistic images of an ideal relationship; most were problematic portraits in some way. Similarly, the idealized images constructed by clerical writers in the prescriptive literature give ample evidence that even the ideal relationship was considerably less than a close affinity or conscious alliance.

Unlike other historians, however, I also explored the relationship from the participants themselves—those clergymen and women who tried to live up to the prescribed gender ideals of their time period. The participants I discovered were mostly anonymous men and women who bore little resemblance to the "emasculated" ministers or the powerful female activists that many historians saw. The personal pastoral relationship for the men and women in this study was a negative one but rarely because it was a too close or "uneasy alliance." The experienced relationship, as revealed in the private writings of pastors, fails to exhibit a specific mission to women or even any attempt to forge close spiritual relationships specifically with female parishioners. Conversely, the private writings of women disclose the opposite side of the same coin: Women were disillusioned, disappointed, and discontented with their spiritual counselors in a variety of ways. Instead of sharing a common purpose and an alliance within a "feminized" church, clergymen and women, deeply divided by the cultural constructions of gender they sometimes struggled to transcend, operated within two overlapping but parallel institutions that we have mistakenly viewed as a single "church."

Notes

INTRODUCTION

1. Nathaniel Hawthorne, *The Scarlet Letter: A Romance* (Boston: Ticknor, Reed, and Fields, 1850); Ann Douglas, *The Feminization of American Culture* (New York: Knopf, 1977). Douglas's work has provided me with a continuing source of inspiration, insight, and sources, notwithstanding the disagreements over interpretation I outline here and throughout this work.

2. Numerous historians have compared image and reality in women's history, among them Carl Degler, "What Ought to Be and What Was: Women's Sexuality in the Nineteenth Century," *American Historical Review* 19 (1974): 1467–90; and Laurel Thacher Ulrich, *Good Wives: Image and Reality in the Lives of Women in Northern New England, 1650–1750* (New York: Knopf, 1982). No one I know has constructed the four-part comparison I outline here, however.

3. Gerda Lerner, "Benefit of Clergy," *New York Times Book Review*, 26 June 1977, 13.

4. Figure 1, "A Present to the Pastor" (by A. Hunt), *New York Daily Graphic*, 14 January 1875.

5. Figure 2, "The Churches and the Women," *New York Daily Graphic*, 16 November 1874. The bottom half of the cartoon, in contrast, shows a Catholic priest welcoming five women and telling them that his church "has always utilized the good work of good women." Figure 3, "Suggestions to Theological Students as to the Relations of the Pastor to the Women of His Church & Congregation," n.d., 3, James H. Fairchild Papers, Box 29, Oberlin College Archives.

6. See, for example, Philip Weiss's essay on tabloid history, "Beethoven's Hair Tells All!" *New York Times Magazine*, 29 November 1998, 108.

CHAPTER 1

1. For example, see the uncritical use of travelers' accounts to describe the pastoral relationship in Ann Douglas, *The Feminization of American Cul-*

ture (New York: Knopf, 1977; New York: Doubleday, Anchor Books, 1988), 100. For a similar argument on the popularity and meaning of seduction novels, see Jan Lewis, "The Republican Wife: Virtue and Seduction in the Early Republic," *William and Mary Quarterly* 44 (1987): 689–721.

2. Alexis de Tocqueville, *Democracy in America*, vol. 2 (1836; reprint, ed. by Phillips Bradley; New York: Random House, Vintage Books, 1945), 225; Frederika Bremer, *The Homes of the New World; Impressions of America*, vol. 2, trans. Mary Howitt (1853; reprint, New York: Johnson, 1968), 67 [emphasis mine], 425; Frances Wright [D'arusmont], *Views of Society and Manners in America; in a Series of Letters from That Country to a Friend in England, during the Years 1818, 1819, and 1820. By an English-woman* (London: Longman, Hurst, Rees, Orme, and Brown, 1821), 421–28.

3. For the antidisestablishmentarian view, see Richard Gooch, *America and the Americans—in 1833–4. By an Emigrant*, ed. Richard Toby Widdicombe (New York: Fordham University Press, 1994), 132–38; Henry Bradshaw Fearon, *Sketches of America. A Narrative of a Journey of Five Thousand Miles through the Eastern and Western States* (1818; reprint, New York: Benjamin Blom, 1969), 167; and Frances Trollope, *Domestic Manners of the Americans*, (1832; reprint, with an introduction by Donald Smalley, New York: Knopf, 1949), 107–14, 124–28. For a sympathetic view of the voluntary church, see Bremer, 212, 219, 639, 646; Francis J. Grund, *The Americans in Their Moral, Social, and Political Relations*, 2 vols. (1837; reprint, 2 vols. in 1, New York: Johnson, 1868), 46. For Wright's correction of previous writers, see 431–35.

4. Bremer, 646–47; Grund, 45–46.

5. Sarah Mytton Maury, *An Englishwoman in America* (London: Thomas Richardson & Son, 1848), 97.

6. Fearon, 46, 113 [emphases in original].

7. Charles Dickens, *American Notes* (1848; reprint, with intro. by Christopher Lasch, Gloucester, Mass.: Peter Smith, 1968), 73.

8. Francis J. Grund, *Aristocracy in America from the Sketch-book of a German Nobleman* (London: Richard Bentley, 1839), 149.

9. Gooch, 132 [emphases in original].

10. Harriet Martineau, *Society in America*, 3 vol. (1837; reprint, New York: AMS Press, 1966), 3: 275–79.

11. Ibid., 290.

12. Ibid., 292. For a brief discussion of nativist sentiment in this period, see David Brion Davis, "Some Themes of Counter-Subversion: An Analysis of Anti-Masonic, Anti-Catholic, and Anti-Mormon Literature," *Mississippi Valley Historical Review* 47 (1960): 205–24.

13. Ibid., 292. Similarly, Henry Fearon took a dim view of the "knitting frolic" in which "the religious females present their minister with a variety of gifts" and then are invited to the preacher's house as a "return for their liberality," 22. Women's charitable activities could easily spill over into the political realm. Carolyn Lawes challenges the view that women's activities were apolitical in her study of antebellum Worcester women's organizations, tracing a sewing circle's transition from support of seminarians to wider political and philanthropic goals, such as foreign missions and antislavery in *Women and Reform in a New England Community, 1850–1860* (Lexington: University of Kentucky Press, 2000), 45–81.

14. Martineau, 292–93. A later visitor to the United States was more explicit in her condemnation of pastors as oppressors of women. Marianne Finch came to attend the Woman's Rights Convention in 1850 and stayed for another year to record the advances and failures in human rights. She, like Martineau, denounced the clergy

for their failure to condemn or, worse, their outright support for slavery. She noted the clergy's support for the oppression of women, too. The biblical text "wives submit yourselves to your husbands" (Ephesians 5:22) was an "especial [favorite] of the American divines." They were anxious to "uphold the Divine right of man—(if he were white)—against the machinations of slaves and women.... From these reverend gentlemen I received much new light on the subject of feminine and slave virtue," she reported with sarcasm. *An Englishwoman's Experience in America* (1853; reprint, New York: Negro Universities Press, 1969), 204–14.

15. Trollope, 124–25, 55–56, 78–80, 170, 207–8, 210–12, 302, 343–44; the quote appears on 75.

16. Ibid., 75. Another conservative female traveler saw few advantages to the voluntary system but reexamined her prejudices against the Catholic church and clergy and found them at least compatible with republicanism, if not preferable to the Protestant church. She believed the Protestant clergy exhibited no loyalty to their congregations and would easily break ties to take a better congregation. In contrast, the celibate Catholic clergy were selfless, especially in their ministry to the sick, since they had no wife or children to distract or worry them. Maury, 97, 78.

17. Trollope, 79–80, 172–73.

18. Ibid., 344.

19. Ibid., 276–77.

20. Ibid., 126–27.

21. *The Compact Edition of the Oxford English Dictionary*, s.v. "bell-wether." See also *The Random House Dictionary of the English Language*, 6th ed. unabridged, s.v. "bellwether," for the note that bellwethers were usually castrated male sheep.

CHAPTER 2

1. Richard Gooch, *America and the Americans—in 1833–4. By an Emigrant*, Richard Toby Widdecombe, ed. (New York: Fordham University Press, 1994), 133. Gooch's reference to "abandoned characters" likely refers to the English immigrant and popular preacher, John Maffitt, whose civil trial in 1822 against a journalist for libel went against him and embarrassed the Methodist church that defended him. See *Correct Statement and Review of the Trial of Joseph T. Buckingham, for an Alledged Libel on the Rev. John N. Maffitt, before the Hon. Josiah Quincy, Judge of the Municipal Court, Dec. 16, 1822* (Boston: William S. Spear, 1822); Benjamin Hallett, *An Exposure of the Misrepresentations Contained in a Professed Report of the Trial of Mr. John N. Maffitt, before a Council of Ministers of the Methodist Episcopal Church, Convened in Boston, December 26, 1822* (Boston: n.p., 1823); *Report of the Trial of Mr. John N. Maffitt, Before a Council of Ministers, of the Methodist Episcopal Church, Convened in Boston, December 26, 1823* (Boston: True & Green, 1823).

2. W. F. Jamieson, *The Clergy a Source of Danger to the American Republic*, 2nd ed. (Chicago: W. F. Jamieson, 1873), 289–93.

3. In the Sermon on the Mount, Jesus warned against "false prophets, who come to you in sheep's clothing but inwardly are ravenous wolves" (Matt. 7:15). The Greek, Aesop, also used the same image in his fable "The Wolf in Sheep's Clothing."

4. For a discussion of the fears and clerical propaganda about infidelity during this period, see Martin Marty, *The Infidel: Freethought and American Religion* (Cleveland: Meridian Books, 1961). For discussions of anticlericalism as a consequence of democratization, see Jon Butler, *Awash in a Sea of Faith: Christianizing the American People* (Cambridge, Mass.: Harvard University Press, 1990), 209–12; and Nathan O.

Hatch, *The Democratization of American Christianity* (New Haven, Conn.: Yale University Press, 1989). For discussions of trial pamphlets as a literary genre, see Daniel A. Cohen, *Pillars of Salt, Monuments of Grace: New England Crime Literature and the Origins of Popular Culture, 1674–1860* (New York: Oxford University Press, 1993); Thomas McDade, compiler, *The Annals of Murder: A Bibliography of Books and Pamphlets on American Murders from Colonial Times to 1900* (Norman: University of Oklahoma, 1961) and "Lurid Literature of the Last Century: The Publications of E. E. Barclay," *Pennsylvania Magazine of History and Biography*, 80 (1956): 452–64; David Ray Papke, *Framing the Criminal: Crime, Cultural Work and the Loss of Critical Perspective, 1830–1900* (Hamden, Conn.: Archon, 1987); Daniel E. Williams, "Rogues, Rascals and Scoundrels: The Underworld Literature of Early America," *American Studies* 24 (1983): 8.

5. The best guide to this case is David R. Kasserman, *Fall River Outrage: Life, Murder, and Justice in Early Industrial New England* (Philadelphia: University of Pennsylvania Press, 1986). Two historical novels demonstrate the continuing interest in this dramatic case. See Mary Cable, *Avery's Knot* (New York: G. P. Putnam's Sons, 1981); and Raymond Paul, *Tragedy at Tiverton* (New York: Viking, 1984).

6. Kasserman's argument emphasizes the political rivalry between the mill owners and the Methodist church, two "emergent institutions" vying for legitimacy in antebellum New England. His bibliography lists sixteen pamphlets, as well as numerous East Coast newspaper reports.

7. Support for Avery's side can be found in Luke Drury, *Report of the Examination of Rev. Ephraim K. Avery* (n.p., 1833); Benjamin Hallett, *A Full Report of the Trial of Ephraim K. Avery* (Boston: Daily Commercial Gazette, 1833), *The Arguments of Counsel in the Close of the Trial* (Boston: Daily Commercial Gazette, 1833), and *Avery's Trial (Supplementary Edition)* (N.p., n.p., 1833); and Avery's own *Vindication of the Result of the Trial of Rev. Ephraim K. Avery* (Boston: David Ela, 1834). For Cornell's side, see William Read Staples, *A Correct Report of the Examination of Rev. Ephraim K. Avery* (Providence, R.I.: Marshall & Brown, 1833); Catherine Williams, the only woman to cover the case, explicitly expurgated her sympathetic depiction of Cornell, in *Fall River, An Authentic Narrative*, Patricia Caldwell, ed. (1833, reprint, New York: Oxford University Press, 1993). Several 1833 broadside songs, all anonymously written and published, also sided with Cornell. "The Factory Maid and the Clove-Hitch Knot" and "Death of Sarah M. Cornell" can be found in the broadside collection of the American Antiquarian Society; "Lines Written on the Death of Sarah M. Cornell" is in the Brown University Library. The forged confession was published as *Explanation of the Circumstances Connected with the Death of Sarah Maria Cornell; by Ephraim K. Avery* (Providence, R.I.: William S. Clark, 1834). *Sarah Maria Cornell, The Fall River Murder*, played at the Richmond Hill Theater for two months in 1833 according to Kasserman, 230. Figure 4, an engraving of Sarah Cornell, is from the *Brief and Impartial Narrative of the Life of Sarah Maria Cornell* (New York: n.p., 1833), reprinted in *Fall River Narrative*, 66. That title does not appear in Kasserman's bibliography. Figure 5, a lithograph of Avery, is from *The Correct, Full and Impartial Report of the Trial of Rev. Ephraim K. Avery, before the Supreme Judicial Court of the State of Rhode-Island, at Newport, May 6, 1833, for the Murder of Sarah M. Cornell* (Providence, R.I.: Marshall and Brown, 1833), reprinted in Kasserman, 77.

8. Figure 6, "A Note Found in Miss Cornell's Bandbox," is in David Melville, *A Fac-simile of the Letters Produced at the Trial of the Rev. Ephraim K. Avery, on an Indictment for the Murder of Sarah Maria Cornell. Taken with Great Care, by Permission of the Hon. Supreme Judicial Court of Rhode Island from the Original Letters in the Office of the Clerk of Said Court* (Boston: Pendleton's Lithography, 1833).

9. Figure 7, "A Minister Extraordinary Taking Passage & Bound on a Foreign Mission to the Court of His Satanic Majesty!" [artist unknown] (New York: Robinson's Lithography, 1833), is at the American Antiquarian Society. Another copy is in the Harry T. Peters America on Stone Lithography Collection in the Department of Cultural History, Museum of History and Technology, Smithsonian Institution. A catalogue from an exhibition in 1972 does not link the print with the Avery case. It predates by two years another Robinson lithograph of the murdered prostitute, "Ellen Jewett," a print that Peters described as the first known "tabloid" print in America, according to Janet A. Flint, *The Way of Good and Evil: Popular Religious Lithographs of Nineteenth-Century America* (Washington, D.C.: Smithsonian Institution, 1972), no. 22. "A Minister Extraordinary" combines cartoon satire with sensationalism, two genres in which Robinson pioneered as a lithographer and apparently came to specialize, according to Helen Comstock, *American Lithographs of the Nineteenth Century* (New York: M. Barrows, 1950), 79–87. Patricia Cline Cohen asserts that Robinson was a "reputable businessman" who was arrested in September 1842 for selling obscene prints and books; see *The Murder of Helen Jewett* (New York: Random House, 1998), 464.

10. Robinson, like Dante Alighieri in the *Divine Comedy*, employed figures from both classical mythology and Christian theology. The winged figure with serpents resembles descriptions of the Furies, mythical females charged with punishing wrongs, especially murder. The ferryman evokes Charon, charged with carrying shades across the Rivers Acheron or Styx to Hades, god of the underworld. In mythology, one realm of the netherworld, Tartarus, was devoted to punishment. In Dante's *Inferno*, Tartarus is the deepest pit in Hell, reserved for Satan and the worst sinners. Thus, Christian artists easily conflated Hades and Satan. Robinson's Satanic landscape swarms with horned and tailed devils, medieval Christian figures who carry out a variety of punishments from scourging and impaling to boiling. See Jane Davidson Reid, *The Oxford Guide to Classical Mythology in the Arts, 1300–1990s* (New York: Oxford University Press, 1993), s.v. "Furies" and "Hades." Robert Guffin and Judy Gunston generously helped me interpret this image.

11. Williams, 31, 64; Williams also imagined the dialogue between Cornell and her doctor when she revealed that her child's father was a minister. "Monstrous," replied the "appalled physician," 19.

12. "The Factory Maid" and "Death of Sarah Cornell," broadside collection at AAS. Figure 8 is "Lines Written on the Death of Sarah M. Cornell," in the Brown University Library.

13. Williams, 60.

14. Mill girls and mill owners all worked hard to assure outsiders that despite their position outside the domestic sphere, the young women still deserved the status of pious and pure true women. See Thomas Dublin, *Women at Work* (New York: Columbia University Press, 1979).

15. The cartoon, figure 9, appears as the frontispiece in John Blunt, *Man-Midwifery Dissected; or, The Family Instructor* (London: Samuel William Fores, 1793) [emphasis in original]. Although the cartoon appeared in an English publication of 1793, the book reached the American side of the Atlantic and the debate still raged well into mid-century before the practice became more acceptable. A later American contribution to the controversy is Samuel Gregory, *Man-midwifery Exposed and Corrected* (New York: George Gregory, 1848). Both sources available from www.dohistory.org. See also Jane B. Donegan, *Women and Men Midwives: Medicine, Morality, and Misogyny in Early America* (Westport, Conn.: Greenwood, 1978).

16. According to Kasserman, Avery tried storekeeping, schoolteaching, and doctoring before he settled on the Methodist ministry as the cheapest, quickest avenue out of farming and into a profession, 76. Of course, the case exacerbated other fears—about adversarial democratic politics, evangelical excess, sectarianism, and the anonymity of the growing urban population—some of the same concerns that preoccupied European travelers. Historians have exploited these other anxieties at some length, but none has shown the way clerical scandal challenged gender ideals as well as political and religious ideals. See Appendix for discussion of what historians saw.

17. The Onderdonk case has largely escaped historians' notice outside Episcopal denominational histories, such as James Elliott Lindsley, *This Planted Vine: A Narrative History of the Episcopal Diocese of New York* (New York: Harper & Row, 1984); and Robert Bruce Mullin, *Episcopal Vision/American Reality: High Church Theology and Social Thought in Evangelical America* (New Haven, Conn.: Yale University Press), 1986. Patricia Cline Cohen examined the case from a feminist perspective in "Ministerial Misdeeds: The Onderdonk Trial and Sexual Harassment in the 1840s," *Journal of Women's History* 7, (1995): 34–57, and generously commented on an earlier version of my work on trials. The following section owes much to her argument and analysis of the broadside in that article.

18. The official record of the trial is in *The Proceedings of the Court Convened under the Third Canon of 1844, in the City of New York, for the Trial of the Right Rev. Benjamin T. Onderdonk, D.D. Bishop of New York on a Presentment Made by the Bishops of Virginia, Tennessee, and Georgia. By Authority of the Court,* (New York: D. Appleton & Co., 1845). Those publications defending Onderdonk include *An Examination of the Proceedings on the Presentment, Trial, and Sentence of the Right Rev. Benjamin T. Onderdonk* (n.p., n.d.[produced by the editor of the *Churchman*, a diocesan publication]); and Benjamin T. Onderdonk, *Bishop Onderdonk's Statement* (New York: Henry Onderdonk, 1845). Those opposing the bishop include John Jay, *Facts Connected with the Presentment of Bishop Onderdonk: A Reply to Parts of the Bishop's Statement* (New York: Stanford & Swords, 1845); and James C. Richmond, *The Conspiracy against the Late Bishop of New York Unravelled* (New York: n.p., 1845).

19. *New York Herald*, 31 December 1844, 3.

20. Cohen offers additional analysis of the figures, 51–53. Figure 10, an oil portrait of the Rev. Onderdonk by William Mount (1830), New York Historical Society; and figure 11, *Black Onder-donk-en Doughlips*, broadside collection, American Antiquarian Society.

21. Cohen makes a similar argument in "Ministerial Misdeeds" but elaborates on the culture of male sexual privilege illuminated by the murder of an 1830s prostitute in *The Murder of Helen Jewett*.

22. *Only Full Report of the Trial of Rev. I. S. Kalloch, on Charge of Adultery, Complete History of the Affair; Doings of the Church; Kalloch's Pulpit Defence; Arrest, Arraignment, Trial, and Result. With Accurate Portraits of Kalloch, and the Beautiful Lady in Black, and the Lecture Room of the Lechmere* (Boston: Federhen, 1857). In fact, the infamous Kalloch went on to a very checkered career. He migrated westward to end up in the 1880s as the socialist mayor of San Francisco and, with his son, involved in a murder trial. Later publications review the case and Kalloch's subsequent career. See William McCann Nielson, *A Faint Idea of a Terrible Life! The Rev. I. S. Kalloch (Mayor of San Francisco) from His Expulsion from College until Now,* 4th edition (San Francisco: J. K. Cooper, 1880); John H. Shimmons, *The Shame and Scourge of San Francisco, or, an Expose of the Rev. Isaac S. Kalloch across the Continent, from Maine to California; the Records of an Evil Life, from Documents of Undeniable Authenticity* (Chicago: n.p.,

1880[?]); M. M. Marberry, *The Golden Voice: A Biography of Isaac Kalloch* (New York: Farrar, Straus, 1947).

23. Figures 12, 13, and 14 are in *Only Full Report of the Trial of Rev. I. S. Kalloch*.

24. I. W. Ayer, *Full Report of R. H. Dana's Argument for Defence in the case of Rev. I. S. Kalloch, Pastor of the Tremont Temple Baptist Church* (N.p., 1857), 3, 9–13. Several other scriptural passages suggest that the *place* a seed is planted determines the fruit that will result. See Mark 4:4–8; Deuteronomy 26:28; Nehemiah 10:35.

25. Discussions of the hotels and their problematic gendered spaces are in Molly W. Berger, "A House Divided: The Culture of the American Luxury Hotel, 1825–1860," in *His and Hers: Gender, Consumption, and Technology*, Roger Horowitz and Arwen Mohun, eds. (Charlottesville: University of Virginia Press, 1998), 39–65; Carolyn Brucken, "In the Public Eye: Women and the American Luxury Hotel," *Winterthur Portfolio* 31 (1996): 203–20. For an additional reading of this image, see Epilogue.

26. Clipping from *New York Staats Zeitung*, Scrapbook on Beecher-Tilton Scandal, Brooklyn Public Library, v. 1, 10; Bowen's remarks were made in private, if at all, and were quoted in "The Beecher-Tilton Scandal," *New York Daily Graphic*, 18 September 1874.

27. Frederika Bremer, *The Homes of the New World; Impressions of America*, vol. 2, trans. Mary Howitt (1853; reprint, New York: Johnson, 1968), 240–41; clipping from the *Liberal Christian*, Scrapbook, Brooklyn Public Library, v. 1, 46. The most recent and most thorough (and impartial) treatment of the case is Richard Wightman Fox, *Trials of Intimacy: Love and Loss in the Beecher-Tilton Scandal* (Chicago: University of Chicago Press, 1999). Other thoughtful treatments are Altina L. Waller, *Reverend Beecher and Mrs. Tilton: Sex and Class in Victorian America* (Amherst: University of Massachusetts Press, 1982); Clifford E. Clark, *Henry Ward Beecher: Spokesman for a Middle-Class America* (Urbana: University of Illinois Press, 1978); and William G. McLoughlin, *The Meaning of Henry Ward Beecher: An Essay on the Shifting Values of Mid-Victorian America* (New York: Knopf, 1970). Paxton Hibben, *Henry Ward Beecher: An American Portrait* (New York: George H. Doran, 1927), is the most unsympathetic portrayal of Beecher.

28. "Will This Be the Result?" a cartoon in the *New York Daily Graphic*, 19 August 1874, featured the Plymouth church committee whitewashing a fence labeled with the scandal. Victoria Woodhull has attracted two recent biographers in Barbara Goldsmith, *Other Powers: The Age of Suffrage, Spiritualism, and the Scandalous Victoria Woodhull* (New York: Knopf, 1998), which contains a print of Beecher surrounded by female acolytes from the author's private collection; and Mary Gabriel, *Notorious Victoria: The Life of Victoria Woodhull* (Chapel Hill, N.C.: Algonquin, 1998). See also Nicola Beisel, *Imperiled Innocents: Anthony Comstock and Family Reproduction in Victorian America* (Princeton, N.J.: Princeton University Press, 1997).

29. Henry Ward Beecher to Theodore Tilton, Oct. 18, 1863, Harriet Beecher Stowe Center; copy of the original, reprinted in *Beecher-Tilton Investigation: The Scandal of the Age* (Philadelphia: Barclay & Co., 1874), 61–63; Theodore Tilton to Henry Ward Beecher, Nov. 30, 1865, *Theodore Tilton vs. Henry Ward Beecher*, 2:738, reprinted in Fox, 329–30; testimony of Henry Ward Beecher quoted in "The Scandal," *New York Daily Graphic*, 2 April 1874, 245. Catherine A. Holland first brought this aspect of the scandal to my attention in "Sex Lives of the Saints? The Beecher-Tilton Scandal, Political Rights, and Intimacy among Men," unpublished paper delivered at Ninth Berkshire Conference on the History of Women, 1993. See also Karen V. Hansen, " 'Our Eyes Behold Each Other': Masculinity and Intimate Friendship in Antebellum New England," in *Men's Friendships*, ed. Peter M. Nardi (Newbury Park, Calif.: Sage, 1993), 35–58.

30. Elizabeth may have anonymously published a poem in the *Independent*, according to Fox, 328–29. Elizabeth Tilton to Theodore Tilton, Jan. 11, 1867 and Feb. 7, 1869; Theodore Tilton to Elizabeth Tilton, Dec. 6, 1866; all reprinted in *Daily Graphic*, 18 September 1874, 569. On companionate marriage, see Karen Lystra, *Searching the Heart: Women, Men, and Romantic Love in Nineteenth-Century America* (New York: Oxford University Press, 1989); Ellen K. Rothman, *Hands and Hearts: A History of Courtship in America* (New York: Basic Books, 1984).

31. Theodore Tilton to Henry Ward Beecher, June 17, 1863, Beecher Family Papers, box 15, folder 615, Yale University Library Manuscripts and Archives, reprinted in Fox, 324–25; Elizabeth Tilton to Theodore Tilton, Jan. 25, 1867; *Theodore Tilton versus Henry Ward Beecher, Action for Crim[inal]. Con[versation]. Tried in the City Court of Brooklyn*, 3 vols. (New York: McDivitt, Campbell, & Co., 1875), 1:499, reprinted in Fox, 266–67.

32. If Elizabeth confessed to the same sin as Catherine Gaunt, then she did not commit adultery. Catherine Gaunt discouraged the romantic love of her priest, but her jealous husband refused to believe the two were innocent. However, Elizabeth might have seen that she failed to do what Catharine had done—check her pastor's love before it became a passion. See Charles Reade, *Griffith Gaunt or, Jealousy* (Boston: Colonial Press, n.d.). The text of Elizabeth's letter of June 29, 1871, from "Theodore Tilton's Sworn Statement" to the Plymouth Church Investigating Committee, in Charles F. Marshall, *The True Story of the Brooklyn Scandal* (Philadelphia: National Publishing Co., 1874), 120–21, is reprinted in Fox, 347. Elizabeth's statement to the Plymouth investigating committee on July 24, 1874, fails to define the exact nature of her confession, "A like confession with hers (namely, Catharine Gaunt's) I had made to Mr. Tilton in telling of my love to my friend and pastor one year before," reprinted in *Daily Graphic*, 18 September 1874, 569.

33. "Tilton's Statement," *Daily Graphic*, 28 July 1874, 187; "Mr. Beecher's Trial," *Harper's Weekly*, 5 June 1875, supplement, 469; "Mr. Beecher," *Harper's Weekly*, 17 July 1875, 574.

34. Figure 15, "Old Lady in a Fog," *Daily Graphic*, 20 August 1874, 347; Figure 16, "The Beecher-Tilton Case," *Daily Graphic*, 22 August 1874, 369; Figure 17, "A Hint to the Plymouth Pastor," *Daily Graphic*, 3 October 1874, 671. In "The Beecher-Tilton Case," *Daily Graphic*, 23 September 1874, 597, the editorial cartoonist returned again to a metaphor of pollution. Public opinion, personified again by a chaste and outraged classical female, turns away from the Gorgon-like devil representing Beecher's and Tilton's statements, declaring the visitor from the underworld has "polluted the air long enough."

35. Figure 18, "How to Make Pastoral Visits and Avoid Slander," *Daily Graphic*, 14 September 1874, 536. For additional examples of comic representations of testimony, see "The Kissing Chorus," *Daily Graphic*, 27 February 1874, 876; and "The Great Brooklyn Collide-oscope," *Daily Graphic*, 4 March 1875, 36. Figure 19, R. Piquet, "Qui Sine Peccato" [he without sin], *Daily Graphic*, 3 April 1875, 259; another example of "high art" reproduction is C. A. Storey, "A Great Scandal in the Olden Time," *Daily Graphic*, 8 August 1874, 271; and A. Hunt, "A Present to the Pastor," *Daily Graphic*, 14 January 1875, 534.

36. Figure 20, "Beecher's Experience in Lap-Land," and Figure 21, "Scene in the Parlor,"from a scrapbook of clippings of the Beecher-Tilton scandal, vol. 1, Brooklyn Public Library, n.p.

37. Figure 22, "A Sample of Spirits," *Daily Graphic*, 4 May 1875. See also "Signs of the Times," *Daily Graphic*, 3 April, 1875, 258, in which an office boy, engrossed in

the newspaper coverage of the trial, informs his boss he'll be ready to work when he's finished reading the "afternoon session" in an hour or two.

38. *Harper's Weekly*, 5 June 1875, 469; 17 July 1875, 574.

39. Figure 23, "Death Struggle on the Ragged Edge," *Daily Graphic*, 11 January 1875. For other cartoons that suggest images of contest or combat, see "The Modern St. Peter," *Daily Graphic*, 28 March 1874, 201; "The Pity of It," *Daily Graphic*, 29 July 1874, 195; "The Great Brooklyn Race," *Daily Graphic*, 12 August 1874, 291; "The Brooklyn Battle," *Daily Graphic*, 15 August 1874, 315; "The Great Brooklyn Gunning Match," *Daily Graphic*, 16 August 1874, 323; "General Butler as a Peace-Maker," *Daily Graphic*, 18 August 1874, 331; and "Discord amongst the Angels," *Frank Leslie's Illustrated Newspaper*, 24 October 1874, 97. Other cartoons posed the trials as spectacles. See "Can He Get Through?" *Daily Graphic*, 14 August 1874, 307, for an image of the trial as a circus; and "The Church 'Mill'-itant," *Daily Graphic*, 5 September 1874, 469, for Plymouth church as a drunken convention. For a discussion of the cultural context of lynching and its use as a social control for both black men and white women, and as a reaction to changing race and gender norms, see Philip Dray, *At the Hands of Persons Unknown: The Lynching of Black America* (New York: Random House, 2002).

CHAPTER 3

1. For a discussion of the history of adultery cases as tort suits, see Laura Hanft Korobkin, *Criminal Conversations: Sentimentality and Nineteenth-Century Legal Stories of Adultery* (New York: Columbia University Press, 1998), chapter 2.

2. The Rev. Barclay's congregation endured rumors about his adulterous conduct but "smuggled it up" for months before formal charges resulted in a trial. See Jacob Kerr, *The Several Trials of the Reverend David Barclay* (Elizabethtown, N.J.: R.&P. Canfield, 1814), 28–29. In a similar manner, the principals in the Beecher-Tilton case managed to suppress the rumors for nearly three years.

3. For an example of a case that produced a public apology from the minister, see "Confession of the Rev. Ray Potter," a broadside probably published in Rhode Island in 1837. The congregation, according to Potter, declined to read his confession in public, "not wishing to wallow in the slough," an indication of the reluctance to publicize such offenses.

4. William Sampson, *The Trial of Mr. William Parkinson, Pastor of the First Baptist Church in the City of New-York on an Indictment of Assault and Battery upon Mrs. Eliza Wintringham* (New York: LBargin and Thompson, 1811), 4–8.

5. Joseph A. Dowling (stenographer), *The Trial of the Rev. William Hogan, Pastor of St. Mary's Church, for an Assault and Battery on Mary Connell* (Philadelphia: R. Desilver, 1822), 19–20; *Decisions of the Council in the Trial of Rev. W. P. Merrill, Pastor of the Free Will Baptist Church, in Portland, with a Statement of Facts, and the Reasons for Such a Decision, in Answer to a Call from Members of Said Church, and Others* (Portland, Maine: Brown, Thurston, 1861), 29.

6. *The Truth Revealed. Statement & Review of the Whole Case of the Reverend Joy H. Fairchild* (Boston: Wright's Steam Press, 1845), 99, 26.

7. *The Trial of the Rev. L. D. Huston, for the Alleged Seduction of Mary Driscoll, Virginia Hopkins, &c.* (Baltimore: n.p., 1872), 38–39, 62–64; *The Truth Revealed*, 93–93. Parkinson also called on the Song of Solomon to persuade Eliza Wintringham that he was "sick *in* love" with her [emphasis in original]. *Trial of Rev. William Parkinson*, 6–8.

8. *The Trial of the Rev. Mr. L. D. Huston*, 38, 62; *Report of the Trial of the Rev. Mr. Van Zandt, Rector of Grace Church, Rochester, N.Y. for the Seduction of Miss Sophia Murdock, a Young and Beautiful Member of His Church* (Philadelphia: n.p., 1842), 6–7. Mothers might be flattered—both pleased and deceived—by pastoral visits and interest in their daughters; more critical neighbors noticed an unhealthy interest in frequent pastoral calls. One woman in Boston recorded Fairchild's twice-weekly calls on a young married neighbor when her husband was out; another noted that he paid unusual attention and gave gifts to her young domestic servant. *The Truth Revealed*, 7. Issachar Grosscup, a Baptist minister in upstate New York, urged a couple in his parish to make an overnight visit to some relatives while he stayed with their adolescent children. The father later claimed that Grosscup took advantage of the parents' trust by seducing their seventeen-year-old daughter; see George L. Whitney, *The Trial of Rev. Issachar Grosscup, for the Seduction of Roxana L. Wheeler* (Canandaigua, N.Y.: n.p., 1848), 6.

9. Huston was accused of seducing another fatherless girl in addition to Mary Driscoll. *Trial of the Rev. L. D. Huston*, 23. The Rev. Van Zandt paid visits and brought gifts to the young Murdock girls, in part because their father was alcoholic and disabled; see *Report of the Trial of the Rev. Mr. Van Zandt*, 4. *The Proceedings of the Court Convened under the Third Canon of 1844, in the City of New York, on Tuesday, December 10, 1844, for the Trial of the Right Rev. Benjamin T. Onderdonk, D.D.* (New York: Appleton, 1845), 17; *Official Report of the Trial of Henry Ward Beecher* (New York: George W. Smith, 1875), 1: 329.

10. *Decisions in the Trial of Rev. W. P. Merrill*, 76. Also see Catherine Read (Arnold) Williams, *Fall River: An Authentic Narrative*, 2nd ed. (Boston: Marsh & Harrison, 1834), 88; and M. M. Marberry, *The Golden Voice: A Biography of Isaac Kalloch* (New York: Farrar, Straus, 1947), 49. In one confused narrative, Mrs. Sarah Reeks sought out her pastor without her husband's knowledge because she and her husband were in desperate financial trouble. The pastor reported that he lent the couple money, ordered a sofa from the husband's workshop, paid a substantial deposit, and never received the goods. The minister claimed his kindness was repaid with charges that he had forged the order, and he defended himself in a slander suit. *The Trial in Full, of Edward Arrowsmith, for Slandering the Character of the Rev. Alexander Cumming, Minister of the Evangelical Independent Church, Rose Street, New York: With the Conviction (by Consent) of George Reeks, for the Same Offence* (New York: S. Wakler, 1819[?]), 34.

11. *The Truth Revealed*, 92–93; *The Trial of Rev. Issachar Grosscup*, 7; *Trial of the Rev. L. D. Huston*, 39. "Hartshorn and laudanum," "penny-royal and tansy steeped in camphor," and "peculiar implements" were all mentioned as agents of abortion in various testimony. See Williams, *Fall River*, 24; David R. Kasserman, *Fall River Outrage: Life, Murder, and Justice in Early Industrial New England* (Philadelphia: University of Pennsylvania Press, 1986), 69; Ammi Rogers, *Memoirs of the Rev. Ammi Rogers*, 6th ed. (Troy, N.Y.: Printed for the author, 1834), 99; Herbert H. Hayden, *The Rev. Herbert H. Hayden: An Autobiography* (Hartford, Conn.: Press of the Plimpton Mfg. Co., 1880), 141. George G. Foster, in his exposé of the New York underworld, *New York by Gas-Light and Other Urban Sketches*, edited by Stuart Blumin (Berkeley: University of California Press, 1990, reprint of 1850 edition), 98–99, includes a story of a young girl who sought aid from her pastor when she discovered her pregnancy. The man helped her to obtain an abortion but exacted sexual favors in return. See also James C. Mohr, *Abortion in America: The Origins and Evolution of National Policy, 1800–1900* (New York: Oxford University Press, 1978).

12. A. E. Drapier, *Trial of Romain Weinzoepflen, Catholic Priest of Evansville, Vanderburgh County, Indiana, on a Charge of Rape Preferred by Mrs. Anna Maria Schmoll* (Louisville, Ky.: W. N. Haldeman & B. J. Webb, 1844), 11–13.

13. Ibid., 198. See also "Clippings on Fr. Roman Weinsoepfel, O.S.B." PCLR, Box 32, folder 21, University of Notre Dame Archives. For an example of the Protestant objection to auricular confession, see C. P. DeLasteyrie, *The History of Auricular Confession. Religiously, Morally, and Politically Considered among Ancient and Modern Nations*, 2 vols. (London: Richard Bentley, 1848).

14. *Poor Mary Pomeroy! The Jersey City Music Teacher: Also, a Full and Authentic Account of the Trial of Rev. John S. Glendenning before the Authorities of Prospect Avenue Church* (Philadelphia: Old Franklin Publishing House, 1874), 49.

15. *The Great Divorce Case! A Full and Impartial History of the Trial of the Petition of Mrs. Sarah M. H. Jarvis, for a Divorce for Her Husband, the Rev. Samuel F. Jarvis* (New York, n.p., 1839), 49, 57; *Report of the Proceedings, on the Petition of Mrs. Sarah M. Jarvis, for a Divorce from Her Husband, Rev. Samuel F. Jarvis*, 2nd ed. (Hartford, Conn.: Review Press, 1839), 72; Williams, *Fall River*, 88; Jacob Harden, *Life, Confession, and Letters of Courtship of Rev. Jacob S. Harden, of the M.E. Church, Mount Lebanon, Hunterdon Co., N.J., Executed for the Murder of His Wife, on the 6th of July, 1860* (Hackettstown, N.J.: E. Winton, 1860); *The Entire and Unabridged Evidence, Given on the Second Inquest, Concerning the Death of Mrs. Priscilla Budge* (Lowville, N.Y.: Lewis County Banner Office, 1860); John Swinburne, *A Review of the Case, the People against Rev. Henry Budge, Indicted for the Murder of His Wife* (Albany, N.Y.: C. Van Benthuysen, 1862); *The Correct, Full and Impartial Report of the Trial of Rev. Ephraim K. Avery* (Providence, R.I.: Marshall and Brown, 1833); *Poor Mary Stannard! A Full and Thrilling Story of the Circumstances Connected with Her Murder* (New Haven, Conn.: Stafford, 1879).

16. *Proceedings of the Court Convened under the Third Canon, 1844*, 15–16, 84; Drapier, 14. Rhoda Davidson claimed, "I had less enjoyment of religion after my intercourse with Mr. F[airchild] than before: the secret that I was keeping troubled me," in *The Truth Revealed*, 26. Sampson, *Trial of Mr. William Parkinson*, 7; Luke Drury, *A Report of the Examination of Rev. Ephraim K. Avery, Charged with the Murder of Sarah Maria Cornell*, (n.p., 1833), 15–16, quoted in Kasserman, *Fall River Outrage*, 104–5.

17. *Proceedings of the Court Convened under the Third Canon, 1844*, 131; *The Truth Revealed*, 93–99. Even Davidson's father deferred to, and sympathized with, the minister when he declined to press suit against his daughter's seducer. "I said I wanted to do what was right, and did not wish to afflict the afflicted" (102).

18. Williams, *Fall River*, 25; *Extraordinary Trial of the Rev. John Seys, Pastor of the Bedford Street Methodist Episcopal Church, New-York City, for an Alledged Assault and Battery on Mrs. Elizabeth Cram*, 2nd ed. (New York: n.p., 1847), 4.

19. Historians of gender and legal theorists have examined the ways that the judicial system displays a profoundly masculine bias. See Michael Grossberg, "Institutionalizing Masculinity: The Law as a Masculine Profession," in *Meanings for Manhood: Constructions of Masculinity in Victorian America*, Mark C. Carnes and Clyde Griffen, eds. (Chicago: University of Chicago Press, 1990), 133–51; Lucinda M. Finley, "Breaking Women's Silence in Law," *Notre Dame Law Review* 64 (1989): 886–910; and Carrie Menkel-Meadow, "Portia in a Different Voice," *Berkeley Women's Law Journal* 1 (1985): 39–50.

20. The procedure is described in Matthew 18:15–17 and in Methodist Episcopal Church, *The Methodist Discipline of 1798, Including the Annotations of Thomas Coke and Francis Asbury*, facsimile edition (Rutland, Vt.: Academy Books, 1979), 109–13, partic-

ularly the discipline of preachers. Bishop Onderdonk's trial, *Proceedings of the Court Convened under the Third Canon, 1844*, 154–56, included a lengthy argument over disciplinary process.

21. For a fuller description of the complexities of these ideals, see Nancy Cott, "Passionlessness: An Interpretation of Victorian Sexual Ideology, 1790–1850," in *A Heritage of Her Own*, Nancy F. Cott and Elizabeth H. Pleck, eds. (New York: Simon and Schuster, 1979), 162–81. See also John D'Emilio and Estelle Freedman, *Intimate Matters: A History of Sexuality in America* (New York: Harper & Row, 1988), 55–84.

22. *Trial of Rev. William Parkinson*, 38; Drapier, *Trial of Romain Weinzoepflen*, 13–15; Clippings on Fr. Roman Weinsoepfel, O.S.

23. Davidson likely referred to Genesis 38:9, the sin of Onan—ejaculating outside the vagina—in *The Truth Revealed*, 93 [emphasis in original]; Hallett, *A Full Report of the Trial of Ephraim K. Avery*, 48, quoted in Kasserman, *Fall River Outrage*, 144, who reported that even the male reporters were upset by the graphic details of questions and testimony. A similar example appears in *The Trial of Rev. Issachar Grosscup*, 14.

24. Sampson, *Trial of Mr. William Parkinson*, 6; *Extraordinary Trial of the Rev. John Seys*, 37; *Proceedings of the Court Convened under the Third Canon, 1844*, 136. See also *The Truth Revealed; Trial of the Rev. Issachar Grosscup;* and Williams, *Fall River*, 1.

25. *Trial of Elder Eleazar Sherman, before an Ecclesiastical Council, Held at the Meetinghouse of the Christian Society in Providence, July 20 and 21, 1835* (Providence, R.I.: H. H. Brown, 1835).

26. *The Truth Revealed*, 95.

27. Sampson, *Trial of Mr. William Parkinson*, 7; *Review of the Trial of Bishop Onderdonk*, 29; *The Truth Revealed*, 26.

28. *Report of the Trial of the Rev. Mr. Van Zandt*, 6, 23. The only document that explicitly ranked the weight of witnesses' testimony in a case against a clergyman stated that a priest was to be believed before a layman, and a man to be believed before a woman, in "Clergy and Religious Records and Cases, 1878–1905, Handling Cases of Dismissal," n.d., *Records of the Archdiocese of Bardstown/Louisville*, Box 7, Folder 15, Archives of the University of Notre Dame.

29. Andrew J. King noted a similar phenomenon in contemporary trials for sexual slander, when judges worked to protect women by reinforcing their domesticity, in "Constructing Gender: Sexual Slander in Nineteenth-Century America," *Law and History Review* 13 (1995): 63–110.

30. Timothy Dwight condemned dueling before an audience of Yale graduates in *The Folly, Guilt, and Mischiefs of Duelling: A Sermon, Preached in the College Chapel at New Haven, on the Sabbath preceding the Annual Commencement, Sept. 1804* (Hartford, Conn.: Hudson & Goodwin, 1805); Henry Slicer condemned it before Congress in "*That Which Is Morally Wrong, Can Never Be Politically Right": A Discourse, in Which Is Considered the History, Character, Causes, and Consequences of Duels, with the Means of Prevention/ Prepared to be Delivered in the Capitol* (Washington City, D.C.: [n.p.], 1838); Joseph Dwight Strong was still railing against the practice on the eve of the Civil War in *A Plea against Dueling: A Discourse Delivered in the First Presbyterian Church, at Oakland, Cal., Sunday, Sept. 25th, 1859* (San Francisco: Towne & Bacon, 1859). No cultural histories yet have probed the role of duels in the nineteenth-century United States, but for discussions of dueling in America and abroad, see Robert Baldick, *The Duel: A History of Duelling* (London: Spring Books, 1970); and Hugh A. Halliday, *Murder among Gentlemen: A History of Duelling in Canada* (Toronto: Robin Brass Studio, 1999). For examples of verbal ripostes in the trials of clergymen, see Jacob Kerr, *The Several Trials of the Reverend David Barclay, before the Presbytery of New-Brunswick, with*

Their Judgment at Oxford (Elizabethtown, N.J.: R. & P. Canfield, 1814); Dowling, *Trial of the Rev. William Hogan; Extraordinary Trial of the Rev. John Seys;* and *Life, Confession, and Letters of Courtship of Rev. Jacob S. Harden*. The displacement of the clergy as moral authority by the legal profession and the trial as spectacle are discussed in Daniel Cohen, *Pillars of Salt, Monuments of Grace: New England Crime Literature and the Origins of Popular Culture, 1674–1860* (New York: Oxford University Press, 1993), 34, 376-7; Richard Wightman Fox, "Intimacy on Trial: Cultural Meanings of the Beecher-Tilton Affair," in *The Power of Culture: Critical Essays in American History*, R. W. Fox and T. J. Jackson Lears, eds. (Chicago: University of Chicago Press, 1993), 102–32; and Grossberg, "Institutionalizing Masculinity."

31. For examples of male experts, see *The Correct, Full and Impartial Report of the Trial of Rev. Ephraim K. Avery*, 163; John Swinburne, *A Review of the Case, the People agt. Rev. Henry Budge*, written and published by a physician who disputed the medical evidence in the case; Whitney, *Trial of Rev. Issachar Grosscup; Report of the Trial of the Rev. Mr. Van Zandt*, 23; Washington Van Zandt, *An Appeal by the Reverend Washington Van Zandt, Late Rector of Grace Church, Rochester* (Auburn, N.Y.: Henry Oliphant, 1843), 21–23; *An Examination of the Proceedings on the Presentment, Trial, and Sentence of the Right Rev. Benjamin T. Onderdonk, D.D., Bishop of the Protestant Episcopal Church in the Diocese of New-York* (n.p., n.d. [produced by the editor of *The Churchman*, the diocesan publication, 1845?], 139. In trials during the early decades of the century, traditional female experts, especially midwives or women who dressed bodies for burial, gave credible reports. But over the course of the century, women played an increasingly smaller role. In an 1879 case, the murdered girl's father employed a female clairvoyant to re-create the scene of the murder and locate the murder weapon, *Poor Mary Stannard!*.

32. Sampson, *Trial of Mr. William Parkinson*, 12–18. Charles P. Nemath, "Character Evidence in Rape Trials in Nineteenth-Century New York: Chastity and the Admissibility of Specific Acts," *Women's Rights Law Reporter* 6 (1980): 214–55, demonstrated that early-nineteenth-century case law discouraged character testimony that was not relevant to the specific rape charge in question. Later in the century, more character testimony was permitted, a trend that continued down to the last three decades of the twentieth century, when feminists protested its use. Although Wintringham's was not a rape case, the judge several times ruled that Parkinson's past history was not relevant but allowed extensive testimony against Wintringham's "reputation for chastity and veracity."

33. Eve's perfidy appears in Genesis 3:1–7 and Potiphar's wife in Genesis 39:7–20. For discussions of gender ideals and behavior in the colonial period, see Nancy Cott, "Eighteenth-Century Family and Social Life Revealed in Massachusetts Divorce Records," in *A Heritage of Her Own*, N. Cott and Elizabeth H. Pleck, eds. (New York: Simon & Schuster, 1979), 107–35; D'Emilio and Freedman, *Intimate Matters*, 3–52; David H. Flaherty, *Privacy in Colonial New England* (Charlottesville: University of Virginia Press, 1972); Mary Beth Norton, "Gender and Defamation in Seventeenth-Century Maryland," *William and Mary Quarterly* 44 (1987): 3–39; Laurel Thacher Ulrich, *Good Wives: Image and Reality in the Lives of Women in Northern New England, 1650–1750* (New York: Oxford University Press, 1983), 87–106. For discussions of working-class sexual ideologies, see Kathy Peiss, " 'Charity Girls' and City Pleasures: Historical Notes on Working-Class Sexuality," in *Powers of Desire: The Politics of Sexuality*, Ann Snitow, Christine Stansell, and Sharon Thompson, eds. (New York: Monthly Review Press, 1983), 74–87; Charles Rosenberg, "Sexuality, Class, and Role in Nineteenth-Century America," *American Quarterly* 25 (1973): 131–53; and Christine

Stansell, *City of Women: Sex and Class in New York, 1789–1860* (Chicago: University of Illinois Press, 1987).

34. Sampson, *Trial of Mr. William Parkinson*, 71. In contrast, see Whitney, *Trial of Rev. Issachar Grosscup*, 70. The plaintiff, the girl's father, was an upstanding patriarch of his church and community. His lawyer emphasized the Revolutionary War heroes in the family and urged the jury to save the women of the community from their own folly and fatuity. Lower-class male plaintiffs (and defendants) suffered a disadvantage in most contests. A. Cheree Carlson argued that wealth and political influence facilitated acquittals of criminal defendants in general in "The Role of Character in Public Moral Argument: Henry Ward Beecher and the Brooklyn Scandal," *Quarterly Journal of Speech* 77 (1991): 38–52. Aggrieved husbands and fathers often found justice in criminal courts rather than civil courts. An "unwritten law" excused injured men who took revenge upon the seducer outside the law. See Robert M. Ireland, "The Libertine Must Die: Sexual Dishonor and the Unwritten Law in the Nineteenth-Century United States," *Journal of Social History* 23 (1989): 27–44; Kermit L. Hall, *The Magic Mirror: Law in American History* (New York: Oxford University Press, 1989).

35. *Proceedings of the Court*, 260, 13; *The Truth Revealed*, 26; Sampson, *Trial of Mr. William Parkinson*, 76–77. See also Dowling, *Trial of Rev. William Hogan*, 181, 197. In a history of cases involving women's psychological injury, Martha Charmallas and Linda Kerber argued that the bias toward physical versus emotional harm, or tangible versus intangible interests, is masculine. See "Women, Mothers, and the Law of Fright: A History," *Michigan Law Review* 88 (1988): 814–64. The level of violence in working-class families may have made it difficult to judge nonviolent injury, according to Pamela Susan Haag, "The 'Ill-Use of a Wife': Patterns of Working-Class Violence in Domestic and Public New York City," *Journal of Social History* 25 (1992): 447–77.

36. Proscriptions against committing "adultery . . . in his heart" appear in Matthew 5:28. Ammi Rogers, *Memoirs of the Rev. Ammi Rogers A.M.*, 6th ed. (Troy, N.Y.: Printed for the Author, 1834), 86–96; *Review of the Trial of Bishop Onderdonk* (Buffalo, N.Y.: Buffalo Commercial Advertiser, 1845), 25; *Review of the Case of Moses Thacher versus Preston Pond, in Charging the Plaintiff with Crime of Adultery; including Letters of Mrs. Jerusha Pond, the Main Witness in the Defence* (Boston: Printed for the Plaintiff, 1838), 21–23, 76, 88. For an example of another clergyman who took his complaints of a conspiracy to the press, see John Whittlesey, *An Authentic Account of the Persecutions and Trials of the Rev. John Whittlesey, of Salem, Connecticut* (New York: n.p., 1845).

37. *The Trial in Full, of Edward Arrowsmith, for Slandering the Character of the Rev. Alexander Cumming* (New York: S. Wakler, 1819?) was published to help the church recoup the costs of the trial since the court awarded the minister only six cents in damages. Similarly, Moses Thacher won only one cent in damages; see *Review of the Case of Moses Thacher*. The New Jersey presbytery explained its reasoning in Kerr, *Several Trials of the Reverend David Barclay*, 318.

38. Sampson, *Trial of Mr. William Parkinson*, 67. The U.S. Constitution, First Amendment, states: "Congress shall make no law respecting an establishment of religion, or prohibiting the free exercise thereof."

39. *Proceedings of the Court*, 17.

40. *Only Full Report of the Trial of Rev. I. S. Kalloch, on Charge of Adultery, Complete History of the Affair; Doings of the Church; Kalloch's Pulpit Defence; Arrest, Arraignment, Trial, and Result. With Accurate Portraits of Kalloch, and the Beautiful Lady in Black, and the Lecture Room of the Lechmere* (Boston: Federhen, 1857), 58; *The Truth Revealed*, 11; *Official Report of the Trial of Henry Ward Beecher*, 798.

41. Alfred Lee, Bishop of Delaware, *A Few Words in Vindication of the Action of the Court of Bishops, Convened at Camden, New Jersey, September, 1853* (Philadelphia: H. Hooker, 1854), 16.

42. *The Truth Revealed*, 51 [emphasis in original]; Joy H. Fairchild, *Farewell Address to the Payson Church, South Boston, Delivered Nov. 22, 1857* (Boston: n.p., 1858); William McCann Neilson, *A Faint Idea of a Terrible Life! The Rev. I. S. Kalloch (Mayor of San Francisco) from His Expulsion from College until Now.* 4th ed. (San Francisco: J. K. Cooper, 1880), 54; *Life, Confession, and Letters of Courtship*, 17–21; Kasserman, *Fall River Outrage*; Swinburne, *The People agt. Rev. Henry Budge*; Herbert Hiram Hayden, *The Rev. Herbert H. Hayden; an Autobiography* (Hartford, Conn.: Press of the Plimpton Mfg. Co., 1880).

43. Drapier, *Trial of Romain Weinzoepflen*, 198. See George W. Dalzell, *Benefit of Clergy in America & Related Matters* (Winston-Salem, N.C.: John F. Blair, 1955), for an explanation and history of this privilege. For anticlerical tracts that made abundant use of these trials, though with questionable accuracy, see M. E. Billings, *The Crimes of Preachers in the United States and Canada from May, 1876, to May 1882*, 2nd annual edition (New York: D. M. Bennett, 1882) and D. M. Bennett, *The Champions of the Church: Their Crimes and Persecutions* (New York: D. M. Bennett, 1878).

CHAPTER 4

1. Elizabeth Tilton to Theodore Tilton, June 29, 1871, in *Theodore Tilton versus Henry Ward Beecher, Action for Criminal Connection Tried in the City Court of Brooklyn*, vol. 1 (New York: McDivitt, Campbell, 1875), 540, 544–45. Charles Reade, *Griffith Gaunt or, Jealousy* (Boston: Colonial Press, n.d.); Ann Douglas, *The Feminization of American Culture* (New York: Alfred A. Knopf, 1977). Elizabeth White perceptively challenged Douglas's use of separate spheres to categorize women as readers and consumers and men as producers, but we can further challenge the Douglas thesis by examining the ways that women readers, not just writers, produced and acted as a result of their reading. Elizabeth Alice White, "Sentimental Heresies: Rethinking *The Feminization of American Culture*," *Intellectual History Newsletter* 15 (1993): 23–31. See also Nina Baym, *Novels, Readers, and Reviewers: Responses to Fiction in Antebellum America* (Ithaca, N.Y.: Cornell University Press, 1984), for an alternative interpretation of sentimental literature, passivity, and market culture.

2. Englishwoman Harriet Martineau's radical prescription departed significantly from the majority view: She advocated breaking down the barriers that confined women to the domestic sphere to increase their opportunities for wider political and intellectual activity and to diminish women's reliance on the church and clergy. See chapter 2. Not all sensational writers were men: Louisa May Alcott was an important exception. David S. Reynolds, *Beneath the American Renaissance: The Subversive Imagination in the Age of Emerson and Melville* (Cambridge, Mass.: Harvard University Press, 1989).

3. Reynolds, 61.

4. Anon., *The Confessions of a Magdalene; or, Some Passages in the Life of Experience Borgia* (New York: n.p., 1831); Maria Monk, *Awful Disclosures of Maria Monk, As Exhibited in a Narrative of Her Sufferings during a Residence of Five Years as a Novice, and Two Years as a Black Nun in the Hotel Dieu Nunnery of Montreal* (New York: Howe & Bates, 1836). The following are similar exposés of corrupt clergy in various denominations: Aesop [pseud.], *The Hypocrite; or Sketches of American Society from a Residence of Forty Years* (New York: Thomas Fox, 1844); Anon., *The Life and Adventures of Oba-*

diah Benjamin Franklin Bloomfield, M.D. . . . Interspersed with Episodes and Remarks Religious, Moral, Public Spirited and Humorous (Philadelphia: Published for the Proprietor, 1818); George Bourne, *Lorette. The History of Louise, Daughter of a Canadian Nun; Exhibiting the Interior of Female Convents* (New York: William A. Mercein, 1833); Charles J. Cannon, *Father Felix: A Tale* (New York: Edward Dunigan, 1845); and *Harry Layden: A Tale* (New York: John A. Boyle, 1842); Mr. DePotter [pseud.], *Female Convents, Secrets of Nunneries Disclosed* (New York: D. Appleton, 1834); Donald Grant Mitchell, *Dr. Johns: Being a Narrative of Certain Events in the Life of an Orthodox Minister of Connecticut* (New York: Charles Scribner, 1866). In addition, clergymen appeared as minor but still corrupt characters in other exposés, such as George G. Foster, *New York by Gas-Light and Other Urban Sketches*, edited by Stuart M. Blumin (Berkeley: University of California Press, 1990, reprint of 1850 edition), 98–99.

5. George Lippard, *The Quaker City; or, the Monks of Monk Hall* (Philadelphia: T. B. Peterson & Bros., 1876), reprinted from *The Quaker City; or, the Monks of Monk Hall. A Romance of Philadelphia Life, Mystery and Crime* (Philadelphia: G. B. Zieber, 1844). Lippard may have drawn inspiration for his diabolical secret society from the anti-Masonry controversy that had roiled through New York and New England fifteen years before. See Paul Goodman, *Towards a Christian Republic: Antimasonry and the Great Transition in New England, 1826–1836* (New York: Oxford University Press, 1988); Ronald P. Formisano and Kathleen S. Kutolowski, "Antimasonry and Masonry: The Genesis of Protest, 1826–1827," *American Quarterly* 29 (1977): 139–65; and David Brion Davis, "Some Themes of Counter-Subversion: An Analysis of Anti-Masonic, Anti-Catholic, and Anti-Mormon Literature," *Mississippi Valley Historical Review* 47 (1960): 205–24.

6. All quotations are from Lippard, *Quaker City* (1876), 270–74.

7. George Lippard, *Memoirs of a Preacher: A Revelation of the Church and Home* (Philadelphia: Joseph Severns 1849); all quotations are from a later edition of the same work entitled *The Memoirs of a Preacher: or, the Mysteries of the Pulpit* (Philadelphia: T. B. Peterson & Brothers, 1864), 52.

8. Karen Halttunen, *Confidence Men and Painted Ladies: A Study of Middle-Class Culture in America, 1830–1870* (New Haven, Conn.: Yale University Press, 1982); John F. Kasson, *Rudeness and Civility: Manners in Nineteenth-Century Urban America* (New York: Hill and Wang, 1990), 103–7. See also Eugenia C. DeLamotte, *Perils of the Night: A Feminist Study of Nineteenth-Century Gothic* (New York: Oxford University Press, 1990); William E. Lenz, *Fast Talk and Flush Times: The Confidence Man as a Literary Convention* (Columbia: University of Missouri Press, 1985); Jane Tompkins, *Sensational Designs: The Cultural Work of American Fiction, 1790–1860* (New York: Oxford University Press, 1985); and Herman Melville's novel, *The Confidence Man: His Masquerade*, ed. Hershel Parker (1857; reprint, New York: W. W. Norton, 1971) for additional discussions and manifestations of this obsession.

9. This discussion draws on several studies of nineteenth-century popular literature, especially Baym, *Novels, Readers, and Reviewers;* Gillian Brown, *Domestic Individualism: Imagining the Self in Nineteenth-Century America* (Berkeley: University of California Press, 1990); Cathy Davidson, *Revolution and the Word: The Rise of the Novel in America* (New York: Oxford University Press, 1986); G. M. Goshgarian, *To Kiss the Chastening Rod: Domestic Fiction and Sexual Ideology in the American Renaissance* (Ithaca, N.Y.: Cornell University Press, 1992); Susan K. Harris, *Nineteenth-Century American Women's Novels: Interpretive Strategies* (New York: Cambridge University Press, 1990); Cynthia Jordan, *Second Stories: The Politics of Language, Form, and Gender in Early American Fictions* (Chapel Hill: University of North Carolina Press, 1989); Mary

Kelley, *Private Woman, Public Stage: Literary Domesticity in Nineteenth-Century America* (New York: Oxford University Press, 1984); David Reynolds, *Faith in Fiction: The Emergence of Religious Literature in America* (Cambridge, Mass.: Harvard University Press, 1981). A very useful catalogue of novels that treat religious topics is Leo O'Connor's *The Protestant Sensibility in the American Novel: An Annotated Bibliography* (New York: Garland, 1992).

10. First published in 1850. The quotations are from Susan Warner, *The Wide, Wide, World*, afterword by Jane Tompkins (New York: Feminist Press, 1987), 341, 181, 417, 154, 217, 239, 454.

11. Ibid., 318, 401, 351 [emphasis in original].

12. Ibid., 561.

13. Ibid., 403.

14. Tompkins's afterword in ibid., 599. Goshgarian has traced the theme of incest, the "double entendre" or the unspoken "(w)hole" of the domestic novel, in Warner and two other best-sellers of the 1850s.

15. For representative men's published memoirs and biographies, see Francis Asbury, *The Journal of the Reverend Francis Asbury: Bishop of the Methodist Episcopal Church* (New York: N. Bangs and T. Mason, 1821); Lorenzo Dow, *The Dealings of God, Man, and the Devil, as Exemplified in the Life, Experience, and Travels of Lorenzo Dow, in a Period of More Than Half a Century* (Norwich, Conn.: William Falkner, 1833); Francis Wayland, *Memoir of the Life and Labors of the Rev. Adoniram Judson, D.D.* (Boston: Phillips, Sampson, 1853). Judson and his wife, both foreign missionaries, were the subject of several popular publications. See Joan Jacobs Brumberg, *Mission for Life: The Story of the Family of Adoniram Judson, the Dramatic Events of the First American Foreign Mission, and the Course of Evangelical Religion in the Nineteenth Century* (New York: Free Press, 1980), chapter 1. See also Scott Evan Casper, *Constructing American Lives: Biography and Culture in Nineteenth-Century America* (Chapel Hill: University of North Carolina Press, 1999). The popular published memoirs listed here all chronicled the ministries of exceptional men and women, and thus I have not included them in my examination of the experienced pastoral relationship in part III. For the problems of using these memoirs as models for one's own ministry, see Isaac Bird Journal, March 30, 1814, Yale University Manuscripts and Archives.

16. Ichabod Spencer, *A Pastor's Sketches; or, Conversations with Anxious Inquirers, respecting the Way of Salvation*, 2nd series (New York: M. W. Dodd, 1855). In this volume, Spencer reported successful conversations with fourteen men and twenty-six women. He more often declined to discuss theology with women than with men, urging them instead to feel rather than think. The fifth chapter, "The Neglected Bible," tells the story of the powerful little tract. For an example of a pastor using tracts instead of conversation, see George Moore Diary, Feb. 3, 1843, and Aug. 4, 1844, American Antiquarian Society. For examples of clergy and women recording their reactions to reading, see Moore, Nov. 4, 1836, and May 2, 1837; John Lloyd Religious Journal, Summer 1842, Princeton Theological Seminary Library; Isaac Bird Journal, Jan. 13, 1814, Yale University Manuscripts and Archives; Hannah Jackson Lowell Cabot Diary, June 1838, Schlesinger Library, Radcliffe College; Frances Quick Diary, April 1, 15, 1855, and May 30, 1858, Schlesinger Library, Radcliffe College.

17. Samuel Hopkins, *Life and Character of Miss Susanna Anthony, Who Died in Newport, Rhode Island, June 23, 1790, in the Sixty-Fifth Year of Her Age*, 2nd ed. (Portland, Maine: Lyman, Hall, 1810), 21; Hopkins, *Memoirs of the Life of Mrs. Sarah Osborn; Who Died at Newport, Rhode Island, on the Second Day of August, 1796, in the Eighty Third Year of Her Age*, 2nd ed. (Catskill, N.Y.: N. Elliot, 1814); Hopkins, ed. *Fa-*

miliar Letters, Written by Mrs. Sarah Osborn, and Miss Susanna Anthony, Late of New-port, Rhode Island (Newport, R.I.: Newport Mercury, 1807). For investigations of women's conversion narratives, see Virginia Lieson Brereton, From Sin to Salvation: Stories of Women's Conversions, 1800 to the Present (Bloomington: Indiana University Press, 1991); Barbara Epstein, The Politics of Domesticity: Women, Evangelicalism, and Temperance in Nineteenth-Century America (Middletown, Conn.: Wesleyan University Press, 1981); Joanna Bowen Gillespie, " 'The Clear Leadings of Providence': Pious Memoirs and the Problems of Self-Realization for Women in the Early Nineteenth Century," Journal of the Early Republic 5 (1985):197–221; and Susan Juster, " 'In a Different Voice': Male and Female Narratives of Religious Conversion in a Post-Revolutionary America," American Quarterly 41 (1989): 34–62.

18. Hopkins, Life and Character, 21, 30–31.

19. Ibid. 74, 33–34, 167–68; Hopkins, Memoirs, 92, 48, 75.

20. Hopkins, Familiar Letters, 86; Hopkins, Life and Character, 34. Both women read independently in tracts and scripture and corresponded and spoke on religious topics with other women. See Hopkins, Life and Character, 26; Hopkins, Memoirs, 26, 50.

21. Hopkins, Memoirs, 75–77.

22. Barbara E. Lacey, "The Bonds of Friendship: Sarah Osborn of Newport and the Reverend Joseph Fish of North Stonington, 1743–1779," Rhode Island History 45 (1986): 126–36; Mary Beth Norton, " 'My Resting Reaping Times': Sarah Osborn's Defense of Her 'Unfeminine Activities,' " Signs 2 (1976): 515–29.

23. For examples of clergy support for female preachers, see Catherine A. Brekus, Strangers & Pilgrims: Female Preaching in America, 1740–1845 (Chapel Hill: University of North Carolina Press, 1998), 229–31, 250, 268–70, 298. Brekus gives many more examples of clergy's criticism of female preaching, however. For an example of clergy's support of female writers, see Ann Douglas, The Feminization of American Culture, 161–162.

24. All quotations are from Harriet Beecher Stowe, The Minister's Wooing, reprint of the 1859 ed. (Hartford, Conn.: The Stowe-Day Foundation, 1978), 163–64, 150.

25. Ibid., 122–23.

26. Ibid., 348–51 [emphasis in original]. The women's power to play the masculine pastoral role is explored in Susan K. Harris, "The Female Imaginary in Harriet Beecher Stowe's The Minister's Wooing," New England Quarterly 66 (1993): 179–98.

27. Stowe, The Minister's Wooing, 85.

28. Ibid., 96–97, 489.

29. H. Trusta [Elizabeth Stuart Phelps], The Sunny Side; or, the Country Minister's Wife (Boston: John P. Jewett, 1851); and A Peep at "Number Five"; or, a Chapter in the Life of a City Pastor (Boston: Phillips, Sampson, 1852); Anon., The Shady Side: or, Life in a Country Parsonage, by a Pastor's Wife (Boston: John P. Jewett, 1853). For more examples of the parsonage novels, see Frederick William Shelton, Peeps from a Belfry; or, the Parish Sketch Book (New York: Charles Scribner, 1855); and The Rector of St. Bardolph's; or, Superannuated (New York: Charles Scribner, 1853); Elizabeth Oakes Smith, Bertha and Lily; or, the Parsonage of Beech Glen. A Romance (New York: J. C. Derby, 1854); [Susan Jocelyn], Lights and Shadows: Parish Sketches by the Pastor's Wife (the 1840 estimate is probably too early) in Peter Fulton, "The Pastor's Wife's Manuscript: A Critical Text and Commentary" (unpublished, edited, and annotated typescript of manuscript in William R. Perkins Library, Duke University, Durham, N.C.). My thanks to Kathy Rudy for this last source. Elias Nason, a Congregational pastor,

read *Sunnyside* in December 1851; Elias Nason Papers, American Antiquarian Society. Frances Quick, a pastor's wife, read the same work to her husband in February 1854; Frances Merrit Quick Diary, Schlesinger Library, Radcliffe College. A clergyman's review of several parsonage novels confirmed their "truthfulness," in *The Christian Examiner*, Nov. 1853.

30. Anon., *The Shady Side*, 197.

31. Trusta, *"Number Five,"* 107.

32. Anon., *The Shady Side*, 321–2, 113.

33. Trusta, *"Number Five,"* 101, 105; Trusta, *The Sunny Side*, 16, 26, 40.

34. Anon., *The Shady Side*, 72.

35. Ibid., 88, 155–56.

36. Ibid., 39 [emphasis in original], 50, 42, 235; Trusta, *"Number Five,"* 208, 202.

37. Herman Melville's *Pierre; or, The Ambiguities* (New York: Harper, 1852) also featured a pastoral relationship.

38. First published in 1850; the quotations are from Nathaniel Hawthorne, *The Scarlet Letter: A Romance* (New York: Penguin Books, 1983), 212. For seventeenth-century scandals that may have inspired Hawthorne, see Frederick Newberry, "A Red-Hot A and a Lusting Divine: Sources for *The Scarlet Letter*," *New England Quarterly* 65 (1987): 256–64. For nineteenth-century fiction and scandals that more probably inspired Hawthorne, see Reynolds, *Beneath the American Renaissance*, 260–63. For Hawthorne's commentary on contemporary issues and ideals, see Sacvan Bercovitch, *The Office of the Scarlet Letter* (Baltimore: Johns Hopkins University Press, 1991).

39. Hawthorne, 94, 180–81.

40. Ibid., 165. Hawthorne first worked this same theme of a minister's ambiguous confession of sin in his 1836 short story, "The Minister's Black Veil."

41. Ibid., 95, 93, 217, 213, 215.

42. Ibid., 78, 83. Hawthorne may have been aware of, and referred to, cases of clerical misconduct that turned into burlesque spectacles (see chapter 4) or generated jokes. One joke that reportedly circulated around New York in the 1840s and 1850s took not very seriously Bishop Benjamin Onderdonk's sexual misconduct, despite his conviction and suspension for immorality. When the gaslights went out during social affairs, some wit would occasionally call out, "Never fear, ladies, the bishop is *not* here!"

43. For an exposition of post-Calvinist theologies in this period, see, for example, Horace Bushnell, *Views of Christian Nurture and of Subjects Adjacent Thereto* (Hartford, Conn.: n.p., 1847); and Charles Finney's 1835 *Lectures on Revivals of Religion Addressed to Ministers of the Gospel*, William McLoughlin, ed. (Cambridge, Mass.: Harvard University Press, 1960). Overviews can be found in Sydney Ahlstrom, *A Religious History of the American People* (New Haven, Conn.: Yale University Press, 1972), chapter 32; and Winthrop Hudson, *Religion in America*, 4th ed. (New York: Macmillan, 1987), chapter 7. For discussions of theology, sexual ideology, and literature in this period, see Goshgarian, *To Kiss the Chastening Rod*, 36–75; and Richard Brodhead, "Sparing the Rod: Discipline and Fiction in Antebellum America," *Representations* (1988): 67–96.

44. Hawthorne, *Scarlet Letter*, 266, 271.

45. Ibid., 275.

46. The details of Matthias's theology, his personal life, and his small cult following came out in several publications at the time of his two highly publicized trials in 1835. He was acquitted in the murder of a male adherent but convicted for assault and battery on his daughter. Paul E. Johnson and Sean Wilentz, *The Kingdom of Mat-*

thias: A Story of Sex and Salvation in 19th Century America (New York: Oxford University Press, 1994), 91–96, take their discussion of Matthias's misogynist theology from William L. Stone, Matthias and His Impostures; or, the Progress of Fanaticism. Illustrated in the Extraordinary Case of Robert Matthews and Some of His Forerunners and Disciples (New York: n.p., 1835), 111–12, 105–8, 131–34, 140, 153–63,160–61, 161n; Gilbert Vale, Fanaticism; Its Source and Influence, Illustrated by the Simple Narrative of Isabella, in the Case of Matthias, Mr. And Mrs. B. Folger, Mr. Pierson, Mr. Mills, Catherine, Isabella, &c., &c. 2 vols. (New York: n.p., 1835), 1: 43; and "The Examination of Robert Mathews Otherwise Called 'Mathias the Prophet,' " in People v. Robert Matthias, October 15, 1834, Indictment Papers, Court of General Sessions, Municipal Archives and Records Center, New York. Peter Cartwright described his exploits in the rich and rollicking memoir, Autobiography of Peter Cartwright: The Backwoods Preacher, ed. William P. Strickland (New York: C & P, 1854).

CHAPTER 5

1. Anonymous reviewer, The Christian Examiner, Nov., 1853.

2. Enoch Pond, The Young Pastor's Guide (Bangor, Maine: E. F. Duren, 1848), 67, 323, 327 [emphasis in original].

3. Gardiner Spring, The Power of the Pulpit; or, Thoughts Addressed to Christian Ministers and Those Who Hear Them (New York: Baker and Scribner, 1848), 430–31, 360–62, 434, 430, 373; Pond, The Young Pastor's Guide, 330, 340, 339, 325 [emphasis in original].

4. Spring, The Power of the Pulpit, 434; Pond, The Young Pastor's Guide, 324, 344, 337–38; Heman Humphrey, Thirty-Four Letters to a Son in the Ministry (Amherst: J. S. & C. Adams, 1842), 63 [emphasis in original]. Pond's complaint about educated parishioners is ironic, since education and access to the scriptures was a basic tenet of Reformed Protestantism and produced periodic challenges to clerical orthodoxy. For an example from the Puritan period, see Selma R. Williams, Divine Rebel: The Life of Anne Marbury Hutchinson (New York: Holt, Rinehart and Winston, 1981). Humphrey was quoting 2 Timothy 4:3–4: "For the time will come when they will not endure sound doctrine; but after their own lusts shall they heap to themselves teachers, having itching ears; and they shall turn away their ears from the truth, and shall be turned unto fables."

5. For examples of lay-clerical tensions during this period and during the colonial period, see David Hall, The Faithful Shepherd: A History of the New England Ministry in the Seventeenth Century (Chapel Hill: University of North Carolina Press, 1972); George Harper, "Clericalism and Revival: The Great Awakening in Boston as a Pastoral Phenomenon," New England Quarterly 57 (1984): 554–66; Ola Winslow, Meetinghouse Hill: 1630–1783 (New York: Macmillan, 1952), 211–12, 214–18; Sidney E. Mead, "The Rise of the Evangelical Conception of the Ministry in America, 1607–1850," in The Ministry in Historical Perspective, H. Richard Niebuhr and Daniel D. Williams, eds. (New York: Harper, 1946), 207–49. Examples of resistance to lay control appear throughout The Methodist Discipline of 1798, facsimile edition (Rutland, Vt.: Academy Books, 1979), 34–35; and in Patrick W. Carey, People, Priests, and Prelates: Ecclesiastical Democracy and the Tensions of Trusteeism (South Bend, Ind.: University of Notre Dame Press, 1983); and Jay P. Dolan, The Immigrant Church: New York's Irish and German Catholics, 1815–1865 (South Bend, Ind.: University of Notre Dame Press, 1983), 87–98. For an example of an early Reformed text advocating a familiar relationship between pastor and parishioner, see Richard Baxter, The Reformed Pastor: A Discourse on the

Pastoral Office, Designed Principally to Explain and Recommend the Duty of Personal In-struction and Catechising (1655; reprint, London: J. Buckland, 1766). Historians who have argued for the "feminization" of American religion in the nineteenth-century fail to note its traditional sources. See Scott, *From Office to Profession*, 47; Ann Douglas, *The Feminization of American Culture* (New York: Knopf, 1977); Barbara Welter, "The Feminization of American Religion, 1800–1860," in *Dimity Convictions: The American Woman in the Nineteenth Century* (Athens: University of Ohio Press, 1976), 83–102.

6. On the decline of permanency, see Daniel Calhoun, *Professional Lives in Amer-ica: Structure and Aspiration, 1750–1850* (Cambridge, Mass.: Harvard University Press, 1965, esp. chapter 4; and Scott, *From Office to Profession*, 3–4, 35, 48, 74–75, 99. For an example of clerical complaints regarding financial support, see Heman Humphrey, *The Duties of Ministers and People: A Sermon, Preached before the General Association of Connecticut, at New-Haven, June 18, 1816* (New Haven, Conn.: Nathan Whiting, 1816). For the decline in deference, anticlericalism, and the effects of democratization in re-ligion during this period, see Nathan O. Hatch, *The Democratization of American Christianity* (New Haven, Conn.: Yale University Press, 1989), 9–10, chapter 2, and Appendix; Paul E. Johnson, *A Shopkeeper's Millennium: Society and Revivals in Roches-ter, New York, 1815–1837* (New York: Hill & Wang, 1978); Alice Felt Tyler, *Freedom's Fer-ment: Phases of American Social History from the Colonial Period to the Outbreak of the Civil War* (New York: Harper & Row, 1944).

7. William Cogswell, *Letters to Young Men Preparing for the Christian Ministry* (New York: Saxton & Miles, 1842), 57.

8. Descriptions of ministerial training in the colonial period and in the nine-teenth century can be found in David Allmendinger, *Paupers and Scholars: The Trans-formation of Student Life in Nineteenth-Century New England* (New York: St. Martin's Press, 1975); Gerald Cragg, "Training the Ministry—The Older Tradition," *Andover Newton Quarterly* 8 (1968): 223–34; Mary L. Gambrill, *Ministerial Education in Eighteenth-Century New England* (New York: Columbia University Press, 1937); James Axtell, *The School upon a Hill: Education and Society in Colonial New England* (New York: Norton, 1974).

9. Allmendinger, *Paupers and Scholars*, 15–32, stressed the familial quality of this relationship but not its link to changing notions of masculinity.

10. For discussions of familial ideology in the colonial and early republican pe-riod, see John Demos, *A Little Commonwealth: Family Life in Plymouth Colony* (New York: Oxford University Press, 1970); Edmund Morgan, *The Puritan Family: Religion and Domestic Relations in Seventeenth-Century New England* (New York: Harper & Row, 1966), 133–60; Shirley Samuels, "Infidelity and Contagion: The Rhetoric of Revolu-tion," *Early American Literature* 22 (1987): 183–91; Melvin Yazawa, *From Colonies to Commonwealth: Familial Ideology and the Beginnings of the American Republic* (Balti-more: Johns Hopkins University Press, 1985), esp. part II.

11. Allmendinger, *Paupers and Scholars* 4–14.

12. Ibid., 121–25.

13. The general catalogue of each early seminary is the best source of curriculum information. See "Assorted Pamphlets and Catalogues on Theological Seminaries," Yale Divinity School, RG 33. See also Robert Wood Lynn, "Notes toward a History: Theological Encyclopedia and the Evolution of Protestant Seminary Curriculum, 1808–1868," *Theological Education* (Spring, 1981): 118–44; Glenn T. Miller, *Piety and Intellect: The Aims and Purposes of Antebellum Theological Education* (Atlanta: Scholars Press, 1990); Natalie Naylor, "Raising a Learned Ministry: The American Education Society: Indigent Students and the New Charity" (unpub. Ph.D. dissertation, Columbia Uni-

versity, 1971); and Naylor, "The Theological Seminary in the Configuration of American Higher Education in the Antebellum Years," *History of Education Quarterly* 17 (1977): 17–30. Both Sidney Mead and Glenn Miller give attention to the controversial and combative atmosphere of seminaries in particular and of evangelical religion in general during this period. For additional examples of theological battles and prominent warriors in the early seminaries, see Sydney E. Ahlstrom, *A Religious History of the American People* (New Haven, Conn.: Yale University Press, 1972), 393–97, 415–22. Notebooks of theological students at various institutions during the period reveal little or no attention to practical pastoral duties. See notebooks in the Robert Acker Clapp Collection (Rochester Theological Seminary, ca. 1856), American Baptist Historical Society, Rochester, N.Y.; Malcolm Douglass Papers (General Theological Seminary, 1848–49), Library at Hobart and William Smith Colleges, Geneva, N.Y.; Elias Henry Johnson Papers (Rochester Theological Seminary, ca. 1868–71), Ambrose Swazey Library, CRDS/BH/CTS/SBI, Rochester, N.Y.; Jonathan Lee Papers (Andover Seminary, 1809–11), Yale Manuscripts and Archives, New Haven, Conn.; John Lloyd's notebook (Princeton Theological Seminary, n.d.) in the Charles Hodge Papers, Princeton Theological Seminary Libraries, Princeton, N.J.; and Charles Swan Walker Papers (Andover and Yale Divinity School, 1867–69), Yale Manuscripts and Archives, New Haven, Conn.

14. Scott, *From Office to Profession*, 66, did not attribute the decline in status of pastoral work to gender issues. H[enry] K[alloch] Rowe, *A History of Andover Seminary* (Newton, Mass.: n.p., 1933), 26, estimated that in the school's first forty years less than two-thirds of Andover's students finished the three-year course. See also E. Brooks Holifield, *A History of Pastoral Care in America: From Salvation to Self-Realization* (Nashville, Tenn.: Abingdon Press, 1983), 118.

15. For the definition of separate spheres, see Nancy Cott, *The Bonds of Womanhood: Women's Sphere in New England, 1780–1835* (New Haven, Conn.: Yale University Press, 1977); and Welter, *Dimity Convictions*. For the shifting definitions of masculinity, see Mark C. Carnes and Clyde Griffen, eds., *Meanings for Manhood: Constructions of Masculinity in Victorian America* (Chicago: University of Chicago Press, 1990); Elizabeth H. Pleck and Joseph H. Pleck, eds., *The American Man* (Englewood Cliffs, N.J.: Prentice-Hall, 1980); E. Anthony Rotundo, *American Manhood: Transformations in Masculinity from the Revolution to the Modern Era* (New York: Basic Books, 1993).

16. George B. Ide, *The Ministry Demanded in the Present Crisis* (Philadelphia: American Baptist Publication Society, 1845), 31–33, 37, 66, 92–93. See also Spring, *The Power of the Pulpit*, 373–74.

17. Archibald Alexander Papers, Princeton Theological Seminary, Pastoral Theology Lecture Notes, Folders 19 and 44; Charles Grandison Finney, *The Memoirs of Charles G. Finney: The Complete Restored Text*, Garth M. Rosell and Richard A. G. Dupuis, eds. (Grand Rapids, Mich.: Academie Books, 1989), 191 [emphasis in original], 102, 269. Finney's evangelical measures were attacked by orthodox Lyman Beecher, *Correspondence. Selections. Lectures of the Rev. Dr. Beecher and Rev. Mr. Nettleton on the "New Measures" in Conducting Revivals of Religion* (New York: G. & C. Carvil, 1828). Finney used his autobiography to continue the defense long after Lyman Beecher of Lane Seminary and Asahel Nettleton of Hartford Seminary had died. For a more thorough discussion of the special concerns of evangelical theological education, see Karin E. Gedge, "Ministry to Women in the Antebellum Seminaries," in *Theological Education in the Evangelical Tradition*, D. G. Hart and R. Albert Mohler Jr., eds., (Grand Rapids, Mich.: Baker Books, 1997), 173–89.

18. Finney, *Memoirs*. H. K. Rowe, *History of Andover Seminary*, described the dif-

ficulty of attracting noted pastors to Andover, 51–53. See also Jonathan Lee Papers, letters to father, April 11 and June 26, 1810, Yale Manuscripts and Archives, complaining of the "infantine state" of the new Andover Seminary and of the school's inability to lure the eminent preacher and pastor Gardiner Spring to the Andover parish. James Harris Fairchild is a good example of the custom of employing graduates as faculty members. Ordained upon graduation from Oberlin, he never held a full-time pastorate before taking up life-long teaching duties at his alma mater. James Harris Fairchild Papers, Biographical Sketch, 1, Oberlin College Archives.

19. Pond, *The Young Pastor's Guide* 204 [emphasis in original]. Manual writers primarily drew on Paul's letters to the Corinthians, Timothy, and Titus, as well as early English Puritans Richard Baxter and Philip Doddridge, continental Protestants Alexandre Vinet and Francois Fenelon, and New England Puritan Cotton Mather, among others. For early sources, see Baxter, *Reformed Pastor;* Adam Clarke, *The Preacher's Manual* (New York: T. Mason and G. Lane, 1837); Cotton Mather, *Manuductio ad Ministerium: Directions for a Candidate of the Ministry* (1726; reprint New York: Columbia University Press, 1938); Edwards A. Park, ed., *The Preacher and the Pastor, by Fenelon, Herbert, Baxter, Campbell* (Andover, Mass.: Allen, Morrill and Wardwell, 1845); A[lexandre] Vinet, *Pastoral Theology; or, the Theory of the Evangelical Ministry,* trans. and ed. by Thomas H. Skinner (New York: Ivison, Blaeman, Taylor, 1871).

20. Spring, *The Power of the Pulpit* 292–95, 312, 422, 304; Cogswell, *Letters to Young Men* 98–101. Both Glenn Miller and E. Brooks Holifield argued that these two qualities were often in conflict, but neither considered the practical consequences of trying to reconcile them.

21. Samuel Miller, *Letters on Clerical Manners and Habits: Addressed to a Student in the Theological Seminary at Princeton, N.J.* (Princeton, N.J.: Moore, Baker, 1835), 16–18, 26–27.

22. Samuel Miller, *Letters,* 33–36 [emphasis in original]. See also William Sprague, *Causes of an Unsuccessful Ministry: Two Sermons, Addressed to the Second Presbyterian Congregation in the City of Albany, August 30, 1829; the Sabbath Immediately Succeeding the Author's Induction as Their Pastor* (Albany, N.Y.: Packard and Van Benthuysen, 1829), 20–21. Though Ann Douglas, *Feminization of American Culture,* 66–67, argued that the clergy's adoption of sentiment and "influence" was a capitulation to "feminization," it was also the adoption of the successful salesman's techniques. Erving Goffman recognized the paradoxical problem in his *The Presentation of Self in Everyday Life* (Garden City, N.Y.: Doubleday, 1959), 249–51. Though he did not specifically address the ministry, Goffman understood that those without a tangible product to sell were at a disadvantage. "The more the individual is concerned with the reality that is not available to perception, the more must he concentrate his attention on appearances." Individuals dwell in a moral world because they are concerned with maintaining the impression that they are living up to community moral standards. "But [as] performers, individuals are concerned not with the moral issue of realizing these standards, but with the amoral issue of engineering a convincing impression that these standards are being realized."

23. Sprague, *Causes of an Unsuccessful Ministry,* 16–17; Spring, *The Power of the Pulpit,* 232. See also Humphrey, *Thirty-Four Letters,* 70; and Samuel Miller, *Letters,* 267–383.

24. Humphrey, *Thirty-Four Letters,* Pond, *The Young Pastor's Guide,* 128.

25. Pond, *The Young Pastor's Guide,* 52, 173, 221; Baxter, *Reformed Pastor,* 40–42; Humphrey, *Thirty-four Letters,* 192, 210–12; Miller, *Piety and Intellect,* 40–41, 90, 148, 161; Spring, *The Power of the Pulpit,* 309.

26. Leonard Bacon, "Inaugural Sermon, March 13, 1825, from the text II Cor, ii 16—'Who Is Sufficient for These Things?' " in *Leonard Bacon: Pastor of the First Church in New Haven*, H. C. Kingsley, Leonard J. Sanford, and Thomas R. Trowbridge Jr., eds. (New Haven, Conn.: 1882), 57.

27. Sprague, *Causes of an Unsuccessful Ministry*, 18, 43; Pond, *The Young Pastor's Guide*, 66; Humphrey, *Thirty-four Letters*, 204.

28. Pond, *The Young Pastor's Guide*, 84, 62, 196–203, 354–56, 374–76; Samuel Miller, *Letters*, 385, 388.

29. Fairchild, "Suggestions to Theological Students as to the Relations of the Pastor to the Women of His Church & Congregation," undated typescript with manuscript corrections, Fairchild Papers, Oberlin College Library Archives, Box 29, Folder 6. Fairchild taught at the college until his death in 1903. Spring, *The Power of the Pulpit*, 309.

30. Archibald Alexander, *Practical Truths* (New York: American Tract Society, 1852[?]), 222. 31. Heman Humphrey's only advice on women in his *Thirty-Four Letters*, 188, was to suggest that though both sexes might meet together in Bible classes, segregating the sexes had advantages. The following manuals contained only passing or no specific reference to women: Richard Baxter's *Reformed Pastor;* Gregory Thurston Bedell, *The Pastor. Pastoral Theology. Experientia Docens, Docet, Docuit* (Philadelphia: J. B. Lippincott, 1880); Theodore L. Cuyler, *How to Be a Pastor* (New York: Baker & Taylor, 1890); James M. Hoppin, *The Office and Work of the Christian Ministry* (New York: Sheldon, 1870); Mather, *Manuductio ad Ministerium;* William Meade, *Lectures on the Pastoral Office: Delivered to the Students of the Theological Seminary at Alexandria, Virginia* (New York: Stanford and Swords, 1849); Park, *The Preacher and the Pastor;* Joseph Parker, *Ad Clerum: Advices to a Young Preacher* (Boston: Roberts Brothers, 1871); William G. T. Shedd, *Homiletics, and Pastoral Theology* (New York: Charles Scribner, 1867). Frederick R. Wynne, *The Joy of the Ministry. An Endeavour to Increase the Efficiency and Deepen the Happiness of Pastoral Work* (New York: James Pott, 1885), 188, suggested that men needed more attention from their pastors than women, although that message is implicit in many of these discussions. For examples of published sermons arguing for women's maternal agency, see Horace Bushnell, *Discourses on Christian Nurture* (Boston: Massachusetts Sabbath School Society, 1847), and "Mary, the Mother of Jesus," in *Sermons on Living Subjects* (New York: Scribner, Armstrong, 1873), 9–36. For examples of women's religiously inspired activism during this period, see Barbara Epstein, *The Politics of Domesticity: Women, Evangelicalism, and Temperance in Nineteenth-Century America* (Middletown, Conn.: Wesleyan University Press, 1981); Nancy Hewitt, "The Perimeters of Women's Power in American Religion," in *The Evangelical Tradition in America*, Leonard I. Sweet, ed. (Macon, Ga.: Mercer University Press, 1984), 233–56; Keith Melder, "Ladies Bountiful: Organized Women's Benevolence in Early 19th Century America," *New York History* 48 (1967): 231–55; Mary P. Ryan, *Cradle of the Middle Class: The Family in Oneida County, New York, 1790–1865* (New York: Cambridge University Press, 1981), chapters 2–3. For the pastoral critique of Finney's "new measures," especially his policy of allowing women to speak in mixed-sex groups, see Charles C. Cole, "The New Lebanon Convention," *New York History* (October, 1950): 385–97; and for the critique of female preaching in general, see Catherine A. Brekus, *Strangers & Pilgrims: Female Preaching in America, 1740–1845* (Chapel Hill: University of North Carolina Press, 1998), esp. chapter 7.

32. Samuel Miller, *Letters*, 317. For the relationship between women and doctors during this period, see Ruth J. Abram, ed., *Send Us a Lady Physician: Women Doctors in America, 1835–1920* (New York: Norton, 1985); Jane B. Donegan, *Women and Men*

Midwives: Medicine, Morality, and Misogyny in Early America (Westport, Conn.: Greenwood, 1978); Edward Shorter, *Bedside Manners: The Troubled History of Doctors and Patients* (New York: Simon and Schuster, 1985). Until the mid-nineteenth century, most women still relied upon a women's healing culture, especially for women's health problems.

33. Samuel Miller, *Letters*, 346, 317.

34. Ibid. Miller and his colleagues at Princeton Seminary—Ashbel Green, Archibald Alexander, and Charles Hodge—produced a body of writings on women analyzed by Ronald W. Hogeland in "Charles Hodge, the Association of Gentlemen, and Ornamental Womanhood: A Study of Male Conventional Wisdom, 1825–1855," *Journal of Presbyterian History* 53 (1975): 239–55. Hogeland apparently missed Miller's pastoral manual, however. Although Hogeland's portrait of old school attitudes toward women is exaggerated, he anticipated my main argument that professionalization slighted women in the pastoral relationship. See Samuel Miller, *A Sermon Preached March 13, 1808, for the Benefit of the Society Instituted in the City of New York for the Relief of Poor Widows with Small Children* (New York: Hopkins and Seymour, 1808); and *The Life of Samuel Miller*, 2 vols. (Philadelphia: n.p., 1869); Ashbel Green, *The Christian Duty of Women, a Discourse Delivered in the Church of Princeton, New Jersey, August 23, 1825, before the Princeton Female Society, for the Support of a Female School in India* (Princeton, N.J.: n.p., 1825).

35. Samuel Miller, *Letters*, 90, 346 [emphasis in original].

36. Cogswell, *Letters to Young Men*, 166. See also *The Clerical Life: A Series of Letters to Ministers* (New York: Dodd, Mead, 1898), 120–25; Samuel Miller, *Letters*, 388, 327, 344; *The Methodist Discipline*, 59–62; Elisha Weaver, *Doctrines and Discipline of the African Methodist Episcopal Church*, 10th rev. ed. (Philadelphia: James H. Bryson, 1860), 75; Clarke, *The Preacher's Manual*, 79.

37. Pond, *The Young Pastor's Guide*, 329, Samuel Miller, *Letters*, 343–44.

38. Alexander Papers, Pastoral Theology Lecture Notes, Folder 15, 16 [emphasis in original], 49.

39. Elam J. Comings Papers, Diary 1837–46, n.p., n.d., Oberlin College Archives. Finney may have been much more forthcoming in lectures than were manual writers. Robert Samuel Fletcher asserts that Finney's pastoral theology course in 1837 consisted of only six lectures, "which were almost entirely devoted to manners and the relation of ministers with the opposite sex." Only later did he expand the topics to include suggestions regarding study habits, business habits, the preparation and delivery of sermons, and pastoral visits, in *A History of Oberlin College from Its Foundation through the Civil War*, vol. 2 (Oberlin, Ohio: Oberlin College, 1943), 728. See also Hoppin, *Office and Work*, 456.

40. Samuel Miller, *Letters*, 158.

41. Fairchild, "Suggestions to Theological Students," 3–17.

42. Samuel Miller, *Letters*, 344; Pond, *The Young Pastor's Guide*, 296–97 [emphasis in original]. For discussions of the importance of marriage for the minister, see Leverett Griggs, *Letters to a Theological Student* (Boston: American Tract Society, 1863), 90–93; *Methodist Discipline*, 25–26 and chapter 21; Mather, *Manuductio ad Ministerium*, 27; Samuel Miller, *Letters*, 318–43; Pond, *The Young Pastor's Guide*, 204–14; Vinet, *Pastoral Theology*, 156–60; and Archibald Alexander's lecture outlines, Box 13, Folder 5. The Discipline of the African Methodist Episcopal Church did not forbid marriage but counseled, "Take no steps toward marrying without consulting your brethren," in Weaver, *Doctrines and Discipline*, 75. George Herbert, *A Priest to the Temple, or, the Country Parson; His Character and Rule of Holy Life* (1652; reprint, London:

T. Roycroft for Benjamin Tooke, 1671), quoted in Park, *The Preacher and the Pastor*, 176, is the only work that recommends celibacy over marriage.

43. Comings's notebook, n.p.; Westervelt's notes, n.p.; Pond, *The Young Pastor's Guide*, 296–97; Samuel Miller, 322.

44. Samuel Miller, *Letters*, 322, 339–40 [emphasis in original].

45. Alexander Papers, Box 13, Folder 5; Samuel Miller, *Letters*, 327–28, 318–19 [emphasis in original]. Despite the fact that he could not recall receiving instruction on the subject of women from Finney during his days as a student, the young James Fairchild wrote his future wife in 1840 that Finney had offered the men (and women) of his pastoral theology class a "*half* dozen or more [suggestions] on the subject of marriage & the qualifications necessary in the wife of a pastor. . . . He spoke at some length on early engagements etc., said much that is true & some things that are not so true," he assured her. James H. Fairchild to Mary Kellogg, Aug. 25, 1840, Fairchild Papers, Oberlin College Archives, quoted in Fletcher, *History of Oberlin College*, 730.

46. Westervelt notes, "On Marriage," n.p., n.d.; Alexander, Lectures on Pastoral Theology, Box 13, Folder 5; Samuel Miller, *Letters*, 333 [emphasis in original].

47. Westervelt; Samuel Miller, *Letters*, 330, 343, 329; Meade, *Lectures*, 220, 212. Oberlin College permitted female students to take theology classes as training for mission work or for the job of pastor's wife but did not grant them degrees in theology or encourage them to seek ordination.

48. Samuel Miller, *Letters*, 329–31 [emphasis mine]. James Hoppin, professor of pastoral theology at Yale for decades and author of a widely used textbook, compressed the whole topic of women into one page on the pastor's wife. She was "thus his good or evil angel," building him up or undermining him. "Besides," he added, her work was "indispensable" in providing "religious counsel to those of [her] own sex" (*Office and Work*, 460–61).

CHAPTER 6

1. Leonard Bacon, "Inaugural Sermon, March 13, 1825, from the Text II Cor., ii 16—'Who Is Sufficient for These Things?' " in *Leonard Bacon: Pastor of the First Church in New Haven*, H. C. Kingsley, Leonard J. Sanford, and Thomas R. Trowbridge Jr., eds. (New Haven, Conn.: 1882), 57.

2. Ibid.

3. Ibid.

4. See, for example, the Isaac Bird Journal, Sept. 23, 1819, Yale Manuscripts and Archives, Isaac Bird Papers. Bird undertook missionary work in Boston during his vacations from Andover "for my own improvement in duties of ministry." Leonard Woods insisted that seminary students be paid for their traveling expenses, even though they preached on occasion for free. Leonard Woods to Isaac Warren, July 28, 1821, George Arents Special Collection, Syracuse University. The letters of Ferdinand DeWilton Ward, a student at Princeton Seminary in the 1830s, to his sister Henrietta Ward, University of Rochester, Special Collections, are good examples of "pastoral activity" within the student's family. Oberlin was the only exception to the all-male seminary. For a discussion of this early "coeducational" community, see Lori Ginzberg, "Women in an Evangelical Community: Oberlin 1835–1850," *Ohio History* 89 (1980), 78–88.

5. George Moore Diary, 1836–1840, Moore Family Papers, American Antiquarian Society.

6. Bird Journal, March 6, 10, 26, 1814.

7. Ibid., March 30, 1814 [emphasis mine].

8. Ibid., March 30, 1814.

9. Ibid., April [?], 1814; March 30, 1814; May 22 and 29, 1814. The novel to which Bird referred is Susanna Rowson's *Charlotte Temple: A Tale of Truth* (Philadelphia: Printed by D. Humphreys for M. Carey, 1794).

10. Edward F. Gurney diary, 13 July 1851, American Baptist Historical Society; Jonathan Lee Diary, 9 July 1816, 190, Yale Manuscripts and Archives; Beecher is quoted in Donald M. Scott, *From Office to Profession: The New England Ministry, 1750–1850* (Philadelphia: University of Pennsylvania Press, 1978), 4. Scott noted that probationary candidates had difficulty determining if their signals were read correctly. If they were misread, then they worried that they were unfit for their vocation.

11. Charles Hodge Diary, 1819–1820, Firestone Library, Princeton University. Not surprisingly, Hodge was one of the leading opponents of the personal and intimate "New Measures" of evangelist Charles Finney.

12. Ephraim Abbott to Mary Holyoke Pearson, Jan. 5, 1812, American Antiquarian Society, Ephraim Abbott Papers. Abbott also recorded the incident in his journal entry of Dec. 24, 1812, Rhode Island Historical Society, quoted in Teresa Anne Murphy, *Ten Hours' Labor: Religion, Reform, and Gender in Early New England* (Ithaca, N.Y.: Cornell University Press, 1992), 94.

13. Abbott to Pearson, Jan. 26, Feb. 7, and Feb. 14, 1812 [emphasis mine].

14. Many of these visits apparently were performed in the company of another seminary student. No doubt this helped to protect the young men from accusations of impropriety while they conducted their work among Boston's lowlife. Bird Journal, May 31, 1814; Sept. 27, 29 [emphasis in original], and Oct. 25, 31, 1819.

15. Ibid., May 15, 1817 [emphasis in original]; Sept. 30, 1819.

16. Moore Diary, Sept. 12, 1843.

17. Charles Swan Walker, Autobiography of Seminary [Andover] Years, Charles Swan Walker Papers, Yale Manuscripts and Archives, Box 3, 300–302.

18. Edward Whiting Gilman Diaries, July 1 and 12, 1851, Gilman Family Papers, Yale Manuscripts and Archives. See also Gilman diary, Sept. 1849; Oct. 10, 1850; Feb. 16, 1851; and Moore diary, July 29, 1840.

19. Gilman diary, Dec. 11, 1853.

20. Ibid., Dec. 11, 1853.

21. Ibid., Dec. 11, 1853.

22. Ibid., Dec. 11, Sept. 25, Sept. 10, 1849.

23. E. Brooks Holifield, *A History of Pastoral Care in America: From Salvation to Self-Realization* (Nashville, Tenn.: Abingdon Press, 1983), 124. Historians of religion and women have long understood the ways that women's public speech threatened patriarchal authority, but only recently have they begun to inquire into the implications of women's less public speech and face-to-face encounters. Women, generally restricted to an oral culture long after men developed written and published discourse, therefore posed a more significant threat to men in that shared oral culture. Women's "heated speech" and "unbridled tongues" signified disorder, both socially and sexually. The research on colonial speech is especially telling, but more needs to be done on nineteenth-century face-to-face dialogue. See David Hall, *Worlds of Wonder, Days of Judgment: Popular Religious Belief in Early New England* (New York: Knopf, 1989); Jane Kamensky, *Governing the Tongue: The Politics of Speech in Early New England* (New York: Oxford University Press, 1997); Carol Karlsen, *The Devil in the Shape of a Woman: Witchcraft in Colonial New England* (New York: Norton, 1987). The only scholar who has tried to reconstruct pastoral conversations between clergy and

women in the colonial period is Laura Henigman, *Coming into Communion: Pastoral Dialogues in Colonial New England* (Albany: State University of New York Press, 1999).

24. Elam J. Comings Diary, 18-37–46, n.p., n.d., Oberlin College Archives; Douglass Family Papers, Malcolm Douglass to David Bates Douglass, April 13, 1848, and May 8, 1847 [emphasis in original], Hobart and William Smith Colleges, Geneva, N.Y.

25. Freeman-Clarke Family Papers, Ferdinand DeWilton Clarke to Henrietta Clarke, July 2, 1833, University of Rochester, Special Collections, Rochester, N.Y.; "The Board say . . ." quoted in Geoffrey C. Ward, "Two Missionaries' Ordeal by Faith in a Distant Clime," *Smithsonian* (August 1990), 118–32.

26. Frederick Gallagher Papers, Mrs. A. to Frederick Gallagher, Feb. 14, 1855 [emphasis in original]; and Margaret Gallagher Diary, both at Bentley Historical Library, University of Michigan, Ann Arbor. I suspect the sincerity of this note, however. Although signed by "Mrs. A.," it is written in a girlish hand and not that of his future wife. The date, Valentine's Day, might be the occasion for flirtatious amusement. The writer explicitly suggested that Gallagher search for a wife among the pious young ladies in his own church. For discussions of courtship in nineteenth-century America, see Karen Lystra, *Searching the Heart: Women, Men, and Romantic Love in Nineteenth-Century America* (New York: Oxford University Press, 1989); and Ellen K. Rothman, *Hands and Hearts: A History of Courtship in America* (New York: Basic Books, 1984). Both authors argue that sexual topics were taboo in public, but not private, communications.

27. Edward J. Gurney Diary, 1851–53, American Baptist Historical Society, Rochester, N.Y., April 29, July 27, Aug. 10, 18, 24, 1851, and May 2, 1852.

28. Ibid., May 2, 1852 [emphasis in original].

29. Ibid., May 13, 1852.

30. Ibid., Nov. 6, 1852.

31. Moore Diary, vol. 1, Aug. 7, 1838.

32. Ibid., Aug. 7, 11, 25, and Sept. 16, 1838.

33. Ibid., Aug. 27, 1838; July 29, 1840.

34. Ibid., vol. 2, Jan. 27, 30, 1842.

35. Ibid., vol. 1, March [?], June 25, July 6, 1840. See Virginia Woolf, *A Room of One's Own; and, Three Guineas* (London: Hogarth Press, 1984), 33: "Women have served all these centuries as looking-glasses possessing the magic and delicious power of reflecting the figure of man at twice his natural size. Without that power probably the earth would still be swamp and jungle." My thanks to Nancy Cott for this reference.

36. Moore Diary, vol. 2, Feb. 4, 1842; Mar. 11, Aug. 17, 1841; Sept. 13, 1842; Dec. 17, 19, 1843.

37. Ibid., vol. 2, Nov. 28, 1843.

38. Ibid., vol. 2, Nov. 28, 1843; May 8, 1844. Moore died three years later, apparently still unmarried, at the age of 36.

39. Elisha Lord Cleaveland, "Record of Ministerial Labors, 1845–1850," March 17, 1846, Elisha Lord Cleaveland Papers, Yale Manuscripts and Archives, Group 139, Box 1, Folder 3a; Elias Nason Diary, June 13, 1853, Elias Nason Papers, American Antiquarian Society.

40. Moore Diary, May 12, 1845; Cleaveland Record, Sept. 3, 1847. For a discussion of Nettleton's career and pastoral methods, see Sherry Pierpont May, "Asahel Nettleton: Nineteenth-Century American Revivalist" (Unpub. Ph.D. dissertation, Drew University, 1969). For Finney's methods, see Charles Grandison Finney, *The Memoirs*

of Charles G. Finney: The Complete Restored Text, Garth M. Rosell and Richard A. G. Dupuis, eds. (Grand Rapids, Mich.: Academie Books, 1989).

41. For Finney's career, see Finney, *Memoirs*; Robert S. Fletcher, *A History of Oberlin College from Its Foundation through the Civil War*, 2 vols. (Oberlin, 1943; reprint, New York: Arno Press, 1971); Lori Ginzberg, "Women in an Evangelical Community: Oberlin, 1835–1850." *Ohio History* 89 (1980): 78–88; Leonard Sweet, *The Minister's Wife: Her Role in Nineteenth-Century American Evangelicalism* (Philadelphia: Temple University Press, 1983). Finney's student Westervelt took notes on his lectures in pastoral theology, which are clearly addressed to both the young men *and* the young women in his class: "Let her try to elevate the society. Let her form societies. Let her have a weekly meeting with the young ladies. Keep a wake [?] to prayer. Inform yourself. Promote female education." All seem to be aimed at young men regarding their wives. But they are followed by specific injunctions to women: "Relieve your husband as far as possible from care. Pray for him as a minister. Be as useful to him as you can in every p[ossible] way. Be sure to pray that you may be profited by your husband." N.p., n.d. See also Ronald W. Hogeland, "Co-Education of the Sexes at Oberlin College: A Study of Social Ideas in Mid-Nineteenth-Century America," *Journal of Social History* (Winter, 1972–73): 160–76.

CHAPTER 7

1. Elizabeth Cady Stanton, Susan B. Anthony, and Matilda Joslyn Gage, eds., *History of Woman Suffrage* (New York: Fowler & Wells, 1881), 532–33. I am indebted to Catherine Brekus for first bringing this speech to my attention. Mary D. Pellauer, *Toward a Tradition of Feminist Theology: The Religious Social Thought of Elizabeth Cady Stanton, Susan B. Anthony, and Anna Howard Shaw* (Brooklyn, N.Y.: Carlson, 1991) takes feminist historians to task for ignoring or downplaying the role of nineteenth-century feminists in contributing to a feminist theology as well as feminist politics.

2. Stanton, Anthony, and Gage, *History*, 533 [emphasis in original].

3. The diaries and correspondence are listed in the bibliography. More than thirty women are represented, although many are not cited because their writing, despite mentioning churchgoing and spiritual concerns, contains so few references to clergymen themselves. These women represent a broad spectrum of women who wrote between 1810 and 1875. They lived mostly in New England and northern states to the west and ranged in age from twelve to seventy-five years. They were unmarried, married, and widowed, mothers and childless women. Some lived with rural farmers as daughters, wives, or servants; several taught school, a few were wealthy matrons or privileged daughters, and two were married to pastors. Only four are African American women. Of those with a strong denominational affiliation, Episcopal, Unitarian, Congregational, Methodist, and Freewill Baptists are represented. One woman became an advocate of spiritualism. Most listened to a variety of preachers from various denominations other than their own. Most attended church regularly, though not all listened to a settled pastor. They led remarkably conventional lives, concerned with their own families or teaching careers and mostly uninvolved in the political, social, and reform movements that historians have discovered occupied many women of the period. They enjoyed no fame or notoriety outside their families and parishes: In short, they were ordinary women.

4. Sally Hitchcock Bliss Journal, July 21–August 25, September 1, 1822; May 11, 1823, American Antiquarian Society.

5. Ibid., Nov. 12, Dec. 25, 1825; Nov. 15, 1826; Jan. 7, 1827.

6. Ibid., May 6, June 24, Oct. 7, Oct. 26, Dec. 30, 1827.

7. Ibid., Nov. 15, 1827; May 20, 1827; Nov. 27, 1828; Feb. 15, 1829.

8. Hannah Lowell Cabot to Sarah Russell, May 1, 1837; Hannah Lowell Cabot to Lydia Cabot, June 18, 1837, Almy Family Papers, Schlesinger Library, Radcliffe College; Helen Marcia Hart Diary, Aug. 23, 1861, Schlesinger Library, Radcliffe College.

9. Ann J. Stoddard Diary, Mar. 4, Mar. 18, Aug. 12, 1866, Schlesinger Library, Radcliffe College; Elizabeth Ellery Dana Diary, Nov. 7, 1858, Dana Family Papers, Schlesinger Library, Radcliffe College.

10. Frances Kingman Holmes Diary, Oct. 1837, p. 28; Aug. 4, 1839, p. 32, Schlesinger Library, Radcliffe College [emphasis mine].

11. Frances Merritt Quick Diaries, Nov. 28, 1858, Schlesinger Library, Radcliffe College [emphasis mine].

12. Ibid., April 15, 1855; July 22, 28, 1858.

13. Sarah Watson Dana Diary, Oct. 27, Sept. 15, 1833 [emphasis in original], Dana Family Papers, Schlesinger Library, Radcliffe College.

14. Quick Diary, Oct. 17, 1858.

15. For overviews of the numerous competing denominations and sects, see Alice Felt Tyler, *Freedom's Ferment: Phases of American Social History from the Colonial Period to the Outbreak of the Civil War* (New York: Harper & Row, 1944); Sydney Ahlstrom, *A Religious History of the American People* (New Haven, Conn.: Yale University Press, 1972); Nathan O. Hatch, *The Democratization of American Christianity* (New Haven, Conn.: Yale University Press, 1989); Jon Butler, *Awash in a Sea of Faith: Christianizing the American People* (Cambridge, Mass.: Harvard University Press, 1990). Also see George Marsden, "Everyone One's Own Interpreter? The Bible, Science, and Authority in Mid-Nineteenth-Century America," in *The Bible in America: Essays in Cultural History*, Nathan O. Hatch and Mark A. Noll, eds. (New York: Oxford University Press, 1982), 80, who argued that the threat of "spiritual anarchy seemed on the verge of realization in nineteenth-century America because of the individual's inclination to claim authority to interpret the Bible for himself or herself." That trend is epitomized by Sarah Moore Grimke's assertion that she had the right "to judge for myself what is the meaning" of the Bible.

16. Sarah Dana Diary, Oct. 27, 1833; Feb. 1, 1834 [emphasis in original].

17. Ibid., Oct. 6, 1833; Sarah Wetmore to Asahel Nettleton, Oct. 8, 182[1?], Asahel Nettleton Papers, Hartford Seminary; Angeline Morehouse to Samuel Morehouse, Nov. 6, n.d., Jennings Collection, Fairfield Historical Society.

18. Wetmore to Nettleton, Aug. 11, 1822.

19. Quick Diary, Oct. 8, 1854; Abigail Morgridge Sewall to Serena Brown, Sept. 26, 1852; Mar. 28, 1859, Sewall Family Papers, Schlesinger Library, Radcliffe College.

20. Sewall to Brown, July 1, 1849; July 4, 1858; July 18, 1859; July 17, 1853; Mar. 17, 1862; July 4, 1858; July 30, 1860.

21. Quick Diary, Sept. 4, 16, 1864; July 11, 1858; Aug. 21, 1864; Oct. 3, 1858 [emphasis in original]; Mar. 11, 1855; Oct. 8, 1854.

22. Harry S. Stout recognized the dramatic qualities in preaching in *The Divine Dramatist: George Whitefield and the Rise of Modern Evangelicalism* (Grand Rapids, Mich.: Eerdmans, 1991); Karen V. Hansen, *"A Very Social Time": Crafting Community in Antebellum New England* (Berkeley: University of California Press, 1994), 211–16, argued that criticisms of ministers revealed the public's attraction to Sunday services as "diversion from everyday work routines." She also discovered, however, that women commented on religious services and recorded their religious philosophies in their diaries more frequently than men (380). For descriptions of masculine values

during this period, see Mark C. Carnes and Clyde Griffen, eds., *Meanings for Manhood: Constructions of Masculinity in Victorian America* (Chicago: University of Chicago Press, 1990); E. Anthony Rotundo, *American Manhood: Transformations in Masculinity from the Revolution to the Modern Era* (New York: Basic Books, 1993); and David Gilmore, *Manhood in the Making: The Emergence of Cultural Concepts of Masculinity* (New Haven, Conn.: Yale University Press, 1990). Carol Gilligan set out her much noted but controversial theory in *In a Different Voice: Psychological Theory and Women's Development* (Cambridge, Mass.: Harvard University Press, 1982). See also Mary Field Belenky, Blythe McVicker Clinchy, Nancy Rule Goldberger, and Jill Mattuck Tarule, *Women's Ways of Knowing: The Development of Self, Voice, and Mind* (New York: Basic Books, 1986).

23. Sarah Dana Diary, Sept. 15, 1833; Quick Diary, Oct. 8, 1854.

24. Frances Kingman Holmes Diary, Oct. 1837.

25. Martha Osborne Barrett Diary, Dec. 31, 1849, James Duncan Phillips Library, Peabody and Essex Museum, Salem, Mass., quoted in Hansen, *Crafting Community*, 216–17; Quick Diary, May 1, 1855.

26. Quick Diary, May 13, 1855.

27. Elizabeth Dana Diary, April 1, 8, 1869; Wetmore to Nettleton, Aug. 11, 1822.

28. Louisa Walter Bishop Hughes Diary, pp. 1, 5, 20–27 (1858–71), Louisa Walter Bishop Hughes Papers, Schlesinger Library, Radcliffe College. Although dozens of women recorded grave illnesses and deaths in diaries and letters, only one mentioned the attendance of a clergyman there. Louisa Hughes reported that her sister, without relatives in Paris, had a "Scotch clergyman" pray with her as she died. These women recorded deaths or illnesses without mentioning a minister in attendance: Helen Marcia Hart Diary, Nov. 28, 1862; Emma Ware to Abigail Sewall, July 19, 1870; Ann J. Stoddard Diary, June 29, 1866.

29. Hughes Diary, 31 (Aug. 1, 1866).

30. Hannah Cabot to Sarah Russell, Feb. 8, 1836 and Sept. [?], 1839; Hannah Cabot to Lydia Cabot, June 1838.

31. Hannah Cabot Diary, Sept. 4, 1839.

32. Ibid.

33. Ibid.

34. Emma V. Brown to Emily Howland, Nov. 29, 1860, Howland Papers, Cornell University Libraries, reprinted in *We Are Your Sisters: Black Women in the Nineteenth Century*, Dorothy Sterlin, ed. (New York: W. W. Norton, 1984), 200–201. Other women of color found black and white ministers with whom they agreed, but also with whom they disagreed, about Christian attitudes toward slavery and abolition. For example, Sarah Parker Remond found a friend and mentor in the Rev. Parker Pillsbury, a white abolitionist from New Hampshire. Sarah Parker Remond, Sept. 18, 1858, Abigail Kelley-Foster Papers, American Antiquarian Society, reprinted in *We Are Your Sisters*, 177. See also *The Journals of Charlotte Forten Grimke*, ed. Brenda Stevenson (New York: Oxford University Press, 1987).

35. Brown to Howland, Nov. 29, 1860.

36. Quick Diary, July 28, 1858.

37. Ibid.

38. Frances Kingman Holmes Diary, Kingman to Rodman, July 26, 1841 [emphasis in original].

39. Kingman to Rodman, July 26, 1841.

40. Quick Diary, copy of letter from Frances Quick to mother, Mar. 9, 1861. Eunice Callender recorded a similar reaction after a visit to a Catholic church. She was

"charmed" by the priest's sermon, thought him "drest most superbly in a delicate gown," and admired his singing voice. "Oh I never heard such a voice or such a preacher," she gushed. "I cannot *describe* him to you." [emphasis in original] She also recorded "ministerial news" in her letters, gossip about the romantic intentions of young preachers, lively arguments on the merits of their preaching, and whether the man and his manner were appropriate subjects for evaluation. Eunice Callender to Sarah Ripley Stearns, Sept. 25, 1811, and April 7, 1806; Dec. 19, 1810; April 2, 1813, Eunice Callender Letters, Schlesinger Library, Radcliffe College.

41. Elizabeth Dana Diary, Feb. 6, 1868. Historians have employed psychoanalytic theory to interpret dreams and trances as expressions of repressed impulses—both aggression and sexual. See John Demos, "Underlying Themes in the Witchcraft of Seventeenth-Century New England," in *Religion in American History: Interpretive Essays,* John M. Mulder and John F. Wilson, eds. (Englewood Cliffs, N.J.: Prentice-Hall, 1978), 86–104; Carol Karlsen, *The Devil in the Shape of a Woman: Witchcraft in Colonial New England* (New York: Norton, 1987). For nineteenth-century ideals of sexual purity, see Nancy Cott, "Passionlessness: An Interpretation of Victorian Sexual Ideology, 1790–1850," in *A Heritage of Her Own,* Nancy Cott and Elizabeth H. Pleck, eds. (New York: Simon and Schuster, 1979), 162–81; Barbara Welter, "The Cult of True Womanhood, 1820–1860," *American Quarterly* 18 (1966): 151–74; and on the difficulty of interpreting nineteenth-century language of sexuality, see Carroll Smith-Rosenberg, "The Female World of Love and Ritual," in *Disorderly Conduct: Visions of Gender in Victorian America* (New York: Knopf, 1985), 53–76.

42. Quick Diary, Sept. 18, 1864; Holmes Diary, Aug. 28, 1842 [emphasis in original].

43. Ahlstrom, *Religious History,* 421. Nettleton's fame in the historical record is eclipsed by the more successful Charles Finney. As a Calvinist in the Edwards-Hopkins vein, Nettleton opposed the "new measures" and emphasis on man's moral agency advocated by Finney.

44. Sarah Wetmore to Nettleton, Oct. 28, 1821 [emphasis in original]; Abby Scofield to Nettleton, n.d.; Almira Hancock, et al., Feb. 21, 1823; Minerva Murphy, et al., to Nettleton, Dec. 16, 1822. Early Methodist itinerants relied on the support and hospitality of numerous women in their travels, according to William T. Noll, "Women as Clergy and Laity in the Nineteenth-Century Methodist Protestant Church," *Methodist History* 15 (1977): 107–21.

45. Ann Waddell to Nettleton, Mar. 28, 1829 [emphasis in original].

46. Mary Anne Mew to Nettleton, Mar. 30, 1832 [emphasis in original].

47. Elizabeth Cook to Nettleton, Mar. 30, 1832; Sarah Lee to Nettleton, June 10, 1826 [emphasis in original]. For examples of women's conventional humility, see Catherine A. Brekus, *Strangers & Pilgrims: Female Preaching in America, 1740–1845* (Chapel Hill: University of North Carolina Press, 1998); Susan Juster, " 'In a Different Voice': Male and Female Narratives of Religious Conversion in Post-Revolutionary America," *American Quarterly* 41 (1989): 34–62; Joanna Bowen Gillespie, " 'The Clear Leadings of Providence': Pious Memoirs and the Problems of Self-Realization for Women in the Early Nineteenth Century," *Journal of the Early Republic* 5 (1985): 197–221; and Frances Holmes Diary, (n.d.) p. 36, copy of letter requesting dismission from her pastor. For a feminist interpretation of women's humility as a developmental stage, see Belenky, Clinchy, Goldberger, and Tarule, *Women's Ways of Knowing,* chapters 1–2. Also see C. Dallett Hemphill, "Age Relations and the Social Order in Early New England: The Evidence from Manners." *Journal of Social History* 28 (1994): 271–

94, for descriptions of the etiquette prescribed for men and women meeting in the "social sphere"—the intermediate space between separate spheres.

48. Samuel Miller, *Letters on Clerical Manners and Habits: Addressed to a Student in the Theological Seminary, at Princeton, N.J.* (Princeton, N.J.: Moore, Baker, 1835), 327.

49. Wetmore to Nettleton, Aug. 20, 182[1?]. The same shift in pronouns also occurred in a letter from Anne S. Rice to Nettleton, May 1, 1830: "If we did not rejoice so much in the cause that detains our dear Mr. Nettleton I know not how I should bear your long delay in coming *home*" [emphasis in original].

50. Wetmore to Nettleton, Oct. 8, 182[1?].

51. Ibid., Oct. 28, 1821, Feb. 10, 1823. She refers to an emotional "parting visit" in her letter of Oct. 15, 1821 as well.

52. Ibid., Oct. 8, 182[1?] [emphasis in original].

53. Ibid. [emphasis in original]

54. Nettleton to Wetmore, Mar. 24, 1822.

55. Ibid.

56. Sarah Wetmore Rand to Nettleton, Jan. 25, 1843. The only letter in the collection from Nettleton to Wetmore is apparently the one she returned to him twenty years later. While it does contain some accounts of his preaching, it also answers her charge of having too many female friends, an issue he may have felt was potentially dangerous, given recent charges of immorality against him.

57. Sherry Pierpont May, "Asahel Nettleton: Nineteenth-Century American Revivalist" (Unpub. Ph.D. dissertation, Drew University, 1969), 115–21, 417. The details of these charges are extremely vague. One surfaced as early as 1818 in Waterbury, Connecticut. Nettleton was accused of seducing a young woman on a sick visit. No formal charges were made, and Nettleton apparently ignored the rumors. Some twenty years later, the same charge resurfaced in company with a more recent one. These accusations merited a hearing by a committee of Connecticut Congregational ministers. Numerous letters by prominent clergymen attesting to Nettleton's good character apparently cleared him. See also John F. Thornbury, *God-Sent Revival: The Story of Asahel Nettleton and the Second Great Awakening,* (Grand Rapids, Mich.: Evangelical Press, 1977); Bennett Tyler, *Memoir of the Life and Character of Rev. Asahel Nettleton* (Hartford, Conn.: Robins & Smith, 1844).

EPILOGUE

1. Figure 14, "The Lecture Room of the Lechmere," *Only Full Report of the Trial of Rev. I. S. Kalloch* (Boston: Federhen, 1857).

2. Linda Kerber, Nancy F. Cott, Robert Gross, Lynn Hunt, Carroll Smith-Rosenberg, and Christine M. Stansell, "Beyond Roles, Beyond Spheres: Thinking about Gender in the Early Republic," *William and Mary Quarterly* 46 (1989): 568.

3. Karin E. Gedge, *Without Benefit of Clergy: Women in the Pastoral Relationship in Victorian America Culture* (Unpub. Ph.D. dissertation, Yale University, 1994), 259–92.

4. For examples of this scholarship, see Robert Redfield, *Peasant Society and Culture* (Chicago: University of Chicago Press, 1956); and Max Weber, *The Sociology of Religion,* trans. Ephraim Fischoff (Boston: Beacon, 1922).

5. Peter W. Williams, *Popular Religion in America: Symbolic Change and the Modernization Process in Historical Perspective* (Englewood Cliffs, N.J.: Prentice-Hall, 1980).

6. George Marsden, *Fundamentalism and American Culture: The Shaping of Twentieth-Century Evangelicalism, 1870–1925* (New York: Oxford University Press, 1980); Walter Rauschenbush, *Christianizing the Social Order* (New York, 1913). For arguments that the late nineteenth century witnessed a "remasculinization" of American Christianity, see Gail Bederman, "The Women Have Had Charge of the Church Work Long Enough: The Men and Religion Forward Movement of 1911–1912 and the Masculinization of Middle-Class Protestantism," *American Quarterly* 41 (1989): 432–65; Margaret Bendroth, *Gender and Fundamentalism, 1875–1980* (New Haven, Conn.: Yale University Press, 1993); Thekla Caldwell, "Women, Men, and Revival: The Third Awakening in Chicago," (Unpub. Ph.D. dissertation, University of Illinois at Chicago, 1991); Betty A. DeBerg, *Ungodly Women: Gender and the First Wave of American Fundamentalism* (Minneapolis: Fortress Press, 1990); and David G. Hackett, "Gender and Religion in American Culture, 1870–1930," *Religion and American Culture* 5 (1995): 127–57.

7. Lucy Mack Smith, *History of Joseph Smith by His Mother, Lucy Mack Smith* (Salt Lake City, Utah: Bookcraft, 1958), 35–36; Joan Iversen, "Feminist Implications of Mormon Polygyny," *Feminist Studies* 10 (1984): 515–22.

8. Joan R. Gundersen, "The Local Parish as Female Institution: The Experience of All Saints Episcopal Church in Frontier Minnesota," *Church History* 55 (1986): 307–22; and "The Non-Institutional Church: The Religious Role of Women in Eighteenth-Century Virginia," *Historical Magazine of the Protestant Episcopal Church* 51 (1982), 347–57. For studies of Catholic women's orders that emphasize the degree to which conflict marked the nuns' relationships with their male clerical superiors, see Daniel A. Cohen, "Miss Reed and the Superiors: The Contradictions of Convent Life in Antebellum America," *Journal of Social History* 30 (1996): 149–84; and Margaret Thompson, "Women, Feminism, and the New Religious History: Catholic Sisters as a Case Study," in *Belief and Behavior: Essays in the New Religious History*, Philip R. Vandermeer and Robert P. Swierenga, eds. (New Brunswick, N.J.: Rutgers University Press, 1991), 136–62.

9. On female preaching, see Catherine A. Brekus, *Strangers & Pilgrims: Female Preaching in America, 1740–1845* (Chapel Hill: University of North Carolina Press, 1998). On ordained women ministers, see Elizabeth Cazden, *Antoinette Brown Blackwell: A Biography* (Old Westbury, N.Y.: Feminist Press, 1983); Cynthia Grant Tucker, *Prophetic Sisterhood: Liberal Women Ministers of the Frontier, 1880–1930* (Boston: Beacon, 1990).

10. On Shakers, see Lawrence Foster, *Women, Family, and Utopia: Communal Experiments of the Shakers, the Oneida Community, and the Mormons* (Syracuse, N.Y.: Syracuse University Press, 1991); Nardi Reeder Campion, *Mother Ann Lee: Morning Star of the Shakers* (Hanover, N.H.: University Press of New England, 1990); Stephen J. Stein, *The Shaker Experience in America: A History of the United Society of Believers* (New Haven, Conn.: Yale University Press, 1992). On spiritualists, see Ann Braude, *Radical Spirits: Spiritualism and Women's Rights in Nineteenth-Century America* (Boston: Beacon, 1989). For accounts of counseling from spirits, see Abigail Sewall to Serena Brown, April 22, 1855; Jan. 29, 1861.

11. Robert Peel, *Mary Baker Eddy: The Years of Authority* (New York: Holt, Rinehart, Winston, 1977), 72–73. See also Stuart E. Knee, *Christian Science in the Age of Mary Baker Eddy* (Westport, Conn: Greenwood Press, 1994); Donald B. Meyer, *The Positive Thinkers: Popular Religious Psychology from Mary Baker Eddy to Norman Vincent Peale and Ronald Reagan* (Middletown, Conn.: Wesleyan University Press, 1988); Ju-

lius Silberger, *An Interpretive Biography of the Founder of Christian Science* (Boston: Little, Brown, 1980).

12. Peel, *Mary Baker Eddy*, 101.

13. Edith L. Blumhofer, "A Confused Legacy: Reflections of Evangelical Attitudes toward Ministering Women in the Past Century," *Fides et Historia* 22 (1990): 49–61; Mary Boys, "Women as Leaven: Theological Education in the United States and Canada," in Elisabeth Schüssler Fiorenza and Mary Collins, eds., *Women—Invisible in Theology and Church* (Edinburgh: T. & T. Clark, 1985); Virgina Lieson Brereton, "Learning in the Margins," in D. G. Hart and R. Albert Mohler, Jr. eds., *Theological Education in the Evangelical Tradition*, D. G. Hart, ed. (Grand Rapids, Mich.: Baker, 1997), 190–99; Jackson W. Carroll, Barbara Hargrove, and Adair T. Lummis, *Women of the Cloth: A New Opportunity for the Churches* (San Francisco: Harper & Row, 1981); Paula D. Nesbitt, *Feminization of the Clergy in America: Occupational and Organizational Perspectives* (New York: Oxford University Press, 1997).

14. For discussions of the role of religion in the "culture wars" of the late twentieth century see Don. S. Browning, K. Brynolf Lyon, and Bonnie J. Miller-McLemore, *From Culture Wars to Common Ground: Religion and the American Family Debate* (Louisville, Ky.: Westminster John Knox Press, 1997); John C. Green, James L. Guth, Corwin E. Smidt, and Lyman A Kellstedt, *Religion and the Culture Wars: Dispatches from the Front* (Lanham, Md.: Rowman & Littlefield, 1996); John Davison Hunter, *Culture Wars: the Struggle to Define America* (New York: Basic Books, 1991); William D. Romanowski, *Pop Culture Wars: Religion & the Roles of Entertainment in American Life* (Downers Grove, Ill: InterVarsity Press, 1996); Kathleen M. Sands, ed., *God Forbid: Religion and Sex in American Public Life* (New York: Oxford University Press, 2000).

15. For contemporary works on Catholic clerical sexual scandals see Jason Berry, *Lead us not into temptation: Catholic Priests and the Sexual Abuse of Children* (Urbana: University of Illinois Press, 2000); Philip Jenkins, *Pedophiles and Priests: Anatomy of a Contemporary Crisis* (New York: Oxford University Press, 1996; Thomas G. Plante, ed., *Bless Me Father for I Have Sinned: Perspectives on Sexual Abuse Committed by Roman Catholic Priests* (Westport, Conn.: Praeger, 1999); Investigative Staff of the *Boston Globe,Betrayal: the Crisis in the Catholic Church* (Boston: Little, Brown, 2002).

APPENDIX

1. For overviews of politics during the first half of the nineteenth century, see Gordon Wood, "The Democratization of Mind in the American Revolution," in *Leadership in the American Revolution*, Gordon Wood, ed. (Washington, D.C.: Library of Congress, 1974). Edward Pessen, *Jacksonian America: Society, Personality and Politics*, rev. ed. (Homewood, Ill.: Dorsey Press, 1978); Harry L. Watson, *Liberty and Power: The Politics of Jacksonian America* (New York: Hill and Wang, 1990); Amy Bridges, *A City in the Republic: Antebellum New York and the Origins of Machine Politics* (New York: Cambridge University Press, 1984); Ronald Formisano, "Deferential-Participant Politics: The Early Republic's Political Culture, 1789–1840," *American Political Science Review* 68 (1974): 473–87; and "Political Character, Antipartyism, and the Second Party System," *American Quarterly* 21 (1969): 683–709.

2. Stuart Blumin, *The Emergence of the Middle Class: Social Experience in the American City, 1760–1900* (New York: Cambridge University Press, 1989); Jeanne Boydston, "The Woman Who Wasn't There": Women's Market Labor and the Transition to Capitalism in the United States, *Journal of the Early Republic* 16 (1996): 183–

206; Christopher Clark, *The Roots of Rural Capitalism: Western Massachusetts, 1780–1860* (Ithaca, N.Y.: Cornell University Press, 1990); Thomas Dublin, *Women at Work: The Transformation of Work and Community in Lowell, Massachusetts, 1826–1860* (New York: Columbia University Press, 1979); Christine Stansell, *City of Women: Sex and Class in New York, 1789–1860* (Chicago: University of Illinois Press, 1987; Mary Ryan, *Cradle of the Middle Class: The Family in Oneida County, New York: 1790–1865* (New York: Cambridge University Press, 1981); Sean Wilentz, *Chants Democratic: New York City and the Rise of the American Working Class, 1788–1850* (New York: Oxford University Press, 1983). On the growth of print culture, see Nina Baym, *Novels, Readers, and Reviewers: Reponses to Fiction in Antebellum America* (Ithaca, N.Y.: Cornell University Press, 1984); Cathy N. Davidson, *Revolution and the Word: The Rise of the Novel in America* (New York: Oxford University Press, 1986); James D. Hart, *The Popular Book: A History of America's Literary Taste* (Westport, Conn.: Greenwood, 1950); Frank L. Mott, *Golden Multitudes: A History of Best-Sellers in the United States* (New York: Macmillan, 1947); Robert A. Rutland, *The Newsmongers: Journalism and the Life of the Nation, 1690–1972* (New York: Dial, 1973); Dan Schiller, *Objectivity and the News: The Public and the Rise of Commercial Journalism* (Philadelphia: University of Pennsylvania Press, 1981); Michael Schudson, *Discovering the News: A Social History of American Newspapers* (New York: Basic Books, 1978); John Tebbel, *Between Covers: The Rise and Transformation of Book Publishing in America* (New York: Oxford University Press, 1987); Jane Tompkins, *Sensational Designs: The Cultural Work of American Fiction, 1790–1860* (New York: Oxford University Press, 1985).

3. Karen Halttunen, *Confidence Men and Painted Ladies: A Study of Middle-Class Culture in America, 1830–1870* (New Haven, Conn.: Yale University Press, 1982); C. Dallett Hemphill, "Age Relations and the Social Order in Early New England: The Evidence from Manners," *Journal of Social History* 28 (1994): 271–94; and "Middle Class Rising in Revolutionary America: The Evidence from Manners," *Journal of Social History* 30 (1996): 317–44; John F. Kasson, *Rudeness and Civility: Manners in Nineteenth-Century Urban America* (New York: Hill and Wang, 1990).

4. Nathan O. Hatch, *The Democratization of American Christianity* (New Haven, Conn.: Yale University Press, 1989); Jon Butler, *Awash in a Sea of Faith: Christianizing the American People* (Cambridge, Mass.: Harvard University Press, 1990).

5. Whitney Cross, *The Burned-Over District* (Ithaca, N.Y.: Cornell University Press, 1965); Paul E. Johnson, *A Shopkeeper's Millennium: Society and Revivals in Rochester, New York, 1815–1837* (New York: Hill and Wang, 1978); Alice Felt Tyler, *Freedom's Ferment: Phases of American Social History from the Colonial Period to the Outbreak of the Civil War* (New York: Harper and Row, 1944).

6. David Allmendinger, *Paupers and Scholars: The Transformation of Student Life in Nineteenth-Century New England* (New York: St. Martin's Press, 1975); James Axtell, *The School upon a Hill: Education and Society in Colonial New England* (New York: Norton, 1974); Burton J. Bledstein, *The Culture of Professionalism: The Middle Class and the Development of Higher Education in America* (New York: Norton, 1976); Daniel Calhoun, *Professional Lives in America: Structure and Aspirations, 1750–1850* (Cambridge, Mass.: Harvard University Press, 1965); Gerald Cragg, "Training the Ministry: The Older Tradition," *Andover Newton Quarterly* 8 (1968): 223–34; James W. Fraser, *Schooling the Preachers: The Development of Protestant Theological Education in the United States, 1740–1875* (Lanham, Md.: University Press of America, 1988); Sidney Mead, "The Rise of the Evangelical Conception of the Ministry in America, 1607–1850," in *The Ministry in Historical Perspective*, H. Richard Niebuhr and Daniel D. Williams, eds. (New York: Harper & Bros., 1946), 207–49; Donald Scott, *From Office to Profes-*

sion: The New England Ministry, 1750–1850 (Philadelphia: University of Pennsylvania Press, 1978). Glenn T. Miller, *Piety and Intellect: The Aims and Purposes of Antebellum Theological Education* (Atlanta: Scholars Press, 1990), shows how changing and competing values complicated the process of educating young men in this period. For professionalization in other areas, see Michael Grossberg, "Institutionalizing Masculinity: The Law as a Masculine Profession," in *Meanings for Manhood: Constructions of Masculinity in Victorian America,* Mark C. Carnes and Clyde Griffen, eds. (Chicago: University of Chicago Press, 1990), 133–51.

7. Melvin Yazawa, *From Colonies to Commonwealth: Familial Ideology and the Beginnings of the American Republic* (Baltimore: Johns Hopkins University Press, 1985); Laurel Thatcher Ulrich, *Good Wives: Image and Reality in the Lives of Women in Northern New England, 1650–1750* (New York: Oxford University Press, 1980).

8. Nancy Cott, *The Bonds of Womanhood: "Woman's Sphere" in New England, 1780–1835* (New Haven, Conn.: Yale University Press, 1977); and "Passionlessness: An Interpretation of Victorian Sexual Ideology, 1790–1850," in *A Heritage of Her Own,* Nancy Cott and Elizabeth H. Pleck, eds. (New York: Simon and Schuster, 1979), 162–81; Dorothy O. Helly and Susan M. Reverby, eds., *Gendered Domains: Rethinking Public and Private in Women's History* (Ithaca, N.Y.: Cornell University Press, 1992); Linda K. Kerber, "Separate Spheres, Female Worlds, Woman's Place: The Rhetoric of Women's History," *Journal of American History* 75 (1988): 9–39; Linda K. Kerber and Nancy F. Cott, "Beyond Roles, Beyond Spheres: Thinking about Gender in the Early Republic," *William and Mary Quarterly* 46 (1989): 565–85; Gerda Lerner, "The Lady and the Mill Girl: Changes in the Status of Women in the Age of Jackson," *American Studies Journal* (Spring, 1969): 5–15; Barbara Welter, "The Cult of True Womanhood, 1820–1860," *American Quarterly* 18 (1966): 151–74; Carroll Smith-Rosenberg, *Disorderly Conduct: Visions of Gender in Victorian America* (New York: Knopf, 1985); Cynthia Eagle Russett, *Sexual Science: The Victorian Construction of Womanhood* (Cambridge, Mass.: Harvard University Press, 1989). For a discussion of the power of separate spheres among other paradigms in women's history, see Manuela Thurner, "Subject to Change: Theories and Paradigms of United States Feminist History," *Journal of Women's History* 9 (1997): 122–46.

9. Barbara Welter, "She Hath Done What She Could: Protestant Women's Missionary Careers in Nineteenth-Century America," *American Quarterly* 30 (1978): 625–38; Barbara Epstein, *The Politics of Domesticity: Women, Evangelicalism, and Temperance in Nineteenth-Century America* (Middletown, Conn.: Wesleyan University Press, 1981); Elizabeth Fox-Genovese, "Two Steps Forward, One Step Back: New Questions and Old Models in the Religious History of American Women," *Journal of the American Academy of Religion* 53 (1985): 465–71; Lori Ginzberg, *Women and the Work of Benevolence* (New Haven, Conn.: Yale University Press, 1990); Richard L. Greaves, ed., *Triumph over Silence: Women in Protestant History* (Westport, Conn.: Greenwood, 1985); Nancy Hewitt, "The Perimeters of Women's Power in American Religion," in *The Evangelical Tradition in America,* Leonard Sweet, ed. (Macon, Ga.: Mercer University Press, 1984), 233–56; and *Women's Activism and Social Change: Rochester, New York, 1822–1872* (Ithaca, N.Y.: Cornell University Press, 1984); Susan Hill Lindley, *"You Have Stept Out of Your Place": A History of Women and Religion in America* (Louisville, Ky.: Westminster John Knox Press, 1996); Keith Melder, "Ladies Bountiful: Organized Women's Benevolence in Early Nineteenth-Century America," *New York History* 48 (1967): 231–55; Redding S. Suggs, *Motherteacher: The Feminization of American Education* (Charlottesville: University of Virginia Press, 1978); Richard A. Meckel, "Educating a Ministry of Mothers: Evangelical Maternal Associations, 1815–1860," *Journal of*

the Early Republic 2 (1982): 403–23; Colleen McDannell, The Christian Home in Victorian America, 1840–1900 (Bloomington: University of Indiana Press, 1986); Ann Taves, "Women and Gender in American Religion(s)," Religious Studies Review 18 (1992): 263–70; and Household of Faith: Roman Catholic Devotions in Mid-Nineteenth-Century America (Notre Dame, Ind.: University of Notre Dame Press, 1986); Mary P. Ryan, Cradle of the Middle Class; Carolyn J. Lawes, Women and Reform in a New England Community, 1815–1860 (Lexington: University of Kentucky Press, 2000); Teresa Anne Murphy, Ten Hours' Labor: Religion, Reform, and Gender in Early New England (Ithaca, N.Y.: Cornell University Press, 1992); William T. Noll, "Women as Clergy and Laity in the Nineteenth-Century Methodist Protestant Church," Methodist History 15 (1977): 107–21. For women's attempts to frame support for women's rights from Christianity, see Nancy Isenberg, " 'Pillars in the Same Temple and Priests of the Same Worship': Woman's Rights and the Politics of Church and State in Antebellum America," Journal of American History 85 (1998): 98–128; Mary D. Pellauer, Toward a Tradition of Feminist Theology: The Religious Social Thought of Elizabeth Cady Stanton, Susan B. Anthony, and Anna Howard Shaw (Brooklyn, N.Y.: Carlson, 1991). For examples of women's rights advocates employing a natural rights rhetoric rather than Christianity, see Jacob Katz Cogan and Lori D. Ginzberg, "1846 Petition for Woman's Suffrage, New York State Constitutional Convention," Signs 22 (1997): 427–39; Rosemarie Zagarri, "The Rights of Man and Woman in Post-Revolutionary America, William and Mary Quarterly 55 (1998): 203–30.

10. David G. Hackett, "Gender and Religion in American Culture, 1870–1930," Religion and American Culture 5 (1995): 127–57; Johnson, A Shopkeeper's Millennium; Paul E. Johnson and Sean Wilentz, The Kingdom of Matthias: A Story of Sex and Salvation in 19th Century America (New York: Oxford University Press, 1994); Richard D. Shiels, "The Feminization of American Congregationalism, 1730–1835," American Quarterly 33 (1981): 46–62; and "The Scope of the Second Great Awakening: Andover, Massachusetts, as a Case Study," Journal of the Early Republic 5 (1985): 223–46; David S. Reynolds, "The Feminization Controversy: Sexual Stereotypes and the Paradoxes of Piety in Nineteenth-Century America," New England Quarterly 53 (1980): 96–106; Darrel M. Robertson, "The Feminization of American Religion: An Examination of Recent Interpretations of Women and Religion in Victorian America," Christian Scholar's Review 8 (1978): 238–46; Harry S. Stout and Catherine A. Brekus, "Declension, Gender, and the 'New Religious History,' " in Belief and Behavior: Essays in the New Religious History, Philip R. Vandermeer and Robert P. Swierenga, eds. (New Brunswick, N.J.: Rutgers University Press, 1991), 15–37.

11. Barbara Welter, "The Feminization of American Religion," in Dimity Convictions: The American Woman in the Nineteenth Century (Athens: Ohio University Press, 1976), 83–102; Amanda Porterfield, "Women's Attraction to Puritanism," Church History 60 (1991): 196–209, helps to undermine assumptions about women's aversion to Calvinist orthodoxy.

12. Ann Douglas, The Feminization of American Culture (New York: Knopf, 1977), 79.

13. Ibid., 10, 42, 111, 110, 99, 103. Douglas's work on sentimental literature has generated much revision among literary historians and feminists, who view the literature in a more positive light, especially for women. See Susan Coultrap-McQuin, Doing Literary Business: American Women Writers in the Nineteenth Century (Chapel Hill: University of North Carolina Press, 1990); and Davidson, Revolution and the Word.

14. Lois Boyd and R. Douglas Brackenridge, Presbyterian Women in America: Two Centuries of a Quest for Status (Westport, Conn.: Greenwood, 1983); Anne M. Boylan,

"Evangelical Womanhood in the Nineteenth Century: The Role of Women in Sunday Schools," *Feminist Studies* 4 (1978): 62–80; Virginia Lieson Brereton, *From Sin to Salvation: Stories of Women's Conversions, 1800 to the Present* (Bloomington: Indiana University Press, 1991); Nancy Cott, "Young Women in the Second Great Awakening," *American Quarterly* 27 (1975): 15–29; Barbara Epstein, *Women, Evangelicalism, and Temperance in Nineteenth-Century America* (Middletown, Conn.: Wesleyan University Press, 1981).

15. A. Cheree Carlson, "The Role of Character in Public Moral Argument: Henry Ward Beecher and the Brooklyn Scandal," *Quarterly Journal of Speech* 77 (1991): 38–52; Clifford E. Clark, *Henry Ward Beecher: Spokesman for a Middle-Class America* (Urbana: University of Illinois Press, 1978); Richard Wightman Fox, *Trials of Intimacy: Love and Loss in the Beecher-Tilton Scandal* (Chicago: University of Chicago Press, 1999); David R. Kasserman, *Fall River Outrage: Life, Murder, and Justice in Early Industrial New England* (Philadelphia: University of Pennsylvania Press, 1986); M. M. Marberry, *The Golden Voice: A Biography of Isaac Kalloch* (New York: Farrar, Straus, 1947); William McLoughlin, "Untangling the Tiverton Tragedy: The Social Meaning of the Terrible Haystack Murder of 1833," *Journal of American Culture* 7 (1984): 75–84; Altina L. Waller, *Reverend Beecher and Mrs. Tilton: Sex and Class in Victorian America* (Amherst: University of Massachusetts Press, 1982).

16. Anthony E. Rotundo, *American Manhood: Transformations in Masculinity from the Revolution to the Modern Era* (New York: Basic Books, 1993), 206; E. Brooks Holifield, *A History of Pastoral Care in America: From Salvation to Self-Realization* (Nashville, Tenn.: Abingdon, 1983), 122; Jane H. Pease and William H. Pease, *Ladies, Women, & Wenches: Choice and Constraint in Antebellum Charleston and Boston* (Chapel Hill: University of North Carolina Press, 1990), 117; Margaret S. Thompson, "Women, Feminism, and the New Religious History: Catholic Sisters as a Case Study," in *Belief and Behavior: Essays in the New Religious History*, Philip R. Vandermeer and Robert P. Swierenga, eds. (New Brunswick, N.J.: Rutgers University Press, 1991), 136–63. See also Gail Bederman, " 'The Women Have Had Charge of the Church Work Long Enough': The Men and Religion Forward Movement of 1911–1912 and the Masculinization of Middle-Class Protestantism," *American Quarterly* 41 (1989): 432–65; Terry D. Bilhartz, "Sex and the Second Great Awakening: The Feminization of American Religion Reconsidered," in *Beliefs and Behavior: Essays in the New Religious History*, Philip R. Vandermeer and Robert P. Swierenga, eds. (New Brunswick, N.J.: Rutgers University Press, 1991), 117–35; Ronald Hogeland, "Charles Hodge, the Association of Gentlemen, and Ornamental Womanhood: A Study of Male Conventional Wisdom, 1825–1855," *Journal of Presbyterian History* 53 (1975): 239–55; Anne Firor Scott, *Natural Allies: Women's Association in American History* (Urbana: University of Illinois Press, 1991); and Carolyn J. Lawes, *Women and Reform in a New England Community, 1815–1860* (Lexington: University of Kentucky Press, 2000) all expose some conflict between women and pastors. So does Laurel Ulrich in *Good Wives* for the colonial period. None explores any *pattern* of conflict in the pastoral relationship, however.

Selected Bibliography

PRIMARY SOURCES

Published Sources: Miscellaneous Crime Literature

Bennett, D. M. *The Champions of the Church: Their Crimes and Persecutions.* New York: D. M. Bennett, 1878.

Billings, M. E. *The Crimes of Preachers in the United States and Canada from May, 1876, to May 1882.* 2nd annual edition. New York: D. M. Bennett, 1882.

Chandler, Peleg W. *American Criminal Trials.* Boston: Charles C. Little and James Brown, 1841–44.

Official Documents of the Presbytery of Albany, Exhibiting the Trials of the Rev. John Chester and Mr. Mark Tucker; together with the Whole Case of the Rev. Hooper Cumming. Schenectady, N.Y.: Henry Stevens, 1818.

Published Sources: Trial Pamphlets, Arranged Alphabetically by Name of Clergyman

Arnold, Samuel

Philandros [pseud.]. *An Astonishing Affair! The Rev. Samuel Arnold, Cast and Tried for his Cruelty. . . .* Concord, N.H.: Luther Roby, 1830.

Avery, Ephraim

Avery, Ephraim K. *Vindication of the Result of the Trial of Rev. Ephraim K. Avery, To Which Is Prefixed His Statement of Facts relative to the Circumstances by Which He Became Involved in the Prosecution.* Boston: David Ela, 1834.

———— [pseud.]. *Explanation of the Circumstances Connected with the Death of Sarah Maria Cornell; By Ephraim K. Avery.* Providence, R.I.: William S. Clark, 1834.

The Correct, Full and Impartial Report of the Trial of Rev. Ephraim K. Avery before the Supreme Judicial Court of the State of Rhode-Island, at Newport, May 6, 1833, for the Murder of Sarah M. Cornell. Providence, R.I.: Marshall and Brown, 1833.

Drury, Luke. *A Report of the Examination of Rev. Ephraim K. Avery, Charged with the Murder of Sarah Maria Cornell.* N.p., 1833.

Hallett, Benjamin F. *A Full Report of the Trial of Ephraim K. Avery, Charged with the Murder of Sarah Maria Cornell, before the Supreme Court of Rhode Island, at a Special Term in Newport. Held in May 1833.* Boston: Daily Commercial Gazette, 1833.

————. *The Arguments of Counsel in the Close of the Trial of Rev. Ephraim K. Avery, Also a Literal Report of the Medical Testimony of Professor Walter Channing and Dr. William Turner.* Boston: Daily Commercial Gazette, 1833.

————. *Avery's Trial* (Supplementary Edition). Np: n.p., 1833.

Hildreth, Richard. *A Report of the Trial of the Rev. Ephraim K. Avery, before the Supreme Judicial Court of Rhode Island. On an Indictment for the Murder of Sarah Maria Cornell.* Boston: Russell, Odiorne, 1833.

Life and Trial of the Rev. Ephraim K. Avery for the Murder of the Young and Beautiful Miss Sarah Maria Cornell. Philadelphia: Barclay, 1877.

Melville, David. *A Fac-simile of the Letters Produced at the Trial of the Rev. Ephraim K. Avery, on an Indictment for the Murder of Sarah Maria Cornell. Taken with Great Care, by permission of the Hon. Supreme Judicial Court of Rhode Island from the Original Letters in the Office of the Clerk of Said Court.* Boston: Pendleton's Lithography, 1833.

Report of a Committee of the New England Annual Conference of the Methodist Episcopal Church, on the Case of the Rev. Ephraim K. Avery, Member of Said Conference. Boston: David Ela, 1833.

Staples, William Read. *A Correct Report of the Examination of Rev. Ephraim K. Avery, Minister of the Methodist Church in Bristol, R.I. Who Was Charged with the Murder of Sarah M. Cornell.* Providence, R.I.: Marshall & Brown, 1833.

The Trial at Large of the Rev. Ephraim K. Avery, for the Wilful Murder of Sarah Maria Cornell, at Tiverton, in the County of Newport, R.I. New York: n.p., 1833.

Williams, Catherine Read Arnold. *Fall River: An Authentic Narrative.* 2nd ed. Boston: Marsh & Harrison, 1834.

Barclay, David

Kerr, Jacob. *The Several Trials of the Reverend David Barclay, before the Presbytery of New-Brunswick, with Their Judgment at Oxford. . . .* Elizabethtown, N.J.: R. & P. Canfield, 1814.

Beecher, Henry Ward

Official Report of the Trial of Henry Ward Beecher. 2 vols. New York: George W. Smith, 1875.

Oliver, Leon. *The Great Sensation: A Full, Complete and Reliable History of the Beecher-Tilton-Woodhull Scandal, with Biographical Sketches of the Principal Characters.* Chicago: Beverly, 1873.

Theodore Tilton Versus Henry Ward Beecher: Action for Crim. Con. Tried in the City Court of Brooklyn, Chief Justice Joseph Neilson, Presiding: Verbatim Report of the Trial. New York: McDivitt, Campbell, 1875.

Williamson, Francis P. *Beecher and His Accusers: A Complete History of the Great Controversy, including the Life of Henry Ward Beecher, together with Pen and Ink Sketches of the Persons Prominently Involved.* Philadelphia: Flint, 1874.

Budge, Henry

The Entire and Unabridged Evidence, Given on the Second Inquest, concerning the Death of Mrs. Priscilla Budge . . . Also: The Evidence Given at the Examination of Rev. Henry Budge, Charged with the Murder of his Wife. . . . Lowville, N.Y.: Lewis County Banner Office, 1860.
Examination as to the Death of Priscilla Budge, before the Coroner and a Jury. New York: n.p., 1860.
Swinburne, John. *A Review of the Case, The People agt. Rev. Henry Budge, Indicted for the Murder of His Wife Priscilla Budge. . . .* Albany, N.Y.: C. Van Benthuysen, 1862.

Cumming, Alexander

The Trial in Full, of Edward Arrowsmith, for Slandering the Character of the Rev. Alexander Cumming, Minister of the Evangelical Independent Church, Rose Street, New York. . . . New York: S. Wakler, 1819[?].

Doane, George Washington

Doane, George Washington. *Protest and Appeal.* Philadelphia: 1852.
Lee, Alfred. *A Few Words in Vindication of the Action of the Court of Bishops, Convened at Camden, New Jersey, Sept. 1853.* Philadelphia: H. Hooker, 1854.
Proceedings of the Court of Bishops, Assembled for the Trial of the Right Rev. George Washington Doane, D.D., L.L.D., Bishop of New Jersey. New York: Stanford & Swords, 1852.

Fairchild, Joy Hamlet

Correspondence between Rev. Nehemiah Adams and Rev. J. H. Fairchild, with Notes and Comments by a Committee of the Payson Church. Boston: 1846.
English, William B. *The Celebrated Trial of Rev. Joy Hamlet Fairchild, for the Alleged Seduction of Miss Rhoda Davidson.* Boston: J. N. Bradley, 1844.
Fairchild, Joy Hamlet. *Remarkable Incidents in the Life of Rev. J. H. Fairchild, Pastor of Payson Church, South Boston. Compiled and Published by Himself with a Portrait.* Boston: Printed for the Author, 1855.
————. *Farewell Address to the Payson Church, South Boston, Delivered Nov. 22, 1857, by Rev. Joy H. Fairchild.* Boston: n.p., 1858.
————. *Iniquity Unfolded! An Account of the Treatment of Mr. Fairchild by the Deacons in South Boston, and Others, Written by Himself.* 2nd edition. Exeter, N.H.: n.p., 1844.
Mr. Fairchild's Trial. Boston: n.p., 1845[?].
The Truth Revealed. Statement & Review of the Whole Case of the Reverend Joy H. Fairchild. . . . Boston: Wright's Steam Press, 1845.
Weeks, J.E.P. *The Trial of Rev. Joy Hamlet Fairchild, on a Charge of Adultery with Miss Rhoda Davidson.* Boston: Boston Daily Times, 1845.

Glendenning, John S.

Poor Mary Pomeroy! The Jersey City Music Teacher; Also a Full and Authentic Account of the Trial of Rev. John S. Glendenning before the Authorities of Prospect Avenue Church: Startling Details. . . . Philadelphia: Old Franklin Publishing House, 1874.

Grosscup, Issachar

Whitney, George L. *The Trial of Rev. Issachar Grosscup, for the Seduction of Roxana L. Wheeler.* . . . Canandaigua, N.Y.: n.p., 1848.

Guild, William

Proceedings in the Case of Elder William B. Guild, of the Third Presbyterian Church of Newark, N.J. New York: Edward O. Jenkins, 1861.

Harden, Jacob S.

Life, Confession, and Letters of Courtship of Rev. Jacob S. Harden, of the M.E. Church, Mount Lebanon, Hunterdon Co., N.J., Executed for the Murder of His Wife, on the 6th of July, 1860. Hackettstown, N.J.: E. Winton, 1860.

Hayden, Herbert Hiram

Hayden, Herbert Hiram. *The Rev. Herbert H. Hayden: An Autobiography.* Hartford, Conn.: Press of the Plimpton Mfg. Co., 1880.
Poor Mary Stannard! A Full and Thrilling Story of the Circumstances Connected with Her Murder. . . . New Haven, Conn.: Stafford Printing, 1879.

Hogan, William

Dowling, Joseph A. [stenographer]. *The Trial of the Rev. William Hogan, Pastor of St. Mary's Church, for an Assault and Battery on Mary Connell.* Philadelphia: R. Desilver, 1822.

Huston, Lorenzo Dow

The Trial of the Rev. L. D. Huston, for the Alleged Seduction of Mary Driscoll, Virginia Hopkins, &c. . . . Baltimore: n.p., 1872.

Jardine, Henry

Harrison, John A., Esq. *Courts of Appeal in Causes Ecclesiastical: Their Necessity Illustrated by the History of the Case of Rev. Henry D. Jardine (deceased).* . . . St. Louis, Mo.: Nixon-Jones, 1886.

Jarvis, Samuel

The Great Divorce Case! A Full and Impartial History of the Trial of the Petition of Mrs. Sarah M. H. Jarvis, for a Divorce from Her Husband, the Rev. Samuel F. Jarvis. . . . New York: n.p., 1839.
Report of the Proceedings, on the Petition of Mrs. Sarah M. Jarvis, for a Divorce from Her Husband, Rev. Samuel F. Jarvis. . . . 2nd ed. Hartford, Conn.: Review Press, 1839.

Kalloch, Isaac

Ayer, I.W. *Full Report of R.H. Dana's Argument for Defence, in the Case of Rev. I.S. Kalloch, Pastor of the Tremont Temple Baptist Church*. N.p., 1857.

Neilson, William McCann. *A Faint Idea of a Terrible Life! The Rev. I. S. Kalloch (Mayor of San Francisco) from His Expulsion from College until Now*. 4th ed. San Francisco: J. K. Cooper, 1880.

Only Full Report of the Trial of Rev. I. S. Kalloch, on Charge of Adultery, Complete History of the Affair; Doings of the Church; Kalloch's Pulpit Defence; Arrest, Arraignment, Trial, and Result. With Accurate Portraits of Kalloch, and the Beautiful Lady in Black, and the Lecture Room of the Lechmere. Boston: Federhen, 1857.

Shimmons, John H. *The Shame and Scourge of San Francisco, or, an Expose of the Rev. Isaac S. Kalloch across the Continent, from Maine to California; The Records of an Evil Life, from Documents of Undeniable Authenticity*. Chicago: n.p., 1880[?].

Maffitt, John

Correct Statement and Review of the Trial of Joseph T. Buckingham, for an Alledged Libel on the Rev. John H. Maffitt, before the Hon. Josiah Quincy, Judge of the Municipal Court, Dec. 16, 1822. Boston: William S. Spear, 1822.

Elsemore, Moses. *An Impartial Account of the Life of the Rev. John H. Maffitt, with a Narrative of the Difficulties Attending His First Marriage and a Circumstantial and Correct History of All the Facts of His Late Marriage to Miss Smith, of Brooklyn, and the Causes of Her Death. . . .* New York: John F. Feeks, 1848.

Hallett, Benjamin F. *An Exposure of the Misrepresentations Contained in a Professed Report of the Trial of Mr. John N. Maffitt, before a Council of Ministers of the Methodist Episcopal Church, Convened in Boston, December 26, 1822*.Boston, n.p., 1823.

Report of the Trial of Mr. John Maffitt, before a Council of Ministers, of the Methodist Episcopal Church, Convened in Boston, December 26, 1823. Boston: True & Green, 1823.

Trial: Commonwealth vs. J. T. Buckingham, on an Indictment for a Libel, before the Municipal Court, City of Boston, December Term, 1822. Boston: New-England Galaxy, 1822.

Matthias, Robert

Drake, W. E. *The False Prophet! The Very Interesting and Remarkable Trial of Matthias . . . for the Murder of Mr. Elijah Pierson. . . .* New York: W. Mitchell, 1835.

————. *The Prophet! A Full and Accurate Report of the Judicial Proceedings in the Extraordinary and Highly Interesting Case of Matthews, alias Matthias, Charged with Having Swindled Mr. B. H. Folger, of the City of New-York, Out of a Considerable Property*. New York: n.p., 1834.

Memoirs of Matthias the Prophet, with a Full Exposure of His Atrocious Impositions, and of the Degrading Delusions of His Followers. New York: New York Sun, 1835.

Stone, William Leete. *Matthias and His Impostures; or, the Progress of Fanaticism, Illustrated in the Extraordinary Case of Robert Matthews and Some of His Forerunners and Disciples*. New York: n.p., 1835.

Vale, G. *Fanaticism; Its Source and Influence, Illustrated by the Simple Narrative of Isabella, in the Case of Matthias . . . A Reply to W. L. Stone*. New York: n.p., 1835.

McDowall, John

History of the Preliminary Proceedings of the Third Presbytery, in the Case of Rev. J. R. McDowall, including the Charges, Specifications, Sentence, &c. New York: New York Observer, 1836.

Merrill, William

Decisions of the Council in the Trial of Rev. W. P. Merrill, Pastor of the Free Will Baptist Church, in Portland. . . . Portland, Maine: Brown, Thurston, 1861.

Onderdonk, Benjamin Treadwell

An Appeal from the Sentence of the Bishop of New York: In Behalf of His Diocese. . . . New York: James A. Sparks, 1845.

An Examination of the Proceedings on the Presentment, Trial, and Sentence of the Right Rev. Benjamin T. Onderdonk, D.D., Bishop of the Protestant Episcopal Church in the Diocese of New-York. n.p., n.d. [produced by the editor of The Churchman, the diocesan publication].

Jay, John. Facts Connected with the Presentment of Bishop Onderdonk: A Reply to Parts of the Bishop's Statement. New York: Stanford & Swords, 1845.

Onderdonk, Benjamin T. Bishop Onderdonk's Statement. New York: Henry Onderdonk, 1845.

The Proceedings of the Court Convened under the Third Canon of 1844, in the City of New York . . . for the Trial of the Right Rev. Benjamin T. Onderdonk. . . . New York: D. Appleton, 1845.

Review of the Trial of Bishop Onderdonk. Buffalo, N.Y.: Buffalo Commercial Advertiser, 1845.

Richmond, James C. The Conspiracy against the Late Bishop of New York Unravelled. New York: n.p., 1845.

Trapier, Paul. Narrative of Facts in the Presentment of the Rt. Rev. Benj. T. Onderdonk, Bishop of New-York. New York: Stanford & Swords, 1845.

Parkinson, William

Sampson, William. Trial of Mr. William Parkinson, Pastor of the First Baptist Church in the City of New-York on an Indictment of Assault & Battery upon Mrs. Eliza Wintringham. New York: Bargin & Thompson, 1811.

Potter, Ray

Potter, Ray. Admonitions from "The Depths of the Earth": or, the Fall of Ray Potter in Twenty-Four Letters. Pawtucket, R.I.: n.p., 1838.

———. Confession of the Rev. Ray Potter. Pawtucket, R.I. [?]: n.p., 1837. Broadside Collection, American Antiquarian Society.

Richards, James

The Documents in the Case of James Richards. New Haven, Conn.: Tuttle, Morehouse & Taylor, 1860.

Rogers, Ammi

Rogers, Ammi. Memoirs of the Rev. Ammi Rogers A.M. a Clergyman of the Episcopal Church, Educated at Yale College in Connecticut, Ordained in Trinity Church in the

City of New-York, Persecuted in the State of Connecticut, on account of Religion and Politics, for Almost Twenty Years; and Finally Falsely Accused and Imprisoned in Norwich Jail, for Two Years, on the Charge of Crimes Said to Have Been Committed in the Town of Griswold, in the County of New-London, When He Was Not within About One Hundred Miles of the Place, and Which He Was Absolutely as Innocent as the Judge Who Pronounced the Sentence, or as Any Other Person in the World. 6th ed. Troy, NY: Printed for the Author, 1834.

Seys, John

Extraordinary Trial of the Rev. John Seys, Pastor of the Bedford Street Methodist Episcopal Church, New-York City, for an Alleged Assault and Battery on Mrs. Elizabeth Cram; with His Portrait and Biographical Sketch. 2nd ed. New York: n.p., 1847.

Sherman, Eleazar

Trial of Elder Eleazar Sherman, before an Ecclesiastical Council, Held at the Meetinghouse of the Christian Society in Providence, July 20 and 21, 1835. Providence, R.I.: H. H. Brown, 1835.

Thacher, Moses

Review of the Case of Moses Thacher versus Preston Pond, in Charging the Plaintiff with Crime of Adultery; including Letters of Mrs. Jerusha M. Pond, the Main Witness in the Defence. Boston: Printed for the Plaintiff, 1838.

Van Zandt, George Washington

Report of the Trial of the Rev. Mr. Van Zandt, Rector of Grace Church, Rochester, N.Y. for the Seduction of Miss Sophia Murdock, a Young and Beautiful Member of His Church. Philadelphia: n.p., 1842.

Van Zandt, Washington. *An Appeal by the Reverend Washington Van Zandt, Late Rector of Grace Church, Rochester*. Auburn, N.Y.: Henry Oliphant, 1843.

Weinzoepflen, Romain

Drapier, A. E. *Trial of Romain Weinzoepflen, Catholic Priest of Evansville, Vanderburgh County, Indiana, on a Charge of Rape Preferred by Mrs. Anna Maria Schmoll.* . . . Louisville, Ky.: W. N. Haldeman & B. J. Webb, 1844.

University of Notre Dame Archives, "Clippings on Fr. Roman Weinsoepfel, O.S.B." PCLR, Box 32, folder 21.

Whittlesey, John

Whittlesey, John. *An Authentic Account of the Persecutions and Trials of the Rev. John Whittlesey, of Salem, Connecticut, Late Ordained Elder of the Methodist Episcopal Church.* . . . New York: n.p., 1845.

Published Sources: Sermons, Tracts and Manuals on Pastoral Ministry

Alexander, Archibald. *Practical Sermons; to Be Read in Families and Social Meetings*. Philadelphia: Presbyterian Board of Publication, 1850.

"Assorted Pamphlets and Catalogues on Theological Seminaries." RG33, Yale Divinity School Archives, New Haven, Conn.

Bacon, Leonard. "Inaugural Sermon, March 13, 1825, from the Text II Cor., ii 16— 'Who Is Sufficient for These Things?' " In *Leonard Bacon: Pastor of the First Church in New Haven*. Edited by H.C. Kingley, Leonard J. Sanford, and Thos. R. Trowbridge Jr. New Haven: n.p., 1882.

Baxter, Richard. *The Reformed Pastor; a Discourse on the Pastoral Office*. . . . 1655. Reprint, abridged and reduced to a new method by Samuel Palmer. London: J. Buckland, 1766.

Bedell, Gregory Thurston. *The Pastor. Pastoral Theology. Experientia Docens, Docet, Docuit*. Philadelphia: J. B. Lippincott, 1880.

Beecher, Lyman. *Correspondence. Selections. Lectures of the Rev. Dr. Beecher and Rev. Mr. Nettleton on the "New Measures" in Conducting Revivals of Religion*. . . . New York: G. & C. Carvill, 1828.

Bushnell, Horace. *Discourses on Christian Nurture*. Boston: Massachusetts Sabbath School Society, 1847.

———. *Sermons on Living Subjects*. New York: Scribner, Armstrong, 1873.

Clarke, Adam. *The Preacher's Manual: Including Clavis Biblica, and A Letter to a Methodist Preacher*. New York: T. Mason and G. Lane, 1837.

The Clerical Life: A Series of Letters to Ministers. New York: Dodd, Mead, 1898.

Cogswell, William. *Letters to Young Men Preparing for the Christian Ministry*. New York: Saxton & Miles, 1842.

Cuyler, Theodore L. *How to Be a Pastor*. New York: Baker & Taylor, 1890.

Douglass, William. *Annals of the First African Church of the United States of America, Now Styled the African Episcopal Church of St. Thomas, Philadelphia*. Philadelphia: King and Baird Printers, 1862.

Finney, Charles Grandison. *Lectures on Revivals of Religion. Addressed to Ministers of the Gospel*. Edited by William McLoughlin. Cambridge, Mass.: Harvard University Press, 1960.

Green, Ashbel. *The Christian Duty of Women*. . . . Princeton, N.J.: 1825.

Griggs, Leverett. *Letters to a Theological Student*. Boston: American Tract Society, 1863.

Hoppin, James M. *The Office and Work of the Christian Ministry*. New York: Sheldon, 1870.

Humphrey, Heman. *The Duties of Ministers and People. A Sermon, Preached before the General Association of Connecticut, at New Haven, June 18, 1816*. New Haven, Conn.: Nathan Whiting, 1816.

———. *Thirty-Four Letters to a Son in the Ministry*. Amherst, Mass.: J. S. & C. Adams, 1842.

Ide, George G. *The Ministry Demanded in the Present Crisis*. Philadelphia: American Baptist Publication Society, 1845.

Mather, Cotton. *Manuductio ad Ministerium: Directions for a Candidate of the Ministry*. 1726. Reprint New York: Columbia University Press, 1938.

Meade, William. *Lectures on the Pastoral Office: Delivered to the Students of the Theological Seminary at Alexandria, Virginia*. New York: Stanford and Swords, 1849.

Methodist Episcopal Church. *The Methodist Discipline of 1798, including the Annotations of Thomas Coke and Francis Asbury*. Facsimile edition. Rutland, Vt.: Academy Books, 1979.

Miller, Samuel. *Letters on Clerical Manners and Habits: Addressed to a Student in the Theological Seminary, at Princeton, N.J.* Princeton, N.J.: Moore, Baker, 1835.

———. *The Life of Samuel Miller*. 2 vols. Philadelphia: n.p., 1869.

Park, Edwards, A., Ed. *The Preacher and Pastor, by Fenelon, Herbert, Baxter, Campbell.* Andover, Mass.: Allen, Morrill & Wardwell, 1845.

Parker, Joseph. *Ad Clerum: Advices to a Young Preacher.* Boston: Roberts Brothers, 1871.

Pond, Enoch. *The Young Pastor's Guide; or, Lectures on Pastoral Duties.* Bangor, Maine: 1844.

Shedd, William G. T. *Homiletics, and Pastoral Theology.* New York: Charles Scribner, 1867.

Spencer, Ichabod. *A Pastor's Sketches; or, Conversations with Anxious Inquirers, Respecting the Way of Salvation.* Second series. New York: M. W. Dodd, 1855.

Sprague, William B. *Causes of an Unsuccessful Ministry: Two Sermons, Addressed to the Second Presbyterian Congregation in the City of Albany, August 30, 1829; the Sabbath Immediately Succeeding the Author's Induction as Their Pastor.* Albany, N.Y.: Packard & Van Benthuysen, 1829.

————. *A Sermon Preached at West Springfield, on the Resignation of the Author's Pastoral Charge, July 26, 1829.* Boston: T. R. Marvin, 1829.

Spring, Gardiner. *The Power of the Pulpit; or, Thoughts Addressed to Christian Ministers and Those Who Hear Them.* New York: Baker & Scribner, 1848.

Vinet, A[lexandre]. *Pastoral Theology; or, the Theory of the Evangelical Ministry.* Translated and edited by Thomas H. Skinner. New York: Ivison, Blaeman, Taylor, 1871.

Weaver, Elisha. *Doctrines and Discipline of the African Methodist Episcopal Church.* Tenth rev. ed. Philadelphia: James H. Bryson, 1860.

Wynne, Frederick R. *The Joy of the Ministry. An Endeavour to Increase the Efficiency and Deepen the Happiness of Pastoral Work.* New York: James Pott, 1885.

Published Sources: Memoirs, Autobiographies, Biographies

Alexander, James W. *Life of Archibald Alexander, D.D.: First Professor in the Theological Seminary at Princeton, New Jersey.* New York: Scribner, 1854.

Cartwright, Peter. *Autobiography of Peter Cartwright: The Backwoods Preacher.* Edited by William P. Strickland. New York: C&P, 1854.

Dow, Lorenzo. *Life and Travels of Lorenzo Dow: In Which Are Contained Some Singular Providences of God, Written by Himself.* Hartford, Conn.: Lincoln & Gleason, 1804.

Finney, Charles Grandison. *The Memoirs of Charles G. Finney: The Complete Restored Text.* Edited by Garth M. Rosell and Richard A. G. Dupuis. Grand Rapids, Mich.: Academie Books, 1989.

Grimke, Charlotte Forten. *Journals of Charlotte Forten Grimke.* Edited by Brenda Stevenson. New York: Oxford University Press, 1987.

Hodge, Archibald Alexander. *The Life of Charles Hodge.* New York: n.p., 1880.

Hopkins, Samuel. *Sketches of the Life of the Late Rev. Samuel Hopkins, D.D. Pastor of the First Congregational Church in Newport, Written by Himself.* Hartford, Conn.: Hudson & Goodwin, 1805.

————. *Life and Character of Miss Susanna Anthony, Who Died in Newport, Rhode Island, June 23, 1790, in the Sixty-fifth Year of Her Age.* 2nd ed. Portland, Maine: Lyman, Hall, 1810.

————. *Memoirs of the Life of Mrs. Sarah Osborn; Who Died at Newport, Rhode Island, on the Second Day of August, 1796, in the Eighty Third Year of Her Age,* 2nd ed. Catskill, N.Y.: N. Elliot, 1814.

Kingsley, H. C., Sanford J., and Trowbridge, Thomas R., Jr., Eds. *Leonard Bacon: Pastor of the First Church in New Haven.* New Haven, Conn.: n.p., 1882.

Osborn, Sarah, and Susanna Anthony. *Familiar Letters, Written by Mrs. Sarah Osborn, and Miss Susanna Anthony, Late of Newport, Rhode Island.* Edited by Samuel Hopkins. Newport, R.I.: Newport Mercury, 1807.

Smith, Lucy Mack. *History of Joseph Smith, by His Mother, Lucy Mack Smith.* Salt Lake City, Utah: Bookcraft, 1958.

Tyler, Bennett. *Memoir of the Life and Character of Rev. Asahel Nettleton.* Hartford, Conn.: Robins & Smith, 1844.

Wayland, Francis. *Memoir of the Life and Labors of the Rev. Adoniram Judson, D.D.* Boston: Phillips, Sampson, 1853.

Published Sources: Novels, Tracts, Travelers' Accounts

Aesop [pseud.]. *The Hypocrite; or, Sketches of American Society from a Residence of Forty Years.* New York: Thomas Fox, 1844.

[Anon.] *Confessions of a French Catholic Priest.* Edited by Samuel F. B. Morse. New York: D. Van Nostrand, 1837.

———. *The Confessions of a Magdalene; or, Some Passages in the Life of Experience Borgia.* New York: n.p., 1831.

———. *Father Oswald: A Genuine Catholic Story.* New York: Casserly, 1843.

Beecher, Henry Ward. *Norwood; or, Village Life in New England.* New York: Charles Scribner, 1868.

Bourne, George. *Lorette. The History of Louise, Daughter of a Canadian Nun; Exhibiting the Interior of Female Convents.* New York: William A. Mercein, 1833.

Bremer, Frederika. *The Homes of the New World; Impressions of America.* Translated by Mary Howitt. 2 vols. 1853. Reprint New York: Johnson, 1968.

Creton, Paul [John Townshend Trowbridge]. *Father Brighthopes; or, an Old Clergyman's Vacation.* Boston: Phillips, Sampson, 1853.

Deland, Margaret. *John Ward, Preacher.* Boston: Houghton Mifflin, 1888.

DeLasteyrie, C. P. *The History of Auricular Confession. Religiously, Morally, and Politically Considered among Ancient and Modern Nations.* 2 vols. London: Richard Bentley, 1848.

DeToqueville, Alexis. *Democracy in America.* 2 vols. 1836. Reprint, edited by Phillips Bradley. New York: Random House, 1945.

Dickens, Charles. *American Notes.* 1848. Reprint, with an introduction by Christopher Lasch. Gloucester, Mass.: Peter Smith, 1968.

Fearon, Henry Bradshaw. *Sketches of America. A Narrative of a Journey of Five Thousand Miles through the Eastern and Western States.* 1818. Reprint, New York: Benjamin Blom, 1969.

Finch, Marianne. *An Englishwoman's Experience in America.* 1853. Reprint, New York: Negro Universities Press, 1969.

Foster, George G. *New York by Gas-Light and Other Urban Sketches.* 1850. Reprint, edited by Stuart M. Blumin. Berkeley: University of California Press, 1990.

Gooch, Richard. *America and the Americans—in 1833–4. By an Emigrant.* Edited by Richard Toby Widdecombe. New York: Fordham University Press, 1994.

Grund, Francis J. *The Americans in their Moral, Social, and Political Relations.* 2 vols. 1837. Reprint (2 vols. in 1), New York: Johnson, 1968.

———. *Aristocracy in America from the Sketch-Book of a German Nobleman.* London: Richard Bentley, 1839.

Hawthorne, Nathaniel. *The Scarlet Letter: A Romance.* Boston: Ticknor, Reed, and Fields, 1850.

Lippard, George. *Memoirs of a Preacher: A Revelation of the Church and Home*. Philadelphia: Joseph Severns, 1849.

———. *The Quaker City; or, the Monks of Monk Hall. A Romance of Philadelphia Life, Mystery, and Crime*. Philadelphia: G. B. Zieber, 1844.

Martineau, Harriet. *Society in America*. 3 vols. 1837. Reprint, New York: AMS Press, 1966.

Maury, Sarah Mytton. *An Englishwoman in America*. London: Thomas Richardson, 1848.

Monk, Maria. *Awful Disclosures of Maria Monk, as Exhibited in a Narrative of Her Sufferings during a Residence of Five Years as a Novice, and Two Years as a Black Nun in the Hotel Dieu Nunnery at Montreal*. New York: Howe & Bates, 1836.

Reade, Charles. *Griffith Gaunt or, Jealousy*. Boston: Colonial Press, n.d.

Reed, Andrew, and Matheson, James. *A Narrative of the Visit to the American Churches of the Deputation from the Congregational Union of England and Wales*. London: Jackson & Walford, 1835.

Savage, Sarah. *Filial Affection; or, the Clergyman's Granddaughter*. Boston: Cummings & Hilliard, 1820.

Shelton, Frederick William. *The Rector of St. Bardolph's; or, Superannuated*. New York: Charles Scribner, 1853.

———. *Peeps from a Belfry; or, the Parish Sketch Book*. New York: Charles Scribner, 1855.

Smith, Elizabeth Oakes. *Bertha and Lily; or, the Parsonage of Beech Glen. A Romance*. New York: J. C. Derby, 1854.

Sterlin, Dorothy, Ed. *We Are Your Sisters: Black Women in the Nineteenth Century*. New York: W. W. Norton, 1984.

Stowe, Harriet Beecher. *The Minister's Wooing*. New York: Derby & Jackson, 1859.

Trollope, Frances. *Domestic Manners of the Americans*. 1832. Reprint, with an introduction by Donald Smalley, New York: Alfred A. Knopf, 1949.

Trusta, H. [Elizabeth Stuart Phelps]. *The Last Leaf from Sunny Side with Memorial of the Author by Austin Phelps*. Boston: Phillips, Sampson, 1853.

———. *A Peep at "Number Five;" or, a Chapter in the Life of a City Pastor*. Boston Phillips, Sampson, 1852.

———. *The Sunny Side; or, the Country Minister's Wife*. Boston: John P. Jewett, 1851.

Ware, Henry, Jr. *The Recollections of Jotham Anderson. Minister of the Gospel*. Boston: The Christian Register Office, 1824.

Warner, Susan. *The Wide, Wide World*. 1850. Reprint, New York: Feminist Press, 1987.

Wright, Frances [D'Arusmont]. *Views of Society and Manners in America; in a Series of Letters from That Country to a Friend in England, during the Years 1818, 1819, and 1820. By an Englishwoman*. London: Longman, Hurst, Rees, Orme, & Brown, 1821.

Unpublished Sources: Clergymen's Journals, Correspondence, Notes

American Antiquarian Society. Ephraim Abbot Papers. Diaries, 1812, 1814. Autobiography. Correspondence.

———. Moore Family Papers. George Moore Diary, 1836–1840, 1840–1844.

———. Elias Nason Papers, 1830–1911.

American Baptist Historical Society. Robert Acker Clapp Collection. Student notebooks, ca. 1856.

_____. Edward F. Gurney Papers. Diary. 1851–53.

_____. Minutes of the Baptist Education Society of the State of New-York.

_____. Records of the Executive Committee; Also Minutes of Meetings of Board, & Faculty Baptist Education Society of the State of New York; March 6, 1822–Dec. 27, 1839. Typescript.

Colgate-Rochester Divinity School/Bexley Hall/Crozier Theological Seminary/St. Bernard's Institute. Ambrose Swazey Library. Elias Henry Johnson Papers. Lecture notebooks, ca. 1868–1871.

_____. Henry Griggs Weston Papers. Mss. Sermon and lecture notes, ca. 1868–1909.

Cornell University Libraries. Department of Manuscripts and University Archives. Daniel B. Fenn Papers. Letter, 1827.

_____. Henry Reeder Papers. Letter from David Reeder, n.d.

Hartford Theological Seminary. Manuscript Collection. Asahel Nettleton Papers. Letters, ca. 1816–1844.

Hobart and William Smith Colleges. Malcolm Douglass Papers. Student notebooks, 1848–49, letters to and from David Bates Douglass, 1846–50.

Oberlin College. Archives. Elam J. Comings, Papers. Diary, 1837–46.

_____. James Harris Fairchild Papers. "Suggestions to Theological Students as to the Relations of the Pastor to the Women of His Church & Congregation." Typescript, n.d.

_____. William A. Westervelt Papers. "Lecture Notes on Pastoral Theology by Dr. Finney." 1 vol. 1843–44[?].

Princeton Theological Seminary Libraries. Archibald Alexander Papers. Lecture Notes on Pastoral Theology, n.d.

_____. John Lloyd Papers. Religious Journal, 1842–48. Spiritual Autobiography, 1848.

Princeton University. Firestone Library. Charles Hodge Papers. Diary, 1819–20. "Certain Evils in Seminary," 1851. Joseph W. Wallace Notebooks on Hodge Lectures.

_____. Samuel Miller Papers. Letters to Miller, ca. 1827–45.

Syracuse University. George Arents Special Collections. Leonard Woods Papers. Letters to Isaac Warren, 1796–1832.

University of Michigan. Bentley Historical Library. Frederick Gallagher Papers. Letters, 1855 and undated.

_____. Theodore Marsh Papers. Autobiography. Letters to Justin Marsh, 1862–63.

University of Notre Dame. Archives. Records of the Archdiocese of Bardstown/Louisville. "Clergy and Religious Records and Cases. 1878–1905. Handling of Cases of Dismissal."

University of Rochester. Special Collections. Freeman-Clarke Family Papers. Letters of Ferdinand DeWilton Ward to Henrietta Ward, 1833–35.

Yale Divinity School Archives. S. W. S. Dutton Papers. Pastoral visitation records, 1855–65.

Yale University. Manuscripts and Archives. Isaac Bird Papers. Journal, 1813–23.

_____. Elisha Lord Cleaveland Papers. "Record of Ministerial Labours," 1845–50.

_____. Edward Gilman Family Papers. Diaries, 1849–58.

_____. Jonathan Lee Papers. Journals and Notebooks, 1810–44.

_____. Charles Swan Walker Papers. Lecture notebooks, 1867–69. Autobiography of Seminary Years.

Unpublished Sources: Women's Diaries, Journals, and Correspondence

American Antiquarian Society. Sally Hitchcock Bliss Journal.
_____. Sarah Lee Diary.
_____. Elizabeth Smith Diary.
Essex Historical Society. Diary of Mary Orne Tucker.
Fairfield Historical Society. Jennings Collection. Angeline Morehouse Letters.
Hartford Seminary. Asahel Nettleton Papers. Letters.
Oberlin College Library. Special Collections. Elizabeth Ford Atkinson Finney Journal.
Peabody Essex Museum. Phillips Library. Martha Osborne Barrett Diary.
Radcliffe College. Schlesinger Library. Almy Family Papers.
_____. Calista Billings Journal.
_____. Eunice Callender Letters.
_____. Dana Family Papers. Elizabeth Ellery Dana Diaries.
_____. Dana Family Papers. Sarah Watson Dana Diary.
_____. Helen Marcia Hart Diary.
_____. Dema M. Higbee Diary.
_____. Frances (Kingman) Holmes Diary.
_____. Louisa Walter Bishop Hughes Diary.
_____. Frances Merrit Quick Diaries.
_____. Emily A. Rice Diary.
_____. Eliza E. Rogers Diary.
_____. Sewall Family Papers. Letters.
_____. Ann J. Stoddard Diary.
_____. Harriet Ann Tappan Diary.
University of Michigan. Bentley Historical Library. Margaret Gallagher Journal.

SECONDARY SOURCES

Abelove, Henry. *The Evangelist of Desire: John Wesley and the Methodists.* Stanford, Ca-
    lif.: Stanford University Press, 1990.
Ahlstrom, Sydney E. *A Religious History of the American People.* New Haven, Conn.:
    Yale University Press, 1972.
Allmendinger, David. *Paupers and Scholars: The Transformation of Student Life in
    Nineteenth-Century New England.* New York: St. Martin's Press, 1975.
Axtell, James. *The School upon a Hill: Education and Society in Colonial New England.*
    New York: Norton, 1974.
Bainton, Roland. *Yale and the Ministry.* New York: Harper & Bros., 1957.
Baym, Nina. *Novels, Readers, and Reviewers: Responses to Fiction in Antebellum America.*
    Ithaca, N.Y.: Cornell University Press, 1984.
Bederman, Gail. " 'The Women Have Had Charge of the Church Work Long Enough':
    The Men and Religion Forward Movement of 1911–1912 and the Masculinization
    of Middle-Class Protestantism." *American Quarterly* 41 (1989): 432–65.
Bednarowski, Mary Farrell. "Outside the Mainstream: Women's Religion and Women
    Religious Leaders in Nineteenth-Century America." *Journal of the American Acad-
    emy of Religion* 48 (1980): 207–31.
Beintema, William J., Ed. *Clergy Malpractice: An Annotated Bibliography.* Buffalo, N.Y.:
    William S. Hein, 1990.
Beisel, Nicola. *Imperiled Innocents: Anthony Comstock and Family Reproduction in Victo-
    rian America.* Princeton, N.J.: Princeton University Press, 1997.

Belenky, Mary Field, Blythe McVicker Clinchy, Nancy Rule Goldberger, and Jill Mattuck Tarule. *Women's Ways of Knowing: The Development of Self, Voice, and Mind.* New York: Basic Books, 1986.

Bendroth, Margaret. *Gender and Fundamentalism, 1875–1980.* New Haven, Conn.: Yale University Press, 1993.

Benedict, Helen. *Virgin or Vamp: How the Press Covers Sex Crimes.* New York: Oxford University Press, 1992.

Berger, Molly W. "A House Divided: The Culture of the American Luxury Hotel, 1825–1860." In *His and Hers: Gender, Consumption, and Technology,* edited by Roger Horowitz and Arwen Mohun. Charlottesville: University of Virginia Press, 1998.

Bilhartz, Terry D. "Sex and the Second Great Awakening: The Feminization of American Religion Reconsidered." In *Beliefs and Behavior: Essays in the New Religious History,* edited by Philip R. Vandermeer and Robert P. Swierenga, 117–35. New Brunswick, N.J.: Rutgers University Press, 1991.

Blauvelt, Martha Tomhave. "Women, Words, and Men: Excerpts from the Diary of Mary Guion." *Journal of Women's History* 2 (1990): 177–84.

Bledstein, Burton J. *The Culture of Professionalism: The Middle Class and the Development of Higher Education in America.* New York: Norton, 1976.

Boyd, Lois, and R. Douglas Brackenridge. *Presbyterian Women in America: Two Centuries of a Quest for Status.* Westport, Conn.: Greenwood Press, 1983.

Boyer, Paul. *Urban Masses and Moral Order in America, 1820–1920.* Cambridge, Mass.: Harvard University Press, 1978.

Boylan, Anne M. "Evangelical Womanhood in the Nineteenth Century: The Role of Women in Sunday Schools." *Feminist Studies* 4 (1978): 62–80.

Boys, Mary. "Women as Leaven: Theological Education in the United States and Canada." In *Women—Invisible in Theology and Church,* edited by Elisabeth Schüssler Fiorenza and Mary Collins, 112–18. Edinburgh: T. & T. Clark, 1985.

Braude, Ann. *Radical Spirits: Spiritualism and Women's Rights in Nineteenth-Century America.* Boston: Beacon Press, 1989.

Brekus, Catherine A. *Strangers & Pilgrims: Female Preaching in America, 1740–1845.* Chapel Hill: University of North Carolina Press, 1998.

Brereton, Virginia Lieson. *From Sin to Salvation: Stories of Women's Conversions, 1800 to the Present.* Bloomington: Indiana University Press, 1991.

———. "Women and Theological Education: Learning in the Margins." In *Theological Education in the Evangelical Tradition,* edited by D. G. Hart and R. Albert Mohler, 190–202. Grand Rapids, Mich.: Baker Books, 1997.

Brodhead, Richard. "Sparing the Rod: Discipline and Fiction in Antebellum America." *Representations* 21 (1998): 67–98.

Brown, Amy Benson. *Rewriting the Word: American Women Writers and the Bible.* Westport, Conn.: Greenwood, 1999.

Brown, Gillian. *Domestic Individualism: Imagining Self in Nineteenth-Century America.* Berkeley: University of California Press, 1990.

Brucken, Carolyn. "In the Public Eye: Women and the American Luxury Hotel." *Winterthur Portfolio* 31 (1996): 203–20.

Brumm, Ursula. "The Motif of the Pastor as an Unsuitable Suitor: The Religious Crisis in American Novels of the Nineteenth Century." *Amerikastudien* 31 (1986): 61–70.

Butler, Jon. *Awash in a Sea of Faith: Christianizing the American People.* Cambridge, Mass.: Harvard University Press, 1990.

Cable, Mary. *Avery's Knot.* New York: G. P. Putnam's Sons, 1981.

Calhoun, Daniel. *Professional Lives in America: Structure and Aspirations, 1750–1850.* Cambridge, Mass.: Harvard University Press, 1965.

Carey, Patrick W. *People, Priests, and Prelates: Ecclesiastical Democracy and the Tensions of Trusteeism.* South Bend, Ind.: University of Notre Dame Press, 1987.

Carlson, A. Cheree. "The Role of Character in Public Moral Argument: Henry Ward Beecher and the Brooklyn Scandal." *Quarterly Journal of Speech* 77 (1991): 38–52.

Carnes, Mark C., and Griffen, Clyde, Eds. *Meanings for Manhood: Constructions of Masculinity in Victorian America.* Chicago: University of Chicago Press, 1990.

Charmallas, Martha, and Linda Kerber. "Women, Mothers, and the Law of Fright: A History." *Michigan Law Review* 88 (1990): 814–64.

Clark, Clifford E. *Henry Ward Beecher: Spokesman for a Middle-Class America.* Urbana: University of Illinois Press, 1978.

Cogan, Jacob Katz, and Lori D. Ginzberg. "1846 Petition for Woman's Suffrage, New York State Constitutional Convention." *Signs* 22 (1997): 427–39.

Cohen, Daniel. *Pillars of Salt, Monuments of Grace: New England Crime Literature and the Origins of Popular Culture, 1674–1860.* New York: Oxford University Press, 1993.

Cohen, Patricia Cline. *The Murder of Helen Jewett.* New York: Random House, 1998.

———. "Ministerial Misdeeds: The Onderdonk Trial and Sexual Harassment in the 1840s." *Journal of Women's History* 7 (1995): 34–57.

Comstock, Helen. *American Lithographs of the Nineteenth Century.* New York: M. Barrows, 1950.

Cott, Nancy. *The Bonds of Womanhood: "Woman's Sphere" in New England, 1780–1835.* New Haven, Conn.: Yale University Press, 1977.

———. "Passionlessness: An Interpretation of Victorian Sexual Ideology, 1790–1850." In *A Heritage of Her Own,* edited by Nancy F. Cott and Elizabeth H. Pleck, 162–81. New York: Simon & Schuster, 1979.

———. "Young Women in the Second Great Awakening." *American Quarterly* 27 (1975): 15–29.

Cragg, Gerald. "Training the Ministry—The Older Tradition." *Andover Newton Quarterly* 8 (1968): 223–34.

Dalzell, George W. *Benefit of Clergy in America & Related Matters.* Winston-Salem, N.C.: John F. Blair, 1955.

Davidson, Cathy N. *Revolution and the Word: The Rise of the Novel in America.* New York: Oxford University Press, 1986.

Davis, David Brion. "Some Themes of Counter-Subversion: Anti-Masonic, Anti-Catholic and Anti-Mormon Literature." *Mississippi Valley Historical Review* 47 (1960): 205–24.

Degler, Carl N. "What Ought to Be and What Was: Women's Sexuality in the Nineteenth Century." *American Historical Review* 19 (1974): 1467–90.

D'Emilio, John, and Estelle Freedman. *Intimate Matters: A History of Sexuality in America.* New York: Harper & Row, 1988.

Demos, John. *A Little Commonwealth: Family Life in Plymouth Colony.* New York: Oxford University Press, 1970.

Douglas, Ann. *The Feminization of American Culture.* New York: Alfred A. Knopf, 1977.

Dublin, Thomas. *Women at Work: The Transformation of Work and Community in Lowell, Massachusetts, 1826–1860.* New York: Columbia University Press, 1979.

Duffy, John J., and Nicholas H. Muller. *An Anxious Democracy: Aspects of the 1830s.* Westport, Conn.: Greenwood, 1982.

Epstein, Barbara. *The Politics of Domesticity: Women, Evangelicalism, and Temperance in Nineteenth-Century America.* Middletown, Conn.: Wesleyan University Press, 1981.

Finley, Lucinda M. "Breaking Women's Silence in Law." *Notre Dame Law Review* 64 (1989): 886–910.

Flint, Janet A. *The Way of Good and Evil: Popular Religious Lithographs of Nineteenth-Century America.* Washington, D.C.: Smithsonian Institution, 1972.

Formisano, Ronald P. "Deferential-Participant Politics: The Early Republic's Political Culture, 1789–1840." *American Political Science Review* 68 (1974): 473–87.

————. "Political Character, Antipartyism, and the Second Party System." *American Quarterly* 21 (1969): 683–709.

Fortune, Marie M. *Is Nothing Sacred? The Story of a Pastor, the Women He Sexually Abused, and the Congregation He Nearly Destroyed.* San Francisco: Harper & Row, 1989.

Foster, Lawrence. *Women, Family, and Utopia: Communal Experiments of the Shakers, the Oneida Community, and the Mormons.* Syracuse, N.Y.: Syracuse University Press, 1991.

Fox, Richard Wightman. *Trials of Intimacy: Love and Loss in the Beecher-Tilton Scandal.* Chicago: University of Chicago Press, 1999.

Fox-Genovese, Elizabeth. "Two Steps Forward, One Step Back: New Questions and Old Models in the Religious History of American Women." *Journal of the American Academy of Religion* 53 (1985): 465–71.

Fraser, James W. *Schooling the Preachers: The Development of Protestant Theological Education in the United States, 1740–1875.* Lanham: University Press of America, 1988.

Gabriel, Mary. *Notorious Victoria: The Life of Victoria Woodhull.* Chapel Hill, N.C.: Algonquin Books, 1998.

Gambrill, Mary L. *Ministerial Education in Eighteenth-Century New England.* New York: Columbia University Press, 1937.

Gedge, Karin E. "Ministry to Women in the Antebellum Seminaries." In *Theological Education in the Evangelical Tradition,* edited by D. G. Hart and R. Albert Mohler Jr., 173–89. Grand Rapids, Mich.: Baker Books, 1997.

Gillespie, Joanna Bowen. " 'The Clear Leadings of Providence': Pious Memoirs and the Problems of Self-Realization for Women in the Early Nineteenth Century." *Journal of the Early Republic* 5 (1985): 197–221.

Gilligan, Carol. *In a Different Voice: Psychological Theory and Women's Development.* Cambridge, Mass.: Harvard University Press, 1982.

Gilmore, David. *Manhood in the Making: The Emergence of Cultural Concepts of Masculinity.* New Haven, Conn.: Yale University Press, 1990.

Ginzberg, Lori. *Women and the Work of Benevolence.* New Haven, Conn.: Yale University Press, 1990.

————. "Women in an Evangelical Community: Oberlin, 1835–1850." *Ohio History* 89 (1980): 78–88.

Goffman, Erving. *Frame Analysis: An Essay on the Organization of Experience.* New York: Harper & Row, 1974.

————. *Interaction Ritual: Essays on Face-to-Face Behavior.* New York: Pantheon, 1982.

————. *The Presentation of Self in Everyday Life.* Garden City, N.Y.: Doubleday, 1959.

Goldsmith, Barbara. *Other Powers: The Age of Suffrage, Spiritualism, and the Scandalous Victoria Woodhull.* New York: Knopf, 1998.

Goshgarian, G. M. *To Kiss the Chastening Rod: Domestic Fiction and Sexual Ideology in the American Renaissance*. Ithaca, N.Y.: Cornell University Press, 1992.

Grossberg, Michael. *Governing the Hearth: Law and Family in Nineteenth-Century America*. Chapel Hill: University of North Carolina Press, 1985.

_____. "Institutionalizing Masculinity: The Law as a Masculine Profession." In *Meanings for Manhood: Constructions of Masculinity in Victorian America*, edited by Mark C. Carnes and Clyde Griffen, 133–51. Chicago: University of Chicago Press, 1990.

Gundersen, Joan R. "The Local Parish as Female Institution: The Experience of All Saints Episcopal Church in Frontier Minnesota." *Church History* 55 (1986): 307–22.

_____. "The Non-Institutional Church: The Religious Role of Women in Eighteenth-Century Virginia." *Historical Magazine of the Protestant Episcopal Church* 51 (1982): 347–57.

Haag, Pamela Susan. "The 'Ill-Use of a Wife': Patterns of Working-Class Violence in Domestic and Public New York City." *Journal of Social History* 25 (1992): 447–77.

Hackett, David G. "Gender and Religion in American Culture, 1870–1930." *Religion and American Culture* 5 (1995): 127–57.

Hall, David. *The Faithful Shepherd: A History of the New England Ministry in the Seventeenth Century*. Chapel Hill: University of North Carolina Press, 1972.

Halttunen, Karen. *Confidence Men and Painted Ladies: A Study of Middle-Class Culture in America, 1830–1870*. New Haven, Conn.: Yale University Press, 1982.

_____. "Early American Murder Narratives: The Birth of Horror." In *The Power of Culture: Critical Essays in American History*, edited by Richard Wightman Fox and T. J. Jackson Lears, 67–101. Chicago: University of Chicago Press, 1993.

Hansen, Karen V. *"A Very Social Time": Crafting Community in Antebellum New England*. Berkeley: University of California Press, 1994.

_____. " 'Our Eyes Behold Each Other': Masculinity and Intimate Friendship in Antebellum New England." In *Men's Friendships*, edited by Peter M. Nardi, 35–58. Newbury Park, Calif.: Sage Press, 1993.

Hardesty, Nancy. *Women Called to Witness: Evangelical Feminism in the Nineteenth Century*. Nashville, Tenn.: Abingdon Press, 1984.

_____. *Your Daughters Shall Prophesy: Revivalism and Feminism in the Age of Finney*. Brooklyn, N.Y.: Carlson, 1991.

Harper, George. "Clericalism and Revival: The Great Awakening in Boston as a Pastoral Phenomenon." *New England Quarterly* 57 (1984): 554–66.

Harris, Susan K. *Nineteenth-Century American Women's Novels: Interpretive Strategies*. New York: Cambridge University Press, 1990.

Hart, James D. *The Popular Book: A History of America's Literary Taste*. Westport, Conn.: Greenwood, 1950.

Hatch, Nathan O. *The Democratization of American Christianity*. New Haven, Conn.: Yale University Press, 1989.

Helly, Dorothy O. and Susan M. Reverby, eds. *Gendered Domains: Rethinking Public and Private in Women's History*. Ithaca, N.Y.: Cornell University Press, 1992.

Hemphill, C. Dallett. "Age Relations and the Social Order in Early New England: The Evidence from Manners." *Journal of Social History* 28 (1994): 271–94.

_____. "Middle Class Rising in Revolutionary America: The Evidence from Manners." *Journal of Social History* 30 (1996): 317–44.

Henigman, Laura. *Coming into Communion: Pastoral Dialogues in Colonial New England*. Albany: State University of New York Press, 1999.

Hewitt, Nancy. "The Perimeters of Women's Power in American Religion." In *The Evangelical Tradition in America*, edited by Leonard Sweet, 233–56. Macon, Ga.: Mercer University Press, 1984.

Hogeland, Ronald. "Charles Hodge, The Association of Gentlemen, and Ornamental Womanhood: A Study of Male Conventional Wisdom, 1825–1855." *Journal of Presbyterian History* 53 (1975): 239–55.

————. "Co-Education of the Sexes at Oberlin College: A Study of Social Ideas in Mid-Nineteenth-Century America." *Journal of Social History* 6 (1972–3): 160–76.

Hibben, Paxton. *Henry Ward Beecher: An American Portrait*. New York: George H. Doran, 1927.

Holifield, E. Brooks. *A History of Pastoral Care in America: From Salvation to Self-Realization*. Nashville, Tenn.: Abingdon Press, 1983.

Ireland, Robert M. "The Libertine Must Die: Sexual Dishonor and the Unwritten Law in the Nineteenth-Century United States." *Journal of Social History* 23 (1989): 27–44.

Isenberg, Nancy. " 'Pillars in the Same Temple and Priests of the Same Worship' Womans' Rights and the Politics of Church and State in Antebellum America." *Journal of American History* 85 (1998): 98–128.

Johnson, Claudia Durst. "Impotence and Omnipotence in *The Scarlet Letter*." *New England Quarterly* 66 (1993): 594–612.

Johnson, Paul E., *A Shopkeeper's Millennium: Society and Revivals in Rochester, New York, 1815–1837*. New York: Hill & Wang, 1978.

Johnson, Paul E., and Sean Wilentz. *The Kingdom of Matthias: A Story of Sex and Salvation in 19th-Century America*. New York: Oxford University Press, 1994.

Jordan, Cynthia. *Second Stories: The Politics of Language, Form, and Gender in Early American Fictions*. Chapel Hill: University of North Carolina Press, 1989.

Juster, Susan. " 'In a Different Voice': Male and Female Narratives of Religious Conversion in Post-Revolutionary America." *American Quarterly* 41 (1989): 34–62.

Kamensky, Jane. *Governing the Tongue: The Politics of Speech in Early New England*. New York: Oxford University Press, 1997.

Karlsen, Carol. *The Devil in the Shape of a Woman: Witchcraft in Colonial New England*. New York: Norton, 1987.

Kasserman, David R. *Fall River Outrage: Life, Murder, and Justice in Early Industrial New England*. Philadelphia: University of Pennsylvania Press, 1986.

Kasson, John F. *Rudeness and Civility: Manners in Nineteenth-Century Urban America*. New York: Hill & Wang, 1990.

Keller, Rosemary Skinner. "Women and the Nature of Ministry in the United Methodist Tradition." *Methodist History* 22 (1984): 99–114.

Kerber, Linda K. "Can a Woman Be an Individual? The Limits of Puritan Tradition in the Early Republic." *Texas Studies in Literature and Language* 25 (1983): 165–177.

————. "Separate Spheres, Female Worlds, Woman's Place: The Rhetoric of Women's History." *Journal of American History* 75 (1988): 9–39.

Kerber, Linda K., and Nancy F. Cott. "Beyond Roles, Beyond Spheres: Thinking about Gender in the Early Republic." *William and Mary Quarterly* 66 (1989): 565–85.

King, Andrew J. "Constructing Gender: Sexual Slander in Nineteenth-Century America." *Law and History Review* 13 (1995): 63–110.

Korobkin, Laura Hanft. *Criminal Conversations: Sentimentality and Nineteenth-Century Legal Stories of Adultery*. New York: Columbia University Press, 1998.

Lane, Roger. "Crime and Criminal Statistics in Nineteenth-Century Massachusetts." *Journal of Social History* 2 (1968): 156–63.

LaSorte, Michael A. "Nineteenth-Century Family Planning Practices." *Journal of Psychohistory* 4 (1976): 163–83.

Lawes, Carolyn J. *Women and Reform in a New England Community, 1815–1860.* Lexington: University of Kentucky Press, 2000.

Lerner, Gerda. "Benefit of Clergy." Review of *The Feminization of American Culture,* by Ann Douglas. *New York Times Book Review,* June 26, 1977, 13.

———. "The Lady and the Mill Girl: Changes in the Status of Women in the Age of Jackson." *Mid-Continent American Studies Journal* 10 (1969): 5–15.

Lewis, Jan. "The Republican Wife: Virtue and Seduction in the Early Republic." *William and Mary Quarterly* 44 (1987): 689–721.

Leys, Marie-Christine. *Apprehending the Criminal: The Production of Deviance in Nineteenth-Century Discourse.* Durham, N.C.: Duke University Press, 1992.

Lindley, Susan Hill. *"You Have Stept Out of Your Place": A History of Women and Religion in America.* Louisville, Ky.: Westminster John Knox Press, 1996.

Lindsley, James Elliott. *This Planted Vine: A Narrative History of the Episcopal Diocese of New York.* New York: Harper& Row, 1984.

Lotz, Roy Edward. *Crime and the American Press.* New York: Praeger, 1991.

Lynn, Robert Wood. "Notes toward a History: Theological Encyclopedia and the Evolution of Protestant Seminary Curriculum, 1808–1868." *Theological Education* 17 (Spring, 1981): 118–44.

Lystra, Karen. *Searching the Heart: Women, Men, and Romantic Love in Nineteenth-Century America.* New York: Oxford University Press, 1989.

Malmsheimer, Lonna M. "Daughters of Zion: New England Roots of American Feminism." *New England Quarterly* 50 (1977): 484–504.

Marberry, M. M. *The Golden Voice: A Biography of Isaac Kalloch.* New York: Farrar, Straus, 1947.

Marsden, George M. "Everyone One's Own Interpreter? The Bible, Science, and Authority in Mid-Nineteenth-Century America." In *The Bible in America: Essays in Cultural History,* edited by Nathan O. Hatch and Mark A. Noll. New York: Oxford University Press, 1982.

May, Sherry Pierpont. "Asahel Nettleton: Nineteenth-Century American Revivalist." Unpublished Ph.D. dissertation, Drew University, 1969.

McDade, Thomas M. [compiler]. *The Annals of Murder: A Bibliography of Books and Pamphlets on American Murders from Colonial Times to 1900.* Norman: University of Oklahoma Press, 1961.

———. "Lurid Literature of the Last Century: The Publications of E. E. Barclay." *Pennsylvania Magazine of History and Biography* 80 (1956): 452–64.

McLoughlin, William. "Untangling the Tiverton Tragedy: The Social Meaning of the Terrible Haystack Murder of 1833." *Journal of American Culture* 7 (1984) 75–84.

Mead, Sidney. "The Rise of the Evangelical Conception of the Ministry in America, 1607–1850." In *The Ministry in Historical Perspective,* edited by H. Richard Niebuhr and Daniel D. Williams, 207–49. New York: Harper, 1946.

Menkel-Meadow, Carrie. "Portia in a Different Voice." *Berkeley Women's Law Journal* 1 (1985): 39–50.

Miller, Glenn T. *Piety and Intellect: The Aims and Purposes of Antebellum Theological Education.* Atlanta, Ga.: Scholars Press, 1990.

Mohr, James C. *Abortion in America: The Origins and Evolution of National Policy, 1800–1900.* New York: Oxford University Press, 1978.

Moran, Gerald F. " 'Sinners Are Turned into Saints in Numbers': Puritanism and Revivalism in Colonial Connecticut." In *Belief and Behavior: Essays in the New Reli-*

gious History, edited by Philip R. Vandermeer and Robert P. Swierenga, 38–62. New Brunswick, N.J.: Rutgers University Press, 1991.

Mott, Frank L. *Golden Multitudes: A History of Best-Sellers in the United States.* New York: Macmillan, 1947.

Mullin, Robert Bruce. *Episcopal Vision/American Reality: High Church Theology and Social Thought in Evangelical America.* New Haven, Conn.: Yale University Press, 1986.

Murphy, Teresa Anne. *Ten Hours' Labor: Religion, Reform, and Gender in Early New England.* Ithaca, N.Y.: Cornell University Press, 1992.

Naylor, Natalie. "Raising a Learned Ministry: The American Education Society: Indigent Students and the New Charity." Unpublished Ph.D. dissertation, Columbia University, 1971.

———. "The Theological Seminary in the Configuration of American Higher Education in the Antebellum Years." *History of Education Quarterly* 17 (1977): 17–30.

Nemath, Charles P. "Character Evidence in Rape Trials in Nineteenth-Century New York: Chastity and the Admissibility of Specific Acts." *Women's Rights Law Reporter* 6 (1980): 214–25.

Newberry, Frederick. "A Red-Hot A and a Lusting Divine: Sources for *The Scarlet Letter.*" *New England Quarterly* 65 (1987): 256–64.

Noll, William T. "Women as Clergy and Laity in the Nineteenth-Century Methodist Protestant Church." *Methodist History* 15 (1977): 107–21.

Norton, Mary Beth. *Liberty's Daughters: The Revolutionary Experience of American Women, 1750–1800.* Boston: Little, Brown, 1980.

Osterud, Nancy Grey. *Bonds of Community: The Lives of Farm Women in Nineteenth-Century New York.* Ithaca, N.Y.: Cornell University Press, 1991.

Papke, David Ray. *Framing the Criminal: Crime, Cultural Work and the Loss of Critical Perspective, 1830–1900.* Hamden, Conn.: Archon Books, 1987.

Paul, Raymond. *Tragedy at Tiverton.* New York: Viking Press, 1984.

Pease, Jane H., and William H. Pease. *Ladies, Women & Wenches: Choice and Constraint in Antebellum Charleston and Boston.* Chapel Hill: University of North Carolina Press, 1990.

Peel, Robert. *Mary Baker Eddy: The Years of Authority.* New York: Holt, Rinehart, & Winston, 1977.

Pellauer, Mary D. *Toward a Tradition of Feminist Theology: The Religious Social Thought of Elizabeth Cady Stanton, Susan B. Anthony, and Anna Howard Shaw.* Brooklyn, N.Y.: Carlson, 1991.

Porterfield, Amanda. *Feminine Spirituality in America: From Sarah Edwards to Martha Graham.* Philadelphia: Temple University Press, 1980.

———. "Women's Attraction to Puritanism." *Church History* 60 (1991): 196–209.

Preston, Jo Anne. "Domestic Ideology, School Reformers, and Female Teachers." *New England Quarterly* 66 (1993): 531–51.

Rabinowitz, Richard. *The Spiritual Self in Everyday Life: The Transformation of Personal Religious Experience in Nineteenth-Century New England.* Boston: Northeastern University Press, 1989.

Rawlyk, George A. *Ravished by the Spirit: Religious Revivals, Baptists, and Henry Alline.* Kingston, Ontario: McGill-Queen's University Press, 1984.

Reverby, Susan M. *Gendered Domains: Rethinking Public and Private in Women's History.* Ithaca, N.Y.: Cornell University Press, 1992.

Reynolds, David S. *Beneath the American Renaissance: The Subversive Imagination in the Age of Emerson and Melville*. Cambridge, Mass.: Harvard University Press, 1989.

_____. *Faith in Fiction: The Emergence of Religious Literature in America*. Cambridge, Mass.: Harvard University Press, 1981.

_____. "The Feminization Controversy: Sexual Stereotypes and the Paradoxes of Piety in Nineteenth-Century America." *New England Quarterly* 53 (1980): 96–106.

Rosenberg, Charles E. "Sexuality, Class, and Role in Nineteenth-Century America." *American Quarterly* 25 (1973) 131–153.

Rothman, Ellen K. *Hands and Hearts: A History of Courtship in America*. New York: Basic Books, 1984.

Rotundo, E. Anthony. *American Manhood: Transformations in Masculinity from the Revolution to the Modern Era*. New York: Basic Books, 1993.

Rowe, H[enry] K[alloch]. *History of Andover Seminary*. Newton, Mass: n.p., 1933.

Ruether, Rosemary Radford, Ed. *Women and Religion in America*. 3 vols. New York: Simon & Schuster, 1974.

Russett, Cynthia Eagle. *Sexual Science: The Victorian Construction of Womanhood*. Cambridge, Mass.: Harvard University Press, 1989.

Rutland, Robert A. *The Newsmongers: Journalism and the Life of the Nation, 1690–1972*. New York: Dial Press, 1973.

Rutter, Peter. *Sex in the Forbidden Zone: When Men in Power—Therapists, Doctors, Clergy, Teachers, and Others—Betray Women's Trust*. New York: Fawcett Press, 1989.

Ryan, Halford R. *Henry Ward Beecher: Peripatetic Preacher*. Westport, Conn.: Greenwood, 1990.

Ryan, Mary P. *Cradle of the Middle Class: The Family in Oneida County, New York: 1790–1865*. New York: Cambridge University Press, 1981.

_____. "A Women's Awakening: Evangelical Religion and the Families of Utica, New York, 1800–1840." *American Quarterly* 30 (1978): 602–23.

Samuels, Shirley. "Infidelity and Contagion: The Rhetoric of Revolution." *Early American Literature* 22 (1987): 183–91.

Saxton, Alexander. *The Rise and Fall of the White Republic: Class Politics and Mass Culture in Nineteenth-Century America*. New York: Verso, 1990.

Scott, Anne Firor. *Making the Invisible Woman Visible*. Urbana: University of Illinois Press, 1984.

_____. *Natural Allies: Women's Association in American History*. Urbana: University of Illinois Press, 1991.

Scott, Donald M. *From Office to Profession: The New England Ministry, 1750–1850*. Philadelphia: University of Pennsylvania Press, 1978.

_____. *Pastors and Providence: Changing Ministerial Styles in Nineteenth-Century America*. Evanston, Ill.: Seabury-Western Theological Seminary, 1975.

Scott, Joan. "Gender: A Useful Category of Historical Analysis." *American Historical Review* 91 (1986): 1053–57.

Shiels, Richard D. "The Feminization of American Congregationalism, 1730–1835." *American Quarterly* 33 (1981): 46–62.

Smith-Rosenberg, Carroll. *Disorderly Conduct: Visions of Gender in Victorian America*. New York: Alfred A. Knopf, 1985.

Stansell, Christine. *City of Women: Sex and Class in New York, 1789–1860*. Chicago: University of Illinois Press, 1987.

Stanton, Elizabeth Cady, Susan B. Anthony, and Matilda Joslyn Gage, Eds. *History of Woman's Suffrage.* New York: Fowler & Wells, 1881.

Stout, Harry S. *The Divine Dramatist: George Whitefield and the Rise of Modern Evangelicalism.* Grand Rapids, Mich.: Eerdmans, 1991.

Stout, Harry S., and Catherine A. Brekus. "Declension, Gender, and the New Religious History." In *Belief and Behavior: Essays in the New Religious History,* edited by Philip R. Vandermeer and Robert P. Swierenga, 15–37. New Brunswick, N.J.: Rutgers University Press, 1991.

Suggs, Redding S. *Motherteacher: The Feminization of American Education.* Charlottesville: University of Virginia Press, 1978.

Sweet, Leonard. *The Minister's Wife: Her Role in Nineteenth-Century American Evangelicalism.* Philadelphia: Temple University Press, 1983.

Taves, Ann. "Women and Gender in American Religion(s)." *Religious Studies Review* 18 (1992): 26–70.

Theriot, Nancy M. *The Biosocial Construction of Femininity: Mothers and Daughters in Nineteenth-Century America.* New York: Greenwood, 1988.

Thompson, Margaret S. "Women, Feminism, and the New Religious History: Catholic Sisters as a Case Study." In *Belief and Behavior: Essays in the New Religious History,* edited by Philip R. Vandermeer and Robert P. Swierenga, 136–63. New Brunswick, N.J.: Rutgers University Press, 1991.

Thornbury, John. *God-Sent Revival: The Story of Asahel Nettleton and the Second Great Awakening.* Grand Rapids, Mich.: Evangelical Press, 1977.

Thurner, Manuela. "Subject to Change: Theories and Paradigms of United States Feminist History." *Journal of Women's History* 9 (1997): 122–46.

Tompkins, Jane P. *Sensational Designs: The Cultural Work of American Fiction, 1790–1860.* New York: Oxford University Press, 1985.

Tucker, Cynthia Grant. *Prophetic Sisterhood: Liberal Women Ministers of the Frontier, 1880–1930.* Boston: Beacon Press, 1990.

Ulrich, Laurel Thatcher. *Good Wives: Image and Reality in the Lives of Women in Northern New England, 1650–1750.* New York: Knopf, 1982.

Waller, Altina L. *Reverend Beecher and Mrs. Tilton: Sex and Class in Victorian America.* Amherst: University of Massachusetts Press, 1982.

Welter, Barbara. "The Feminization of American Religion." In *Dimity Convictions: The American Woman in the Nineteenth Century,* 83–102. Athens: Ohio University Press, 1976.

———. "The Cult of True Womanhood, 1820–1860." *American Quarterly* 18 (1966): 15–74.

———. "She Hath Done What She Could: Protestant Women's Missionary Careers in Nineteenth-Century America." *American Quarterly* 30 (1978): 625–38.

White, Elizabeth Alice. "Sentimental Heresies: Rethinking *The Feminization of American Culture.*" *Intellectual History Newsletter* 15 (1993): 23–31.

Williams, Daniel E. "Rogues, Rascals and Scoundrels: The Underworld Literature of Early America." *American Studies* 24 (1983): 5–19.

Williams, Peter W. *Popular Religion in America: Symbolic Change and the Modernization Process in Historical Perspective.* Englewood Cliffs, N.J.: Prentice-Hall, 1980.

Winslow, Ola. *Meetinghouse Hill: 1630–1783.* New York: Macmillan, 1952.

Wood, Gordon S. "The Democratization of Mind in the American Revolution." In *Leadership in the American Revolution,* edited by Gordon Wood. Washington, D.C.: Library of Congress, 1974.

Woolf, Virginia. *A Room of One's Own; and, Three Guineas*. London: Hogarth Press, 1984.

Yazawa, Melvin. *From Colonies to Commonwealth: Familial Ideology and the Beginnings of the American Republic*. Baltimore, Md.: Johns Hopkins University Press, 1985.

Zagarri, Rosemarie. "The Rights of Man and Woman in Post-Revolutionary America." *William and Mary Quarterly* 55 (1998): 203–30.

Index

Abbott, Ephraim, 146–47
abolition of slavery. *See* anti-slavery
abortion, 57, 206, 230n. 10
African Americans, 35, 91, 95, 147, 148, 183–84, 251n. 34
   racial stereotyping of, 35
African Methodist Episcopal Church, 130, 245n. 42
Alexander, Archibald, 120, 127, 131, 134
Allmendinger, David, 117
American Education Society, 116, 117, 122
Anthony, Susan B., 48
Anthony, Susanna, 90–92
anti-slavery, 17, 36, 40, 77, 94, 96, 183, 212, 214, 251n.34
Avery, Ephraim, 23, 25, 26–32, 47, 51, 57, 59, 63, 70, 218, 226n.16
Awful Disclosures at the Hotel Dieu (Monk), 81

Bacon, Leonard, 125, 141–42
Baptists, 36–39, 53, 54, 56–57, 168–69
Barclay, David, 51, 229n.2
Barrett, Martha, 177
Barrows, Emily, 54, 56–57
Beecher, Henry Ward, 3, 26, 39–48, 52, 56, 70, 72, 77, 78, 106, 218

Beecher, Lyman, 146
"Beecher's Experience in Lap-Land," 46
bellwether, 20–21
benefit of clergy, 6, 73, 104
"Benefit of Clergy" (Lerner), 5
benefit of doubt, 72, 73
Bird, Henry, 148–49
Bird, Isaac, 144–45, 147, 148–49, 153, 246n.4
birth control, 63
Blackwell, Antoinette Brown, 203
Bliss, Sally, 165–68, 176, 178, 187
Bowen, Henry, 39
Brekus, Catherine, 92
Bremer, Frederika, 12, 13, 39
Brown, Emma, 183–84
Brown, John, 183
Budge, Henry, 51, 59
Bushnell, Horace, 170
Butler, Mrs., 56, 59

Cabot, Hannah, 168, 181–83
Calhoun, Daniel, 115
Callender, Eunice, 251–52n.40
Calvinism, 96, 167, 198, 201, 216, 217, 219
cartoons, 47–48
Cartwright, Peter, 88, 106

Catholicism, 57–58, 133, 151–52, 206, 212, 219, 223n.16
celibacy, 58, 133, 154, 192, 203–4, 223n. 16
Channing, William Ellery, 15, 181–83
children, 125, 207
Christianity, 24, 200–201
Christian Science. *See* Church of Christ, Scientist
Church of Christ, Scientist, 204–05
Church of England, 13
Church of Latter-Day Saints, 55, 159, 201–2
"Churches and the Women, The," 7
Civil War, 77–78, 210
Clap, Rev. Mr., 90
Clarke, Ferdinand, 154
Cleaveland, Elisha, 161
Clergy
    accounts of pastoral duties, 141–62
    clerical privilege, 71
    clerical sin, 61
    competition and dissension among, 114
    condescension toward women, 150–51
    decline in permanency in ministry, 115
    decline in respect for, 114
    disestablished minister, 93–96
    education of, 111–13, 116–20, 143, 213
    experiences with women, 148–53
    ideal pastor, 121–26
    ideal pastor to women, 126–33
    as "martyr," 97–100
    "masculinization" of, 52, 65–70, 199
    ministrations to sick and dying, 145, 148, 179–80, 251n.28
    as novice pastors, 143–48
    in pastoral role, 141–62
    pastor's wife, 133–37, 153–57, 160–62, 246n.48, 249n.41
    as "physicians of souls," 124
    pious memoirs, 88–97
    preaching, 123–24
    professionalization of, 111–21, 135–37, 199, 213
    sexual scandals among, 23–74, 198
    travelers' views on, 12–20
    trials of, 23–74, 198, 218, 233nn.29–30, 234n.32
    "uneasy truce" with women, 199, 217

women's experience with, 163–95
    See also specific clergymen
Clinton, President William Jefferson, 206
cognitive dissonance, 54
Cogswell, William, 116, 122, 130
Cohen, Patricia Cline, 35, 226n. 17
Comings, Elam J., 153
Comstock laws, 40
confession, auricular, 57–58
Confessions of a Magdalene, The, 81
congregational polity, 115
Connell, Mary, 54
conspiracies, 69–70
Cook, Elizabeth, 189
Cornell, Sarah Maria, 26–31, 59, 60, 63
Cott, Nancy, 199
courtship, 134
Cram, Elizabeth, 60, 63
Cummings, Alexander, 52

Dana, Elizabeth, 169, 178, 186
Dana, Richard Henry, 37–38
Dana, Sarah, 170–71, 175, 178
"Dark Underdonkation," 34–35
Davidson, Rhoda, 55, 57, 60, 63, 64, 231nn.15–16
"Death Struggle on the Ragged Edge," 48
democracy, 11, 14, 18, 21
denominational affiliation
    of clergy in trials, 51–52
    of women in study, 249 n.3
    See also specific clergymen and women
de Tocqueville, Alexis, 12
Dickens, Charles, 14, 15
disestablished minister, 93–96
Doane, George Washinton, 51, 72
Dorland, Louisa, 58
Douglas, Ann, 3, 4, 5, 78, 79, 84, 91, 92, 93, 123, 158, 160, 199, 216–17, 218, 235n.1
Douglass, Malcolm, 153–54
Driscoll, Mary, 55, 56, 230n.8
Dwight, Timothy, 144

Eddy, Mary Baker, 204–5
elderly, 125
Emerson, Ralph Waldo, 182

Fairchild, James H., 7, 126–27, 129, 132, 243n.18, 246n.45
Fairchild, Joy Hamlet, 51, 54–55, 59, 60, 64, 69, 70, 71–72, 230n.7
Fall River Narrative (Williams), 63
Fearon, Henry, 14, 19, 222n.13
feminine role. *See* women
Feminization of American Culture (Douglas), 5, 216–17
Finch, Marianne, 222–23n.14
Finney, Charles, 106, 120, 121, 131, 133, 134, 153, 161–62, 183–84, 203, 245n.39, 246n.45, 249n.41
Finney, Elizabeth, 162
First Amendment, 24, 71, 212
Fish, Joseph, 92
Fletcher, Robert Samuel, 245n.39
Foster, George, 80
free love, 40, 77

Gallagher, Frederick, 155, 248n.26
Garrison, William, 183
gender difference, 175, 205–6
gender equality, 206
gender ideology, 5, 7, 25, 31–32, 33, 35, 42, 48, 52, 62, 67–68, 101, 112–13, 137, 153, 205, 208, 213
gender role, 203, 213
Gilded Age, 218
Gilligan, Carol, 175, 182
Gilman, Edward Whiting, 150–52
Glendenning, John S., 51
Goffman, Erving, 243n.22
Gooch, Richard, 15, 23, 223n.1
Goshgarian, G.M., 87
Griffith Gaunt (Reade), 42–43, 77, 78–79, 106–7, 228n.32
Grimke, Sarah Moore, 250n.15
Grosscup, Issachar, 51, 230n.7
Grund, Francis, 13, 15
Guild, William, 51
Gundersen, Joan, 202
Gurney, Edward, 145, 155–56, 157

Hackett, David, 201
Halttunen, Karen, 83
Hansen, Karen V., 250n.22
Harden, Jacob, 51, 71, 73
Harper's Weekly, 46, 47
Hawthorne, Nathaniel, 3, 84, 101–5

Hayden, Herbert Hiram, 52, 57, 59
"A Hint to the Plymouth Pastor," 45
Hodge, Charles, 146, 147
Hogan, William, 51
Hogeland, Ronald W., 245n.34
Holifield, E. Brooks, 152, 218
Holmes, Rev. Mr., 185
homosexuality, 63, 133, 206–8
homosociality, 41
Hooker, Isabella Beecher, 40
Hopkins, Samuel, 90–92, 96
Hoppin, James, 246n.48
hotels, 38–39, 227n.25
"How to Make Pastoral Visits and Avoid Slander," 45
Howland, Emily, 183
Hughes, Louisa, 180, 251n.28
Humphrey, Heman, 114, 244n.30
Huston, Lorenzo Dow, 51, 55, 56, 57, 230n.8
Hutchinson, Anne, 92

Ide, George, 119
incest, 56, 82, 87
industrialization, 211, 218
intellect, 122, 123

Jamieson, W.F., 24
Jarvis, Samuel, 51
Jefferson, Thomas, 211

Kalloch, Isaac, 25, 36–39, 51, 70, 71, 72–73, 197, 226n. 22
Kasserman, David, 218, 226n.16
Kasson, John, 83
Kingman, Frances, 169, 176, 185–86, 187

"Lady in Black," 37
lay misconduct, 61
Lawes, Carolyn, 222n13
Lechmere Hotel (Mass.), 37–39, 197–98
Lectures on Pastoral Duties (Pond), 121
Lee, Alfred, 72
Lee, Ann, 203
Lee, Jonathan, 146
Lee, Sarah, 189
Lerner, Gerda, 5
"Lines Written on the Death of Sarah M. Cornell," 30
Lippard, George, 82–84

literature, 75–107
  clergy as "benevolent despot" in, 84,
    85–88
  clergy as "reverend rake" in, 80–85
  disestablished minister in, 93–96
  parsonage novels, 97–101
  pious memoirs, 88–97
  sentimentalism, 78, 79, 84–85
  See also specific literary works

Maffitt, John, 51, 52, 172
Man-Midwifery Dissected (Blount),
  frontispiece, 31–32
Mann, Horace, 157
manners, 122–23
marriage, 133–37, 153–57, 160–62
Marsden, George, 250n. 15
Martineau, Harriet, 14, 15–19, 21, 198,
  222n.14, 235n.2
Matthias, Robert, 51, 106, 239–40n.46
Maury, Sarah, 13–14
McFarland, Mrs. Daniel, 40
Meade, William, 135
Melville, Herman, 96
Memoirs of a Preacher, The (Lippard), 82–
  83
meritocracy, 115
Merrill, William, 51, 54, 57
Methodists, 212
Mew, Mary Anne, 188–89
middle class, 83–84, 211
Miller, Samuel, 123, 125, 126, 128–29,
  130–31, 133–34, 135, 152
minister. See clergy
"Minister Extraordinary Taking Passage
  & Bound on a Foreign Mission"
  (Robinson), 28–29
Minister's Wooing, The (Stowe), 93–96
Moby Dick (Melville), 96
Monk, Maria, 81–82
Moore, George, 143, 149–50, 156–61
Moulton, Emma, 43
Moulton, Frank, 43
morality, 25, 61, 103, 104, 175, 182, 215
Morehouse, Angeline, 172
Mormons. See Church of Latter-Day
  Saints
Mount, William Sydney, 34

Nason, Elias, 161
National Woman's Rights Convention
  (Syracuse, N.Y.), 163, 203
neglect, 5
Nettleton, Asahel, 161, 165, 187–95, 233n.
  30, 253nn.56–57
New York Daily Graphic, 6–7, 44, 45, 46
nuns, 202, 205, 219

Oberlin College, 183, 203
"Old Lady in a Fog," 44
Onderdonk, Benjamin, 25, 32–36, 51, 59,
  60, 64, 66, 68, 70, 71, 72, 226n.17,
  239n.42
Osborn, Sarah, 90–92

Parker, Theodore, 183
Parkinson, William, 51, 53, 59, 64, 67,
  68, 69, 71
parsonage novels, 97–101
pastor. See clergy; pastoral relationship
pastoral relationship
  in experience, 4, 139–95
  historical context for, 209–15
  historiography on, 215–20
  as ideal, 4, 109–37
  in literary imagination, 4, 75–107
  negative perception of, 3–74
  in pastoral theology, 109–37
  See also clergy
Paul (apostle), 122, 145, 154, 243n.19
Pease, Jane, 219
Pease, William, 219
Peep at "Number Five", A; or, a Chapter in
  the Life of a City Pastor (Phelps), 97
Phelps, Elizabeth Stuart, 97
Phillips, Wendell, 183
piety, 122, 123
Pillsbury, Parker, 251n.34
pious memoirs, 88–97
Pomeroy, Mary, 58
Pond, Enoch, 112, 113, 114, 115, 119, 121,
  125, 130, 133
Pond, Jerusha, 69–70
"Poor Man's Guide and Friend"
  (Alexander), 127
"Present to the Pastor, A," 6
Price, Abigail, 163–65, 171, 172, 176, 177,
  199, 203

Protestantism, 61, 115, 211–12
public accusation, 61–63
"Public Opinion," 44
Puritanism, 101, 103, 104

Quaker City, or The Monks of Monk Hall,
    The (Lippard), 82
"Qui Sine Peccato," 46
Quick, Frances, 169–71, 172, 174–75,
    176, 177–78, 184–85, 186, 187

Reade, Charles, 78
Reeks, Sarah, 230n.9
"Relations of the Pastor to the Women of
    his Church" (Fairchild), 7, 126–27
religion
    Abbott on, 147
    "declension" of, 215–16
    "democratization" of, 211
    denominational histories, 200
    elite masculine leadership in
        institutional, 200
    as social orientation, 202
    as source of danger to American
        republic, 24
    travelers' reports on, 12–13
    See also clergy; pastoral relationship
Remond, Sarah Parker, 251n.34
Restell, Madame, 57
"reverend rake," 80–85
Reynolds, David, 80–81
Richardson, Albert D., 40
Robinson, Henry R., 28
Rogers, Ammi, 51, 57, 69
Rotundo, Anthony, 218

Sabbath schools, 114
"Sample of Spirits," 46
Scarlet Letter, The (Hawthorne), 3, 101–5
"Scene in the Parlor," 4
Schmoll, Anna Maria, 57–58, 59, 62
Scott, Donald, 118
Second Great Awakening, 212, 216
seminaries, 111–13, 116–20, 143, 213, 241–
    42n.13
sentimentalism, 78, 79, 84–85
separation of church and state, 71
Sewall, Abigail, 173–74, 204

sexual harassment, 35, 207
sexual misconduct by clergy, 23–74
sexuality, 7–8, 18–19, 87–88, 95–96,
    105, 130–32, 136, 152, 155, 161, 186,
    193, 206–7
sexual submissiveness, 62
Seys, John, 51
Shady Side, The, 97
Shakers, 203–4
Sherman, Eleazar, 51, 63
sin, 61, 104
Sketches (Spencer), 89
slavery, 77, 183–84, 211, 251n.34
Smith, Lucy Mack, 201–2
Spencer, Ichabod, 89, 237n.16
spiritual equality of men and women,
    127
spiritualists, 204
Sprague, William, 124, 125
Spring, Gardiner, 114, 117, 122, 124, 127
Stoddard, Ann, 168–69
Stowe, Harriet Beecher, 40, 77, 78, 93–
    97
Sunnyside, The (Phelps), 97, 98

Tennent, Gilbert, 90, 91
Thacher, Moses, 52, 69–70
theology, differences in, 3, 32–33, 39, 96,
    103–4, 118–20, 167, 170–71, 173–74,
    198, 204, 212–13, 216–17
Thompson, Margaret, 219
Tilton, Elizabeth, 41–46, 56, 77, 78, 79,
    88, 106–7, 228nn.30–32
Tilton, Theodore, 40–46, 78, 106
Tompkins, Jane, 87
Trollope, Frances, 12, 18–20, 21, 23, 80,
    90, 106, 198
Turner, Bessie, 45

Uncle Tom's Cabin (Stowe), 77, 96
urbanization, 211

Van Zandt, George Washington, 51, 64–
    65
verdicts as equivocal, 32, 34, 36, 41, 50–
    52, 70–74

Waddell, Ann, 188
Walker, Charles Swan, 150

Warner, Susan, 85, 87

Weems, Mason Locke, 81

Weinzoepflen, Romain, 51, 57, 69, 70, 73

Wetmore, Sarah, 171, 172, 179, 190–95,
253n.56

Wheeler, Roxanna, 57

White, Elizabeth, 235n.1

Whitefield, George, 90

Whittlesey, John, 51

Wide, Wide World, The (Warner), 85–88

Williams, Catherine, 27, 29–30, 31, 63

Williams, Peter, 200

Wintringham, Eliza, 53, 59, 62, 63, 64,
67, 68, 69, 233n. 30

"without benefit of clergy," 6, 70–74. See
also benefit of clergy

women
autonomy in religious views, 92, 171,
201
clergy's attempts to guide, 148–53
in colonial era, 213
disillusionment of, 59, 199, 220
experience with clergy, 163–95
"feminization" of, in trials, 52–65,
198
hotel accommodations for, 38
ideal pastor to, 126–33
marginalization of, 60
mute suffering, 60
notions of inferiority, 67–68, 131
participation in "non-institutional"
church, 202
in pastoral role, 86, 91–92, 94–95, 98,
102–4, 133–37, 163–65, 167
pastoral theology regarding, 126–33
public speech, 247n.23
restricted sphere of, 17
sexual submissiveness, 62
travelers' views on, 12
trial process as hostile to, 63

Woodhull, Victoria, 40

Woods, Leonard, 246n.4

Wright, Frances, 12

Wright, Samuel Osgood, 171